CAMBRIDGE
EXAMINATIONS
PUBLISHING

OBJECTIVE
first certificate

Second edition

Annette Capel **Wendy Sharp** **Self-study Student's Book**

CAMBRIDGE
UNIVERSITY PRESS

Map of Objective First Certificate Student's Book

TOPIC	LESSON FOCUS	EXAM SKILLS	GRAMMAR	VOCABULARY
Unit 1 **Fashion matters 8–11** Fashion; describing people	1.1 Speaking and listening 1.2 Grammar	Paper 5 Speaking: 2 Comparing photographs Paper 4 Listening: 3 Matching Paper 3 Use of English: 4	Comparison Adverbs of degree	Appearance and clothing Phrasal verbs
Exam folder 1 12–13		Paper 3 Use of English: 4 Key word transformations		
Unit 2 **The virtual world 14–17** Computer games; the Internet	2.1 Reading 2.2 Grammar	Paper 1 Reading: 1 Skimming and scanning	-*ly* adverbs Review of present tenses	Computers Compound nouns Positive and negative adjectives
Writing folder 1 18–19		Paper 2 Writing: 1 and 2 Informal letters and emails		
Unit 3 **Going places 20–23** Travel	3.1 Listening Pronunciation: word stress 3.2 Grammar	Paper 5 Speaking: 2, 3 Paper 4 Listening: 2 Sentence completion Paper 3 Use of English: 4	Modals 1: Obligation, necessity and permission	Travel and holidays Travel collocations Expressions with *do* Prepositions of location
Exam folder 2 24–25		Paper 3 Use of English: 3 Word formation		
Unit 4 Our four-legged friends 26–29 Animals; pets	4.1 Reading 4.2 Grammar and vocabulary	Paper 1 Reading: 3 Matching Paper 4 Listening: 1 Multiple choice	*as* and *like*	Animals and pets Compound adjectives Expressions with *time*
Writing folder 2 30–31		Paper 2 Writing: 1 Transactional letters and emails 1 (formal)		
Unit 5 Fear and loathing 32–35 Narration: frightening experiences	5.1 Listening Pronunciation: past tense endings 5.2 Grammar	Paper 4 Listening: 1 Short extracts Paper 3 Use of English: 2	Review of past tenses: Past simple Past continuous Past perfect	Fear Irregular verbs
Exam folder 3 36–37		Paper 3 Use of English: 2 Open cloze		
Unit 6 **What if? 38–41** Winning prizes	6.1 Reading 6.2 Grammar and vocabulary	Paper 1 Reading: 2 Gapped text-sentences Paper 3 Use of English: 1	Adverbs of frequency Review of conditionals with *if*	Winning Phrases with *in* Parts of speech
Writing folder 3 42–43		Paper 2 Writing: 2 Stories 1		
Revision Units 1–6 44–45				
Unit 7 **Life's too short 46–49** Sport	7.1 Grammar 7.2 Listening Pronunciation: question tags	Paper 3 Use of English: 3 and 4 Paper 4 Listening: 3 Matching	Gerunds and infinitives 1 Question tags	Sport Phrases expressing likes and dislikes
Exam folder 4 50–51		Paper 3 Use of English: 1 Multiple choice cloze		

TOPIC	LESSON FOCUS	EXAM SKILLS	GRAMMAR	VOCABULARY
Unit 8 **Downshifting 52–55** Modern lifestyles	8.1 Reading 8.2 Grammar and vocabulary	Paper 5: Speaking: 2 and 3 Paper 1 Reading: 1 Multiple choice questions	*used to* and *would*	Jobs and work Word formation Expressions with *get* Phrasal verbs with *get*
Writing folder 4 56–57		Paper 2 Writing: 2 Essays 1		
Unit 9 **The hard sell 58–61** Advertising	9.1 Grammar 9.2 Listening and speaking Pronunciation: sentence stress	Paper 3 Use of English: 4 Paper 5 Speaking: 3 Shared task	Modals 2: Speculation and deduction Order of adjectives	Products and promotion Adjective–noun collocations
Exam folder 5 62–63		Paper 4 Listening skills for FCE		
Unit 10 **The final frontier 64–67** Space	10.1 Reading 10.2 Grammar	Paper 1 Reading: 2 Gapped text-sentences	Review of future tenses	Space Signposting words in texts Phrases with *at*
Writing folder 5 68–69		Paper 2 Writing: 2 Articles 1		
Unit 11 **Like mother, like daughter 70–73** Family	11.1 Speaking and listening 11.2 Vocabulary and grammar	Paper 5 Speaking: 1 Giving personal information Paper 4 Listening: 4 Multiple choice	*like* Adverb or adjective? Past and present participles	Personality *-ed/-ing* adjectives Phrasal verbs Cinema
Exam folder 6 74–75		Paper 4 Listening: 1 Short extracts		
Unit 12 **A great idea 76–79** Technology and inventions	12.1 Reading 12.2 Grammar and vocabulary	Paper 1 Reading: 3 Multiple matching Paper 3 Use of English: 4	The passive	Inventions Verb collocations
Writing folder 6 80–81		Paper 2 Writing: 2 Reviews		
Revision Units 7–12 82–83				
Unit 13 **Education for life 84–87** Education	13.1 Listening 13.2 Grammar	Paper 5 Speaking: 2 Paper 4 Listening: 3 Multiple matching Paper 3 Use of English: 4	Reported speech Reporting verbs Reported questions	School and education Expressions with *make*
Exam folder 7 88–89		Paper 4 Listening: 2 Sentence completion		
Unit 14 **Career moves 90–93** Working life	14.1 Reading 14.2 Grammar	Paper 5 Speaking: 2 Paper 1 Reading: 3 Multiple matching	Perfect tenses	The workplace Negative prefixes Expressions with *all* and *the whole*
Writing folder 7 94–95		Paper 2 Writing: 2 Applications 1		
Unit 15 **Too many people? 96–99** The environment	15.1 Listening Pronunciation: numbers 15.2 Grammar and vocabulary	Paper 5 Speaking: 4 Paper 4 Listening: 2 Sentence completion Paper 3 Use of English: 2 and 3	Countable and uncountable nouns *Some, any, no*	The environment Word formation Expressions with uncountable nouns
Exam folder 8 100–101		Paper 4 Listening: 3 Multiple matching		

TOPIC	LESSON FOCUS	EXAM SKILLS	GRAMMAR	VOCABULARY
Unit 23 **Unexpected events** 146–149 Natural disasters	23.1 Listening Pronunciation: intonation 23.2 Grammar	Paper 4 Listening: 2 Sentence completion Paper 3 Use of English: 2 and 4	Intensifiers *I wish / If only* *wish/hope*	The natural world Phrasal verbs with *off* Verb–noun collocations
Exam folder 12 150–151		Paper 1 Reading: 2 Gapped text-sentences		
Unit 24 Priceless or **worthless? 152–155** Art	24.1 Reading 24.2 Grammar and vocabulary	Paper 1 Reading: 1 Multiple choice Paper 3 Use of English: 3	Adverbs and word order	Art Verb collocations Words often confused
Writing folder 12 **156–157**		Paper 2 Writing: 2 Articles 2		
Revision Units 19–24 158–159				
Unit 25 **Urban decay, suburban** **hell 160–163** City life	25.1 Listening and speaking 25.2 Grammar	Paper 4 Listening: 2 Sentence completion Paper 3 Use of English: 1 Paper 5 Speaking: 4	Mixed conditionals	City life Words with *up-* Words with *re-*
Exam folder 13 164–165		Paper 1 Reading: 3 Multiple matching		
Unit 26 **Getting around 166–169** Transport	26.1 Reading 26.2 Grammar and vocabulary	Paper 1 Reading: 3 Multiple matching Paper 3 Use of English: 2	Inversion Relative pronouns: *who, whom, whose*	Means of transport Phrases with *get*
Writing folder 13 **170–171**		Paper 2 Writing: 2 Essay 2		
Unit 27 **Material girl 172–175** Famous people	27.1 Listening Pronunciation: intonation 27.2 Grammar and vocabulary	Paper 4 Listening: 4 Multiple choice Paper 3 Use of English: 3	Revision of tenses Time expressions	Famous people Phrasal verbs and expressions
Exam folder 14 176–177		Paper 5 Speaking: Complete test		
Unit 28 Sense and **sensitivity 178–181** Popular psychology	28.1 Reading and vocabulary 28.2 Grammar	Paper 1 Reading: 2 Gapped text-sentences Paper 3 Use of English: 2	Number and concord	Colour Phrasal verbs with *out* Verbs and adjectives followed by prepositions
Writing folder 14 **182–183**		Paper 2 Writing: 2 Applications 2		
Unit 29 **Newshounds 184–187** The media	29.1 Listening 29.2 Vocabulary	Paper 4 Listening: 3 Multiple matching Paper 3 Use of English: 1		The media English idioms
Exam folder 15 188–189		Paper 2 Writing: 1 and 2		
Unit 30 Anything for **a laugh 190–193** Humour	30.1 Reading 30.2 Grammar and vocabulary	Paper 1 Reading: 3 Multiple matching Paper 3 Use of English: 2	*rather* The grammar of phrasal verbs	Humour
Writing folder 15 **194–195**		Paper 2 Writing: 1 Transactional letters and emails 3 (formal)		
Revision Units 25–30 196–197				
Grammar folder 198–208 **Self-study folder 209–288**				

Content of the First Certificate Examination

The Cambridge First Certificate examination consists of five papers, each of which is worth 40 marks. It is not necessary to pass all five papers in order to pass the examination. There are five grades: Pass – A, B, C; Fail – D, E.

As well as being told your grade, you will also be given some indication of your performance i.e. whether you have done especially well or badly on some of the papers.

Paper 1 Reading 1 hour

There are three parts to this paper and they are always in the same order. Each part contains a text and a comprehension task. The texts used are from newspaper and magazine articles, fiction, guides and reviews. For general reading skills for FCE see Exam folder 10.

Part	Task Type	Number of Questions	Format	Objective Exam folder
1	Multiple choice	8	You must read a text followed by multiple choice questions with four options A, B, C or D.	11 (138–139)
2	Gapped text	7	You must read a text with sentences removed. You need to use the missing sentences to complete the text.	12 (150–151)
3	Multiple matching	15	You must answer the questions by finding the relevant information in the text or texts.	13 (164–165)

Paper 2 Writing 1 hour 20 minutes

There are two parts to this paper. Part 1 is compulsory, you have to answer it. In Part 2 there are four questions and you must choose one. Each part carries equal marks and you are expected to write between 120–150 words for Task 1 and 120–180 for Task 2.

Part	Task Type	Number of Tasks	Task Format	Objective Writing Folder
1	Question 1 a transactional letter or email • formal/informal	1 compulsory	You are given a situation which you need to respond to by letter or email. You may be given some extra information in the form of notes which you need to use in your answer.	2 (30–31); 8 (106–107); 15 (194–195); **Exam folder 15** (188–189)
2	Questions 2–4 • an article • an informal non-transactional letter • a letter of application • a report • an essay • a review • a story Question 5 Writing one of the above types of task: • There is a choice of two set books, with a question on each.	4 choose one	You are given a choice of topics which you have to respond to in the way specified.	Essays 4 (56–57); 13 (170–171); Articles 5 (68–69); 12 (156–157); Reviews 6 (80–81); Reports 11 (138–139); Letters of Application 7 (94–95); 14 (182–183); The set book 9 (118–119); Stories 3 (42–43); 10 (132–133); **Exam folder 15** (188–189)

Paper 3 Use of English 45 minutes

There are four parts to this paper, which test your grammar and vocabulary.

Part	Task Type	Number of Questions	Task Format	Objective Exam folder
1	Multiple choice gap-fill mainly testing vocabulary	12	You must choose which word from four answers completes each of the 12 gaps in a text.	4 (50–51)
2	Open gap-fill, testing mainly grammar	12	You must complete a text with 12 gaps.	3 (36–37)
3	Word formation	10	You need to use the right form of a given word to fill the gaps in a text containing 10 gaps.	2 (24–25)
4	'Key' word transformations testing grammar and vocabulary	8	You must complete a sentence with a given word, so that it means the same as the first sentence.	1 (12–13)

Paper 4 Listening about 40 minutes

There are four parts to this paper. Each part is heard twice. The texts are a variety of types either with one speaker or more than one. For general listening skills for FCE see Exam folder 5.

Part	Task Type	Number of Questions	Task Format	Objective Exam folder
1	Multiple choice	8	You hear short, unrelated extracts, each about 30 seconds with either one or two speakers. You must choose an answer from A, B or C.	6 (74–75)
2	Sentence completion	10	You hear either one or two speakers and this part lasts about 3 minutes. You must write a word or short phrase to complete the sentences.	7 (88–89)
3	Multiple matching	5	You hear five unrelated extracts with a common theme. Each lasts about 30 seconds. You must choose the correct answer from a list of six.	8 (100–101)
4	Multiple choice	7	You hear either one or two speakers talking for about 3 minutes. You must choose an answer from A, B or C.	9 (112–113)

Paper 5 Speaking about 14 minutes

There are four parts to this paper. There are usually two of you taking the examination and two examiners. This paper tests your accuracy, vocabulary, pronunciation, and ability to communicate and complete the tasks.

Part	Task Type	Time	Format	Objective Exam folder
1	The interviewer asks each candidate some questions.	3–4 minutes	You are asked to give information about yourself.	14 (176–177) Complete speaking test (Parts 1–4)
2	Each candidate talks to the interviewer for about 1 minute.	3–4 minutes	You have to talk about two pictures and then comment on the other candidate's pictures.	see above
3	Candidates have to discuss a task together.	3–4 minutes	You are given some material – diagrams, pictures, etc. to discuss with the other candidate.	see above
4	Candidates offer opinions relating to the task they've just completed.	3–4 minutes	The interviewer will join in with your discussion.	see above

1·1 Fashion matters

1a 1b

1 What sort of clothes do you prefer to wear? Do you ever have to wear things you don't really like? If so, why? Talk with a partner.

2 In pairs, describe what people in the class are wearing today. Then list topic vocabulary under these headings, adding to the words given.

Clothes: suit, sweatshirt, ...
Footwear: (flat/high-)heeled shoes, ...
Jewellery: bracelet, pendant, ...
Headgear: beret, helmet, ...
Materials: woollen, leather, ...
Hairstyle: curly, spiky, ...
Appearance: stylish, smart, ...

Vocabulary spot

List topic vocabulary in sets like these, using headings to help you learn the words and their meanings.

3 Work in pairs. Each student chooses a pair of photos, for example, 1a and 1b. Take it in turns to describe what each person is wearing and say something about their appearance.

Exam spot

In Part 2 of Paper 5, each candidate is given a pair of photos to talk about on their own. The task will involve comparing and contrasting the two photos, rather than just describing each one.

4 In the same pairs, compare the two people in your pair of photos. Talk about their age, their clothes, their hair, or even imagine their personality! These examples may help you.

The one on the left is younger than the one on the right.
This girl's clothes are not as stylish as the other one's.
He/She has longer hair than the other one.
This man seems to be less serious than the man in the suit.

5 As a class, summarise what you said about the people.

Listening

6 🎧 You are now going to hear some short recordings, where five of the people in the photos talk about what they like to wear. Say who is speaking in each case.

Here is an example: Speaker 1 is the man in photo 3b. Look at the photo of him as you listen.

In this transcript of what Speaker 1 says, some words and phrases are highlighted. This is to show that parts of an exam recording may make you think that other answers are possible. This is why you must listen carefully and check when you listen a second time.

I'm not a suit man *– even for work, I can get away with casual stuff, though I still **like my clothes to look smart**. I love shopping – my favourite place is Paul Smith in Covent Garden. I bought a really nice woollen shirt there recently. Clothes are important to me, but they need to be comfortable as well as **stylish**.*

7 🎧 Now listen to the other four speakers and match the correct photo to each speaker. Note down any words and phrases that help you to decide. Compare your answers with another student when you have finished.

Speaker 2 ☐   Speaker 4 ☐
Speaker 3 ☐   Speaker 5 ☐

Vocabulary

In the recordings, there are several examples of phrasal verbs. For example, Speaker 1 says:

   … even for work, I can **get away with** *casual stuff.*

Phrasal verbs are used a lot in informal English.

8 🎧 Listen to Speakers 2–5 again and list the nine phrasal verbs you hear. Then match them to these short definitions.

   a be seen very clearly
   b join or combine things
   c return
   d wear smarter clothes than usual
   e keep money for something special
   f reduce
   g get dressed in something
   h go somewhere for entertainment
   i know the most recent facts about something

Corpus spot 👁

Many phrasal verbs contain irregular verbs. Be careful with past tense forms – the *Cambridge Learner Corpus* shows FCE candidates often make mistakes with these.

I **took off** my coat and sat down.
NOT   I ~~taked~~ off my coat and sat down.

9 Now choose six of the phrasal verbs to complete this letter, using each of them once only.

What advice would you give the writer? Discuss in pairs.

Dear Jayne

Last night, Maria, Sally and I
(1) .... clubbing.
Because I was late back from work,
I quickly (2) ....
that black skirt of mine and a
T-shirt, but the other two really
(3) .... ! Maria
chose a beautiful purple dress and
sprayed her hair gold. Sally
(4) .... the
most outrageous outfit – red leather
shorts, a bright green top and high-
heeled, knee-length boots with stars
on. When we got there, they both
(5) .... on the
dance floor and I looked very
ordinary in comparison.

Honestly, I can't (6) ....
.... them –
they're so fashion-conscious. What
would you do in my position?

1·2

Comparison

1 Read this short text about the fashion industry. Do you agree with its viewpoint?

Why is it that fashion houses design their clothes for the youngest and skinniest men and women? We may not actually want to look like supermodels, but it is a fact that the most emaciated figures have dominated the world's catwalks for a very long time. It seems it is not in the interests of the fashion industry to represent an 'average' person. Although 'slimmer' may not always mean 'more desirable' in the real world, fashion succeeds because it carries with it that image of the least attainable figure.

2 Think about these comparison structures.

-er than	more … than	the most …
the -est	less … than	the least …

- Why do we say *younger than* but **less** *serious than*; and *the youngest* but *the **most*** *emaciated*?
- Which common adjectives can we either add *-er/-est* to or use *more/most* with?
- What are the spelling rules for forming the comparative and superlative of words like *slim* and *skinny*?

Check the Grammar folder whenever you see this:

G···❯ **page 198**

Corpus spot

Correct the mistakes that FCE candidates have made with comparatives in these sentences.

a What are the better clothes to wear at the camp?
b He is famouser than all the others in the film.
c You look more tired and thiner.
d I would like to buy a much more better one.
e It's now more easy to get there.
f This is even worser than before.

3 Give the comparative and superlative forms of these adjectives.

bright	brighter	the brightest
large	....	....
thin	....	....
dirty	....	....
casual	....	....
outrageous	more/less outrageous	....
good	....	the best
bad	worse	....
far	....	....

4 Now complete the following sentences by using one of the adjectives in exercise 3, choosing either the comparative or the superlative form.

a There's no way you can fit into my shoes – you take a .... size than I do!
b Jake wears .... clothes of any of us – take his pink and purple ties, for example!
c Don't dress up for the club tonight – everyone's looking .... there nowadays.
d You can't put those jeans on again – they're .... pair I've ever seen!
e I'm a bit worried about Sally. She doesn't eat a thing and so she's getting .... than ever.
f Australia is .... place I've ever travelled to.
g Have you painted this room recently? Everything's looking a lot .... than before.
h Market stalls often offer slightly .... value for money than shops.

Grammar extra

Note the use of *a lot* and *slightly* in sentences g and h. These are adverbs of degree, which are commonly used with comparative adjectives. Some adverbs of degree are also used with superlative adjectives, as in this example:

*Kate Moss is **by far** the most famous model of the 1990s.*

Put these adverbs of degree into the following sentences. Which one can be used with both comparative and superlative adjectives?

a bit	a great deal	much

a This ring is only .... more expensive and it's .... nicer than the others.
b Tracksuits may be .... warmer, but shorts are .... the best for running in, whatever the weather.

G···❯ **page 198**

5 *not as … as / not so … as*

You used this structure to compare the people in the photos in the last lesson. Now compare these photos of cars in the same way, choosing suitable adjectives from the ones below to describe them.

EXAMPLE: *The Beetle is not as fast as the Ferrari.*

| comfortable | elegant | fast | practical | sexy |

Comparison of adverbs

6 Identify the comparative adverbs in this short newspaper article and then explain how they are formed.

(G) ⋯⟶ page 198

BOY MEETS GIRL

Androgenous clothing design is a familiar idea nowadays, although it is perhaps the term 'unisex' that is more commonly used by the fashion industry. Traditional dress restrictions for men and women are becoming blurred, largely because gender roles in today's society are defined less strictly than they were.

With menswear designer Lee Copperwheat, Pam Blundell produces the *Copperwheat Blundell* label. She says, 'I design trousers for women and Lee will re-cut them for men. We have even started doing unisex pieces, such as trousers and raincoats, in six different sizes to fit everybody.' Many other designers work in this way, with the result that similar lines for men and women are now much more readily available.

What do you feel about these sorts of clothes? Do you think that unisex clothing will still be in fashion in five years' time? Why?/Why not?

7 Now practise using all these comparison structures. Complete the second sentence so that it has a similar meaning to the first sentence, using the word given. **Do not change the word given.** You must use between two and five words including the word given. There is an example at the beginning (0).

0 Mary is shorter than her brother.
not
Mary is ……*not as tall as*…… her brother.

1 These sunglasses cost a bit less than my last pair.
were
These sunglasses …………………………
than my last pair.

2 Coco Chanel was an extremely talented designer.
most
Coco Chanel was one of …………………………
………………………… in the world.

3 That supermodel is only 17 – I thought she was older.
as
That supermodel is not …………………………
I thought.

4 It takes much less time to travel by train than by car.
lot
Travelling by train …………………………
travelling by car.

5 This jewellery shop is the cheapest one I've found.
expensive
This jewellery shop is …………………………
all the ones I've found.

6 Suzanne's host at the dinner party wasn't as elegantly dressed as she was.
more
At the dinner party, Suzanne was far …………………………
………………………… her host.

7 I preferred you with curlier hair.
straight
I preferred your hair when it wasn't
………………………… is now.

8 John wears smarter clothes now he has a girlfriend.
less
John dressed …………………………
he didn't have a girlfriend.

Exam folder 1

Paper 3 Part 4 Key word transformations

In this part of the Use of English paper you are tested on both grammar and vocabulary. There are eight questions and an example at the beginning. You can get up to two marks for each question.

1   Read the Part 4 exam instructions below and then look at the example (0).

Complete the second sentence so that it has a similar meaning to the first sentence, using the word given. **Do not change the word given.** You must use between two and five words, including the word given.

Here is an example **(0)**.

0   This is the most exciting holiday I've ever had. < *First sentence*

   exciting < *key word – this never changes*

   I've never had a .... one.

The second sentence must mean the same as the first when it is complete.

The gap can be filled by the words 'more exciting holiday than this', so you write:

| 0 | M O R E | E X C I T I N G | H O L I D A Y | T H A N | T H I S |

ANSWER:
I've never had a ...*more exciting holiday than this*... one.
   1 mark   +   *1 mark*

Write only the missing words IN CAPITAL LETTERS **on the separate answer sheet**.

---

2   Think about what is important in this exam task. What advice would you give another student about answering Part 4 in the exam?

3   Now read the advice given in the bullet points.

Advice

- Read the first sentence carefully.
- Think about how the key word given is commonly used.
- Complete the gap with a possible answer. You can use the question paper for rough answers.
- Count the number of words you have used in the gap. You must use not less than two and not more than five, including the word in bold. Note that a contracted form such as 'don't' counts as **two** words.
- Read the completed second sentence to check it means the same as the first.
- Ask yourself whether the words in the gap fit the sentence grammatically.
- Transfer your answer (just the words in the gap) to the answer sheet.

4   Complete these transformations, using exactly the number of words in brackets (this includes the word given). There is an example at the beginning (0).

---

o   Have you got a brooch that is cheaper than this one?
less (4)
Have you got *a less expensive brooch* .... than this one?

1   'A club has just opened in Leeds,' said Maria to Sally.
told (5)
Maria .... club in Leeds.

2   I returned the dress to the shop because it was badly made.
took (3)
Because the dress was badly made, I ....
to the shop.

3   Some shops try really hard to help you.
effort (3)
Some shops really .... to help you.

4   Fifty years ago, cars were slower than they are nowadays.
as (5)
Fifty years ago, cars .... they are
nowadays.

5   People wear casual clothes where I work.
up (4)
People .... where I work.

6   It's a lot easier to learn a language by visiting the country where it's spoken.
much (4)
You can learn a language .... you visit
the country where it's spoken.

7   Peter Høeg writes the best novels in Danish today.
far (4)
Peter Høeg is by .... of Danish novels
today.

8   The stall didn't sell much jewellery because of its high prices.
highly (3)
The jewellery on the stall was so .... not
much was sold.

The virtual world

1 Do you agree with the following statement? Talk to another student, giving your opinion.

Computer games are anti-social and violent, and their users are mindless nerds.

nerd /nɜːd/ *noun* [C] *informal* someone, especially a man, who is not fashionable and who is interested in boring things • **nerdy** *adjective informal* boring and not fashionable

2 🎧 Now listen to this extract from a radio interview with a university lecturer. Does he have the same view of computer games as you have? What are his reasons?

3 When you are looking for specific information, you can ignore any parts of a text that do not relate to this task. Running your eyes over a text in this way is called scanning.

Scan the four short reviews of computer games, to decide quickly which game is:

a the worst	**c** the least expensive
b the best	**d** the most informative.

Where did you find this information? How much of each review did you need to look at?

Exam spot

In Paper 1, there is a lot of text to read and the time allowed is only one hour. By **skimming** and **scanning** the text, you can increase your reading speed and find answers more efficiently. These skills are essential in Part 3, the matching task.

1

The idea is brilliant: set in the Wild West, this is a clone of perhaps the most popular game ever, *Doom*. Probably the best thing about this game is its introduction, with unusual camera angles, excellent sound effects and just about every Western cliché there ever was. It goes downhill when you get into the game itself. You spend your time creeping around deserted buildings, endlessly shooting at hundreds of bad guys. You collect ammunition, health points and other things that you can use to solve puzzles. But once you finish one level of the game, on you go to another one which is remarkably similar. It's a case of 'Been there, done that' – eight times! However, while you're playing, you can always listen to the background music, which is terrific. Turn up the volume and enjoy it.

THE VERDICT: *Makes you yawn at times, but good fun for fans of Westerns.* ***** £45**

2

Did you know that car games have a poor relation? Yes, it's their motorbike cousins! Somehow motorbike games never provide the same thrill as car games. But this version comes very close and is easily the best available. There are eight different bikes, nine long tracks and a choice of race styles: Grand Prix or the muddier scrambling type. The intelligence and speed of your 23 computer opponents is high, which guarantees a game demanding enough for the most advanced racer. So get on your bikes!

THE VERDICT: *A super-slick bike racer that does not disappoint.* ******* £40**

3

Ice is very useful. It keeps food cold in your freezer and combines perfectly with Coca-Cola. Tragically, of course, the passengers of the Titanic experienced the downside of ice. Namely that if a ship hits a big piece of ice, the ship comes off worse. The real-life setting of the Titanic disaster may seem a joyless subject, but there is plenty of historical fact and, thankfully, no gory detail. This is a first-person adventure, with a real sense of atmosphere. Unfortunately, though, just as you start solving a few puzzles, the ship goes down. As the technology improves, games of this type are becoming more and more elaborate, but here there is just too little to do. What a missed opportunity!

THE VERDICT: *If you're interested in the history of the ship, you will definitely learn something – if not, give it a wide berth!* **** £40**

4 To get an idea of what a paragraph or whole text is about, you should read it through quickly, rather than word by word. This is called skimming.

In groups of four, choose one review each and skim it to find out what sort of game is described. Briefly describe the game to the others.

5 Find words or phrases which mean the same as a–j. The review number is given in brackets.

   a an exact copy (1)
   b a frequently-used idea (1)
   c deteriorates (1)
   d bullets (1)
   e a feeling of excitement (2)
   f challenging (2)
   g gloomy (3)
   h complex (3)
   i walk with heavy steps (4)
   j vulnerable to (4)

6 In review 3, the writer talks about the *downside of ice*. What exactly does this mean? Here are some more compound nouns using 'up' and 'down'. Which three words are used in connection with computers?

upturn	breakdown
upgrade	crackdown
set-up	letdown
back-up	downloading

4

This game is so bad that I am sitting here unwilling to even write about it! But the magazine pays me to, so I must. Here goes … You are a bird-headed robot and you want to control a number of cities. To do this, you have weapons, a shield and the ability to jump higher than the non-bird-heads. You stomp around at a slow pace, searching for something to shoot at. When you do find something, you end up at the mercy of the interface as well as the enemy. The control system is useless. The graphics are appalling. The cities are flat and bare. The task is truly boring. What more can I say? It's coming out next month!

THE VERDICT: *Avoid.* *** £35**

7 Use the words from the box in exercise 6 to complete sentences a–h.

   a This game is a complete ....! It cost me over £40 and it is really boring.
   b I can't find the original file and I forgot to make a .... , so I'm starting the whole document again.
   c .... music from a legal source means that the performers don't miss out on earnings.
   d Jean is new to the department and doesn't understand the .... yet.
   e The .... in the economy is good news for all of us.
   f There was a serious .... in communication and the peace talks collapsed.
   g You should buy this .... for your software. Then your computer wouldn't crash so often!
   h 'Zero tolerance' means a total .... on crime.

Grammar extra

-*ly* adverbs

All the adverbs below were used in the reviews of computer games. Write down their related adjectives and then say what the spelling rules are for forming these adverbs.

endlessly	tragically	remarkably	easily	truly

Some adverbs do not end in -*ly*. The most common of these are *fast*, *hard*, *late* and *well*.
Note also the adverbs *hardly* and *lately*, which have different meanings.

Explain the meaning of the adverbs used below.

a I hardly slept last night.
b I found it hard to sleep last night.

c There have been a lot of good films lately.
d We were late for the film, which had already started.

G ···⟩ page 198

Corpus spot

Correct any spelling mistakes that FCE candidates have made with adverbs in these sentences.

   a Unfortunatelly, I'm quite busy at the moment.
   b If I were you, I would definitly spend my evenings reading by the fireside.
   c You just have to say your name and the computer opens the door automaticly.
   d Entering the restaurant, you immediatly feel comfortable.
   e We realy started to work hard the morning before the show.
   f You must adjust the laser extremily carefully to get it in the correct position.
   g I would like more information, especialy about accommodation.
   h The computer completly takes hold of our lives.

2·2

Review of present tenses

1 Here are some examples from the reviews of computer games. Look at the underlined tenses in a–j and identify them as present simple or present continuous. Then complete the statement about present tenses, using the letters a–j once only.

  a It goes downhill when you <u>get into</u> the game itself.
  b While <u>you're playing</u>, you can always listen to the music.
  c Motorbike games never <u>provide</u> the same thrill.
  d It <u>keeps</u> food cold in your freezer.
  e If a ship <u>hits</u> a big piece of ice, the ship <u>comes off</u> worse.
  f Games of this type <u>are becoming</u> more and more elaborate.
  g I <u>am sitting</u> here unwilling to even write about it.
  h But the magazine <u>pays</u> me to.
  i You <u>stomp around</u> at a slow pace.
  j It's <u>coming out</u> next month.

> The present .... tense is used for permanent situations (examples .... and ....) or to talk about actions which are habitual or repeated (examples .... and ....). This tense is also used in time clauses introduced by words such as *until, once, as soon as,* .... (example ....). Note also that it is used in both parts of zero conditional sentences, as in this example and in example ....
>
> On the other hand, the present .... tense is used for temporary situations (example ....), situations that are changing or developing (example ....), and for events or actions happening now (example ....).This tense can also be used to talk about the future (example ....).

G ···⋮> page 198

2 Read these sentences and correct any tense errors.

  a Home computers are becoming more and more popular.
  b This week, the shop sells all software at 20% off.
  c Don't switch off the computer as I'm downloading a film.
  d As soon as you are playing this game, you realise the graphics are tremendous.
  e When you buy a new computer, you are getting a lot of free software.
  f Many children prefer computers to books.

3 Choose the correct present tense for each of these sentences, using the verbs in brackets.

  a My new game is sensational – as soon as you .... a level, you .... something completely different to do. (finish, get)
  b Generally, computer manuals ...., although some are still very long and difficult to follow. (improve)
  c An upgrade for this application .... soon. (come out)
  d In the latest version, a dragon .... overhead and .... dramatically when you .... it. (fly, explode, hit)
  e Online sales .... increasingly important for the company. (become)
  f Back-up copies .... time to prepare, but they are essential. (take)
  g It is said that computers .... life easier. (make)
  h If a computer ...., you .... the file you .... on unless you .... it regularly. (crash, lose, work, save)

4 Skim this extract from an article about 'googlewhacking'. Then fill each gap with a suitable present tense of one of the verbs below. Use each verb once only. There is one extra verb you do not need.

add   become   believe
change   create   encourage
find out   google   mean
~~refer~~   sound   spend   submit
update

Compare your answers with another student.

In which spaces can both the present simple and the present continuous be used? Is there any change in meaning?

Which of the verbs that you used do not have a present continuous form? Do you know any more verbs like this?

Verbs not normally used in the continuous tenses are called 'stative' verbs.

G ⋯⋮➔ page 199

5 Read these statements and say whether you agree or disagree with each one, giving your reasons.

a Some people hate computers because they don't understand them.
b Computers belong to the 21st century; books don't.
c The Internet seems to offer an enormous amount of helpful information, but in fact, a lot of it is dangerous, particularly for children.
d People forget that computers may have a health risk.
e The virtual world is becoming more important in our daily lives.

Google

Gary Stock, a very experienced Internet user, has come up with the new term 'googlewhack', which (0) <u>refers</u> to a single entry on a Google search page. It (1) .... increasingly difficult for googlewhackers like Gary to achieve their aim: the appearance of the message "Results 1-1 of 1" on their computer screen. For one thing, people (2) .... new web pages and (3) .... existing ones all the time, which in turn (4) .... more and more entries on Google. Also, anyone who (5) .... their googlewhack to a website (6) .... another entry just by doing that.

Perhaps all of this (7) .... like a waste of time, but Gary Stock (8) .... that googlewhacking is a meaningful activity that (9) .... people to surf the web again, just like during the early days of the Internet. According to many, Google (10) .... our lives by broadening our knowledge of the world. People certainly (11) .... about new or unusual things by googlewhacking – from 'bartok nosepieces' to 'jillionaire incinerate'! But if you (12) .... these phrases on your computer today, will they still be googlewhacks?

Vocabulary

6 These adjectives have all come up in this unit.

appalling   brilliant   demanding   elaborate   excellent
joyless   popular   sensational   sophisticated   terrific
tremendous   useless

Divide them into two basic meaning groups, positive and negative. If you are not sure which group to place a word in, use a dictionary.

Some of these adjectives may be useful in the next writing task on pages 18–19.

Vocabulary spot

List new words in a vocabulary notebook and add to them when you can. It can be helpful to include a sentence showing how the word is used.

Writing folder 1

Informal letters and emails

1 Look at the extracts below. Which two would you describe as informal? How did you decide?

A
I want to let you all know about our staff get-together last week. It's a pity more of you weren't there as it was a terrific occasion. Why not come along next time? There's free coffee and biscuits!

B
This is to inform you of the decisions taken at last week's meeting. Please note that all members of this department are strictly required to be present at such meetings and action may be taken in future to ensure this.

C
Anyway, let me tell you about the party Jack is having on Saturday. Well, just about everyone is coming – even that weird guy Sam from college! Jack says he wants us all to be there, so you'd better not miss it. Why not come down for a few days? You can stay at my place if you want.

Decide for each extract who could have written it, who it was probably written to and why.

Exam spot

In Paper 2, you may have to write an informal letter or email. Think carefully about who you are writing to and why, before you decide whether to use informal language. In Part 2, you may be given an extract from a friend's letter or email to reply to, which can also give you clues about a suitable style.

2 Read this writing task and find the style clues.

Here is part of a letter from an English friend:

Guess what? My parents have given me some money for passing my exam, so I can splash out on something really special. I can't choose between buying a new computer game or saving up a bit more and getting some clothes. Which do you think would be better? And can you suggest what exactly I should get?

Write a suitable letter to your friend. (120–180 words)

3 The sample answer below would get a low mark, for several reasons. What are they?

Dear Frankie

What brilliant news in your letter! I wish to offer you congratulations about the exam. Moreover, how nice to have some spare cash.

You say you can't decide if to buy a computer game or some clothes. Don't you think that if you choose some new clothes you must save up a bit more money first? Clothes are not as cheap than computer games and I know you like expensive designer outfits. If you choose computer game, which one? There are so many available and to my mind they are all the same. In my opinion you should spend the money in something else. Why don't you get yourself a new dictionary, for example? Then it would be easier for you to study, wouldn't it?

I hope you will consider my suggestion seriously and I look forward to receiving a reply from you in due course.

Yours sincerely

Correct the errors in paragraph 2 and rewrite paragraphs 1 and 3 in an appropriate style.

4 How will you answer this task? Work in pairs.

Content ideas

Decide whether you think your friend should buy a game or clothes and note down some reasons to support your view. Then think about one specific game or item of clothing. What is special about it? Compare your ideas.

Game: topic, best points, price
Clothes: material, colour, style

Language input
You need to include these functions:

Congratulations   Opinion   Advice/Suggestion

Organisation

A letter needs adequate paragraphing, to make it easy to follow. In the sample answer, paragraph 2 is too long and the ideas in it are muddled. It is important to plan what you are going to say in note form before you start writing.

- Use this plan for your letter.
    - Opening formula
    - Paragraph 1 Initial greetings and congratulations
    - Paragraph 2 Opinion about which item the friend should buy
    - Paragraph 3 Description of one specific item
    - Paragraph 4 Final remarks
    - Closing formula
- Try to use linkers within each paragraph, to improve the flow of the letter. Choose appropriate ones from the linkers in 5 opposite to present your ideas in a clear order.
- Do not include any postal addresses, as they are not needed in the exam.

Style

Here are some typical features of informal writing. There is at least one example of each in the sample.

Contracted forms, for example, *I'm, don't*
Phrasal verbs
Phrases with *get, take, have*, etc., for example, *take a look*
Short sentences
Simple linking words, for example, *Then*
Direct questions, for example, *What about …?*
Some exclamation marks (not too many!)

Editing your work

It is important to read through what you have written and put right any mistakes. Check your work for the following:

a Is the grammar accurate?
b Is the spelling correct?
c Is there enough punctuation?
d Is the style consistent?

The first letters of the five headings above spell out the word C-L-O-S-E. It is important to think about these five elements (Content, Language, Organisation, Style, Editing) for all FCE Paper 2 tasks. And the word 'Close' will also remind you to finish a piece of writing, for example by signing off a letter. Some candidates in the exam forget to do this and lose marks.

Formal or informal?

Write *Inf* next to the expressions that are informal.

1 Initial greetings
It was great to hear from you. ....
I am writing with reference to your letter. ....
Thanks for writing to me. ....

2 Congratulations
Well done! ....
I would like to offer congratulations on ....
Let me congratulate you on ....

3 Opinion
In my opinion ....
To my mind ....
I hold the view that ....
Personally, I have no doubt that ....
My own thoughts are ....

4 Advice/Suggestion
Why not try ....
What about trying ....
It is recommended that you ....
You could ....
I urge you to ....
I suggest that ....
If I were you ....

5 Linkers
Moreover ....
Also ....
Then again ....
Furthermore ....
Better still ....
As well as that ....
What's more ....
Additionally ....

6 Endings
Do drop me a line if you have time. ....
I look forward to hearing from you without delay.
....
Hope to hear from you soon. ....
Keep in touch. ....
I hope to hear from you at your earliest convenience.
....

7 Opening and closing a letter
Match these opening and closing formulae and say when you should use each of them.

Dear Jayne	*Yours faithfully*
Dear Sir	*Yours sincerely*
Dear Ms Jones	*Love*

Going places

1 Discuss these photographs with a partner. What types of holiday do they show?

2 Now compare the two photographs.

Student A	Student B
What sorts of people would enjoy these holidays?	What are the advantages and disadvantages of each of these holidays?

3 Where do you usually spend your holidays? Why?

Exam spot

In Part 2 of Paper 4 you will be asked to complete some sentences. You will need to write a word or short phrase and you will hear the passage twice. The words you write down are in the order you hear them. There is no need to make any changes to these words.

Listening

4 You are going to hear a man being interviewed on the radio about a cruise he recently took to the Antarctic. In groups note down the kind of travel vocabulary that you think you will hear. Explain your words to the rest of the class. For example:

Cruise: ship, captain, ...
Trip: voyage, journey, ...

5 🎧 Read through the questions 1–10 very carefully and, in pairs, try to predict what word or words you might need to fill each gap. Now listen to the interview.

1 The temperature was usually around ....
2 The name of the ship was the ....
3 The cupboards in the cabins were situated ....
4 The nationality of the expedition leader was ....
5 The weather in this area is sometimes ....
6 Steve enjoyed seeing the different types of ....
7 The only people, besides tourists, in the region are working at a ....
8 The only evidence of the fishing industry is empty ....
9 The cruise ships are forbidden to get rid of .... in the area.
10 It's important that tourists don't disturb the ....

6 Do you approve of tourists being allowed to go to unspoilt areas of the world? Would you go to these places if you had the opportunity?

Vocabulary

7   All the words in the box below are to do with travel and holidays. With a partner, put them into the following categories:

   a boats   **c** seaside
   b movement   **d** people   **e** accommodation

journey	caravan	campsite	canoe
flight	courier	hotel	yacht
cliff	bed and	crossing	sightseers
liner	breakfast	holiday-makers	coast
shore	voyage	travel agent	sand
ferry			

Vocabulary spot

It is useful to remember words which go together. These are called 'collocations'. For example, you *go on holiday, on a trip,* etc.

8   Link the verbs in list A with suitable nouns in list B. There is sometimes more than one answer.

   A
   take   book   catch   set   board   get   go

   B
   skiing   a trip   sightseeing   sail   a ship
   a plane   a tan   a hotel   a flight

9   In the listening, you heard the expression *do more good than harm.* Now look at some other expressions with *do.* Complete the sentences below, putting *do* into the correct tense.

do someone a favour	do your best
do your homework	do business with
do military service	someone
do the shopping	do something for a living

   a I've always found that they are a very good company to ....
   b What does your father ....?
   c We don't have to .... in Britain.
   d I usually .... at my local supermarket.
   e I'd forgotten my wallet, so Pete .... and lent me some money.
   f I always try to .... when I ...., but I don't always get a good mark.

Pronunciation

Look at this word from the interview: ANT**ARC**TIC
The middle syllable of the word is stressed. This means that it is slightly longer when you say it. It doesn't mean you need to make it louder!
In English the stress pattern in words is variable.

10   In pairs decide where you would put the main stress on these words from the listening. If you're not sure, listen again to the interview.

recent	expedition	deserted
temperature	injection	untouched
comfortable	scientists	excursions
passenger	biscuits	permitted
atmosphere	industry	experience

11   Read this dialogue through to yourself and mark the stress on the words in italics. Then work with a partner. Take a role each and read out the dialogue.

   Travel Agent: Good morning, can I help you?
   Customer: Yes. Have you got any *brochures* on *Africa*? I'm a keen *photographer* and I'd like to spend some time *photographing* the *animals*.
   Travel Agent: Well, we can offer you *various package* deals. What kind of *accommodation* would you prefer?
   Customer: Oh, a good *hotel*. I don't like to be *uncomfortable* – I'm not the camping type.
   Travel Agent: Well, I think we have *something* here to suit you. Let's see. We have two weeks in *Kenya*. It looks very *attractive*, I don't think you'll be *disappointed*. They also *guarantee* plenty of *wildlife*.
   Customer: That sounds good. Thanks. I'll take the *brochure* and have a look at it tonight.

12   🎧 Listen to the recording to check your pronunciation.

Modals 1: Obligation, necessity and permission

1 Look at the extracts (a–g) from the listening and then decide which extract goes with phrases 1–6.

   a you should take warm clothes
   b you really need a windproof coat
   c you don't have to socialise if you don't want to
   d cruise ships are not allowed to go where they like
   e they have to carry scientists to lead the excursions
   f small parties are permitted to land
   g you've got to keep away from the wildlife

What word or phrase in a–g means:

   1 There's no choice.   4 It's allowed.
   2 It's necessary.   5 It's not necessary.
   3 It's forbidden.   6 It's a good idea.

2 In small groups talk about the following sentences. Decide why some sentences use *must* and others use *have to*.

   a I must remember to buy a newspaper on my way home.
   b The doctor says I have to try to take more exercise.
   c All cars must be left in the car park, not on the road.

   G ⋯⟶ page 199

3 Imagine you are **extremely** rich. In pairs discuss your holidays in the places shown, using *must, have to,* and *don't have to*. Talk about transportation, accommodation, food, activities, entertainment and people.

> *When I go to Los Angeles I tell my secretary that I must stay at the Beverley Wiltshire hotel. My suite must have a private swimming pool and jacuzzi. Luckily I don't have to queue at the airport as I have a private jet, and a limousine to meet me. Even though I'm very rich I still have to take a passport like everyone else.*

Corpus spot

Be careful with modal verbs – the *Cambridge Learner Corpus* shows FCE candidates often make mistakes with these.

   I **must fill in** an application form for a visa.
   NOT I ~~must to fill in~~ an application form for a visa.

   I **don't have to show** my passport at the border any more.
   NOT I ~~haven't to show~~ my passport at the border any more.

Correct the mistakes that FCE candidates have made with obligation and necessity.

   a You needn't to be worried about me.
   b Another thing, should I to take my camera with me?
   c You needn't smoke in this part of the restaurant; it's a no smoking area.
   d It must be nice when I am older.
   e We have get to the exhibition early or we won't get a ticket.
   f You don't have to swim off the rocks because it's dangerous.
   g My doctor says I need give up smoking.
   h Lisa must to buy a ticket before getting on the bus.
   i I don't have to be late or I'll miss my plane.

4 With a partner, talk about the following situations.

EXAMPLE: *I'm going to travel abroad.*
   – *I need a new passport.*
   – *I have to have an injection.*
   – *I must pack my bag.*
   – *I should buy a new pair of sunglasses,*
      but I don't think I have time.

a It's the weekend tomorrow.
b I'm 18 today.
c My friend is getting married soon.
d I started a new job last week.
e I've won the lottery.
f I'm going to learn to drive a car.

5 You can use *permit*, *allow*, *let* and *can* to express permission. Notice that both *permit* and *allow* are followed by *to*, and *let* and *can* aren't.

What did your parents let you do when you were younger?
What are you allowed to do when you are 18 in your country?

Using *permit*, *allow*, *let* or *can* once only, complete these sentences. You may need to add other words.

a I wasn't .... to go on holiday with my friends until I was sixteen.
b You .... stay at this campsite without booking in advance.
c Peter .... me borrow his large suitcase when I went shopping in New York.
d They .... us to board the plane early because we only had hand luggage.

6 There are two past forms of *need*. One is *didn't need to do* and the other is *needn't have done*. Look at these examples and in pairs discuss what you think the difference in meaning is.

a I didn't need to go to the bank this morning, as I had enough money to do the shopping.
b I needn't have rung to tell him about the air traffic control strike because he told me he had already heard about it on the radio.

G ⋯⋮➤ page 199

Exam spot

Remember that a contraction – *don't, isn't* – counts as two words.

7 Complete the second sentence so that it has a similar meaning to the first sentence, using the word given. **Do not change the word given.** You must use between two and five words, including the word given.

1 The travel agent said, 'All passengers for Marseilles must change trains in Paris.'
   to
   The travel agent said that all passengers for Marseilles ....
   trains in Paris.

2 I went to the bank but it wasn't really necessary.
   gone
   I ....
   the bank.

3 I wasn't allowed to go on holiday with my friends last year.
   let
   My parents ....
   on holiday with my friends last year.

4 This is a 'no swimming area'.
   permitted
   You ....
   in this area.

5 It's a good idea to have health insurance when you go on holiday.
   get
   You .... before you go on holiday.

6 British passport holders no longer need a visa to visit the USA.
   have
   British passport holders ....
   a visa to visit the USA any more.

G rammar extra
Prepositions of location

Complete the following sentences with these prepositions of location.

on	in	into	off	at	across

a The hotel had a swimming pool .... its roof.
b I arrived .... the airport very early in the morning.
c When I walked .... the hotel I was amazed by the decoration.
d I arrived .... Spain last Tuesday.
e We showed our passports as we went .... the frontier.
f I found a bank .... the town centre.
g We sat .... the terrace drinking coffee.
h There was a notice .... the wall telling us about trips.
i I jumped .... the pool to cool off.
j Singapore is an island .... the coast of Malaysia.

Exam folder 2

Paper 3 Part 3 Word formation

In this part of the Use of English paper you are given a short text with ten gaps and an example. At the end of some of the lines there is a word in capitals which you will need to change so that it will make sense when it is put in the gap in the same line. In the example below, you are given the verb 'arrive' and it needs to be changed into the noun 'arrival' in order for the sentence to make sense.

EXAMPLE:	Their plane's late ..... was due to a thunderstorm during the flight.	ARRIVE
ANSWER:	Their plane's late ARRIVAL was due to a thunderstorm during the flight.	

You need to read the sentence carefully to decide what kind of word is missing – is it a noun, a verb, an adjective or an adverb? In English we often use prefixes (words that go in front of a word) and suffixes (words that go at the end of a word) to change the type of word it is.

Prefixes

1   The following prefixes all give the meaning of NOT when they come before a word. We often put *il-* before words beginning with *l*, *ir-* before words beginning with *r*, and *im-* before words beginning with *p*. Take care with this rule though, as there are exceptions.

il-	un-	in-
dis-	ir-	im-

Which prefix do we use to make these adjectives negative?

a satisfied	j legible
b relevant	k accessible
c patient	l responsible
d complete	m pleased
e legal	n realistic
f possible	o perfect
g comfortable	p regular
h honest	q literate
i popular	

2   What meaning do you think these prefixes give to the word that follows? Can you think of some more examples?

a *mini*-skirt	f *under*done
b *non*-stop	g *anti*-freeze
c *re*train	h *ultra*-conservative
d *sub*way	i *out*live
e *un*tie	

Suffixes

3   NOUNS – Typical noun suffixes are:

-ation	-ion	-ness	-ship	-ity
-ism	-ence	-ment	-al	

Make these words into nouns.

a happy	f popular
b intelligent	g friend
c approve	h social
d repeat	i pay
e inform	

4   Not all nouns follow the above pattern. Make nouns from these words.

a true	c die
b succeed	d high

5   ADJECTIVES – Typical adjectival suffixes are:

-ible	-able	-y	-al
-ive	-ful	-less	-ous

Make these words into adjectives.

a wind	d peace
b attract	e eat
c hope	

6 VERBS – Typical verb suffixes are:

-ve	-ist	-en
-ise	-ize	-ify

Make these words into verbs.

a wide   **c** sympathy
b behaviour   **d** clear

In British English you will nearly always be correct if you use *-ise*.

7 ADVERBS – Adverbs are usually formed by adding the suffix *-ly* to the adjective. However, there are some exceptions.

Make these words into adverbs.

a hard   **d** peace
b good   **e** fast
c slow   **f** true

8 Read through the passage on the right and think about what kind of words you need to make. For example, 0 is a noun (publication). List the parts of speech for 1–10 and then complete the task.

1 = a verb
2 =
3 =
4 =
5 =
6 =
7 =
8 =
9 =
10 =

Advice

- Read through the passage carefully to get an idea of what it is about.
- Decide what kind of word is missing – is it an adjective, verb, noun or adverb?
- Make sure that your choice makes sense in the sentence. Some words may need to have a negative prefix.
  EXAMPLE: The waitress took ages to bring us the menu and I found her very rude and .... HELP
  ANSWER: UNHELPFUL
- Check that you have spelt the words correctly.
- You MUST write your answers IN CAPITAL LETTERS.

A MAP MAKER

Example: | o | P | U | B | L | I | C | A | T | I | O | N | | | | |

The (**0**) ..... of the first atlas was in 1595. The man **PUBLISH**

who (**1**) ..... this collection of maps was called Gerardus **PRODUCT**

Mercator. Born in 1512, his father was a shoemaker called

Hubert Kremer. Mercator spent his (**2**) ..... in Flanders, where **YOUNG**

he became known as an (**3**) ..... talented map-maker. **EXTREME**

Besides teaching mathematics to the students at the

University of Louvain, he also earned extra money

making (**4**) ..... instruments. **SCIENCE**

In 1544 he was briefly imprisoned for his (**5**) ..... beliefs **RELIGION**

and, fearing for his family's (**6**) ....., he went to live in the **SAFE**

Rhineland, where he lived for the rest of his life.

His first atlas, published in 1538, was so (**7**) ..... that it was **SUCCEED**

translated into a (**8**) ..... of European languages. However, **VARY**

although Mercator spent time updating his map with new

data, it was still (**9**) ..... because the earth is round. **ACCURACY**

As maps are flat, it is virtually (**10**) ..... to have correct scale, **POSSIBLE**

area and direction on one map.

4·1 Our four-legged friends

1 Before doing this questionnaire, discuss your feelings about animals in general and having a pet.

Pet Questionnaire

1 Which kind of pet would you prefer to have and why?
- **a** A dog
- **b** A cat
- **c** A budgerigar
- **d** A goldfish
- **e** Something exotic like a snake or a tarantula
- **f** None. I object to people keeping animals as pets.

2 Which country keeps the most dogs as pets?
- **a** The UK
- **b** The USA
- **c** France

3 Which country keeps the most cats as pets?
- **a** Sweden
- **b** The UK
- **c** Germany

4 If someone owns a dog, do you think that they should
- **a** be made to buy a licence for it?
- **b** have to do a training course?
- **c** only allow the dog out on a lead?
- **d** be allowed to keep it in an apartment?
- **e** be free to do what they want as dog owners?
- **f** do none of these?

2 What do you think would be the best pet for the people in pictures 1–4?

3 You are going to read four texts about different pets. Read the introduction below to find out who the four pets have been to see recently.

Nowadays more and more pet owners are spending their hard-earned money on sorting out their pets' psychological problems. 'Owners come to us when they've tried everything they can with no result,' says Dr Mugford, one of Britain's leading animal behaviourists. 'We find that most owners can be trained to deal with behavioural problems in one 90-minute session, although it does take a lot of hard work and commitment to see the results. Dogs are the most receptive to therapy. Cats can be tricky, and the chances of success with anything more exotic depend on the problem and the creature's personality.'

4 Skim texts A–D. Where are they from?

- **a** an article
- **b** an encyclopedia
- **c** a pet-care book
- **d** a novel

Exam spot

First of all read through the texts quickly to get an idea of where they come from and what they are about. Remember this is called 'skimming'.

5 Now scan the texts A–D to find the information to answer questions 1–11. Underline the words or phrases that give you the answers.

EXAMPLE: *Which owner was embarrassed by a pet?*
      A Brett   **B** Rosemary
      C Fiona   **D** Vicki
ANSWER: D (*I spent the whole time going red in the face and apologising to people.*)

Which owner

1 had some trouble with accommodation because of a pet? [1]

2 thinks the pet is completely cured? [2]

3 was attacked by a pet? [3]

4 got a pet when it was very young? [4]

5 had to learn new ways of behaviour? [5]

6 wanted a pet because of loneliness? [6]

7 believed the pet might die? [7]

8 had to teach a pet who was the boss? [8]

9 wasn't given any help by the therapist? [9]

10 wasn't worried about the pet's health? [10]

11 bought nice things for their pet? [11]

A | Brett

Brett got his pet Doberman, called Sonny, from an organisation which rescues dogs that have been badly treated by their previous owners. 'The day after Sonny arrived he refused to let me into the house after work, and when I fought my way in he bit me. It was like an all-out war. I didn't know what to do, but I'd had Dobermans before and I know they're very bright dogs and I felt he deserved a chance. I finally went to see an animal behaviourist and although it took over two years of tremendously hard work, Sonny is much better. The therapist started by retraining me. I had to ignore Sonny's bad behaviour. He had to learn that I was in charge. It's been the hardest job I've ever done, and although Sonny can still be a bit tricky, he's a different dog these days.'

B | Rosemary

Rosemary had always wanted a parrot, so a year ago she acquired William from an advertisement in a newspaper. 'I needed a bit of company as I'm a pensioner living on my own, so at first I was delighted to get William. Well, three weeks after I got him, he suddenly started barking like a dog. The flats where I live don't allow dogs and William made such a loud barking noise that my neighbour reported me. Then William started repeating the arguments he must have heard at his previous owners'. They were a young couple getting divorced. William shouted "Steve, you're a liar! Don't go Steve, I love you Steve" (Steve was the husband's name). I took William to see an animal behaviourist who said he was in good condition, but she couldn't do anything for him and she thought that in time he'd forget his past owners and start copying the noises I make. In fact, I like opera and William has now started to sing along, as I do when I'm listening, although he can only manage the high notes at present.'

C | Fiona

Fiona, who works as a nurse, has a Siamese cat called Tooting. She's spent over four years trying to cure Tooting of anorexia, a problem you have if you don't eat. 'There was a time when I thought Tooting wouldn't survive, he was so painfully thin. His previous owner told me that Tooting had been on antibiotics because he had problems with his teeth and gums. I'd do everything to tempt him to eat – buy him fresh prawns and salmon, then hand-feed it to him. In the end I saw an animal behaviourist who said that Tooting had profound anxiety about eating because he now associated it with pain. So I had some of his teeth extracted and I was given a pain-relieving electrical device that he wears when he eats. It's been pretty successful, and Tooting is eating fairly normally again.'

D | Vicki

Vicki has a dachshund called Yoda. 'At about six months Yoda suddenly became really wild. She'd rush up to anyone – especially if she thought they were doing something she regarded as odd, such as sitting on the grass or sunbathing – and start barking. She'd chase passers-by, particularly if they were carrying umbrellas, and stand and bark at objects like post-boxes and tin cans on the pavement. I spent the whole time going red in the face and apologising to people. But I knew enough about dogs to suspect that Yoda's problem was due less to being very aggressive than to excessive fear. As I'd got her as a puppy from a reputable breeder, I knew there was nothing basically wrong with her. I only had one consultation and Yoda was immediately better. I was given a device called an Aboistop, which fits on a dog's collar. Each time Yoda barks it squirts lemon essence, which isn't at all harmful but dogs don't like the smell. It has worked like a dream.'

---

6 **What do you think about behaviour therapy for animals? Is it popular in your country? What would you do if:**

   a your dog kept barking at people?

   b your dog tried to bite people?

   c your cat clawed the furniture?

   d your parrot wouldn't speak?

7 **What words related to a–h occur in texts A–D?**

   a organise (A)   e success (C)

   b trick (A)   f aggression (D)

   c advertise (B)   g excess (D)

   d argue (B)   h reputation (D)

4·2

as and *like*

1 Read the explanations below. Some of the examples are taken from the article you have read in 4.1.

- *As* is used to refer to a person's (or animal's) profession:
  I knew he'd been trained as a guard dog …
  Fiona, who works as a nurse, …

- *Like* is only used for comparison or similarity:
  … he suddenly started barking like a dog. (He's actually a parrot.)
  It was like an all-out war.
  It has worked like a dream.

- *Like* and *such as* can be used to mean *for example*:
  … and bark at objects like post-boxes …
  … such as sitting on the grass or sunbathing …

- Some verbs can be followed by *as*:
  … something she regarded as odd …

  Other verbs of this type are *refer to, use, be known, describe, class, accept* and *treat*.

- *As* is normally followed by a subject and verb, while *like* is followed by a noun or pronoun:
  … as I do when I'm listening …
  He was crying like a baby.

  (In British English it is becoming more common to hear *like* followed by a subject and verb. This is acceptable in American English.)

G ┄┄⟩ page 199

Corpus spot 👁

The *Cambridge Learner Corpus* shows FCE candidates often confuse the use of *like* and *as*.

> I would like to work **as** a babysitter.
> NOT I would like to work ~~like~~ a babysitter.

Sometimes students use *like* or *as* when it isn't necessary to do so.

> It was a small flat that looked empty.
> NOT It was a small flat that looked ~~like~~ empty.

> I expected the water to be crystal clear.
> NOT I expected the water to be ~~as~~ crystal clear.

---

2 Complete the following sentences, using *as*, *like* or nothing, as appropriate.

a The strange man looked .... a burglar.
b I know it sounds .... foolish, but I want to buy a tiger.
c You can work .... full-time in my shop.
d The new shopping centre is very big – it's .... an airport terminal.
e She could play the piano just .... a professional.
f He went to the fancy dress party dressed .... a gorilla.
g Pete regarded his cat .... a member of the family.

Compound adjectives

3 A compound adjective is an adjective which has two parts and is usually written with a hyphen. Many have a present or past participle in the second part of the compound, as in this example from 4.1:

hard-earned money – money which you work hard to earn.

Work through the questions in a–d with a partner.

a
1 Who do you think our 'four-legged friends' are?
2 What is a man-eating tiger?
3 How would you describe a cat which has blue eyes, long hair and a bad temper?
4 What about an animal with two toes and a back covered in scales?

b
Do you know anyone who is:
1 left-handed?
2 cross-eyed?
3 bad-tempered?
4 sharp-tongued?
5 narrow-minded?

Compound adjectives are very useful for describing people, both for character and physical characteristics. Describe someone in your family.

EXAMPLE: My mother's a brown-eyed, curly-haired, woman. She's left-handed. She's a broad-minded and self-confident person.

c

Some compound adjectives have a preposition in the second part of the compound, as in this phrase from 4.1: 'all-out war' – total war.

1 Where would you sit at a drive-in movie?
2 How would you feel if you were hard-up?
3 How much money do you need to have to be well-off?

Can you think of some more examples?

d

The article in 4.1 talked about a '90-minute session' with the therapist. Notice that *minute* is singular not plural.

How would you describe:

1 a journey which was fifty kilometres long
2 a girl who is twelve years old
3 a film which lasts 75 minutes
4 a car which costs £35,000
5 a pause which lasts ten seconds

Listening

4 🎧 You overhear some conversations about animals. For questions 1–3, decide which is the right answer, A, B or C.

1 Which animal does the man own?
  A a bird
  B a snake
  C a rabbit

2 What problem does the woman have with her dog?
  A The neighbours are frightened of it.
  B It is always ill.
  C She hasn't time to take it for walks.

3 What does this man think about zoos?
  A He likes visiting them.
  B He thinks they should free the animals.
  C He believes they are doing a good job.

Vocabulary

Vocabulary spot

Use an English–English dictionary to look up words you don't know.

5 Decide which of the words below belong with each of these animals.

parrot   cat   dog   horse

perch	foal	mane	feather
hoof	fur	neigh	purr
bark	paw	kennel	puppy
stable	whiskers	kitten	wing
squawk	claw	beak	

6 There are many common expressions with 'time' in English, as in this example from the article about the four pets.

… that in time he'd forget his past owners

to spend time	to kill time
to pass the time	to have a good time
to take time off	to tell the time
time for breakfast/lunch	ten times three
in time	behind the times
at times	from time to time
four times as much	a time when
to waste time	

Complete the sentences a–h with one of the expressions above.

a Her ideas on women working are completely
....

b I usually don't have enough ...., so I grab a sandwich on the way to work.

c He says he never puts on weight, but he eats three .... as I do.

d .... people will realise that not spending enough on education will only lead to disaster.

e Although Peter decided not to come to the concert with us he said he hoped we would ....

f I always take a book to the doctor's surgery to .... while I'm waiting.

g She was given a watch as soon as she learnt to
....

h I really hate .... doing stupid exercises.

Writing folder 2

Transactional letters and emails 1

Question 1 in Paper 2 is compulsory – all exam candidates have to answer it. 'Transactional' means that the letter or email has a particular purpose, and will require further action by its reader, usually in the form of a written response. The letter or email must be based on the information given in the question. Examples of transactional letters and emails include: writing to a school to request details about a language course; complaining to a company about a holiday; replying to a friend about arrangements for a party. The letter or email could be formal or informal. For the examination there is no difference in the way you write a letter or an email.

1   Look at the following extracts and decide what the writer is doing in each. (Some may be used twice, while others are not used at all.)

a   complaining   d   giving information
b   suggesting   e   asking for information
c   correcting information

1

> I must point out that the article in your newspaper about our International Club gave some misleading information. We actually meet once a week, not once a fortnight and we begin at 8 o'clock, not 9 o'clock. You also gave the impression that the club was just for young people. In fact, we are very happy to welcome people of all ages.

2

> I have always enjoyed working with animals and have spent every summer working as a riding instructor at a local stable. I am available for interview from May 19th this year and I include the names and addresses of two people who would be willing to give me a reference.

3

> As I've already said, I think the general standard of accommodation in your hotel is good. However, I think that you should spend more time on staff training as I found some of your staff, especially those in the restaurant, to be unhelpful and on one occasion, quite rude.

2   Read this example of a Part 1 task.

You have just returned from a trip to Florida. You flew there and back with Ocean Air. You decide to write to the airline to complain about your flight.

Read the advertisement and the notes you have made. Then write a letter to the airline, using all your notes.

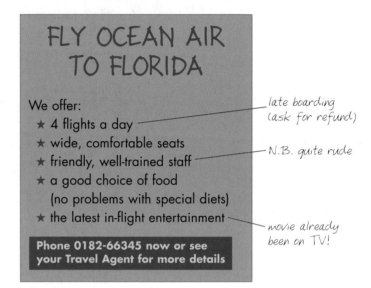

> FLY OCEAN AIR TO FLORIDA
>
> We offer:
> ★ 4 flights a day — *late boarding (ask for refund)*
> ★ wide, comfortable seats
> ★ friendly, well-trained staff — *N.B. quite rude*
> ★ a good choice of food (no problems with special diets)
> ★ the latest in-flight entertainment — *movie already been on TV!*
>
> **Phone 0182-66345 now or see your Travel Agent for more details**

Write your **letter** in 120–150 words. Do not include any postal addresses.

3   In pairs, discuss what you are being asked to do.

• Do you need to write a formal or an informal letter? How do you know?
• Do you know the name of anyone at the company? How will you begin and end the letter? What kind of tone will your letter take (rude, polite, etc.)?
• How are you going to organise the letter? For example: How many paragraphs? What kind of linking words?
• Which points do you think are the most important?
• Are there any points you think you can leave out?
• Is there anything you think it would be a good idea to add?

4   With a partner decide what is wrong with the following letter. For example, there are punctuation mistakes, so *a* is ticked (✓). Do the same with b–j.

   a   punctuation ✓
   b   paragraphing ☐
   c   length ☐
   d   grammar ☐
   e   vocabulary ☐
   f   opening and closing phrases ☐
   g   content points ☐
   h   spelling ☐
   i   tone (level of politeness, formality) ☐
   j   linking words ☐

Dear Sir,

I am writing to complain about the flight to Florida that I made with your airline on 12th June this year. We were three hours late boarding the plane. No one was able to tell us why. Another problem was the flight attendant. She was very unhelpful. I had problems with my hand luggage. She told me she was too busy to help me. I demand some compensation for the problems I had flying with your airline. If you don't send me the money immediately, I will call my lawyer.

Yours faithfully

---

5   With a partner decide which of these sentences you would use in a formal letter and why. You must remember that your letter must have a 'positive effect' on the person reading it.

   a   I want you to give me back my money.
   b   I look forward to hearing from you in the near future.
   c   The food was OK.
   d   I have decided not to fly with your company again.
   e   I would be grateful if you could send me a refund.
   f   The service was satisfactory.
   g   If you don't do what I tell you, there's going to be trouble.
   h   I would appreciate an apology from your company.
   i   Hi Steve!
   j   See you soon.
   k   Dear Sir or Madam
   l   And, another thing, I won't fly with you again because it wasn't very comfortable.

Abbreviations

6   You will sometimes find abbreviations given in the Part 1 task. Decide what the following common abbreviations mean. Use your English–English dictionary to help you.

   a   RSVP   f   Sq., Ave, St, Rd   k   Dr
   b   e.g.   g   PTO   l   c/o
   c   etc.   h   kgs, kms   m   approx.
   d   N.B.   i   nos.   n   cont'd
   e   tel.   j   max., min.   o   mins

7   Another type of transactional letter or email task is correcting information, usually from a newspaper article. Look at this task. Write your answer in 120–150 words in an appropriate style.

In the summer you had a job at a work camp in Kirby in England. A friend in Kirby has just sent you this article from the local newspaper. You decide to write an email to the newspaper to correct some of the information in the article.

Read the article and the notes you have made. Then, write an email to the newspaper, using **all** your notes.

> **Student Slaves at Workcamp**
> All summer some 30 foreign students were working long hours for little more than pocket money on a local farm. Sleeping in old tents and with only one shower between 30 people, the students spent their days picking fruit and vegetables. It's a disgrace that visitors to this country who come to these so-called 'international workcamps' should have to put up with such dreadful conditions.
> I think that

> *Notes*
> – *max. 15 students*
> – *mornings only, weekends free*
> – *modern, wooden buildings with showers*
> – *fun, great atmosphere*

Write an email. You must use grammatically correct sentences with accurate spelling and punctuation in a style appropriate for the situation.

5.1 Fear and loathing

1 What frightens you? Say how you feel about the things in the picture.

2 Imagine a frightening situation and tell another student the story as though it really happened to you. Use some of the language below.

> I felt … a bit uneasy / anxious / jumpy / tense / on edge.
> I was … really shocked / scared stiff / scared to death.
> I was … absolutely terrified / petrified.
> It was … hair-raising / spine-chilling / so scary / really creepy / very spooky.
> I went … to pieces / white / pale / rigid with fear.
> I became … hysterical / a nervous wreck.

3 Write a title on the board that summarises the story you have just heard. As a class, choose the three most frightening titles. The students who have listened to these accounts should tell the class what happened, using *he/ she* … .

Listening

4 🎧 Listen to this recording, where a man is talking about something frightening that happened to him. Say where the man was and how long he spent there.

Now listen again and describe in detail what happened to the man. Use these questions to help you.

1 Why was he in the building?
2 What time of day was it?
3 How far did the lift go?
4 Which two things did he try to do?
5 Why was he there for so long?

> ### Exam spot
>
> Part 1 of Paper 4 consists of eight short extracts. For each extract, there is one multiple choice question. The eight questions will test different things, for example who is speaking, how he or she feels, where the recording is taking place, or what it is about.

5 Here is the question for the extract you have just heard.

    1 You will hear a man talking about something frightening that happened to him. What was his first reaction?
      A He sat down and cried.
      B He decided to call for help.
      C He tried to keep calm.

All three options are mentioned in the extract. Listening out for sequence words – that is, words which tell you what happened when – will help you to decide what his **first** reaction was.

🎧 Listen once more to the extract and note down any sequence words and phrases. Which one signals the answer?

6 🎧 Now look at these questions. Before you listen, think about the words in bold and decide what you will need to listen out for.

    2 You will hear a woman talking about something that happened in her home. When was she **most** scared?
      A When she heard a burglar upstairs.
      B While she was watching a horror film.
      C When she suddenly saw a frog.

    3 You hear a man talking about how to deal with fear. **Who** is he?
      A an ex-teacher
      B an ex-pilot
      C an ex-actor

    4 You hear a woman describing what happened to her on a journey. **Where** did she **end up** that night?
      A on a country road
      B in hospital
      C at her house

    5 You hear a man being interviewed about a sailing accident. What was the **worst** part of his experience?
      A being cold
      B feeling hungry
      C avoiding sharks

    6 You hear a woman talking on the radio about an incident abroad. **Why** was she able to **escape**?
      A She was by the door.
      B She wasn't noticed.
      C She had a radio.

7 🎧 How much can you remember about the last account? Discuss with a partner what happened and note down everything in the order it happened. Then listen to extract 6 to check your notes.

Pronunciation

8 In the extracts you have just heard, there are a number of examples of verbs with regular past tense endings. Although the spelling of these is always the same, *-ed*, the pronunciation is different, according to which letter precedes the ending.

🎧 Listen to extract 1 again. All the regular verbs which occur in it are listed below in order. Underline the verbs which contain the sound /ɪd/, for example, *started*.

pressed	screamed
noticed	hammered
started	helped
shuddered	realised
pushed	happened
lifted	called
shouted	

Can you explain the reason for the /ɪd/ ending?

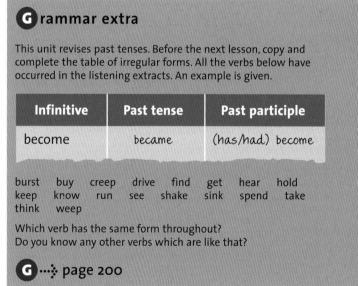

ⓖrammar extra

This unit revises past tenses. Before the next lesson, copy and complete the table of irregular forms. All the verbs below have occurred in the listening extracts. An example is given.

Infinitive	Past tense	Past participle
become	became	(has/had) become

burst   buy   creep   drive   find   get   hear   hold
keep   know   run   see   shake   sink   spend   take
think   weep

Which verb has the same form throughout?
Do you know any other verbs which are like that?

ⓖ ⋯⋗ page 200

Review of past tenses

1 Look at examples a–j, which come from the listening in 5.1. Decide which tenses they contain. Where there are two different tenses in the same sentence, list both.

past simple	(PS)
past continuous	(PC)
present perfect tense	(P)
past perfect tense	(PP)

a I'd had this interview for a job.
b I got in the lift and pressed the button.
c I've never been in one since.
d I was watching a horror movie.
e It was her footsteps I had heard.
f While I was putting the books away, I found something else.
g The others were looking at a map on the table, but I was standing by the back window.
h I knew they hadn't seen me.
i When I realised they had gone, I ran inside.
j You have recently sailed around the world.

Look again at the examples containing two different tenses. Can you explain why each tense is used? Think about when each action happened.

Past simple/Past continuous
The most important difference between these two tenses is the duration of an action. For example, in example *f* above, the past continuous describes an action that happened over a longer time period than the second action, which happened at a specific moment and may have interrupted the longer continuous activity:

———————X————————

While I was putting the books away … I found something else.

Like the present continuous tense, the past continuous is used to describe temporary situations, as in example *d*.

————————————————X

I was watching a movie. … I turned off the TV.

Note that this use can be an effective way of setting the scene at the beginning of a story, as in example *g*.

————————————————X

The others were looking at a map … Six of them burst in.

2 Complete this text using the verbs in brackets, in either the past simple or past continuous tense.

Quite late one evening I (1) .... (walk) home alone from college. The wind (2) .... (blow) hard and it (3) .... (pour) with rain, so there (4) .... (be) no one around. Anyway, this big black van (5) .... (drive) past me and (6) .... (stop), just where the road (7) .... (curve) round. I (8) .... (decide) to go on, though I (9) .... (feel) increasingly uneasy. However, as soon as I (10) .... (get) close to the van, it (11) .... (drive) off. This (12) .... (happen) twice more further down the same road. Each time, the van (13) .... (pull up) fifty metres ahead of me, (14) .... (wait) until I almost (15) .... (draw up) with it and then (16) .... (pull away) again. By this stage I (17) .... (be) absolutely petrified. So I (18) .... (stand) for a moment under a tree. The rain (19) .... (come down) in torrents now. I (20) .... (shake) and (21) .... (wonder) what to do next, when a policeman (22) .... (come) past. He (23) .... (push) his bike because of the heavy rain. I (24) .... (grab) him by the arm and (25) .... (make) him stop. Then I completely (26) .... (go) to pieces. While he (27) .... (try) to calm me down, I (28) .... (hear) the van drive off, thankfully for the last time. I've never walked home on my own since.

Past simple/Past perfect
The past perfect is used for actions in the past that occur earlier than the time period that is being described, as in example *i*:

When I realised they <u>had gone</u>, I ran inside.

3 Complete these sentences with the verbs in brackets, in either the past simple or past perfect tense.

a We .... (spend) the previous night in a really creepy hotel in the middle of nowhere, so we .... (decide) to stay in a place in town.

b Jenny .... (tell) us in great detail what .... (happen) to her on the mountain and .... (explain) why she .... (find) it so scary up there.

c I .... (keep) still for over half an hour and I .... (think) it .... (be) safe at last to come out of my hiding place.

G ⋯⟶ page 200

4 Look at this set of four pictures from an action story. Describe what happened in each scene, starting with the last one (4), and making reference back to what had happened earlier. Remember to use a range of past tenses.

5 Read this extract from the thriller *The Big Sleep*, ignoring the gaps for the moment. Why do you think the man telling the story wasn't frightened of the gun? Turn to page 45 to find out if you are right!

The gun pointed at my chest. Her hand seemed to **(0)** ....be........ quite steady. I laughed **(1)** .... her. I started to walk towards her. I saw her small finger tighten on **(2)** .... trigger and grow white at the tip.

I was about six feet away from her **(3)** .... she started to shoot. The sound **(4)** .... the gun made a sharp slap, a brittle crack in the sunlight. I didn't see any smoke. I stopped again **(5)** .... grinned at her.

She fired twice more, very quickly. I don't think **(6)** .... of the shots would have missed. There were five in the little gun. She **(7)** .... fired four. I rushed her.

I didn't want the last one in my face, **(8)** .... I swerved to one side. She gave it to me quite carefully, **(9)** .... worried at all.

I straightened up. 'My, but you're cute,' I said.

Her hand **(10)** .... holding the empty gun and began to shake violently. The gun fell **(11)** .... of it. Her mouth began to shake. Then her whole face **(12)** .... to pieces.

6 Now fill each gap, choosing a suitable word from the box below. There are three words you do not need.

and	any	at	because	had	has
not	of	out	so	some	the	was
went	when				

Can you put these words into grammatical categories? For example, *and* is a conjunction. These words are typical of the kinds of words that are tested in Part 2 of Paper 3.

Exam folder 3

Paper 3 Part 2 Open cloze

In this part of the Use of English paper you are asked to complete a text containing 12 gaps. You must write only one word in each gap. The missing word is usually a grammar word, but occasionally, vocabulary is tested. There is an example at the beginning. You must write your answers in CAPITAL letters.

It is very important to read through the text carefully before you decide to write anything down. Sometimes the answer to a gap depends on what is said later in the paragraph. Many students lose marks for not reading through carefully enough. Also look at the title so you get some idea of what the text is about. The title is there to help you.

1   Read this text through at least twice and then choose the best title from the three below.

   1 **DON'T TAKE THE RISK!**
   2 **NOTHING TO WORRY ABOUT**
   3 **BALANCING THE RISKS**

Example: `o` `O` `N` ☐☐☐☐☐☐☐☐☐☐☐☐

What are the chances of slipping **(0)** .... a banana skin, being hit by lightning or being struck by a meteorite? These are not the sort of unlucky events that most people **(1)** .... their time thinking about, **(2)** .... perhaps one has already happened to them.

However, **(3)** .... surprising number of people have, **(4)** .... some time in their lives, imagined aliens kidnapping them. Some even have recurring nightmares about it, whereas relatively **(5)** .... are afraid of dying from flu, even **(6)** .... it is more likely to happen. No doubt many people **(7)** .... go rock climbing will be among the people drinking bottled water on the grounds that it is safer **(8)** .... water from the tap.

Amazingly, our fear of flying outweighs our fear of driving, **(9)** .... the statistics show that going by plane is much safer. The best explanation is that people dread far more the possibility of dropping **(10)** .... of the air than of crashing on land.

(11) .... an attempt to educate us all in the real and imagined risks of life, the British government has asked scientists to construct a scale of risk that the public can use to compare any new and unfamiliar risks, **(12)** .... as those involved in taking new medicines, in terms of real events.

2 Now try to fill in the gaps. If you need help, look at the following clues.

   0 *on* (to slip on something)
   1 A collocation – *to ..... time doing something.*
   2 A linker which means *if not* – read the sentence very carefully.
   3 What kind of article should go here?
   4 A prepositional phrase. Which preposition?
   5 *Some* began the sentence; now you have a contrast with *relatively .....* How many? Remember the word it refers to is *people.*
   6 Part of a linker – there are two possible answers. Just write one down.
   7 Read the sentence carefully and you'll see that a relative pronoun is needed. There are two possible answers. Only write one down.
   8 a word used in comparisons
   9 another linker
   10 a preposition
   11 a preposition
   12 '..... as' means 'for example'.

Advice

- Remember to think about what type of word is needed in the gap, e.g. verb, preposition, article, pronoun.
- Check whether it should be singular or plural, past or present, etc.
- Check that when you add a word, it makes sense in the sentence and the text.
- You must only write **one** word.
- No contractions (*can't, don't*, etc.) are allowed.
- Your word must be correctly spelt.
- Always write something down, however difficult the gap may seem.
- You must write your answers IN CAPITAL LETTERS.
- You will need to transfer your answers to an answer sheet. Make sure you have transferred each answer correctly.

What if?

Exam spot

In Part 2 of Paper 1, you will have to complete a *gapped text*, where seven sentences have been removed. This type of text has a clear development of ideas, and may also have a time sequence. You should look out for words that refer back and forwards in the text, such as *it* and *this*, as well as references to time. This will help you to fit the text together.

1 Read this quote from the article below and suggest what the article might be about. Which are the key words that help you to decide?

> **I normally arrive at the winner's home around Sunday lunchtime, having got up early and driven for hours. If I left on a Saturday, after the draw, I wouldn't get there until the middle of the night.**

2 Now read the article quickly to see if you are right. Ignore gaps 1–4 for the moment.

3 What is the writer's job? Read the article again and describe to a partner what the man does on Sunday. Notice the time references in the article.

4 These four sentences have been removed from the article. Which two include a time reference? Use this information to help you fit sentences A–D into the correct gaps (1–4).

> A The bigger the win, the more mood swings there are.
> B All this is very understandable.
> C My initial visit lasts about two hours.
> D Then the subject of publicity comes up.

Which sentence refers back to the previous paragraph?

I usually arrive to find about eight adults sitting waiting, plus a lot of kids. It's always a very crowded room and the atmosphere is pretty tense. My nerves are on edge, too. The first thing I say is 'Can I take my jacket off?' and they always say 'Would you like a cup of tea?'

1 Then I leave them to it, having given them a little handbook we've prepared called *Out of the blue – it's you!* They seldom bother to read it but they tend to feel that by holding it they've established some sort of bond with us – the whole thing becomes more real to them because they've actually got something in their hands.

I check into a local hotel, leaving them to talk among themselves, then return later that evening. On this second visit, I usually have to go over all the same points I did the first time around. It seems they can't take things in because of the shock.

2 Winners often burst into tears when the press call. If I'm still in the house, I always go to the door and deal with reporters. In many ways, the effect of a sudden win is similar to that of a sudden death in the family.

Immediately, everything in their life changes. There's confusion, anxiety, emotional panic – they don't know what to do next, what the future holds, how to behave or where to go.

The behaviour of jackpot winners the first week is fairly standard. They won't be able to sleep, they'll pick at their food. Curiously, there can also be a sense of guilt. They'll sometimes say 'I didn't want to win this much, you know. If I'd won less, I'd have been much happier. Why did it happen to me?'

3 Most people buy lottery tickets for the fun of it, they never really expect to win. If they do win big money, they don't know how to cope. So it's vital for me to take my time, go slowly, repeat everything. If I appear to be in control, it gives them more confidence.

The first important question I'm asked by winners is 'When will we get the money?' They're often surprised when I reply 'Tomorrow!' But it's true. If they take their ticket to Camelot's regional office on the Monday, they'll get the money, immediately.

4 I make it clear that it's completely their decision. I just try to point out the pros and cons. I go over the chances of them keeping their win secret. I ask how many friends and relations they've already told – which is usually lots – and they say 'But if any of our friends were asked for information, they wouldn't talk.' They don't like it when I suggest the opposite. Once, two tabloid newspapers were offering £10,000 for such information. There are very few people who can resist that kind of temptation, friends or not.

Personally speaking, if I won the jackpot I'd go public. With luck, you can control the publicity. Otherwise, eventually it leaks out and you have no control. One of my winners has managed to keep it a secret so far, but mentally he's in a really terrible state. He's paranoid – he thinks people are following him, he is suspicious of everyone, he can't sleep for recurring nightmares. He's scared to buy a new car in case people start asking him questions. The poor bloke's life has been turned upside down and he's gained nothing, except the money in the bank, of course.

5 Scan the article to answer these questions about lottery winners. Use the time clues in the questions to direct you to the right part of the article.

   a Why does the man have to repeat things during his second visit?
   b How do jackpot winners behave initially?
   c What usually happens when the man first arrives at the house?
   d When can winners claim their prizes?

6 Explain the meaning of these words and phrases from the article, guessing their meaning from context if necessary. The line numbers are given in brackets.

   a bond (14)   **f** paranoid (77)
   b cope (46)   **g** suspicious (79)
   c in control (48–49)   **h** recurring (80)
   d resist (69)
   e leak out (74)

   Find the phrase *emotional panic* (line 32). What exactly does this mean?

7 Look closely at the final two paragraphs of the article and discuss these questions.

   Should lottery winners receive so much publicity?
   What are the pros and cons of winning the lottery?
   If you won the jackpot, would you go public?

Useful language

As I see it …
To my mind …
In my opinion …
For one thing … .
For another thing …
On the one hand … .
On the other hand …
The main advantage is …
One drawback is …

Conditionals with *if*

1 🎧 You are going to listen to four short extracts, where people talk about winning the lottery. How would their lives change if they won?

2 These examples from the article in 6.1 are all conditional sentences. Say what the contracted verb forms are in each sentence and explain how the sentences differ in their use of tenses.

a If I won the jackpot, I'd go public.
b If I'd won less, I'd have been much happier.
c If they do win big money, they don't know how to cope.
d If they take their ticket to Camelot's regional office on the Monday, they'll get the money.

Match a–d to conditional types 0–3.

0 A situation that happens often.
1 A situation that may happen in the future.
2 A situation that is unlikely to happen.
3 A situation that could have happened in the past, but didn't.

G ⋯⋮ page 200

3 Match the two halves of each sentence.

1 If you did more revision, …
2 If it snows, …
3 If I have time, …
4 If Helen comes round, …
5 If there had been a vote, …
6 If they finish early, …
7 If you swam regularly, …
8 If I'd known about the risk, …

a we'll get the toboggan out.
b she'll be able to tell you.
c Sam and Bernie usually have a coffee.
d you'd pass the exam.
e I'd never have eaten seafood.
f they would have lost.
g I like to walk to work.
h your body would be in better shape.

Conditionals with *unless*

4 Read these examples and explain the meaning of *unless*.

a We'll miss the start of the match unless Juan arrives soon.
b Unless you've already got tickets, you won't be able to get in.

Corpus spot

Correct any mistakes with *unless* that FCE candidates have made in these sentences. Tick the correct sentences.

a There will be no improvement in my tennis unless I don't get some training.
b I will not remain silent about the letter unless you give me my money back.
c People hardly ever use candlelight today unless there isn't anything wrong with the power supply.
d There isn't much to do in the city unless you haven't got friends.
e You must stop working so hard unless you don't want to end up in hospital sooner or later.
f If there were no televisions, we wouldn't know much about other countries unless we visited them.

5 Correct the eight mistakes with tenses in this story and fill gaps 1–10 with *if* or *unless*. The first ones have been done for you.

Yesterday was a very bad day. (1) ...If.... it ~~wasn't~~ hadn't been raining, perhaps it wouldn't have been so difficult. The thing is, I never drive to work (2) .... it's raining. But it was pouring and I needed to get to an important meeting, so I took the car. It broke down on the way. (3) .... I had it serviced regularly, I know it won't be so unreliable, but garages charge so much these days that I don't bother. I decided to call the breakdown company on my mobile phone. Well, I would have done that (4) .... my mobile hasn't run out of battery! Never mind, I thought, (5) .... I'll find a public phone, I'll be able to call from there (6) .... it's out of order! It was, so I can't! By this time, I was in a panic. What will my boss say (7) .... I didn't get to the meeting? With him, (8) .... people arrive on time, he will get really angry with them. Luckily, a taxi pulled up. 'Mason Square,' I shouted, 'and (9) .... you will do the journey in under ten minutes, I'll pay you double!' 'Forget it,' said the driver. 'The centre of town's gridlocked. (10) .... you would pay me £50, I couldn't get you there in time.' So I ended up late for the meeting and the boss was furious with me.

6 Talk to a partner. Take it in turns to finish these sentences. Then tell the class what your friend said.

   a Unless I get up early tomorrow, …
   b If I had enough money, …
   c My life would be a lot easier if, …
   d If I hadn't come to class today, …

Vocabulary Phrases with *in*

7 All these phrases have come up in this unit. Check you know their meaning with a partner. Then choose four of them to complete the sentences below.

take (something) in	in fact
in control	in case
in a state/in a panic	have it in for
in time	(someone)

   a I don't want to go to that restaurant tonight.
   .... , I never want to go there again!
   b Always take your umbrella .... it rains.
   c People who work at home often feel more .... of their time.
   d Are we .... for the 7.15 performance?

Write three example sentences containing the other phrases.

   e ....
   f ....
   g ....

8 Look at the words in the box. They form four sets and each four words have a similar meaning. Can you group them into the four categories in the table? Be careful: some words can be more than one part of speech. Think carefully about their meanings when you decide which category to put them into.

on	tiny	received	experiment	
by	light	in	accepted	trial
gathered	try	welcomed	delicate	
to	gentle	attempt		

Nouns	Verbs	Prepositions	Adjectives

Now read the short newspaper article below. There are four spaces in it. Decide which part of speech is required in each gap. Then choose the correct option to fill each one from your four sets of words.

Could it possibly be YOU?

THE NATIONAL LOTTERY

Camelot is to make a final (1) .... today to track down the winner of an unclaimed £2.1 million jackpot prize. A (2) .... plane will fly over Hull trailing the banner: '£2 million winner – is it you?' for two hours at lunch time.

The city became the focus of attention after a local newspaper (3) .... an unsigned letter from an elderly local widow saying she did not want the prize. Her reason was that 'the fuss would finish me off'. If the money is not claimed (4) .... 11pm it will go into the lottery's good causes fund.

Writing folder 3

Stories 1

In Part 2 of Paper 2, you may be asked to write a short story. The first or last sentence of the story is given in the question and you must remember to include this. Make sure that the story you write fits with the sentence.

1 Look at these two questions. Discuss with a partner what tenses you would need to use in each story.

a You have been asked to write a short story for your college magazine. The story must begin with the following sentence:

If he hadn't answered the phone, it would have been just another ordinary day.

b You have decided to enter a short story competition. The rules say that the story must end with the following sentence:

Suddenly, he woke up and realised it had been a nightmare.

2 Now read this sample answer, which works for both questions. Notice which tenses have been used. You can ignore the underlined words and gaps for the moment.

If he hadn't answered the phone, it would have been just another ordinary day. But he had lifted the receiver and had heard the news that turned his life upside down. His girlfriend had been taken hostage and her kidnappers were demanding $1,000,000.

He was in shock but he still moved fast. He found his father's gun and (1) went out of the flat. A bus was pulling away and he managed to jump on. He travelled downtown to the city's biggest bank. As he (2) went in through the glass doors, people looked at him (3)............................. Then someone noticed the gun and screamed. 'If you don't move, you won't get hurt,' he shouted (4)........................... 'I want a million dollars, now. Hand it over.' He waved the gun around (5)...........................

They stuffed the cash from the safe in a bag. He grabbed it, left the building and headed for the river, where the kidnappers were waiting. He ran and ran, endlessly, but the river got further and further away. He was crying now.

Suddenly, he woke up and realised it had been a nightmare.

3 Look at numbers 1 and 2 in the text. To get a good mark in the exam, you need to use a range of vocabulary. Choose suitable words to replace the ones given from the sets below. These words have all come in previous units so you should know them!

1 **A** rushed   **B** shuddered   **C** hammered
   D stomped
2 **A** carried   **B** threw   **C** burst   **D** turned

Now choose suitable adverbs for gaps 3–5, from the ones below. More than one answer is possible. Decide with a partner which three words fit best together.

anxiously	desperately	nervously
suspiciously	tragically	wildly

4 Look at the picture sequence below and re-arrange sentences a–i in the order of the pictures. Then include suitable sentence openers from 1–6 where needed. There is one extra opener you do not need.

a … a crowd of people had gathered and were watching her anxiously as she struggled to reach the bank.

b … she heard someone whimpering below her and when she looked down from the bridge, she saw a small boy in the deepest part of the river, waving his arms helplessly.

c … she thought he was dead but when he coughed and his legs started to move, she knew he had saved his life.

d It was a fast-flowing river and she had to swim harder than she had ever swum before, to get to him before it was too late.

e As Jean walked towards the bridge, she was thinking of all the things she could do now that the school holidays had arrived.

f Although he was panicking, she was able to grab him and she started to pull him back to the bank.

g It was a beautiful summer's day, the sun was shining and the birds were singing.

h … she jumped off the bridge and dived into the rushing water.

i … she managed it and threw both herself and the boy onto the warm grass.

1 Eventually
2 Suddenly
3 Without a second thought
4 By now
5 At first
6 Last but not least

5 Now do this writing task.

You have decided to enter a short story competition. The rules say that the story must begin with the following sentence:

As soon as he got out of the car, Martin felt uneasy.

Write your **story** in 120–180 words.

Spend a few minutes noting down ideas for your story and then discuss your notes with a partner. Suggest how your partner's story could be improved. Then list relevant vocabulary you could both use, including a range of verbs, adjectives and adverbs.

Write your story, being careful to include the given sentence accurately and where you are told to.

After you have written your story, remember to check the spelling, punctuation and grammar.

Units 1–6 Revision

Topic review

1 Together with a partner, read these sentences and discuss which are true for you, giving more details. Try to use as much of the vocabulary and language as you can from the units you have just studied.

   a I always get out of bed early in the morning.
   b If I had some money, the first thing I would buy is a fast car.
   c I'm worse at English than I am at Maths.
   d I'm always getting into trouble for forgetting things.
   e I'm not afraid of anything!
   f I think I'm broad-minded.
   g I must try to work harder.
   h I like to follow fashion.
   i Books interest me more than computer games.
   j Package holidays are not for me.

Grammar

2 Use only one word to fill each of the gaps in the following passage.

> Most (**0**) ..*of*.. us go a little crazy when we jet off (**1**) .... holiday but some, it would seem, go completely mad. They see giant rats eating through their luggage and even lose their mother-in-law in (**2**) .... back of a stolen caravan. So says WorldCover Direct, the holiday insurer. These are just (**3**) .... of the claims the company (**4**) .... received in the past 12 months.
>
> A director said, 'One of our policyholders skied into a tree (**5**) .... he was on holiday and made a claim for injuries. What he didn't mention was that he (**6**) .... blind and in the process of testing a new radar system for blind skiers.'
>
> But what (**7**) .... you were in the Mediterranean in August and had had (**8**) .... much sun? Take a dip in the pool, sit in the shade for a while – or phone your holiday insurance company requesting repatriation (**9**) .... you were 'feeling a bit hot'? One holiday maker, (**10**) .... was in Spain, did just that. Another policyholder made a claim because he and (**11**) .... wife had missed their flight. He failed to mention that she was prevented (**12**) .... boarding because she had a baby pig in her hand luggage!

Phrasal verbs

3 Complete the following sentences using the appropriate verb.

UP
   a If Elizabeth had been able to .... up just a little more money, she would have bought a faster computer.
   b When you manage to find his address, ... me up and let me know what it is.
   c Come just as you are, there's really no need to .... up.
   d We followed the signs to the beach without having any idea of where the road would .... up.
   e I don't know how you .... up with the noise from your neighbours – it would drive me mad!

OUT
   f Tourist guides often carry umbrellas so that they .... out in a crowd.
   g Sheila decided to get a travel agent to .... out all her holiday arrangements, rather than trying to book the tickets herself.
   h Pete spent a long time trying to .... out how to get his dog to stop barking.
   i 'I don't know how you can .... out looking like that,' Sue's mother said.
   j It was so foggy last night I could hardly .... out the lines on the road.

Now look at these mixed examples and replace the verb or phrase in italics with a phrasal verb or compound noun. You may have to add another extra word.

k If you want to look good in that outfit, you'll have *to reduce* the amount of chocolate you eat.

l The newspaper is saying that there has been *an improvement* in British Airways' share price.

m I really hate shops that make you feel guilty when *you return* clothes that shrink in the wash or fall to pieces.

n We decided *to start the journey* to the castle at midnight, in the hope of seeing the ghost.

o He was in hospital for a while but he's now back at work – it didn't seem to take him long *to recover from* being bitten by that dog.

Revision of present and past tenses

4 Read through this text and put the verbs in the correct tense.

The statistics on the safety of flying **(1)** ...... (BE) immensely comforting. It **(2)** ...... (SEEM) that the chances of being involved in an accident **(3)** ...... (BE) a million to one – the equivalent of flying safely every day for 95 years. Try telling that to the white-faced, petrified aerophobic, who **(4)** ...... (SEE) every frown on a stewardess's face as a portent of disaster. For some years now, psychologist Henry Jones **(5)** ...... (TRY) to tell them, and he **(6)** ...... (DO) a lot more besides. He **(7)** ...... (DEVELOP) both a theory and practice for treating air travel anxiety. Apparently, it **(8)** ...... (BE) a widespread phobia. One American survey **(9)** ...... (PUT) it as the fourth most common fear, preceded only by snakes, heights and storms. Jones **(10)** ...... (HAVE) nearly 500 clients during the last decade. Before they **(11)** ...... (COME) to him, some of his clients **(12)** ...... (never FLY), others **(13)** ...... (HAVE) just one bad experience after years of flying. One man **(14)** ...... (TAKE) over 200 flights a year for five years and **(15)** ...... (never WORRY) up till then. Then, one day on a flight to Chicago the pilot **(16)** ...... (ANNOUNCE) that they were going to turn back because of an engine fault. The man then **(17)** ...... (HAVE) a panic attack and **(18)** ...... (TRY) to get off the plane in mid-air. After Jones's course, the man **(19)** ...... (OVERCOME) his fears and **(20)** ...... (MANAGE) to fly again.

5 Complete the second sentence so that it has a similar meaning to the first sentence using the word given. Do not change the word given. You must use between two and five words, including the word given.

1 Andrea said she would only go dancing if her mother bought her a new outfit.
   unless
   Andrea said she ....
   her mother bought her a new outfit.

2 I have never seen such a terrible film before.
   worst
   This is the ....
   seen.

3 I'm sorry I didn't meet you at the airport – my car wasn't working.
   met
   I ....
   at the airport, if my car had been working.

4 This party is 'evening dress' only.
   allowed
   You ....
   dress casually for this party.

5 I'm not as frightened of flying as I am of ghosts!
   than
   I'm ....
   I am of flying.

6 It was a mistake for me to buy you that computer game.
   bought
   I ....
   that computer game.

7 The play started before we could get there.
   had
   The play ....
   when we got there.

8 I need to wear glasses to drive.
   see
   I can't ....
   my glasses.

> **5.2 exercise 5**
> The man talks about the incident later in the story. He says:
> 'All five chambers are empty. She fired them all. She fired them all at me. From a distance of five or six metres. Cute little thing, isn't she? Too bad I had loaded the gun with blanks.'

Life's too short

Gerunds and infinitives 1

1 Identify the equipment in pictures a–n, and name each sport.

2 With a partner ask and answer these questions.

   a What sport can't you stand watching?
   b What sports do you really enjoy watching?
   c What sportsperson are you keen on seeing play?
   d What sports have you either taken up or given up recently?
   e Do you mind watching a sport if the weather is cold and windy?
   f Do you feel more like playing sports on holiday than during the rest of the year?

3 A gerund, which is a verb used as a noun, always ends in -ing, but not all -ing forms are gerunds. They can be present participles or adjectives as well. What is the -ing form in these sentences?

   a I pulled on the climbing rope to show I was safe.
   b Anna was running along the track when she tripped and fell.
   c Snowboarding is a very popular sport.

4 Look at these sentences:

   a I enjoy going swimming.
   b After learning to ice-skate, I'm going to learn to play ice hockey.
   c I want to take up rowing.
   d Climbing is a fairly safe sport nowadays.
   e It's not worth going to watch our local football team because they always lose!

Find an example of a gerund above which:

   1 follows a preposition.
   2 is the subject of the sentence.
   3 follows an expression.
   4 follows a verb.
   5 follows a phrasal verb.

5 When we put a verb after a preposition, we usually use a gerund. Complete the following sentences with a preposition and one of the verbs below.

learn	teach	drop	get	do	play	swim

   a She had difficulty .... to the meeting on time.
   b Steve is very proud .... to do deep sea diving so quickly.
   c I'm very keen .... the children to ride their bikes.
   d The boy was in trouble .... his muddy sports clothes on the changing room floor.
   e I believe .... some exercise every day in order to keep healthy.
   f You don't have to be good .... to enjoy it.
   g I'm looking forward .... against him again soon.

G ···⟩ page 201

6 Infinitives are forms like (*to*) *do*, (*to*) *say*. They are usually used with 'to', but not always.

Look at the following sentences which show the more common uses of the infinitive.

a I'm going to the pool *to have* my swimming lesson.

b I want *to enrol* for netball practice next term.

c They are unlikely *to hold* the Olympics in Cambridge.

d They let me *do* the judo classes even though I had never done it before.

e You must not *run* with the ball in some sports.

f We encouraged them *to run* faster by cheering loudly.

Now say which of the above:

1 follows an adjective?
2 follows a modal auxiliary?
3 follows a main verb?
4 is used to express purpose?
5 has an infinitive without 'to'?
6 follows the object of a verb?

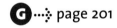 page 201

Corpus spot

Be careful with gerunds and infinitives – the *Cambridge Learner Corpus* shows FCE candidates often make mistakes with these.

> I look forward to **hearing** from you.
> NOT I look forward to ~~hear~~ from you.

Correct the mistakes that FCE candidates have made with gerund and infinitive forms in these sentences.

a I suggest to take the easier route.
b Do you want go out with me?
c I'm used to sleep in a tent.
d There's no point play today.
e I suggest you to go to the sports centre.
f I like play hockey.
g I recommend you going there.
h I hope hearing from you soon.
i I am interested to apply for this job of personal trainer.
j I should give up to swim every morning.

7 Read through this email and put the verbs in brackets in the correct form and give your reasons.

> Send Chat Attach Address Fonts Colors Save As Draft
>
> To: Jill Campbell
> Cc:
> Subject: Trip to Mont Blanc
>
> Dear Jill,
>
> I've just got back from (**1**) .... (climb) Mont Blanc in the Alps and I must (**2**) .... (tell) you what a great time I had. On (**3**) .... (arrive) in Chamonix we were introduced to our guides. We were then kitted out with ice-axes, crampons and climbing boots and were sent straight out into two days' (**4**) .... (train) in and around the Le Tour glacier. The guides used this time (**5**) .... (assess) our ability (**6**) .... (make) the ascent and (**7**) .... (teach) us the basics of (**8**) .... (mountaineer), such as how (**9**) .... (use) an ice-axe and how to best (**10**) .... (work) in a team.
>
> The first day consisted of (**11**) .... (climb) for five hours from the Nid d'Aigle to the Gouter Hut. I thought I'd be too cold (**12**) .... (sleep) but in fact that wasn't a problem at all! Day 2 started at 2 am with a four and a half hour walk to the summit. (**13**) .... (reach) the summit was only a third of the day's work. The descent route included (**14**) .... (jump) across gaps in the ice and took seven hours.
>
> I'm really looking forward to (**15**) .... (see) you next weekend so I can (**16**) .... (tell) you all the details.
>
> Love, Sue

8 Complete the second sentence so that it has a similar meaning to the first sentence, using the word given. **Do not change the word given. You must use between two and five words, including the word given.**

1 The newspapers said that he had pushed the other player.
   accused
   The newspapers .... the other player.

2 The pitch isn't dry enough to play on.
   too
   The pitch .... play on.

3 It wasn't easy for me to learn how to paraglide.
   difficulty
   I .... how to paraglide.

4 'I wouldn't go diving by yourself, if I were you,' the instructor said.
   advised
   The instructor .... diving by myself.

5 I prefer to go on walking holidays than lie on a crowded beach.
   rather
   I .... walking holidays than lie on a crowded beach.

1 Discuss these questions with a partner.

a Who do you think is the greatest football player/golfer/athlete/tennis player/racing driver of all time? Why?

b Do you think that some sports are easier than others? Why?

c What sports would you consider to be dangerous? Why?

d Have you ever seen or tried a dangerous sport? What was it?

Notice that when you talk about sport you usually ask, 'Which sport do you do?' and you say, 'I go swimming', 'I play football'.

Which sports do you use with 'go' and which with 'play'?

Exam spot

Part 3 of Paper 4 consists of six questions and five short extracts linked by a theme. You need to match each extract to one of six options, A–F. There is one extra option that you do not need.

Listening

2 🎧 Listen to this extract, where a woman is talking about a sport she has recently taken up. As you listen, try to work out what the sport is. What clues did you hear?

3 🎧 Now you're going to hear the first speaker again and also four other people talking about dangerous sports. For questions 1–5, choose from the list of statements A–F what each speaker states. There is one extra letter which you do not need to use.

Speaker 1 [1] Speaker 3 [3] Speaker 5 [5]
Speaker 2 [2] Speaker 4 [4]

A I'm always looking for something new.
B I've always enjoyed taking risks.
C It's not as dangerous as some ordinary sports.
D Knowing I might be killed makes it more enjoyable.
E It puts some excitement in my life.
F I wanted to prove to everyone that I could do it.

4 Listen again. What dangerous sports do the speakers mention? Are they popular in your country?

5 Match the sport with the place.

a track   1 golf
b pitch   2 athletics
c course   3 tennis
d court   4 football
e rink   5 skiing
f slopes   6 ice-skating

Pronunciation

6 🎧 In the extracts you have just heard there are some examples of question tags. Listen to these sentences.

That <u>could</u> be pretty scary, <u>couldn't it</u>?
I guess they <u>needed</u> to have a bit of excitement in their lives, <u>didn't they</u>?

Question tags are formed from the auxiliary verb and the personal pronoun. We use it when we are not sure of something or to ask for agreement. If the sentence is positive then the tag is usually negative and vice versa.

Steve's played football for ten years, hasn't he?
She couldn't get a place on the team, could she?

Quite often the tag isn't a real question.

EXAMPLE: *It's a nice day, isn't it?*

This is usually used by English people to start a conversation at a bus-stop or on a train. Don't just answer with 'yes' or 'no'!

The following tags often cause problems.

a Somebody's here, aren't they?
  (*Somebody/everybody/nobody* take '*they*')
b Nobody's coming, are they? (*nobody* is negative)
c Let's go sailing, shall we? (*let's* means '*we shall*')
d It hardly/scarcely ever rains here, does it? (*hardly* and *scarcely* are negative)
e That's the man, isn't it? (Subject is '*that*')
f He'd rather go skiing, wouldn't he? (*would rather*)
g I'd better get some new trainers, hadn't I? (*had better*)
h I've got better at running, haven't I? (*have got* = possession)
i She has lunch at 12.00, doesn't she? (full verb)
j Don't do that, will you? (polite order)
k I'm right, aren't I?

The meaning of a question tag changes with the intonation. Compare examples a and b.

a 'It's a nice day, isn't it?'

b 'You haven't got change for £5, have you?'
  In *a*, which isn't a real question, the intonation is falling, whereas in *b*, where it is a real question, the intonation rises.

7 You are the Editor of a local newspaper. Interview someone in the class for a job as a sports reporter on your paper. Find out as much as you can about them (where they live, what sports they play or enjoy watching, how old they are, etc.). First of all ask them questions to which you know the answer.

So, your name is ...., isn't it?
You're .... years old, aren't you?
You enjoy playing ...., don't you?

Then try asking some questions to which either you don't know or you're not sure of the answer.

You've worked in (country), haven't you?
You met (sportsman/woman) last year, didn't you?
You can play (sport), can't you?
You've visited (city), haven't you?

8 Decide what the question tag should be in these sentences.

a You'd rather go to the cinema than to a football match, ...?
b I'm awful at tennis, ...?
c You can't see where I hit the ball, ...?
d You will try to win, ...?
e Everyone wants to take part in the Olympics, ...?
f There will be a game on Saturday, ...?
g Don't forget the tickets, ...?
h You've got a racket, ...?
i You have a game tonight, ...?

9 Change the word in capitals to fit the sentence. Read through the text carefully before you do the exercise.

With some personal fitness trainers charging as much as £150 an hour, it's not surprising that only the rich and (1) .... (FAME) can afford the kind of one-to-one that will (2) .... (SURE) they work out enough to stay in shape. However, the idea that they are only for the elite is about to be shattered by *Get Motivated*, a new London-based company that charges just £25 for an hour with a (3) .... (QUALIFY) trainer. I decided to put this scheme to the test and asked *Get Motivated* to send a personal trainer to my home for a (4) .... (TRAIN) session. When 23 year old Stephanie arrived, I was sceptical about her (5) .... (YOUNG), but what followed was a very (6) .... (DEMAND) hour. Stephanie grew up in Australia and has a degree in human (7) .... (MOVE) studies and a diploma in (8) .... (EDUCATE) – the minimum (9) .... (QUALIFY) *Get Motivated* requires. Stephanie says that what appeals most to her about the GM scheme is that it gives her the (10) .... (FREE) to design her own sessions for clients.

Do you think you'd like a personal trainer? Why?/Why not?

10 You heard these words in the listening extracts. In pairs talk about what kind of words they are and then change them into nouns.

a dangerous
b frightened
c risky
d aggressive
e protective
f nervous
g terrifying
h exciting

Exam folder 4

Paper 3 Part 1
Multiple choice cloze

In this part of the Use of English paper you must choose one word or phrase from a set of four (A, B, C or D) to fill a gap in the text. There are twelve gaps and an example. The text always has a title, which will give you some help in telling you what it is about before you start reading.

Below are some examples of the type of words that are tested in this part of Paper 3.

Expressions

1 I .... to the conclusion, after failing to win any matches, that I would do better to give up playing tennis altogether.
   A drew   B got
   C formed   D came
   D is the right answer. The expression is *to come to a conclusion*. You can *form a conclusion, draw a conclusion*.

Verb/Adjective + preposition

2 I .... at the airport so late that my plane had already taken off.
   A got   B arrived
   C reached   D came
   B is the right answer. *Came* and *get* are followed by *to*; *reached* doesn't take a preposition.

Phrasal verbs

3 He was lucky to be kept .... at the factory when most of the other workers lost their jobs.
   A back   B on
   C off   D up
   B is the answer. *To be kept on* means to be retained in employment. The other phrasal verbs here, *keep back, keep off* and *keep up* all exist but mean something different.

Linking words

4 You'd better write your invitations to the party today .... you want people to reply by next week.
   A unless   B while
   C if   D otherwise
   C is the answer. *Unless* means *if not, otherwise* means *or else* and *while* is used in a different type of clause.

Vocabulary

5 I changed some of my money into foreign .... and also took some travellers' cheques.
   A income   C currency
   B funds   D revenue
   C is the right answer. All the other words are connected with money, but are used differently.

Advice

- Always read the text all the way through before you try to fill in any gaps.
- Make sure you read each sentence carefully so that you don't miss any important words.
- Always put down an answer even if you're not completely sure that it's correct.
- Make sure you transfer your answers to the answer sheet correctly.

For questions 1–12, read the text below and decide which answer (A, B, C or D) best fits each gap. There is an example at the beginning (0).

Example:

O A dates   **B** belongs   **C** exists   **D** comes

| 0 | A | B | C | D |

The History of Football

Football or soccer, which is so popular all over the world, (0) .... back to the Middle Ages. At that (1) .... it was very different from the game we play today. Any number of players could (2) .... part and the matches usually developed into a free-for-all. In its modern (3) ...., football is less than two hundred years old.

In 1846 the first rules to govern the game were drawn up at Cambridge University. The number of players was (4) .... to 11 per side, which made things much more orderly than before. Later, in 1863, the Football Association was (5) .... up to help promote the game in Britain.

The game is played on a grass or artificial (6) .... with a goal net at each end. The (7) .... is to move the ball around the field, (8) .... the feet or head, until a player is in a (9) .... to put the ball into the net and score a goal.

Professional football is not only the most popular (10) .... sport in the world, (11) .... also more people actually play football themselves than any other team sport. In 1904 FIFA, the world governing (12) .... of football, was founded. It organises the World Cup tournament every four years.

1	**A** season	**B** time	**C** term	**D** stage
2	**A** play	**B** make	**C** take	**D** do
3	**A** form	**B** shape	**C** fashion	**D** pattern
4	**A** limited	**B** checked	**C** counted	**D** defined
5	**A** put	**B** set	**C** born	**D** called
6	**A** court	**B** pitch	**C** course	**D** track
7	**A** object	**B** reason	**C** focus	**D** purpose
8	**A** by	**B** to	**C** of	**D** with
9	**A** place	**B** point	**C** position	**D** spot
10	**A** witness	**B** audience	**C** spectator	**D** viewer
11	**A** because	**B** but	**C** while	**D** so
12	**A** body	**B** band	**C** collection	**D** group

Vocabulary spot

When you learn new vocabulary, write it down in an organised way. Do not just write down an individual word with its translation into your language.

It's important to understand how a word is used, not just its meaning.

Verbs – Find out what comes after a verb. Is it a gerund/clause/infinitive with *to*/without *to*/a preposition?
Nouns – Is the noun countable or uncountable? This affects the grammar of the sentence.
Phrasal verbs – Learn the phrasal verb in context, that is, in a sentence.
Collocations – Organise these separately in sections according to topic or verb. For example, *to pay* – a bill, a compliment, attention *house* – household, housewife, housework

8·1 Downshifting

1 How do you feel about working conditions today? Do you think that things have got better or worse? Why?

2 Work with a partner and each look at one pair of photos. Say how you think working life has changed in the last 100 years and why.

3 *Downsizing* is when a company reduces staff or offices in order to become more efficient. Skim the article to find out what *downshifting* is.

Exam spot

Part 1 of Paper 1 is a text with 8 multiple choice questions, where you have to choose the answer to a question or finish a sentence from four given alternatives. You should read the text and the questions carefully, because this part of the exam tests detailed understanding. It is helpful to underline the words in the text which contain the answers to the questions.

4 Read the article again more carefully and answer question 1. Then look at the explanation below – were you right?

1 According to the writer, people are beginning to rethink their lives because
   A they feel too dependent on their possessions.
   B they are worried about the amount of rubbish they throw away.
   C they want to spend time doing other things.
   D their families object to their working so hard.

The answer is C. – 'leaving them precious little time or energy for family or leisure.'
A is likely but not the real reason.
In B the writer thinks that the *reader* would be worried, rather than people in general.
D is probably true but also not the answer to the question.

As you move around your home take a good hard look at its contents. It's likely that your living room will have a television set and a DVD player, and your kitchen a washing machine and tumble drier, maybe also a microwave oven and electric toaster. Your bedroom drawers will be stuffed with almost three times as many clothes as you need. You almost certainly own a car and a home
10 computer, holiday abroad at least once a year and eat out at least once a week. If you could see the volume of rubbish in your dustbin over a year, you would be horrified.

Now, perhaps, more than ever before, people are wondering what life is all about, what it's for. The single-minded pursuit of material success is beginning to trouble large numbers of people around the world. They feel the long-hours work culture to make
20 more money to buy more things is eating up their lives, leaving them precious little time or energy for family or leisure. Many are turning to alternative ways of living and downshifting is one of them.

According to a national consulting group, this new approach to work coincides with radical changes in the employment market, where a job is no longer guaranteed and lifetime employment can only be achieved by
30 taking personal responsibility for your career.

Six per cent of workers in Britain took the decision to downshift last year, swapping their highly pressured, stressful positions for less demanding, less time-consuming work which they believe gives them a better-balanced life.

One couple who downshifted is Daniel and Liz. They used to work in central London. He was a journalist and she used to work for an international bank. They would commute every
40 day from their large house in the suburbs, leaving their two children with a nanny. Most evenings Daniel wouldn't get home until eight or nine o'clock, and nearly twice a month he would have to fly to New York for meetings. They both earned a large amount of money but began to feel that life was passing them by.

Nowadays, they run a farm in the mountains of Wales. 'I always wanted to have a farm here,' says Daniel, 'and we took almost
50 a year to make the decision to downshift. It's taken some getting used to, but it's been worth it. We have to think twice now about spending money on car repairs and we no longer have any holidays. However, I think it's made us stronger as a family, and the children are a lot happier.'

Liz, however, is not totally convinced. 'I used to enjoy my job, even though it was hard work and long hours. I'm not really a country
60 girl, but I suppose I'm gradually getting used to looking after the animals. One thing I do like though is being able to see more of my children. My tip for other people wanting to do the same is not to think about it too much or you might not do it at all.'

Now answer questions 2–5, underlining the words in the article that give you the correct answer, and saying why the other three choices are wrong.

2 What does the writer say about the employment market?
  A There aren't many jobs nowadays.
  B It's difficult to keep a company job for life.
  C You have to look hard to find a job yourself.
  D It's changing all the time.

3 When Daniel was a journalist he used to
  A live in central London.
  B dislike his job.
  C miss his children.
  D be highly paid.

4 What has Daniel's reaction been to moving to Wales?
  A He's happy that he's now fulfilled an ambition.
  B He felt at home on the farm almost immediately.
  C He misses the holidays they used to have abroad.
  D He is sorry that they made the decision to move too quickly.

5 Daniel and Liz both agree that the move
  A was difficult to organise.
  B has improved family life.
  C to a farm was expensive.
  D has been a total success.

There will often be a question on an item of vocabulary such as a word which is unusual or idiomatic, or one that is used by the writer in a special way. You should work out the meaning by looking at the context around the word itself.

6 What does the word 'tip' in line 64 mean?
  A a good idea   B a clue   C a word of advice
  D a warning

Sometimes a 'reference' question is included, which tests your understanding of words such as 'it' and 'this'. You must read the lines before and after the word carefully to decide what it is referring to.

7 What does 'it' in line 66 refer to?
  A her tip   B her job   C having animals
  D downshifting

The final question often asks 'Who was this text written by?' or 'Who is likely to read this text?', which tests your overall understanding.

8 Why was this text written?
  A To warn people of the problems of downshifting.
  B To tell people how to downshift.
  C To make people aware of a new social trend.
  D To prove that having a good job doesn't make you happy.

Giving an opinion
Personally, I think that …
If you ask me, I …
On the one hand, I think that …, but on the other I think …
Well, first of all, … secondly …, finally …
Generally, I agree/disagree with …

Asking for an opinion
How do you feel about …?
Don't you agree that …?

Agreeing
I agree entirely.   You're right.
Absolutely!   Oh, quite!
Of course.

Disagreeing (Try not to say 'You're wrong!')
Well, I'm not sure I agree with you.
You have a point, but …
I understand your view, although I …
Mmm, I don't see it quite like that.

---

5 Do you think Daniel and Liz made the right decision? Why?/Why not? Are people beginning to downshift in your country? What are the advantages and disadvantages of downshifting?

6 Decide whether you think the following statements are true or false or whether you don't know. Then, in pairs, discuss your answers, using some of the expressions in the box opposite.

  a Modern working conditions are destroying the quality of life.
  b Most professional people suffer a great deal of stress.
  c Stress is worthwhile if you get what you want.
  d Success always brings happiness.
  e People are very materialistic nowadays.
  f Younger people see life completely differently from their parents.

7 Look at the article again and find words in each paragraph that are similar in meaning to the words below:

Paragraph 1: amount   filled   appalled
Paragraph 2: determined   hunt
Paragraph 3: way   basic
Paragraph 4: exchanging
Paragraph 5: outskirts
Paragraph 6: manage

8.2

used to and would

1 Read examples a–c and then decide which rule(s) in 1–3 apply.

  a Daniel and Liz used to work in central London. (USED TO + DO)

  b They would commute every day. (WOULD + DO)

  c I'm gradually getting used to looking after the animals. (BE/GET USED TO + DOING)

  1 To talk about something in the past that doesn't happen now. This could be something permanent.

  2 To mean *to be/get accustomed to*.

  3 To talk about a repeated action in the past which doesn't happen now. Note that the action must be repeated and this form is normally used for narrative.

Notice that *be used to* describes a state and *get used to* expresses a change in state.

Corpus spot

The *Cambridge Learner Corpus* shows FCE candidates often make mistakes with *used to*.

I **used to** live in London.
NOT   I ~~use~~ to live in London.

2 Correct the following sentences, if necessary.

  a Some years ago the capital of South Vietnam would be Saigon.

  b People used to work very long hours in the steel industry.

  c Britain would have a large manufacturing industry.

  d People are now used to working harder for less money.

  e It takes a long time to get used to do a new job.

  f My grandmother was used to work very long hours when she was a girl.

  g When I worked for the BBC, I would have to start at 7.30 am.

  h John has never got used to having a woman boss.

G ⋯⊳ page 201

Listening

3 In pairs, discuss what each of the jobs below involves. Then listen to the five extracts and decide which jobs the speakers used to do.

> astronaut   chef   dentist   pop singer
> detective   plumber   surgeon
> window-cleaner   zoo-keeper

Speaker 1   1
Speaker 2   2
Speaker 3   3
Speaker 4   4
Speaker 5   5

4 Imagine you have recently changed jobs. Tell your partner all about your old job, without saying what it was. Your partner has to guess the job.

Vocabulary

5 What jobs or professions are linked to these five places? For example, a bank has a manager, cashiers, secretaries, computer operators, a security guard, etc.

1 a cruise ship ....

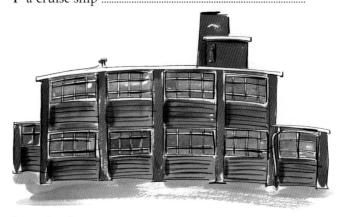

2 a school ....

6 *Get* is a very common verb especially in spoken English and is often used instead of other **verbs**. Rewrite the sentences without using *get* either as a verb or in a phrase.

EXAMPLE: *Jon used to have a BMW, but now he's got a Mercedes.*

ANSWER: *Jon used to have a BMW, but now he owns a Mercedes.*

a Nurses have got to wear a uniform.
b They get breakfast in the canteen every morning.
c I'm getting promoted next month.
d We take it in turns in our department to get everyone coffee in the morning.
e I got a letter from my boss asking me to go to a conference in Los Angeles.
f Jane usually gets home from work about 7.30 pm.
g Some students need to get their hair cut before they attend an interview.
h Sue has managed to get a man to come and service the photocopier on Tuesday.

3 a hospital ....

4 a department store ....

5 a sports centre ....

7 Phrasal verbs with *get*. Complete the sentences using the endings below.

| my new boss   your exams |
| being made redundant   much money |
| his new job   his guards |

a The prisoner got away from ....
b I get on well with ....
c I hope you get through ....
d He never got over ....
e My nephew is getting on well with

....

f While I'm doing an apprenticeship, I'll have to get by without ....

Now replace the phrasal verb in each sentence with a suitable form of one of these verbs.

make a success of	escape
like	manage
recover from	pass

8 Look back at the article in 8.1 and find four examples of compound adjectives. (These were covered in Unit 4.)

9 Make changes to these words, which have all come up in this unit.

a horrified — verb ....
— noun ....

b success — verb ....
— negative adjective ....

c energy — adjective ....
— adverb ....

d national — noun ....
— verb ....

e employment — negative adjective ....
— verb ....

f responsibility — adverb ....
— negative adjective ....

g decision — adjective ....
— verb ....

h commute — noun ....
— noun ....

Writing folder 4

Essays 1

In Part 2 of Paper 2, you may be asked to write a discursive essay, that is one that argues for and/or against some topic, or one where you are asked your opinion. You must write between 120 and 180 words. You are usually asked to write this essay following a class discussion on a topic. Here is a typical exam question.

Your teacher has asked you to write an essay giving your views on the following question:

Should companies give men and women equal opportunities to have time off work to look after their children?

Write your **essay**.

---

1 The following sentences are all from an essay on the subject above. Put them in the right order.

A This already happens in some parts of the world, particularly in Scandinavia, where both men and women are offered maternity leave.

B Not only would the family benefit from this flexibility, but also companies, which would have happier workers.

C In conclusion, therefore, I believe that both parents should be given the choice of deciding who will stay at home and who will go back to work.

D Although companies in my country, and men, might take a while to accept this idea, I think that it is an inevitable part of social change.

E In the past, and also nowadays in many countries, it was always the man who went out to work leaving his wife at home to take care of the children.

F I'd like to begin this essay by saying that I think both parents should be encouraged to take an active part in looking after their children.

G However, society is beginning to change and there needs to be more flexibility both at home and at work.

2 Now decide which sentences should go into:

Paragraph 1 – Introducing the topic
Paragraph 2 – Setting out the arguments or giving reasons
Paragraph 3 – Drawing a conclusion

3 Read this statement and the essay which follows:

People nowadays have to work too hard.

First of all, I'd like to say that, in general, the people in my country don't tend to work as hard as people in some other countries. Most of our population works in the service industry – in banks, hotels and insurance. **And** there is very little heavy industry and most manufacturing is fully automated. **And** they usually only work about 35 hours a week and have four weeks' holiday a year. **But** in some countries the situation is totally different. People have to work in old-fashioned factories, which are dirty and likely to give them illnesses as they get older, or they work in the fields using animals rather than tractors. I think that people in my country have been lucky up until now. **But** things are beginning to change. There are fewer jobs and people are being made redundant. **So** people have to work harder to keep their jobs. **So,** in conclusion I'd like to say that I agree that people nowadays have to work too hard.

Decide which word or phrase you could use from the box below instead of the words in bold. For example for the first *And* you could use 'In addition', or 'Moreover', but you couldn't use 'As well as'. Why is this?

Think about other changes you may need to make to the text in order to use some of these linkers.

in addition	nevertheless
moreover	in contrast
as well as	on the other hand
as a result	therefore
however	

4 Where could you put the expression *not only … but also*?

5 Where do you think the essay should be divided into paragraphs?

Useful expressions

To begin
First of all, …
In my opinion, …
I'd like to begin by saying that …
Many people think/believe/say that …

To finish
In conclusion, …
I'd like to conclude by saying that …
To sum up, …

Advice

- Read the question carefully.
- If the question asks for your experience, don't forget to give examples.
- Remember to organise your essay. It shouldn't be a string of sentences but a logical answer to the question.
- Don't forget to use paragraphs (three is about right).
- Check your spelling, grammar and punctuation.
- Use linking words.
- Check you have really answered the question.
- Count your words or make sure you know how many lines of your handwriting make 120–180 words.

6 In pairs, think about the following essay topic and make some notes using the questions below.

Your teacher has asked you to write an essay discussing the following statement.

Stress can be reduced by playing sport.

- Do you have any personal experience of this?
- Think of some examples.
- Can playing sport when you feel stressed be bad for your health?
- Are there other things to help reduce stress which are better than sport?
- How do you feel about the title – do you agree completely/partly or do you disagree totally?
- Any conclusions – in general/personally?

Now organise your notes into:

- an introduction
- some reasons/arguments/personal experience
- a conclusion
Which linking words are you going to use?

The hard sell

Modals 2: Speculation and deduction

1   Look at the advert opposite. What do you think it is selling? Discuss your ideas with a partner, using some of these openers.

Well, it could be advertising …
Or perhaps it might be for …

I think it must be a …
It can't be for … because …

Look at page 83 to find out if you guessed correctly.

2   The modal verbs in the first pair of examples above indicate that the speaker is unsure about something. It is also possible to use *may*, though less common. However, *can* is not used in this way.

Is the speaker unsure in the second pair of examples? Which words tell you?

Now look at this example. Is the speaker unsure?

It couldn't possibly be an advert for chocolate.

Does the meaning change if the full stop is replaced by a question mark? Say the sentence and the question aloud to your partner. The question would sound better with extra words at the end. Which words?

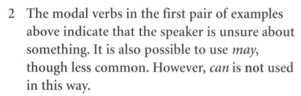 page 201

3   Now read the text about a TV advert and underline examples of the modals used in 1.

4   Explain the meaning of these words from the text.

a   voice-over   d   verdict
b   jingle   e   brand
c   celebrity   f   cunning

Why is the title of Bob's article appropriate?

The best ad missed the boat at Cannes

This is the title of an article by Bob Garfield, an American expert on advertising. He was writing about the International Advertising Film Festival, which takes place at the same time as the main film festival in Cannes.   5

For Bob, the best ad of the year was from Delvico Bates, Barcelona, for *Esencial* hand cream. The ad shows a woman riding her bike, which has a very squeaky chain. The woman gets off the bike, opens her jar of *Esencial* and rubs some of the cream onto   10
the chain. Then she rides away – but the squeak remains. Why? Because, as the voice-over says, '*Esencial* moisturizes, but it has no grease.'

Why is this ad so good? It can't be for its special effects, because there aren't any. Might it be the   15
music? No, there isn't even a jingle. Could it be that the woman is a celebrity? No. Bob's verdict: 'It's a vivid demonstration of brand non-attributes. Inspired. Cunning. Brilliant.' In other words, by showing failure in a different context, the quality of   20
the product is reinforced – grease is good for bike chains, but not for the skin.

So surely this ad must have won at Cannes? No. The simple truth is that it couldn't win, because the agency failed to enter it in time for the festival   25
deadline!

5 In the final paragraph, it says *So surely this ad must have won at Cannes?* Here, the modal is referring to a past action. Say whether the speaker is sure or unsure in sentences a–c below.

   a The latest Sony ad must have cost a fortune to produce.
   b There's one ad showing a man sitting in an armchair on a mountain peak. That couldn't have actually happened – it must be down to special effects.
   c Advertising has come a long way in the last forty years. Television audiences of the 1960s might have been totally overwhelmed by an action-packed ad of today!

G ⋯⋗ page 202

6 Complete the second sentence so that it has a similar meaning to the first sentence, using the word given. Do not change this word. Use between two and five words, including the word given.

   1 It isn't possible for this to be a real location.
     be
     This .... a real location.

   2 If you read the slogan, it sounds as if it's about shampoo.
     must
     Reading the slogan, ... about shampoo.

   3 I'm not sure, but I think it's *Radiohead* singing that jingle.
     might
     That jingle .... by *Radiohead*.

   4 I'm sure that recent advert for computers had an enormous budget.
     must
     That recent advert for computers
     .... an enormous budget.

   5 I bet Rafael Nadal earned a lot for that car advert.
     paid
     Rafael Nadal .... a lot for that car advert.

   6 They didn't use Tom Cruise on the voice-over – the voice was deeper than his.
     been
     It .... Tom Cruise on the voice-over – the voice was deeper than his.

Vocabulary spot

Write down important collocations in your vocabulary notebook. Try using visual diagrams, like this one:

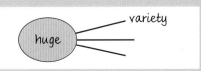

7 Look at the adjectives below. Which ones collocate with each of the nouns given? List the phrases that are possible, for example *huge variety*. You can use some in the role play that follows.

huge	variety
high	message
low	idea
deep	budget
shallow	market
narrow	character
wide	picture
	view
	voice

8 Role play: XK trainers. Get into small groups and read your instructions (A or B). Then spend a few minutes listing useful vocabulary, using a dictionary if necessary. When groups A and B are both ready, have a face-to-face discussion.

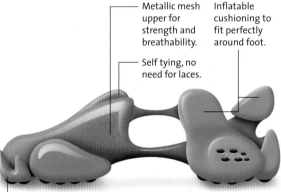

Metallic mesh upper for strength and breathability.

Inflatable cushioning to fit perfectly around foot.

Self tying, no need for laces.

Shock absorbing gel pumped into undersole to absorb impact.

Group A Advertising agency
A leading manufacturer of sports shoes, XK, is about to start selling a new type of trainer. Your agency hopes to get the contract for the TV commercial and you need to prepare your ideas. As there is a big budget for this, you should use famous people and exotic locations! Prepare to meet XK.

Group B turn to page 83.

9·2

Listening

1 Is there one commercial that you really like? Or one that you just can't stand? Briefly describe a commercial to your partner and say why you like it or loathe it.

2 🎧 You are going to hear two people talking about some commercials they have seen. In Part 1, which of these aspects are mentioned by the speakers? Tick the ones you hear.

a a puzzling beginning
b a good storyline
c a dramatic ending
d an out of the ordinary setting
e a surprising location
f a well-known personality
g a powerful slogan
h an extravagant production

Grammar extra
Order of adjectives

The woman talks about *a graceful silver vehicle*. Which of the two adjectives is used to give an opinion? Can the order of these adjectives be changed?

Underline the adjectives used in slogans a–d and then identify them according to the types below. What is the rule for opinion adjectives?
a The classic British motorbike
b The sensational new CD from Jack Johnson
c Our popular full-length navy cotton nightshirt
d Bite-sized biscuits with a delicious creamy filling

OPINION
DESCRIPTION: SIZE SHAPE AGE COLOUR NATIONALITY MATERIAL
Descriptive adjectives are usually in the order above. It is quite unusual to have four adjectives in a row (as in example c). More commonly, any additional descriptive information is given in a separate phrase (as in example d).

Decide whether the following adjectives are in the correct order. Reorder them where necessary.
a a black huge dog
b an awful old woollen coat
c the Italian famous singer
d a red large apple
e an elaborate wooden square box
f a sophisticated new novel by a Scottish tremendous author

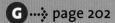 page 202

Pronunciation *Sentence stress*

3 🎧 Look at these extracts from Part 1. Certain words were stressed by the speakers for emphasis. Listen again and underline the stressed words.

a It must have cost a fortune to make.
b … it's just another car advert!
c … the beginning is a bit misleading.
d He eats it, so it must be good.
e … the one that had a whole team of top footballers from around the world!
f … the budget must have been huge … all for one advert!
g But the company probably earned millions of dollars in increased sales …

4 🎧 Listen to Part 2, where one particular advert is discussed. Answer the questions below by writing W for woman, M for man, or B for both in the boxes.

1 Who didn't like the Bacardi advert? ☐ 1
2 Who was surprised by part of the advert? ☐ 2
3 Who thinks that adverts need to contain something unusual? ☐ 3
4 Who agrees that Ray was an effective character? ☐ 4
5 Who liked the music in the advert? ☐ 5

5 🎧 Listen to Part 2 again. Explain the following phrases in your own words.

a brilliantly put together
b a striking image
c stick in your mind
d the right ingredients
e exotic location
f made an impact on
g getting the message across
h dig into your pocket

6 In pairs, decide on the important factors that make a TV or film advert successful.

Speaking

Exam spot

Part 3 of Paper 5 is a 'shared task', where you must have a discussion with the other candidate and then try to decide together on a solution to the task. It is acceptable to 'agree to disagree', however! Remember to give your partner a chance to speak during this Part.

a

b

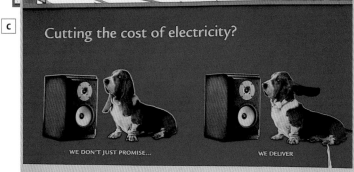

c

d

e

f

7 Look at the six photographs. Identify what product each billboard is advertising and discuss how effective it is at selling the product. Then decide which two adverts are the most effective, giving reasons for your choice.

8 Spend some time looking at the photographs and note down useful vocabulary for each one. Remember that when you do the task, you will have to give an opinion about them rather than describe them. Include relevant words and phrases from earlier in the unit.

9 Think about how to structure the discussion so that you and your partner have equal opportunities to take part. Try to use some of the phrases below to achieve this.

Would you like to start?
What do you think about the second one?
Why don't you continue?
But what about you?
Is that your view too?
Okay, now we have to decide. Shall I summarise?

10 Try to speak together for about three minutes. Make sure you allow enough time within this to decide on the two adverts, so that the task is completed. Give clear reasons for your choice.

11 Tell the class which adverts you both chose and say why.

Exam folder 5

Listening skills for FCE

You will need to develop a range of listening skills and strategies for FCE Paper 4. These include:

Before you listen
- Using the information in the rubric and in the questions to give you an idea of what each recording will be about
- Predicting key language and possible answers from the questions

While you listen
- Listening for overall meaning
- Listening for specific information
- Recognising important signals and markers in a long recording
- Recognising 'paraphrase' – text that means the same as something in the question
- Understanding the opinions or attitudes of speakers
- Writing down words that you hear
- Guessing the meaning of words and phrases you don't know

After you listen
- Checking your answers
- Transferring your answers accurately to the answer sheet

Remember that you will hear everything twice. Because of this, there is no need to panic! If you miss an answer, you can listen for it the second time.

For information about Paper 4, see *Content of the First Certificate Examination* on page 7.

1 🎧 Match the Part 1 rubrics 1–4 with recordings A, B and C. One rubric isn't needed.

1 You hear part of a lecture on advertising. What is the lecturer describing?
2 You hear someone being interviewed on the radio about his working life. Why did he decide to start his own company?
3 You hear a woman talking about an athletics event. What is she unhappy about?
4 You hear a man talking about telephone selling. How does he deal with these calls?

2 For the rubric you didn't use, underline topic nouns that you might hear in the box below.

| boss | brand | commuter | display | jump | manager |
| market | prize | race | slogan | stress | track |

3 🎧 Look at these Part 2 sentences and find words and phrases in the recording script below that relate to the underlined words and phrases. Can you predict what the missing words are? Then listen and write one or two words in each gap.

As an example of making a scientific claim, the speaker talks about an advertisement for 1 ....

The most important message in the advertisement for the car is to do with 2 ....

When targeting teenagers in advertisements, products are often linked to 3 .... which others would find unacceptable.

Advertisements aimed at parents may include young children or 4 .... and .... , as they connect with their role as carers.

Recording script

To support the suggestion that one product is better than its competitors, the existence of actual proof is often mentioned. In one case, involving the promotion of **1** xxxxxxxxxxxx , reference was made to an unnamed university research project, which analysed shades of white.

It must be true that there are more advertisements focusing on our love of driving than on anything else. While the messages of freedom and mobility are always important, it is above all the aspect of **2** xxxxxxxxxxxx that is stressed in this particular one. We are supposed to believe that this car will take us to new places in society and change our role for ever.

Advertisers adopt different strategies as far as young people between the ages of 15 and 19 are concerned. For this population, it is not about conforming but about the complete opposite of that. Indeed, products for this age group are frequently connected with **3** xxxxxxxxxxxxxx, the kind that older people such as parents might well disapprove of.

Turning to mothers and fathers as consumers, advertisements targeting these people often reinforce the experience of bringing up a family. An advert that links its product to young children or even, interestingly enough, to **4** xxxxxxxxxxxx , will probably succeed because these images appeal directly to motherly or, perhaps less commonly, fatherly instincts!

4 Transfer your answers to this sample answer sheet. Be careful with spelling.

Part 2		Do not write here
9		1 9 0
10		1 10 0
11		1 11 0
12		1 12 0
13		1 13 0

5   In Part 3, you may need to understand the overall meaning or main idea of a recording. Listen to the following extracts and decide for each one what topic is being discussed.

Speaker	Topic
1	
2	
3	
4	
5	

6   You may need to understand a speaker's opinions or attitude, which may be signalled in different ways. Listen to the five extracts again and list any examples of the signalling language a–c.

a a verb   I think ....
....
....

b an adjective plus preposition
          keen on ....
....
....

c a phrase   From my point of view ....
....
....

7   You will need to recognise paraphrase in Part 4 in particular. Suggest other ways of wording the key information in these questions about a new sports stadium. Then listen to the interview with the architect and check your ideas. Listen again to answer the questions.

1 The biggest benefit of the new stadium is that
  A it will seat more people than before.
  B play will continue in bad weather.
  C growing conditions will be improved.

2 What, according to the architect, is a problem at the moment?
  A the weight of the roof
  B the schedule for building work
  C the increased cost of the project

The final frontier

1 Describe what is happening in the pictures and compare the people. Will the general public be able to go into space by 2015? Why?/Why not?

2 Discuss these questions in small groups, explaining your opinions in detail.

- Do you think you will ever take a holiday in space?
- Should governments spend tax-payers' money on space travel?
- Why are there so many satellites orbiting the Earth? Will this technology become more important, in your view?

3 You are going to read an article on space travel. Quickly skim the article for its general meaning, ignoring the missing sentences. Why do NASA and the SFF have different priorities?

Exam spot

In Part 2 of Paper 1 you first need to understand what the text is about and how it develops, so skim the main text from which the sentences have been removed. Then underline key words and phrases in sentences **A–H** and look for links to these in the main text. Check that the extra sentence doesn't fit anywhere.

CHEAP ACCESS TO SPACE

'Cheap' is an important word in space technology nowadays and re-usable rockets will be a key way of controlling costs. They will deliver things to orbit, bring stuff back to Earth and then go up again, perhaps with machinery for a space factory, or even carrying tourists.

NASA, the US government-owned space program, plans to develop such a rocket. 1 ____ Since this will require different technology, it is more likely that people outside the NASA program will develop re-usable rocket design.

Rick Tumlinson, co-founder of the Space Frontier Foundation (SFF), firmly believes that it is time for businesses to get involved. 2 ____ '25 years after the Wright brothers, people could buy a commercial plane ticket, but 25 years after landing on the Moon, we sat around watching old astronauts on TV talking about the good old days.' However, this situation is due to change. Recently, Tumlinson was one of only 20 guests invited to the White House to hear the President

announce his plans to return to the Moon and explore Mars.

Using his high profile, Tumlinson is going to try to prove a point. Space is our destiny, he says, so why not get on with it? 3 ____ For example, Rotary Rocket is working on something that would be launched like a rocket but return like a helicopter. Pioneer Rocketplane believes there could be a billion dollar market in taking packages from one side of the planet to the other in an hour.

4 ____ 'Our goal is to become a delivery service to low Earth orbit that will radically re-align the economics of doing business in space. Satellites will be our parcels; our vehicles will be orbiting as efficiently as air freight carriers.'

The SFF ran a survey on the internet called 'Cheap Access to Space', where it asked American taxpayers for their opinions on the current US space program and future priorities for space transportation. Its own

4 Seven sentences have been removed from the article. Choose from the sentences A–H the one which fits each gap. There is one extra sentence, which you do not need to use. Work through the text, using the underlined phrases in sentence A to help you decide whether it fits in any of the gaps. Discuss your ideas with a partner.

5 Now underline the words and phrases in sentences B–H that link to the text and decide on your answers.

A At the same time, the SFF accepts that NASA's missions could bring other scientific benefits.

B Several companies already have blueprints for getting into space and back cheaply.

C Commercial activity such as this is what the private sector should be doing.

D However, its immediate priority is missions to Mars from the Moon.

E Here again, private companies may well prove them wrong in the very near future.

F This is not a matter of budgets or schedules, but of fundamental purpose and design.

G He sees the NASA program as a bit of a dinosaur.

H Another company, Kistler Aerospace, has similar plans.

Vocabulary

6 Go through the text again to find words related to a–j. An example is given. Try to use some of these words in the speaking practice in exercise 7.

a use   *re-usable*
b commerce
c economy
d deliver
e efficient
f end
g reverse
h settle
i appropriate
j afford

7 Discuss these questions.

- Do you think the SFF is right to encourage the commercial development of space? Why?/ Why not?
- What benefits and drawbacks might this bring?

view is that it is impossible for NASA to offer an 'open frontier'. [5] NASA is 'elitist and exclusive', whereas the SFF believes in opportunities for everyone: 'a future of endlessly expanding new choices'.

The SFF wants to see 'irreversible human settlement' in space as soon as possible and maintains that this is only going to happen through free enterprise. It is inappropriate for government-sponsored astronauts to be building buildings and driving trucks. [6]

Once space transportation becomes affordable, mass space travel will be possible. Many people believe that by 2015, space tourism will have become a viable industry. However, US government officials don't see a future for space tourism. [7] David Ashford, Managing Director of Bristol Spaceplanes Limited, once said that space tourism would begin ten years after people stopped laughing at the concept. People have already stopped laughing.

10·2

Review of future tenses

1 Look at examples a–e from the article on space and identify the future forms listed 1–4 below. What other tense is used in examples f and g to refer to the future?

1 *going to* future
2 future simple
3 future continuous
4 future perfect

a Re-usable rockets will deliver things to orbit and bring stuff back to Earth.
b This is only going to happen through free enterprise.
c Our vehicles will be orbiting as efficiently as air freight carriers.
d Many people believe that by 2015, space tourism will have become a viable industry.
e Tumlinson is going to try to prove a point.
f NASA plans to develop such a rocket.
g However, this situation is due to change.

2 Which of the examples a–g mention the following?

1 a prediction about the future
2 a planned event that is expected to happen soon
3 an event that has not yet happened but will happen within a certain period of time
4 an intention to do something

3 Why can the present continuous be used in the following example?

Tumlinson is giving the opening speech at Friday's conference.

4 How are predictions about the future expressed in these two examples?

a Private companies may well prove them wrong.
b There could be a billion dollar market in taking packages from one side of the planet to the other in an hour.

5 Why is *would* used in this example instead of *will*?

David Ashford once said that space tourism would begin 10 years after people stopped laughing at the concept.

G ⋯⟩ page 202

6 Choose the correct option in italics in these sentences and explain why it is correct.

a Within the next twenty years, the cost of space travel *will be falling / will fall* dramatically.
b In the near future, it's likely that adventure holidays *won't be / aren't going to be* limited to remote places on Earth.
c People *will / may* one day have the opportunity to go to distant planets, but first we need to discover a way of travelling faster than the speed of light.
d Our 7-day travel program is due to depart on December 1, 2015 and *will carry / will have carried* you 100 km into space.
e I've decided I *am going to book / will book* a trip into space as soon as I can afford it.
f The Americans always said they *would fly / will fly* to Mars.
g Sooner or later people *will live / will be living* in space.
h Alpha, the International Space Station, *will have been / will be* up in space for ten years this time next week.

7 What will we wear in the future? Read these FCE candidates' ideas and then complete the summary, using the future perfect of the verbs in the box. One verb isn't needed.

A new technology will change fabrics so they will change their colour during the day. People will be even more concerned with pollution and harmful UV rays, so their clothes will have built-in protective filters to help them keep healthy.

You may think that people will wear silver clothes like in science-fiction movies but I think everyone will wear very colourful balloons. They will use a special gas inside the balloons to make them fly.

become	fill	include	manage	rise	take

One person predicts that pollution (1) .... to a dangerous level, but optimistically suggests that manufacturers (2) .... some form of protection against this in their clothes. The other writes about people flying in their clothes, explaining that these 'balloons' (3) .... with gas to lift them off the ground. Neither feels that clothes (4) .... a uniform colour such as the silver of so many futuristic films. In fact, one person believes that a development in technology (5) .... place to create materials that can change colour while they are being worn.

What are your own ideas about future clothes? Talk to a partner.

Listening

8 🎧 You are going to hear three people talking about the future. Decide whether each speaker has a positive or a negative view of what life for human beings might be like.

Speaker 1 ....
Speaker 2 ....
Speaker 3 ....

Which speaker is closest to your own ideas about the future? Why?

Vocabulary Phrases with *at*

9 Speaker 2 used the preposition *at* in three different ways:

I'm reading one of his sci-fi ones at the moment.
They live for at least three hundred years.
There will always be some country at war with another.

Choose the correct phrase for each of these sentences and explain the meaning of the incorrect options.

1 Hurry up, we'll be locked inside the building unless we leave
....
A at first **B** at once
C at last

2 Jordi is looking forward to the move, but ...., I know he'll miss his friends here.
A at least **B** at present
C at the same time

3 For the first time in ten years, this war-torn country is now ...., thanks to the skills of the negotiators on both sides.
A at peace **B** at war **C** at rest

4 Journalists often get scientific facts slightly wrong, but this article is inaccurate reporting ....
A at his laziest **B** at its worst
C at their best

Notice, as in the last example, that *at* is commonly used with a pronoun and a superlative.

Writing folder 5

Articles 1

1 Look at these titles of articles about the future. Which article would you most like to read? Why?

2 Match the titles to the opening paragraphs A–D. Do all four paragraphs fit their titles well? Why?/Why not?

Aliens are coming ...

3 – 2 – 1 Lift off!

Is anybody there?

A lifelong ambition

A

Imagine being launched in a rocket towards that final frontier. Strapped into your seat in a shiny silver capsule, you feel the power of the engines as they carry you up and away. And soon, you are orbiting around the earth, covering vast distances and looking down on the planet you call home.

C

Our planet is going to be invaded – not by little green men but by a revolutionary new form of transport! Next week sees the launch of a worldwide advertising campaign, for a vehicle that could completely change our life on earth.

B

I want to go up into space. I think it may be possible for ordinary people to go up into space soon. I read something about space travel. I want to be one of the first to go. I hope I can go up into space.

D

On some nights, I open my window and <u>watch</u> the stars. It's a <u>nice</u> thing to do. Sometimes I stay there for ages, wondering what the universe holds. It makes me feel <u>small</u>. Space is a <u>big</u> place. There are <u>a lot of</u> galaxies apart from our own – so there must be other life?

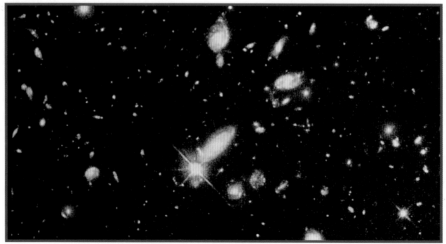

Hubble Space Telescope image of distant galaxies

3 Look again at paragraph D. How could it be improved? Choose words and phrases from the pairs below to replace the words underlined. In each pair, both a and b fit the text correctly, so the final choice is up to you!

a	b
stare at	gaze at
wonderful	brilliant
unimportant	humble
vast	huge
so many	an enormous number of

What parts of speech are the words in a–d below? Insert all these words into paragraph D where they fit best.

a cloudless   beautiful   twinkling
b forms of
c very   such
d truly   surely

Read through the paragraph once more. Could any sentences be joined together? Write out a final version.

4 Paragraph B is a poor attempt at an opening paragraph. Why? Rewrite it, making the following improvements, along with any others of your own.

- Order the ideas more clearly.
- Join any short sentences together.
- Include a first sentence that links back to the title.
- Replace any repeated words, e.g. *want: wish, hope.*
- Use a variety of sentence openers.
- Add suitable words to describe and emphasise.

Exam spot

An article is not an essay! It is written for a wider audience and will appear in a certain type of magazine. Read the exam question carefully to find out where the article may be published and who will read it. Choose a suitable style and use a range of language to make your article interesting to read.

5 Now look at this exam question.

You see this notice in an in-flight magazine and decide to enter the competition.

GALAXY TRAVEL COMPETITION

What forms of transport will we be using in 50 years' time?

Where will we take our holidays?

Write us an article, giving us your views on both of these questions. Science fiction writer John T. Price will choose the most original article, which will receive a prize of $1,000 and be published in our magazine next year.

Write your **article**. (120–180 words)

6 Answer these questions about the writing task.

a Which **two** topics do you need to write about?
b What is meant by 'forms'?
c Should the style be serious or lively?
d How many paragraphs should you write?

7 Plan your article before you start writing. Make content notes for each paragraph and think of a suitable title. Look back over Units 9 and 10 for relevant vocabulary and grammar. Then write your article in 120–180 words. Don't be afraid to use your imagination!

11·1 Like mother, like daughter

1   Look at these photos of famous people and their children. Do you think the children resemble their mother or father? What similarities or differences can you see?

2   With a partner try to find out as much as you can about each other. When you ask about each other's family also ask these questions:

Who do you most look like in your family? Do you sound like anyone in the family when you answer the telephone? Who do you take after in character?

For extra practice take it in turns to think of a famous person but don't tell your partner who it is. Your partner has to ask you personal questions to try to find out your identity. Try not to make it too easy!

Listening

3   🎧 You are going to hear an interview with the daughter of a Hollywood film star.

The recording will be stopped when you hear the following words.

… *some of the kids I knew did.*

Now look at question 1.

1   For her 14th birthday, Hannah
   A took some friends to see a Harrison Ford film at the cinema.
   B went to watch the making of a film.
   C was given whatever she wanted.

Here are some things to think about.
• Did she go to the cinema? How do we know?
• Did she meet Harrison Ford?
• How did her parents treat her?
• Did she have any brothers and sisters?

4   Decide on the correct answer. Which sentence in the interview tells you?

Remember that a wrong answer often repeats the same vocabulary you hear in the recording, and might be true but doesn't actually answer the question.

5 🎧 Now continue listening to the rest of the interview and answer questions 2–7.

2 How did Hannah's mother feel when Hannah said she wanted to be an actress?
   A She wasn't keen on her doing it.
   B She wasn't discouraging.
   C She didn't think she was serious about it.

3 What does Hannah say about the comparison with her mother?
   A They have the same shaped eyes.
   B They are both tall.
   C Their noses are similar.

4 Hannah and her mother both think that
   A they look identical.
   B they do look a bit alike.
   C people are completely wrong.

5 How did Hannah feel about her mother's attitude to acting?
   A She was a bit upset.
   B She was angry.
   C She understood.

6 Why was Hannah encouraged to train to be an accountant?
   A Her mother had had a bad experience with money.
   B Hannah needed to learn the importance of saving.
   C Her mother considered it a useful profession.

7 How does Hannah's mother sound?
   A very demanding
   B slightly foreign
   C like her daughter

6 🎧 Now listen to the interview again. What adjective or adjectives does Hannah use to describe:

a her childhood in Hollywood?
b how her mother had felt when she first arrived in Hollywood?
c part of her nose?
d her mother talking about acting?
e the quality they both possess?
f her mother's attitude to money?
g her mother's voice?

Grammar extra

You've heard already the expression *to look like* + a noun phrase which means *to resemble* or *to take after physically*.

EXAMPLE: *She looks like her mother.*

Now look at these two questions.
A What's he/she like?
B What does he/she like?

Decide which of the words below can be used to answer the questions.

| tall | swimming | friendly | hamburgers |
| watching TV | photography | amusing | |

7 Find out who in your class is from a family the same size as yours, and then form a group. For example, if you are an only child, go to part of the room with others who are only children. Talk to the others in your group about what your family is like, how you feel about the size of your family and what effect, if any, it has had on you. Talk about your place in the family, and whether it's best to be the eldest, youngest, only one, middle child and so on.

8 Are there any special characteristics that run in your family? Is there anything you all like/dislike? Does it look as if you will:

a grow bald/have white hair when still quite young?
b get fat?
c live a long time?
d wear glasses?
e follow in your parents' footsteps (do the same things as your parents have done)?
f have good health?

11·2

Describing personality

1 Use one of the adjectives in the box to answer questions a–n.

sociable generous bad-tempered lazy
considerate optimistic loyal cheerful
self-conscious unreliable conceited
amusing aggressive sensible

How do you describe a person who:

a has a very good opinion of him/herself?
b is usually happy?
c looks on the bright side of things?
d buys you expensive presents?
e never does anything stupid?
f would never upset you?
g never turns up on time?
h really worries what people think of them?
i gets out of bed on the wrong side in a morning?
j tells jokes?
k likes fighting with people?
l doesn't want to get out of bed in the morning?
m will stand by you if you are in trouble?
n enjoys the company of other people?

2 Which of the adjectives above are positive, and which are negative? What are their opposites?

In pairs, say which of these adjectives you would use to describe:

a yourself   d your teacher
b your parents   e your best friend
c your brothers/sisters   f your worst enemy

Vocabulary spot

Extend your vocabulary by thinking of adjectives with opposite meanings. Remember to use a negative prefix if necessary.

Phrasal verbs

3 Replace the words in bold with the correct form of one of the phrasal verbs in the box.

fall out with	pick up	look on	grow up
stand by	turn up	put off	

EXAMPLE: Fred **had an argument** with his best friend. Fred **fell out with** his best friend.

a I **learnt** a bit of Spanish when I was on holiday in Chile.
b Susan **lived** in Shanghai **when she was young**.
c He tried to **discourage** them **from** seeing the film, as it was very violent.
d Pete usually **arrives** at work looking a bit of a mess.
e My boss **supported** me when I had some trouble at work.
f Most people would **see** film stars as being rich and spoilt.

Adverb or adjective?

Normally adverbs are used with verbs.

EXAMPLE: Hannah acts beautifully.
This tells you how she acted.

However, with certain verbs it's sometimes necessary to use adjectives. These verbs are usually connected with our senses – look, sound, taste, feel, and smell. Other verbs include be, appear and seem, and become.

EXAMPLE: 'Hannah is **beautiful**.' and 'Hannah looks **beautiful**.'

4 With a partner discuss what you would say in these situations.

EXAMPLE: You're eating a lemon. It tastes sour.

a You're listening to a love song. It sounds …
b You're walking by the sea. It smells …
c You're walking home late at night. It feels …
d You're eating spaghetti. It tastes …
e You're looking through a travel brochure. It looks …
f You're wearing a designer suit. It feels …

5 Some of these verbs can have two meanings. Look at the underlined verbs and explain the differences.

   A The actress <u>looked</u> angry when she read the bad review.

   B The actress had <u>to look</u> at her co-star angrily at one point in the film.

   A I <u>feel</u> fine.

   B I <u>felt</u> the water carefully to see if it was hot enough.

In examples A, 'looked' and 'feel' mean 'seemed'. In examples B, 'to look' and 'felt' are both actions. If the verb means 'seemed', then an adjective is used after it. If the verb is used for an action, then it is followed by an adverb.

Complete these sentences using an adverb or an adjective.

   a The food tasted ....

   b I felt the soft fur on the rabbit very ....

   c I don't feel very ....

   d Ann looked .... to see if there was any traffic, before crossing the road.

   e Noises can sound quite .... at night.

   f Your coat looks ....

   g He looked at her .... when she entered the room.

   h The rabbit appeared .... out of the hat.

Past and present participles

Corpus spot

Be careful with -ed and -ing adjectives – the *Cambridge Learner Corpus* shows FCE candidates often make mistakes with these.

> My friend was very **excited** about going to Hollywood on holiday.
> NOT My friend was very ~~exciting~~ about going to Hollywood on holiday.

> In our home we want to do many things otherwise we feel very **bored**.
> NOT In our home we want to do many things otherwise we feel very ~~boring~~.

6 When Hannah is talking about her mother and her attitude to acting she says she became quite embarrassed. Hannah means that her mother became a bit red or maybe blushed and wasn't sure what to say. What would it mean if Hannah had said 'my mother became quite embarrassing'?

Can you finish these sentences which explain what the grammatical rule is?

   1 to talk about how we feel about something we use ....

   2 to talk about the person or thing that is causing the feeling we use ....

 ⋯⋗ page 202

Speaking

7 In pairs talk about how you feel when you watch the following:

   a soap operas   e films about aliens
   b westerns   f cartoons
   c Disney films   g foreign films with
   d Frankenstein movies   subtitles

EXAMPLE: *I am bored by soap operas. They're so appalling.*

Use some of these adjectives.

bored/boring	excited/exciting
disturbed/disturbing	thrilled/thrilling
horrified/horrifying	appalled/appalling
shocked/shocking	revolted/revolting
moved/moving	gripped/gripping

Exam folder 6

Paper 4 Part 1
Short extracts

In this part of the Listening paper you will hear eight unconnected short recordings of about 30 seconds each. There will be either one or two speakers. For each question, you have to decide which is the correct answer from three possible options. Both the question and the options are recorded, which gives you time to think about the recording that is coming up. Each recording is repeated.

You should make the best use of the time available. Read through each question as you hear it and underline any key words. Think about what to listen out for during the pause before each recording starts. After you have listened once, choose the option that you think is correct. As you listen for the second time, check that the other two options are definitely wrong.

If you do not know the answer to a question, keep calm and move on to the next one. At the end of the Listening test, you will have time to transfer your answers to an answer sheet. For any questions you haven't been able to answer, make a guess – there is a one in three chance of your being right!

1 Look through these questions and underline the key words.

You will hear people talking in eight different situations. For questions 1–8, choose the best answer (**A**, **B** or **C**).

1 You hear this advertisement on the radio for a new magazine. Who is the magazine aimed at?
A gardeners
B cooks
C climbers

2 As you leave the cinema, you overhear this conversation. What is the man's opinion of the film?
A It is longer than necessary.
B It has a weak storyline.
C Its actors are disappointing.

3 You overhear a woman talking on the phone. What sort of person is she?
A unhappy
B impractical
C disloyal

4 You hear this interview on the radio. Why did the man give up his job?
A to recover from stress
B to reduce his expenses
C to move somewhere quiet

5 You overhear this conversation in a hotel. Why has the woman come down to reception?
A to ask for another room
B to order some food
C to complain about the service

6 You hear this radio report about a football match. What happened at the match?
A Some fans ran onto the pitch.
B A player was badly injured.
C The referee stopped the match.

7 You hear this interview on the radio. Where is it taking place?
A in a clothes shop
B at an exhibition
C on a beach

8 You overhear this woman talking about an evening course. What does she enjoy most?
A doing maths
B watching videos
C having coffee

2 🎧 Now listen and answer the eight questions. Remember that each recording is repeated. When you have finished, check your answers.

3 Fill in the extract from the answer sheet for Part 1 below with your answers.

Part 1			
1	A	B	C
2	A	B	C
3	A	B	C
4	A	B	C
5	A	B	C
6	A	B	C
7	A	B	C
8	A	B	C

Advice

- Think about possible contents for each question as you listen.
- Choose your answers at the first listening.
- Check your answers at the second listening.
- Keep calm and make a guess if necessary.
- Remember to transfer your answers to the answer sheet at the end of the listening test.

A great idea

1 How technology-minded do you think you are? Try this questionnaire to test your response to modern technology. Answer yes or no to all the questions.

? ? ? ? ? ? ? ? ? ? ?

1 Have you ever felt anxious about:
a down escalators stopping suddenly?
b leaving a TV set plugged in?
c putting food in a microwave oven?

2 Do you call an expert when:
a the lights fuse?
b the drains are blocked?
c you need a plug putting on something?

3 Do you use:
a a laptop?
b an electric toothbrush?
c a digital camera phone?
d an iPod/MP3 player?
e an electric tin-opener?

4 When you speak to voicemail do you:
a talk naturally?
b keep it brief?
c put the phone down when you realise it's voicemail?
d keep repeating yourself?

5 If you put money in a vending machine and nothing happens do you:
a kick it viciously?
b put more money in?
c walk away resignedly?
d ring up the owners?

Scoring

1 2 points for Yes
  0 points for No
2 2 points for Yes
  0 points for No
3 2 points for No, 0 for Yes
4 a=0, b=0, c=2, d=1
5 a=2, b=1, c=0, d=0
The higher your score, the more uneasy you are with technology. In fact, you're a technophobe! A low score indicates you are at home with new developments and gadgets. You're a technophile!

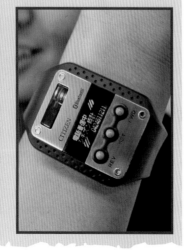

Vocabulary spot

When you read a text you may find that some words are unfamiliar to you. Don't immediately reach for your dictionary! Try to work out the meaning of an unknown word from its context, that is, the words around it.

2 With a partner, work out the meaning of the words in italics below.

a Houses in hot countries have *shutters* at the windows to keep out the sun.
b The *forerunner* of ice-cream was frozen snow.
c Batman wears *a mask* so no one will recognise him.
d Her flat was very *compact*, but everything fitted in very neatly.
e You know when you reach Paris because you can see that famous *landmark*, the Eiffel Tower.
f There were several *factors* in his decision to move abroad – the most important being that he could get a job more easily.

Exam spot

In Part 3 of Paper 1 you will need to be able to understand paraphrase – that is to match words or phrases with words or phrases of similar meaning.

3 You are going to read a magazine article about the Kodak camera and its inventor, George Eastman. You will have to decide which section of the article mentions each question. First of all, skim the text quickly for general meaning. Now look at the first question below the article.

What other words can be used instead of 'suggestion'? You need to find someone who worked with Eastman who suggested something. The answer is in section **A**.

Now answer questions 2–12 in the same way.

GEORGE EASTMAN AND THE KODAK CAMERA

A Photography became available to the man in the street around 1888 when the Kodak camera was introduced by an American, George Eastman (1854–1932). When Eastman was 24, he made plans for a holiday to Santo Domingo. A co-worker proposed he made a record of the trip, so Eastman bought a camera. It was as big as a microwave oven and needed a heavy metal stand. There were also chemicals, glass tanks and a heavy plate holder to carry. The complete outfit was 'a pack-horse load', as Eastman later described it.

B In the end, Eastman didn't get to Santo Domingo but instead became completely absorbed in photography and sought to simplify the complicated process. He worked in a bank during the day and experimented at home in his mother's kitchen at night. In 1880 Eastman leased the third floor of a building in Rochester and began to manufacture 'dry plates', which were a form of camera film which was easier to process. His goal was to invent a camera 'as convenient as a pencil' and in 1888 he finally achieved this objective with the invention of the Kodak camera. It was advertised as 'the smallest, lightest and simplest of all Detective cameras' – a popular term in the 1880s for cameras which were so small and light they could easily be held in the hands.

C Eastman's faith in the importance of advertising was unbounded. The camera was advertised in leading papers and periodicals of the day – with the adverts written by Eastman himself.

He coined the phrase 'you press the button, we do the rest' and within a year it became a well-known catchphrase.

D It was very easy to take a photograph with the Kodak camera, requiring only three simple steps: turning the key (to wind on the film); pulling the string (to set the shutter); and pressing the button (to release the shutter and make the exposure). There was no viewfinder. To take a photo you just pointed the camera at a subject. However, a circular mask had to be used in the camera, placed in front of the film, because definition at the edge of the image area was poor. As a result, the camera produced distinctive, round photographs.

E The technology of the Kodak camera was not especially revolutionary. It was not the first hand camera, nor was it the first camera to be made solely for roll film. What makes it a landmark in the history of photography, is that it was the first stage in a complete system of amateur photography. It was sold already loaded with enough film to take 100 photographs. After the film had been exposed, the entire camera was sent to the factory, where it was unloaded and the film developed and printed. The camera was reloaded with fresh film, and returned to its owner together with the negatives and a set of prints. Before this, photographers had had no alternative but to do the developing and printing themselves. As a result, few ordinary people had taken up photography.

Which section mentions

a suggestion made by a colleague? `1` [ ]

the introduction of a slogan? `2` [ ]

a desire to make the method of producing photographs easier? `3` [ ]

a disadvantage of the Kodak camera? `4` [ ]

an admission that the new camera wasn't particularly ground-breaking? `5` [ ]

a belief that publicity was essential? `6` [ ]

the actions required to photograph something? `7` [ ] `8` [ ]

the reason why the average person hadn't taken up photography previously? `9` [ ]

the way in which certain cameras were described in the 19th century? `10` [ ]

the need for transportation for old-style cameras? `11` [ ]

an ambition achieved? `12` [ ]

12·2

The passive

1 Which of the verbs in bold in these sentences from the passage are in the passive?

  a It **was sold** already loaded with enough film …
  b His goal **was** to invent a camera …
  c … they **could** easily **be held** in the hands.
  d After the film **had been exposed**, the entire camera **was sent** to the factory …
  e … few ordinary people **had taken up** photography.
  f It **was advertised** as …

2 How is the passive formed and why is it used?

G ⋯⋰ page 202

3 Fill the spaces in the newspaper article opposite with the passive form of one of the verbs below.

dissolve	store	fill	supply
persuade	disperse	encourage	use
talk into	ask	issue	hope make up

by or *with*?

4 What do you think the rule is for when we use *by* and when we use *with*?

Shakespeare wrote Romeo and Juliet. Romeo and Juliet was written by Shakespeare.
Money can't buy happiness. Happiness can't be bought with money.

Change the following in the same way.

  a Mud covered the kitchen floor.
  b A cat scratched him.
  c A car ran him over.
  d Bulldozers smashed down the old house.
  e They are rebuilding the school using a new type of brick.

5 It isn't always necessary to use *by*. Which sentences are correct and which need *by* … to complete them?

  a Jurassic Park was produced
  b A new road is now being built round the town
  c She was given a job
  d He was murdered
  e She is being operated on
  f The fire is said to have been started

G ⋯⋰ page 203

Shops with the sweet smell of success

It began with the smell of freshly baked bread. A supermarket with a sharp nose for business believed people **(1)** .... to spend more money if they smelled something pleasant. The idea was so successful that hundreds of other shops **(2)** .... to do the same. The smells of engine oil, leather and burning rubber **(3)** .... to launch and sell a new car, while banks and hotels **(4)** .... often .... with pleasant fragrances such as apple and lavender. Sports shops believe that customers **(5)** .... spending more money if they can smell the scent of freshly mown grass.

These business scents **(6)** .... by two companies, BOC Gases and Atmospherics. The fragrances **(7)** .... in carbon dioxide and **(8)** .... via air conditioning, or **(9)** .... in discreet cylinders and released when needed.

BOC Gases is working with British firms to see how well the fragrances are doing. Soon customers **(10)** .... with questionnaires, and it **(11)** .... their answers will provide a clearer idea of the relationship between scents and increased sales. A spokesman for the company said: 'Any smell you want **(12)** .... for you. We **(13)** (constantly) .... for the same smells, like coffee and bread, but we want people to think of other things.'

Corpus spot

Take care when using the passive – the *Cambridge Learner Corpus* shows FCE candidates often make mistakes with this.

> The hotel **was opened** by a famous film star.
> NOT The hotel ~~opened~~ by a famous film star.

Correct the mistakes that FCE candidates have made with the passive in these sentences.

  a The house painted blue.
  b The mobile was not answer.
  c My laptop has bought for me two months ago.
  d He born in June.
  e The meeting has cancelled.

6 Where would you see the following notices?

a All crockery and cutlery to be returned after use.

b **You are requested not to smoke.**

c RESERVED FOR MEMBERS

d Packet should be opened at the other end.

e LOST TREASURE FOUND IN GARDEN

7 In pairs ask and answer these questions.

   a Has your photo ever been in a newspaper?

   b It is said that in the future most people will work from home. Do you agree?

   c Can you explain how paper is produced?

   d Where was your watch made?

   e What were you given for your last birthday?

8 Link the following pieces of information using a passive.

   a John Lennon – New York

   b gunpowder – China

   c telephone – half a billion people

   d Tutankhamun – Lord Caernarfon

   e satellites – 1957

   f Olympic Games – London

   g togas – the Romans

   h leather – cows

9 Complete the second sentence so that it has a similar meaning to the first sentence, using the word given. Do not change the word given. You must use between two and five words, including the word given.

Exam spot

When you have a key word transformation from active to passive or passive to active, it is important to keep in the same tense as the original sentence.

1 Inventors don't like people copying their ideas.
object
Inventors .... being copied.

2 Why were the students mixing up those chemicals in the lab yesterday?
being
Why .... up in the lab yesterday?

3 They made her hand over her notebooks.
was
She .... her notebooks.

4 People say that the local camera shop is very good.
supposed
The local camera shop ....
very good.

5 My boss told me of his decision yesterday.
informed
I .... decision yesterday.

6 Fewer people smoke these days.
decrease
There .... the number of people who smoke these days.

10 In the article in 12.1, the collocation *to take a photo* is used.

Look at the words in the boxes and decide which of the verbs below each can go with. Some can go with more than one, but usually with a different meaning. Find out the meanings of the collocations.

come   take   tell   fall

a story	into money	turns	ill
a seat	advantage of	asleep	apart
a lie	the time	notice of	an interest
to a conclusion	to a decision	in love	a long time
the difference	offence	the truth	

Listening

11 🎧 You are going to hear four people talking about different inventions. Decide in each case what you think the invention is.

Writing folder 6

Reviews

In Part 2 of Paper 2 you may be asked to write a review, for example of a concert, film, play, or TV programme you have seen. A review is a type of article, and is generally published in a magazine or posted on a website. It can be either serious or light-hearted, and should contain both information and opinion.

1 Think of the best and worst films you have seen recently. List their good and bad points. Then tell your partner about each film.

2 Look at the notes about two films below. Which film did the writer prefer, A or B?

A	B
fascinating storyline	boring love scenes
historical events	appalling dialogue
shocking violence	complicated plot
tremendous soundtrack	terrible costumes
excellent acting skills	dull characters
interesting locations	unrealistic ending
frighteningly realistic	disappointing special effects

3 Read the film review opposite and complete gaps 1–7 with one of the sets of phrases in exercise 2.

4 A positive review usually ends with a recommendation, as in the review opposite. Which of the recommendations below are grammatically correct? Tick them and correct the other sentences.

a I suggest you to see this film immediately.
b This film is highly recommended.
c The movie has much to recommend it.
d I will advise you not to miss this film.
e I suggest that you see this film without delay.
f I strongly advise you to go and see the film.
g I could recommend this film to you.

One of the best films I have seen recently is *The Last King of Scotland*, starring Forest Whitaker. His performance as Idi Amin is (1) .... and cleverly illustrates how strange Amin's behaviour was at times. Alongside Whitaker, newcomer James McAvoy displays some (2) .... as the young Scottish doctor Nicholas Garrigan, who arrives in Uganda just as Amin takes power and who eventually becomes his personal doctor.

Uganda has some amazing landscape and the film's (3) .... show us the real beauty of the country. The (4) .... , based on a novel by journalist Giles Foden, blends fact and fiction in a very clever way, sweeping us along with the (5) .... that were such a tragedy for Uganda in the 1970s. There are a number of scenes of (6) .... and the film is frequently disturbing because of this, but at the same time it is totally gripping.

Last but not least, there is a (7) .... , with a wide range of African music that will have you dancing in your seat at times. I thoroughly recommend this film to you.

5 Complete these sentences with information of your own, using passive forms of the verbs in brackets. Try to vary the tenses you use.

a The film .... (direct)

b This wonderful story .... (set)

c All of the costumes .... (design)

d The main character .... (play)

e The supporting cast .... (choose)

f Most of the music .... (compose)

g A subtitled version .... (show)

h The screenplay .... (nominate)

6 Now read this exam question.

You have seen this announcement on your college noticeboard.

We want your reviews now!

Have you enjoyed a particular programme on TV recently? Or is there one that you just can't stand? Either way, why not write a review for the college website? Include plenty of information about the programme and give us your opinions on it, good or bad.

Email your review to Sam at the Student Office: sam@unitel.ac

Write your **review**.

7 Which programme will you write about? List as many nouns as you can to do with each type of programme below.

comedy: jokes,
documentary: photography,
game show: quiz,
reality show: celebrities,
soap opera: drama,

8 Make a paragraph plan before you start writing. Remember to name the programme at the start. Use some of the language in exercise 2 and include a recommendation unless your review is negative. Write 120–180 words.

Units 7–12 Revision

Grammar

1 For questions 1–12, read the film review below and think of the word which best fits each gap. Use only one word in each gap.

The best film I have seen is LA Confidential, starring Kim Basinger and Kevin Spacey. It was set **(1)** .... 1950s Los Angeles and **(2)** .... the budget wasn't particularly extravagant, the film had very powerful images and seemed totally authentic. **(3)** .... example, the costumes looked just like what people **(4)** .... have worn; the cars seemed to **(5)** .... exactly what people **(6)** .... to drive around in. **(7)** .... of the actors played their parts extremely well, and Kim Basinger in particular gave **(8)** .... truly outstanding performance. The film was absolutely gripping, largely **(9)** .... the storyline was so carefully put together. There were several ingredients: **(10)** .... only the obvious **(11)** .... like murder and blackmail, but also corruption, Hollywood lifestyles, and some moving family histories. **(12)** .... is an impressive film. See it!

Topic review

2 Read these sentences and say which are true for you, giving more details. Don't be afraid to use your imagination!

   a I used to be different from how I am now.
   b Next weekend I'm going to do something dangerous!
   c I look like a famous film star.
   d It must have been difficult looking after me when I was younger.
   e I can't stand getting behind with my work.
   f School used to be really boring.
   g At home, I was always made to finish my food.
   h By this time next year I'll have passed FCE.
   i I really enjoy watching adverts on TV.
   j I find it hard to believe that the Earth has been visited by aliens.

Vocabulary

3 Two common verbs are used in these sentences. Decide what they are and fill the gaps, using a suitable verb form.

   a We're .... used to living in a village now.
   b Jane .... on really well with her boss.
   c Don't .... offence – I'm only trying to help!
   d After Bill was made redundant, he soon learned to .... by with less money.
   e You should .... advantage of the opportunity to go to America while your aunt is living there.
   f I finally .... a letter from the company last week, offering me a refund.

g There's no point offering Jim any advice – he'll .... no notice of it!

h The engineer .... the whole thing apart and eventually found the problem.

4 Decide which is the odd one out in these sets and say why.

a disturbing, terrifying, cunning, appalling
b voice-over, jingle, slogan, campaign
c surgeon, sister, plumber, porter
d fancy, detest, loathe, hate
e deep, wide, huge, shallow
f pitch, rink, court, track
g intend, pretend, expect, hope
h extravagant, economical, affordable, cheap

Phrasal verbs

5 Complete these sentences with the correct verbs.

ON
a The property market is .... on favourably by investors.
b It must be really hard to .... on in advertising – it's such a competitive business.
c If you .... on going to the party, I suppose I'd better give you a lift.

OFF
d Sales of electric cars could .... off very soon.
e I'm going to use the exercise bike in the gym later to .... off that huge lunch!
f Jenny .... me off seeing that film; she said it was very shocking.

Writing

6 Read paragraphs A–C and decide what type of writing each one is, choosing from 1–4.

1 letter   3 article
2 story   4 essay

A
> To sum up, in my opinion people should work fewer hours in the future. By doing this, unemployment could be reduced and working parents would be able to spend more time with their children. Moreover, life would be less stressful, which must be a benefit to society in the end.

B
> She suddenly noticed something shiny on the sand just in front of her. It was a small metallic object, about the same size as a mobile phone, but unlike anything she had ever seen before. Without a second thought, she picked it up and put it in her pocket, planning to take the strange thing home to show her brother. That was Maria's first big mistake.

C
> Have you ever thought of joining a gym? I recently did and it changed my life. I used to come home from my job and just sit watching TV, but now, I work out every evening. My friends say my personality has changed. Before, I would be rather aggressive whenever my day had been bad, but now, they say I'm much better tempered.

Which paragraph

• is an opening?
• is a conclusion?

1 Look at this pair of photographs, which show two different classrooms in Britain. Talk to a partner about the differences and say which school is closer to your own learning experience.

2 Now talk to each other about your schooldays. You should each describe:

a a school you attended (its size, location, atmosphere)
b a teacher you remember well
c something at school that you particularly enjoyed
d someone at school that you found really annoying

Report your partner's answers to the class. For example:

X told me/said that he/she …
X spoke about/talked about his/her …
X thinks/feels/remembers that he/she …
X claims/believes strongly/is convinced that …

Which tenses did you use to report what you heard?

3 Report David's confession below as reported speech, being careful to use suitable past tenses.

EXAMPLE: *David said that it wasn't Simon's fault. …*

'It isn't Simon's fault! I want to describe what really happened. I was inside the classroom during break and I saw a group of my friends outside. I went over to the window and tried to get their attention. I waved at them but they didn't see me, so I hammered on the window. I know glass is breakable but I just didn't think. When my hand went through I panicked. I wasn't hurt and I wanted to avoid getting into trouble, so I put Simon's bag over the hole and left the room. I'm sorry I haven't told anyone the truth until now.'

Listening

4 You are going to hear a radio interview with two work colleagues, Sandra Wilson and Mike Tripp, who also used to attend the same school.

First, read the reported statements 1–8 below.

1 Sandra explained that she had disliked Mike because of his attitude to school.
2 Sandra accused Mike of deliberately forgetting certain things he had done at school.
3 Mike explained that he had known at the time how irritating he was.
4 Mike wished he had worked harder at school.
5 Mike said that he had left the science exam because he couldn't answer the questions.
6 Mike felt that his father had expected him to do well when he left school.
7 Mike admitted that the school careers teachers had been quite helpful.
8 Mike mentioned that his father had helped him financially in starting his business.

🎧 Now listen to the recording and tick the statements that are true. Compare your answers and listen again to check.

5 In the recording Sandra talked about some of Mike's friends who didn't *make it*. What exactly does this mean? In which other situations might you use this expression?

There are a number of other expressions with *make*. Complete these reported statements of how Mike set up his business, using a suitable phrase from the ones below.

make an impression	make a profit	make a success of
make a start	make use of	

a Mike said that he had .... in a small way while still at school.
b He admitted that he had .... the school computer in his lunch breaks.
c He explained that he had .... on some cheap flights.
d He said that he had .... the business from the start.
e He complained that the careers teachers at school had not .... on him.

6 Below are some short descriptions of the first jobs some famous people had. See if you can work out which job was done by each person.

7 In the extracts there are several words commonly found in letters of application, which will be dealt with in the next Writing folder. Underline any words you think may be useful. Check their meaning in an English–English dictionary and look for further examples of their use.

Madonna

Agatha Christie

Tom Cruise

Annie Lennox

A
His parents divorced when he was 12 and his mother was left to bring up four children single-handed. All four kids had jobs – his three sisters worked for different local restaurants, while he cut grass and did a paper round. It probably took him a year to earn what he can now make in a single day.

B
He inherited the family sculpting business but showed little interest in it. He had no talent for stonework whatsoever and so, not surprisingly, the business went downhill fast. Instead, it was his determination to solve the twin mysteries of life and death that led him to be considered the wisest man alive.

C
On leaving school at 17, the only jobs available were in the local fish factory. The smell was appalling and working on the filleting machine made her constantly want to throw up. She escaped to London in the end and found employment as a waitress.

D
He became an apprentice on a cargo ship at the age of 17 and his very first experience was gained on a voyage to Rio de Janeiro. Altogether he spent five years at sea. He devoted his spare time to his hobby, which was ultimately to become a full-time career, but only once he was 35.

E
She worked long hours at a hamburger restaurant and was so poor that she had to search through the dustbins after work for any thrown-out food. She also sold ice-cream and was a coat-check girl at the *Russian Tea Rooms* in New York.

F
Initially, she took a position as an unpaid assistant in a chemist's shop, and later qualified in pharmacy. Her duties gave her a sound knowledge of poisons, that would subsequently be extremely relevant.

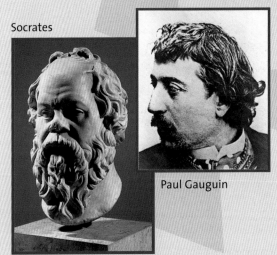

Socrates

Paul Gauguin

Reporting

1 Look at quotes a–c and explain why the tenses underlined have been used in reporting them.

a 'I can't remember much about my first school; my mother will, though.'
Greg claimed that he <u>couldn't</u> remember much about his first school, but thought that his mother <u>would</u>.

b 'When Jack moved to secondary school he became less motivated.'
His mother said that Jack <u>had become</u> less motivated when he <u>had moved</u> to secondary school.

c 'Girls are now doing better than boys at school.'
The expert said girls <u>are</u> now doing better than boys at school.

G ···⟶ page 203

2 Decide which structures can be used after the following reporting verbs, giving examples. Two are done for you.

accuse *She accused him of cheating.*
admit   *He admitted (to) being wrong.*
        He admitted (that) he was wrong.

apologise	promise
argue	refuse
claim	say
deny	suggest
explain	urge
insist	warn

Corpus spot

Be careful when using reporting verbs – the *Cambridge Learner Corpus* shows FCE candidates often make mistakes in the structures that follow them. Here are two of the most common mistakes.

My father suggested **that I should read** this wonderful story.
NOT My father ~~suggested me to read~~ this wonderful story.

I phoned my boyfriend and I **explained my secret to him**.
NOT I phoned my boyfriend and I ~~explained him my secret~~.

3 Match the quotes a–d with the reported statements 1–4.

a 'I visited my old school recently and it was much smaller than I remembered.'
b 'Perhaps we should educate parents about how they can help their children.'
c 'We belong to an anti-learning culture.'
d 'I'll make more of an effort.'

1 She complained that society doesn't encourage education.
2 He promised to work harder.
3 She explained that she had been back and had found it very different.
4 He suggested showing parents what to do.

Listening

Exam spot

Part 3 of Paper 4 is a matching task with one extra option. Before the recording starts, read options **A–F** and predict what you might hear.

4 You will hear five different callers to a radio phone-in giving their views about educational performance in Britain. For questions 1–5, choose from the list (A–F) what each person says.

First, read A–F and predict what the speakers might say.

A Changes in society explain why boys and girls have different career ambitions.
B The recently improved academic performance of girls should be recognised.
C Boys can miss out on the influence of men while they are growing up.
D Limited opportunities at school are affecting some children's development.
E Parents tend to raise boys and girls differently from a young age.
F A different approach is needed to the early stages of learning.

5 Listen to Speaker 1. Then complete this summary using present tenses. Match the content to one of the options A–F.

The first speaker claimed that there (1) .... too many women teachers in British schools and argued that boys (2) .... men as role models. He also suggested boys (3) .... more by broken marriages than girls.

6 🎧 Now listen to Speakers 2–5 and note down the main points each person makes. Then report their views by writing summaries similar to the one in exercise 5. Match your summaries to A–F and write your choices below.

Speaker **2**   Speaker **3**   Speaker **4**   Speaker **5**

7 🎧 As you listen again, listen out for words or phrases that mean the same as a–h. The number of the extract is given in brackets.

a are usually (1)   e dealt with (3)
b make good progress (2) f referring to (4)
c misbehaving (2)   g make longer (4)
d earners (3)   h applaud (5)

8 Discuss these questions:

- Are girls doing better at school than boys in your country? Why?/Why not?
- How should the problem of underachievement be tackled?

Ⓖrammar extra

Reported questions usually involve changes in word order. Look at the questions below and how they have been reported. Then report questions a–e.

What's the answer to number 14?
He asked what the answer to number 14 was.

Where are the cassette boxes?
He asked where the cassette boxes were.

When did this term start?
She asked when this term had started.

Are there enough books to go round?
He asked if there were enough books to go round.

Should I repeat the question?
She asked whether she should repeat the question.

a Why are girls gaining more university places?
   He asked ...
b In what ways was the situation different twenty years ago?
   He asked ...
c Will things get better in the future?
   He asked ...
d Should British children spend more time at nursery?
   He asked ...
e Why haven't we faced up to this problem?
   He asked ...

---

9 Complete the second sentence so that it has a similar meaning to the first sentence, using the word given. Don't change the word given. You must use between two and five words, including the word given.

1 'You put that frog on my chair, didn't you, Charlie?' said Sally.
of
Sally ....
that frog on her chair.

2 'Stop misbehaving or you'll be sent to the head,' the teacher said to Johnny.
warned
The teacher ....
or he would be sent to the head.

3 At the interview, Kate was asked how well she had done in her exams.
did
The interviewer asked Kate, 'How well
....
in your exams?'

4 'Please try to stay awake during the lesson,' the teacher told them.
urged
The teacher ....
asleep during the lesson.

5 Susan denied wasting her time at school when she was younger.
said
Susan ....
her time at school when she was younger.

6 'Have you tidied up in the science lab?' the headmaster asked them.
tidied
The headmaster wanted to know
....
in the science lab.

7 'I'm sorry, I've forgotten my homework,' Nicholas said.
apologised
Nicholas ....
his homework.

8 Stephen told me he would see me the next day at the lecture.
see
'I ....
at the lecture,' Stephen said.

Exam folder 7

Paper 4 Part 2 Sentence completion

Advice

- You must write down the actual words that you hear. Do not spend time trying to say things 'in a different way'. If you do that you will probably miss the next answer.
- If you cannot do one question it is very important not to worry; you will, after all, hear the piece twice. Leave the difficult question and come back to it later.
- You will only need to write very little – one, two, or three words.
- Minor spelling mistakes are accepted. However, you should check your spelling before transferring your answers to the answer sheet.
- Always try to write something, even if you're not sure that it's the correct answer.

In this part of the Listening paper you hear either a monologue or a conversation. The task will be to complete a set of sentences.

1 Before you listen, read through the question paper and try to predict what the answers are going to be. Together with a partner, try to do this now, and then see how many of the answers you predicted correctly at the end of the exercise.
These clues may help you.

   1 What sort of jobs would people who work with a famous chef have?
   2 What type of skills should a person doing this job have?
   3 What sort of thing do you 'follow'?
   4 A hotel name.
   5 What does 'attend' collocate with?
   6 What can someone 'make'?
   7 Where might you have lunch? Listen carefully to this one as you may hear more than one place.
   8 Another way of saying 'cope with'?
   9 What sort of things do you try to resist?
   10 The name of another job.

2 🎧 You will hear part of a radio interview with a woman called Christine Whitelaw. For questions 1–10, complete the sentences.

The right job

Christine's occupation is that of [1] to a chef.

Christine is skilled at [2] very quickly.

Christine followed a [3] when she first

left school.

Christine's first job was at a hotel called the [4]

In order to get her present job, Christine had to attend [5]

After lunch, Christine spends her time doing correspondence and

making [6]

If Christine has a working lunch with Patrick they eat it

in the [7]

Christine's previous hotel experience taught her how to cope with

the [8]

Christine finds it difficult to resist all the [9]

where she works.

Christine says that she wouldn't want to change her job and work

as a [10]

Career moves

1 Identify the jobs in the photos and say what skills are important in each one. Which job would you prefer and why?

2 Check you know the meaning of these words and then choose three to complete the quotes below.

> calculating   concerned   insecure   flexible
> self-motivated   academic   redundant

a A career used to be for life. Once you had left school, you found a job and worked your way up the career ladder. Today, the job market is far more .... , and no one knows what tomorrow may bring.

b You have to be ready to accept change, in short be .... , if you are going to stay in the job market. There's a positive side to this – instead of feeling that you have to stay in the job you've been trained to do, you have more freedom to move around and try different things.

c Women are more willing to take career risks, partly because they are less .... with status, but also because they like to experiment. It's just a question of saying: I think I can do this. And then giving it a go.

3 Do you view these trends in the job market positively or negatively? In what other ways has the job market changed?

4 You are going to read a magazine article about five women who have recently changed careers. For questions 1–15, choose from the women (A–E). They may be chosen more than once. There is an example at the beginning (0).

Which of the women

studied while working?	1 [ ] 2 [ ]
expects to earn more eventually?	3 [ ]
gets by on less money?	4 [ ]
used to own a company?	5 [ ]
travelled in her original job?	6 [ ]
like meeting people in their work?	7 [ ] 8 [ ]
enjoys her new lack of routine?	9 [ ]
took some time to get on top of her work?	10 [ ]
now work from home?	11 [ ] 12 [ ]
used to work in government?	13 [ ]
found their previous job stressful?	14 [ ] 15 [ ]

5 Now answer these questions about the women.

a Why do you think Amanda felt increasingly *discontented* in her old job?
b How might Linda become *demotivated*?
c In what context does Sue describe her salary as *unimaginable*?
d How might Petra's new life seem *uncertain* and *insecure* to some people?
e Why did the fact that Helen had had her own business make her seem *unemployable*?
f Why would an *immature* applicant be *unsuitable* for Helen's job as a registrar?

6 Choose suitable negative prefixes for these words.

> practical   capable   organised   dependent
> successful   honest   loyal   patient

Meet five women who have changed careers

A — Amanda, 39

I had been working in sales for twelve years when I suffered an ankle injury that was to change my whole life. Someone suggested alternative medicine and I was so impressed by the treatment that I began evening classes out of interest. I had reached a point in my life where things had to change. In many ways I had it all: a company car, foreign business trips, my own house, job security. But at 33, I felt increasingly discontented. So I persuaded my boss to let me work a four-day week and did homeopathy classes on the remaining day. It took four difficult years to qualify, as I was studying 25 hours a week on top of my job. Although my income has reduced by a third, my overheads are lower too. As for the BMW, I don't miss it at all!

B — Linda, 34

I'd always wanted to have my own business, but something had held me back. I did various jobs in marketing, including four years in the cosmetics industry. When I was made redundant last year, I knew the time was right. I'd had my own colours done and I'd found it fascinating, so I used my redundancy money to buy a 'House of Colour' franchise. My work is very sociable and the best thing of all is that I answer to no one but myself. Everything is based here in the house, so I have to be incredibly organised and self-motivated. I'm nothing like as tense as before, despite giving it my all. The only downside is the money, although in all seriousness I reckon the takings will have overtaken my previous salary by next year. I hope so, anyway!

C — Sue, 34

I'd never seen myself as academic. Hairdressing seemed glamorous and I wanted a car, so I went to work in a salon as an apprentice. It paid very little, but I had fun. Then my husband announced that he was moving to London. That was the catalyst I'd been waiting for. I stayed put and took English and Law at night school. I was spending 45 hours a week in the salon and working for exams as well. I lost ten kilos in weight, but for all the stress of studying, I knew I was doing the right thing. After leaving college I went into market research. My confidence has always been low and it was three years before I felt I'd cracked the job. My present earnings would have been unimaginable back in the salon.

D — Petra, 45

I worked for three cabinet ministers, earning £60,000 a year, but at the cost of having to work a 65-hour week. When I turned 35, it hit me: I've worked here for nearly 15 years and I've probably got 25 to go. If I'd added up the hours they would probably have been equivalent to 40 normal working years! I decided to save as much as possible, and then get out. It sounds very calculating, but it had to be. Choosing to take redundancy has given me new opportunities. I've set up the spare room as an office and I'm currently editing a collection of family letters, which is something I'd always wanted to do. People who need certainty and structure would find my new life very difficult, but all in all, I feel I've made the right decision.

E — Helen, 53

My family had been in the leather business since 1906 and the company eventually passed to me. I loved the work, but the business was a huge responsibility and I worried constantly. When small shops failed, our own revenue dropped. By 1994 it was hopeless and I went into voluntary liquidation. My friends said I would be unemployable, not just because of my age but because I'd run my own business. However, I've been working as a registrar* for the past three years. The original advert sought a mature, understanding person to deal with people from all walks of life, which was tailor-made for me! Although I miss my business, I've experienced two different careers, and it's marvellous to have another job which needs genuine commitment.

*a person who keeps official records of births, marriages and deaths

Grammar extra

There are a number of expressions with *all* in the article. Say how *all* is used in a–h.

- I had it all (A)
- I don't miss it at all! (A)
- the best thing of all (B)
- giving it my all (B)
- e in all seriousness (B)
- f for all the stress (C)
- g all in all (D)
- h all walks of life (E)

Sometimes, *all* is confused with *whole*. In this example, it is not possible to use *all*.

an ankle injury that was to change my whole life.

Now complete these sentences using *all* or *whole*. Where it is possible to use either, write both alternatives. Add any words necessary.

a The firm acknowledged .... 279 applications the same day.
b The recession had affected .... car industry, causing many redundancies.
c .... world depends on electronic communications nowadays.
d Accountants have a powerful voice in .... companies.
e We had been staring at figures on screen .... day and .... us were fed up.
f There are disadvantages to .... jobs.

What rules can you make about the use of *all* and *whole* on the basis of these examples?

G ⤷ page 203

14·2

Perfect tenses

1 Explain the differences in meaning in these sentences and identify the tenses used.

a I have never sent an email.
b I never sent an email in my last job.
c I had never sent an email until I started working here.
d I will have sent over 500 emails by the end of this week!

2 Now look at these examples of perfect tenses from 14.1. Identify their uses, choosing from 1–7.

a I had been working in sales for twelve years.
b My income has reduced by a third.
c I'd always wanted to have my own business.
d The takings will have overtaken my previous salary by next year.
e That was the catalyst I'd been waiting for.
f My confidence has always been low.
g If I'd added up the hours …
h I've set up the spare room as an office.
i I've been working as a registrar for the past three years.
j I've experienced two different careers.

1 talking about a recent event or situation
2 talking about an event or situation which started in the past but is still true
3 emphasising the duration of a recent event or situation
4 talking about an event or situation that happened earlier than the past time being described
5 emphasising the duration of an event or situation which took place earlier than the past time being described
6 used in a conditional structure
7 talking about an event that will happen within a specified future time

Which perfect tense has not been exemplified in a–j? Give an example of this tense.

G ···⫶ page 203

3 Choose the correct tense in a–h below.

a What I *have been showing / had been showing* you today is only part of our huge range of products.
b Last week, the company *was voted / has been voted* top supplier for the third time.
c Since she started college, Sara *has studied / has been studying* every night, including weekends.
d On Friday, I *have been working / will have been working* in the department for exactly a year.
e The end of year results were not as bad as the directors *had feared / have feared*.
f By May, eight new designs *have been launched / will have been launched*, increasing our sales potential.
g Our sales director *has made / made* some appalling decisions and frankly, we'd be better off without him!
h They *were waiting / had been waiting* for the fax all day but when it came through the final page was missing.

Corpus spot

Correct any mistakes with tenses in these sentences written by FCE candidates. Two sentences are correct.

a I felt very sorry after I've seen your report.
b Some months ago he has directed a movie.
c Their fans want to know what has been happening to them.
d For thousands of years our civilisation is making progress.
e When I left your house in Ljubljana, I've decided to visit the lakes.
f Some friends of mine have been working there last summer.
g If I hadn't met you, I wouldn't have been able to find my way home.
h The Astrid Hotel is closed since last year.

Listening

4 🎧 You are going to hear five people talking about relevant experience for particular jobs. Note down skills and qualities mentioned by each person.

Speaker 1: office administrator
Speaker 2: interpreter
Speaker 3: shop assistant
Speaker 4: first-aid worker
Speaker 5: cook

What other skills and qualifications would be useful in each job?

5   Now read the role play instructions for Student A or B.

Student A
You are about to attend an interview for a job which you really want, working at an international sports event in Australia, next summer. The job will be one of the five described in Listening 4 on page 92, but you don't know exactly which one yet! Spend a few minutes thinking about relevant experience and qualifications.
Remember to be enthusiastic at the interview and explain why you think you would be suitable.

Student B
You are going to interview someone for a job at a major international sports event in Australia. Tell the interviewee what the job involves (choose one of the five described in Listening 4 on page 92). Then ask the interviewee about relevant experience (including knowledge of English), qualifications, general commitment, and suitability for the job you have in mind.

Then decide on a scale of 0–5 (5 being the most positive) how your interviewee has performed, according to these criteria:

Experience   Qualifications   Commitment   Inter-personal skills   Enthusiasm

6   Skim the article below to decide who it is aimed at. Then put the verbs in brackets into the correct perfect tense.

How to survive in business today

By the beginning of this century, the stripping away of management layers and large-scale staff redundancies **(1)** .... (shrink) companies radically. In some ways, this harsh new reality **(2)** .... (bring) bosses and workers closer together. At the same time, there **(3)** .... (never, be) so many small businesses starting up, with the result that, since 2005, a staggering 60 per cent of the working population **(4)** .... (work) in small groups, usually of five or less. Alongside these trends, the need to apply psychology in the workplace **(5)** .... (grow) constantly. 'Jobs for life' **(6)** .... (cease) to exist, and in contrast, survival skills at work **(7)** .... (become) absolutely essential. A group of streetwise employees **(8)** .... (tell) us their top tips on how to survive in the office.

• Fax or email people at night – it will look as though you **(9)** .... (put in) extra hours.

• Never stay later than the boss – it's too obvious and it **(10)** .... (know) to cause widespread office discontent.

• Try to remember people's names – recent studies **(11)** .... (show) that this simple gesture makes people think more highly of you.

• Spend money on good clothes – a survey by Hays Personnel Services **(12)** .... (find) that 42% of men and 52% of women think well-dressed people have a career advantage.

• Become known as a safe pair of hands rather than a high-flying genius – in ten years' time, you **(13)** .... (give) the top job while your flashy colleagues **(14)** .... (claim) unemployment benefit for at least five years.

• Be concise in meetings – if you **(15)** .... (ramble on) at length, the chances are that you won't have got your message across.

Writing folder 7

Applications 1

1 Give the adjectives related to these nouns, using your dictionary if necessary.

motivation ....
commitment ....
determination ....
cheerfulness ....
enthusiasm ....
energy ....
organisation ....
talent ....
skill ....
confidence ....

2 Read this advertisement. Decide which skills would be essential for the job, choosing from the nouns above and adding ideas of your own.

WANTED

Friendly, English-speaking people to work as restaurant and bar staff on our Mediterranean cruise ships

Tell us about
◆ why you would like to work for us
◆ any relevant experience you may have
◆ personal qualities that would be useful on board.

Contact ZY Cruises, PO Box 500, Southampton SO4 5TR, quoting reference PM44.

---

3 Now read these two letters of application. Has each applicant covered all the necessary points? Who would stand a better chance of getting the job?

A

Dear Sir or Madam

I have just seen your advertisement for jobs on board your cruise ships (reference PM44) and I would like to apply. I am a 20-year-old Swede with determination and commitment. I have often thought of spending time at sea and your job seems the perfect opportunity.

Although I have no on board experience, I have been working as a waiter in a local restaurant for the last 18 months and I have also had some experience of bar work. My knowledge of English is quite good, as I have been attending classes for the last six years. I would like to add that I have visited many parts of the Mediterranean myself and could talk to guests confidently during the voyage.

As for other personal qualities which might be useful on board a ship, I am an organised and easy-going person, so sharing a cabin with other crew members would not be a problem.

I am sure I would make a success of this job and I hope you will consider my application.

Yours faithfully
Pernilla Axelsson

B

Dear Mr or Mrs

I saw the job you advertised and I want to give it a go. I love the idea of going on a cruise and I'm just the person you need. I never thought of working on a ship but it sounds fine.

By the way, I've worked in a bar, though I didn't enjoy it that much. I wouldn't mind being a waiter on your ship though. Do the staff eat the same food as the guests? I've heard it's very good.

You ask about me. Well, I tell good jokes. I'm always cheerful and I think you would have to be, stuck on a ship for so long.

Write to me soon.

Harry

4 Make improvements to the second letter, rewriting it according to these guidelines.

a Change the opening and and closing formulae. Make sure the style is formal throughout.

b Rewrite the first sentence to make it clear which job is being applied for. Remember to use the present perfect!

c Edit the first and second paragraphs to make them sound more positive. Build up the information about previous experience, including some reference to learning English.

d Write a new third paragraph on personal qualities, using some of the adjectives and nouns in exercise 1.

e Try to write around 180 words in all.

Exam spot

If you choose to write a letter of application in Part 2 of Paper 2, you do not need to write any addresses. Remember to cover all the points in the question and try to sound positive about yourself. You should use a formal style, with an appropriate open and close.

5 Now look at this exam question. Underline the parts of the task that you need to cover. Remember to plan your answer before you start writing.

You see the following advertisement in an international magazine.

Can you answer YES to these questions?

▼ *Do you speak English confidently?*
▼ *Do you enjoy visiting new places?*
▼ *Do you get on well with people?*

If so, we would be interested in hearing from you! We are looking for energetic and cheerful guides to lead our 15-day coach tours round Europe. Tell us why you would be suitable.

Apply to: Europewide Coach Tours, PO Box 23, London W1X 6TY, stating where you saw our advertisement.

Write a **letter of application** in 120–180 words.
Do not include any postal addresses.

15·1 Too many people?

1 Have you ever visited a place that is famous for being beautiful or interesting and been disappointed when you arrived? Think of some of the problems that people cause, like litter, for example.

What do you think should be done to stop places being spoiled?

Is there somewhere in your country that you think needs to be protected?

Listening

2 🎧 You will hear a woman talking about some of the problems faced by the Grand Canyon National Park Service. Complete the sentences.

The Grand Canyon is located in the [___1___] part of Arizona.

The canyon is [___2___] deep from top to bottom.

The Grand Canyon National Park was opened in [___3___]

[___4___] people a year visit the Grand Canyon National Park.

The park introduced an electric [___5___] to help solve the problem of parking.

In the summer the park is affected by [___6___] brought by southwesterly winds.

The park also suffers from a lack of [___7___] and this sometimes has to be brought in by truck.

The temperature of the Colorado river is now [___8___] all year round.

There are now larger [___9___] in the river because of the number of boulders in it.

The Grand Canyon is often said to be one of the [___10___] in the world.

Vocabulary

3 In the listening you heard the following words that are connected with **water**.

floods	dam	reservoir
rapids	drought	river

Now sort out the following words into these categories:

a throw away   **b use again**

recycle	litter	junk
rubbish	bottle bank	
second-hand		

Vocabulary spot

Think of different meaning categories and write down all the words you know for each one. Compare your lists in groups, to check spelling and learn more words.

4 How green are you?

   a What do you do with the rubbish in your household?

   b Are you economical about using water and electricity? Why?/Why not?

   c How would you feel if you had to walk or cycle everywhere?

   d What do you think about being a vegetarian?

   e What's your opinion of people who wear real fur coats?

5 Make nouns, verbs and adverbs from these adjectives.

> longest   weakest   deepest
> strongest   widest   shortest

Now complete this text, using an appropriate form of the word in capitals.

Oil on beaches, vehicle exhaust fumes, litter and many other waste (**1**) .... **PRODUCE** are called pollutants, because they pollute our environment. Pollutants can affect our health and harm animals and plants. We pollute our (**2**) .... **SURROUND** with all kinds of (**3**) .... **CHEMIST** waste from factories and power stations. These substances are the (**4**) .... **WANT** results of modern living. Pollution itself is not new – a hundred years ago factories sent out great clouds of (**5**) .... **POISON** smoke.

(**6**) .... **FORTUNATE**, pollution has spread to the land, air, and water of every corner on Earth.

(**7**) .... **SCIENCE** have much to learn about pollution, but we do know more about how to control it. We can also reduce pollution by recycling waste and using biodegradable materials which (**8**) .... **EVENTUAL** break down in the soil and (**9**) .... **APPEAR**.

Pronunciation

6 🎧 Listen again to the woman talking about the Grand Canyon. Write down all the numbers that she mentions.

7 🎧 Now practise saying these numbers and then listen to the recording to check your pronunciation.

Measurement
13km
30cm
0.5km
2.5m
153 kilos
1m 53cm
$\frac{1}{2}$
$\frac{1}{4}$
$\frac{2}{3}$

Dates
1st May 1899
3rd August 2000
12th February 2004
25th December 1990
the 15th century
4/5/45

Money
10p
£1.45
$50

'0'
'0' can be pronounced in different ways in English.
Telephone number –
012-323-66778
Football score – 3–0
Tennis score – 40–0
Science and temperature –
0 degrees Celsius

Telephone numbers
01256-311399
00-44-324-667012

Maths
$2 + 6 = 8$
$3 - 2 = 1$
$4 \times 4 = 16$
$10 \div 2 = 5$
20%
3°
$\sqrt{16}$

8 Now answer the following questions. Then get into teams and make up your own questions about numbers.

   a What's your date of birth?

   b What's your telephone number?

   c What's your address?

   d How tall are you?

   e How much do you weigh? (You don't have to be honest.)

   f When did man first walk on the moon?

   g What's the average temperature in summer in your country? In winter?

   h What's the population of your country?

   i How many people are there in a football team?

15·2

Countable and uncountable nouns

1 Decide which words in the following pairs are countable.

a	land	country
b	spaghetti	meal
c	recommendation	advice
d	travel	journey
e	job	work
f	money	coin
g	lightning	storm
h	weather	temperature
i	English	verb
j	vehicle	traffic
k	seat	furniture
l	hair	hairstyle
m	luggage	suitcase
n	mountain	scenery
o	information	note

Which four words can be both countable and uncountable?
What is the difference in meaning?

Corpus spot

Be careful with uncountable nouns – the *Cambridge Learner Corpus* shows FCE candidates often make mistakes with these.

I have a lot of **homework** tonight.
NOT I have a lot of ~~homeworks~~ tonight.

These uncountable nouns are the ones which FCE candidates make most mistakes with.

information
advice
transport
knowledge
equipment
homework
furniture
stuff
accommodation
luggage

G ⋯⟶ page 203

2

Plural countables or uncountables e.g. coins or money
plenty of, a lot of, lots of

Uncountables e.g. money
much, little
a great/good deal of, a large/small amount of

Plural countables e.g. coins
many, (a) few, several
a great/good/small number of

All verbs, determiners and pronouns referring to uncountable nouns are singular:

A **great deal** of research **has been done** into the pollution produced by cars in cities. Unfortunately, very **little** of **it is taken** seriously by politicians.

Use this information to correct the following sentences where necessary.

a How much of the tourists actually realises the problems they cause?

b Little of the soils can be used for cultivation now the trees have been cut down.

c A large number of equipment are needed to camp at the bottom of the Canyon.

d Few luggages can be carried on the back of a donkey down the dirt tracks.

e A large number of rainforests is being cut down every year.

f The amount of traffic are causing too many congestions in major cities.

g Much governments believes that nuclear power are the key to future energy problems.

h The Park Ranger gave me several good advices about camping in the national park.

i Little people nowadays wear fur coats.

3   Both these pairs of sentences are correct, but there is a difference in meaning. What is it?

I make few mistakes with English grammar.
I make a few mistakes with English grammar.

I have little time to watch the TV at the weekend.
I have a little time to watch the TV at the weekend.

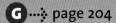 **Grammar extra**

some* and *any* and *no

Look at the following sentences and decide what the rule is for using *some* and *any* and *no*.

a   At lunchtime the Prime Minister announced some of the government's plans for reducing congestion in cities.
b   I haven't been able to see any stars in the sky recently because of light pollution.
c   Would you like me to give you some information on ways you can cut down on using water?
d   Have you any idea of the amount of food that is wasted each day in the developed world?
e   No amount of persuasion will make some people use public transport rather than private cars.
f   Have you got any/some change for the phone?

G ⋯⋗ page 204

Vocabulary

4   Expressions like *a piece of* or *a bit of* are often used to limit an uncountable noun. However, these words aren't very precise and it is better to use the right expression.

EXAMPLE: *in a shop you ask for a loaf of bread*
   at home you ask for a slice of bread

Which of the words on the left are used with the uncountable nouns on the right?

shower	clothing
slice	lightning
item	rain
glass	cake
clap	string
pane	people
ball	glass
flash	chocolate
crowd	water
bar	thunder

5   Using the information in this unit, complete the following sentences.

a   Would you like .... chocolate to take on your trip? – Yes, could you put in a couple of ....
b   Did you have .... bad weather over the weekend? – Yes, heavy rain and enormous .... of lightning.
c   .... of the football hooligans spent Saturday night smashing all the .... of glass in my local school.
d   I used to have short .... , but I've decided to grow it.
e   Could you give me .... about travelling in India?
f   My bank always refuses to change .... that I bring back from abroad.
g   Even though .... vehicles use unleaded petrol nowadays, it doesn't make it any pleasanter to sit in heavy ....

G ⋯⋗ page 204

6   For questions 1–12, read the text below and think of the word which best fits each gap. Use only one word in each gap. There is an example at the beginning (0).

The Pyramids

On (**0**) ..*the*.. great rocky plain of Giza in Egypt, stand (**1**) .... of the world's most remarkable buildings – three pyramids. There are quite a (**2**) .... other pyramids in Egypt, but these three are the largest and most famous. They were erected more than 4,000 years (**3**) .... and, while other great monuments have fallen into ruins, these pyramids have stood the test of time.

As the Egyptians believed (**4**) .... life after death, each ruler had a great (**5**) .... of his treasure buried with him. (**6**) .... the pyramids are enormous, the rooms inside are very small, because the pyramids themselves consist chiefly of solid stone. The largest, the Great Pyramid at Giza, was built by King Khufu in about 2500 BC and is still mostly intact. Its original height was almost 147 metres, and it weighed more (**7**) .... seven billion kilograms.

The pyramids were made (**8**) .... huge blocks of stone (**9**) .... were quarried, trimmed to a fairly regular shape, transported to the construction site and then piled on top of (**10**) .... another with astonishing precision. It used to be believed that over 100,000 men (**11**) .... been needed to build the pyramids, but now the scientists think the true figure (**12**) .... nearer 10,000.

Exam folder 8

Paper 4 Part 3 Multiple matching

In this part of the Listening paper you hear five short extracts, usually monologues, which are all related to each other in some way. It may be that they are all speaking about the same subject or experiences. Another possible link may be function or feeling or job. You need to match each extract to one of six options. You hear the extracts twice, and it is very important that you take the opportunity to check your answers carefully during the second listening. One mistake could affect two answers.

1 🎧 You are going to hear the first speaker talking about his experience of education. Look at the statements A–F and decide which one is true for the first speaker.

A I really enjoyed meeting new people.

B My attitude to studying had been wrong.

C It taught me how to cope with money.

D I'm not sure what I want to do now.

E I realised I worked better in a freer environment.

F I had to work harder than I expected.

The answer for Speaker One is B. Now look at the recording script. The part containing the answer is underlined.

Advice

- Don't sit looking out of the window while you're waiting for the recording to start. Read the questions carefully.
- Try to predict what each person might say.

Recording script

Speaker 1:
When I started my last year at school, I didn't take it seriously enough. <u>I should've chosen subjects which were useful rather than ones I liked or that sounded easy.</u> By the time exams came I'd given up and I did very badly. I knew I'd have to work hard but I wasn't able to catch up with my friends. Because I failed at science I can't be a teacher, which is what I really want to do. I'm doing a part-time job in order to make ends meet and next year I'll be starting evening classes to get better qualifications.

Look carefully at the options.

A I really enjoyed meeting new people. – *He doesn't mention new friends.*

B My attitude to studying was wrong. – *Right answer.*

C It taught me how to cope with money. – *Money is mentioned (to make ends meet) but nothing is said about learning what to do with money.*

D I'm not sure what I want to do now. – *He's going to study so this isn't the answer.*

E I realised I worked better in a freer environment. – *This isn't mentioned at all.*

F I had to work harder than I expected. – *This isn't the answer as he knew he had to work hard.*

King's College, Cambridge

2 🎧 Listen to the other speakers and for questions 2–5, choose from the list A–F which each speaker states. (Remember that B has already been used.) Use each letter only once. There is one extra letter which you do not need to use.

Speaker 2 [ ] 2
Speaker 3 [ ] 3
Speaker 4 [ ] 4
Speaker 5 [ ] 5

3 Now look at the recording script for Speakers 2–5 and underline the parts which give you the answers.

Recording script

Speaker 2:
I left school and moved to a college to take my final exams. It was the best decision I could have made. At the college nobody seemed to care about homework and this really motivated me. I had to plan my work myself – there was no one to make you do it and no one to check up on what you'd done. I was still dependent on my parents for money – but that was OK. I learned a lot about real life there – things like getting on with people and organising your time – which has been really useful now I'm working.

Speaker 3:
When I left school I didn't have a particular career in mind so I decided to do Environmental Studies at university, mainly because I'd enjoyed geography at school. I didn't really like the course at university and I did think about leaving, but instead I changed courses, which was easier than I expected. I think university was useful in that I learnt how to live alone and how to budget, and as I'm an underpaid teacher now, that really helps.

Speaker 4:
I had no difficulty choosing what I was going to do – my parents are both doctors and ever since I was small I also wanted to do that. They really encouraged me and I did well at school and got into a good medical school fairly easily. It was surprisingly tough at medical school, but I had some good friends and we pulled through together. I think the doubts only began to set in when I graduated and got my first job in a hospital. I began to wonder if I'd missed out because I'd been so focused on becoming a doctor. So now I'm doing some voluntary work in Africa which I'm really enjoying.

Speaker 5:
I decided to take a year off after doing my last year at school. I'd had enough of revising and sitting in a library so I decided to go off to Australia for nine months and earn a bit of money. I've got relatives there who put me up when I first arrived and found me a job. It wasn't doing anything particularly interesting, but the great part was that I was getting to know people who were completely different to the ones I'd known back home. I really recommend taking a year out, but you need to have a firm plan or it could end up a waste of time.

Eat to live

1 Make a list of what you normally eat in a day. Compare your list with a partner.

2 What do you think someone in the following countries eats?

   • Japan • Alaska • USA

3 🎧 Now you are going to hear three women talking about the food they normally have. Listen and make brief notes about what they eat.

   Which person's diet would you like to try?

4 You are going to read an article from a newspaper, talking about a new food product that is aimed at children. Seven sentences have been removed from the article. Choose from the sentences A–H the one which fits each gap (1–7). There is one extra sentence which you do not need to use.

Akiko (Japan)

Breakfast	Lunch	Dinner

Kunu (Alaska)

Breakfast	Lunch	Dinner

Gayle (USA)

Breakfast	Lunch	Dinner

Tasty Vegetables for Kids

Flavoured frozen vegetables – including chocolate-tasting carrots – went on sale yesterday. 1 [   ] This is in response to a plea from Gordon McVie, director general of the Cancer Research Campaign charity, for a solution to unhealthy eating habits among young people.

2 [   ] It found that many mothers had all but abandoned the struggle to get their children to eat vegetables.

'We know that a third of all cancers are diet related and potentially preventable,' said McVie, who has lent his name to the new range of vegetables. 3 [   ]

The idea for the 'wacky' vegetable grew out of an impromptu discussion in January between Professor McVie and Malcolm Walker, chairman of Iceland Frozen Foods. They talked about why frozen vegetables could not incorporate some of the flavours used to market packets of crisps. 4 [   ]

5 [   ] Interestingly, the majority rejected a number of potential lines, including bubble gum broccoli, prawn cocktail cauliflower and toffee apple

5 Look back at the article and, using your dictionary to help you, find the words that mean:

   a given a special taste
   b what you eat
   c natural and artificial chemicals
   d helpings
   e covering

6 In English we often use the expression *off*. What other word can you use in these phrases? There is an example first to help you.

   EXAMPLE: *The milk was off. – sour*

   a The waitress told us the spaghetti was off today.
   b The meat was off.
   c The waiter was a bit off with us.
   d I'm off cakes at the moment, I'm on a diet.

7 In groups discuss these questions.

   a What do you think of the idea of flavouring fruit and vegetables? Would it be popular in your country? Why?/Why not?
   b What is your favourite food?
   c Do you think you have a healthy diet?
   d Are you or could you become a vegetarian?
   e What are the typical national dishes in your country?
   f Is there anything you can't stand or aren't allowed to eat?
   g When you were a child did you eat the same things as your parents? Why?/Why not?

sweetcorn. The company declined to comment on the flavouring process, except to say it had made use of 'natural' additives and had not altered the vegetables' underlying taste or nutritional value. 'In fact, there has been no genetic meddling and our market research shows that children and parents are very keen,' said Barbara Crampton, an Iceland spokeswoman.

Professor McVie said the recommendations of specialists for a healthy life were that children and adults should eat five portions of fruit and vegetables a day. The study came up with an amazing result. [6 ____]

The big supermarkets, responding to increasing public awareness of the problem of children not wanting to eat their 'greens', have started to repackage fresh produce to appeal more directly to children. [7 ____] Both the Tesco and Sainsbury chains are also developing vegetables with sauces and coatings aimed at children.

Professor McVie said he hoped the flavoured vegetables might encourage children to move on to more traditional forms of vegetables, in the same way that fish fingers encouraged children to try fish.

A These have always proved popular with children.

B A study for the charity was carried out among working class families last year.

C Safeway, for example, recently introduced a children's range of miniature fruit and vegetables with softer flesh and skin.

D Researchers are experimenting with 'super-vegetables' which contain more vitamins.

E It found that for most children this was achieved on only one day a year – Christmas Day.

F The products were extensively market-tested on children aged 7 to 10.

G He believes that unless the British public understands this, there will be potentially serious health implications for the future.

H Also available are baked-bean-flavoured peas, cheese and onion cauliflower, and pizza sweetcorn.

16·2

The article

1   Look at these nouns from the listening in 16.1:

| waiter   noodles   fish   cheese   lunch |

Which of these nouns are
- singular countable?
- plural countable?
- uncountable?

Which of them take
- *a/an* (the indefinite article)?
- *the* (the definite article)?
- nothing?

2   Link the sentence in A with the rule in B. Some rules can be used more than once.

A

d   1   He's a waiter.
f   2   The Earth is egg-shaped.
g   3   The United States exports wheat.
c   4   The British love curry.
b h 5   He's the best chef in Bangkok.
a   6   I usually go to a restaurant that overlooks the River Thames.
e g 7   The Rocky Mountains are great for skiing.
i   8   I hate fast food.
j k 9   There's a restaurant on the corner – it's the restaurant with a red sign.
e   10   Football always makes me hungry.

B

a   *the* is used with rivers/oceans/seas/mountain ranges
b   *no article* is used with most streets/villages/towns/cities/countries/lakes/single mountains
c   *the* is used with national groups
d   *a/an* is used with jobs
e   *no article* is used with sports
f   *the* is used when there is only one of something
g   *the* is used for countries in the plural e.g. The Netherlands
h   *the* is used with superlatives
i   *no article* is used when a noun is used generally
j   *a/an* is used when something is mentioned for the first time
k   *the* is used when a noun has already been mentioned

3   Read through this article and decide whether to use *a/an*, *the* or nothing in the gaps. Some gaps can have more than one answer.

'I'll have what he's having.' That's what (1) .... diners sometimes tell (2) .... waiters when another customer is served (3) .... meal that looks delicious. Wouldn't it be simpler if you could see every dish on (4) .... menu before making up your mind? In (5) .... Japan, that's exactly what diners can do. There, (6) .... restaurant displays of real-looking fake food, called *sanpuru*, serve as (7) .... three-dimensional menu.

At one time, restaurants in Japan used to display real food to advertise (8) .... restaurant's specialities, and to allow customers to 'preview' their meal. (9) .... displays also meant that (10) .... foreigners unable to read (11) .... Japanese menu could figure out (12) .... best thing to order. In the 1930s (13) .... first fake foods were made from (14) .... wax. Eventually such fake foods replaced (15) .... real foods. Today *sanpuru* are made from vinyl, (16) .... kind of plastic.

4   Decide whether you need to use an article or not in these sentences.

a   I went to .... hospital to see a friend who was ill.
b   I went to .... hospital when I was knocked off my bike.
c   I go to .... library once a week.
d   She always goes to .... bed early.
e   I often get hay fever in .... summer.
f   The shops in my town always close for .... lunch.
g   My father used to go to work by .... bike.
h   When are you going on .... holiday?
i   Tom never gets to .... work on time.
j   He earns £800 .... week.
k   I'll visit you in .... October.
l   I can't play .... football very well.
m   Ronald Reagan once held .... office of president.

n My uncle goes to .... prison to teach the prisoners computer skills.

o I've played .... flute ever since I was a child.

G ⋯⋯⦂ **page 204**

Possession

1 When we are talking about people we use *'s* or *s'*:
my sister's boyfriend, the visitors' cars
In the first example there is only one sister so the apostrophe
is before the *s*. In the second example the apostrophe is after the *s* because there is more than one visitor.

2 *'s* is also used when we are talking about time or distance:
a month's holiday, a kilometre's walk

3 We usually use *of* when we are talking about objects or position:
the back of the room, the film of the book
Also for when a container has something in it:
a bottle of milk

4 Quite often we use a noun to describe another noun when it describes either the kind, use or place:
a pear tree, a coffee cup, a shop window

5 Correct the following sentences where necessary.

a The father of my husband works in an Italian restaurant.
b I looked through the restaurant's window but couldn't see anyone.
c He was sitting at the front of the terrace.
d I bought a magazine of cooking.
e I'm sure we all always look forward to pay day.
f Most waiters get tips to help supplement their day's pay.
g Can I have a coffee cup and a piece of that delicious cake, please?
h The boss of my company is having a big party to celebrate his birthday.

Listening

6 🎧 Listen to a man talking about how to make his favourite dish.
The first time you listen, write down the ingredients you hear.
The second time you listen, write down the method of making the dish.
Now, using the basic vocabulary from the listening, tell your partner how to prepare your favourite dish. Notice you need to use the imperative – *do, put, cut,* etc.
Remember to use articles correctly.

Writing folder 8

Transactional letters and emails 2

This question is compulsory – all candidates have to answer it. 'Transactional' means that the letter or email will require further action by its reader, usually in the form of a written response. The letter or email must be based on the information given in the question.

1   When you write a letter or email it is important that you keep in the same style all the way through. Read through this letter and, with a partner, decide which is the best alternative, a or b, in 1–10 below. The first one has been done for you.

> Dear Pete,
> (1) ...~~Thanks a lot~~... for coming along
> (2) .... plans for the new student café on campus. I really think we all
> (3) .... and I hope that we can
> (4) .... some ideas for interesting menus. (5) .... asking your friend Marco Brown, the TV chef, to open the café on Saturday.
> (6) .... when we open, and I think the café will (7) .... with the students. Anyway, (8) ....
> (9) ....
> (10) ....
>
> George

  1 **a** I am writing to thank you
     (**b**) Thanks a lot
  2 **a** to discuss the
     b to talk about
  3 **a** found it very useful
     b thought it was extremely productive
  4 **a** come up with
     b propose
  5 **a** We all appreciate your
     b Thanks a million for
  6 **a** I feel sure everyone will have an enjoyable time
     b It's certain to be a great night

  7 **a** go down well
     b prove very popular
  8 **a** that's all for now
     b I will contact you again at some point
  9 **a** See you soon
     b I look forward to seeing you in the near future
10 **a** Yours faithfully
     b Best wishes

2   Look at this exam question.

You have received an invitation and map from your friend Anna. You want to go to her party but you need to find out some information. Read the information and the map, and look at the notes you have made. Then write an email to Anna, using all your notes. You must use grammatically correct sentences with accurate spelling and punctuation in a style appropriate for the situation.

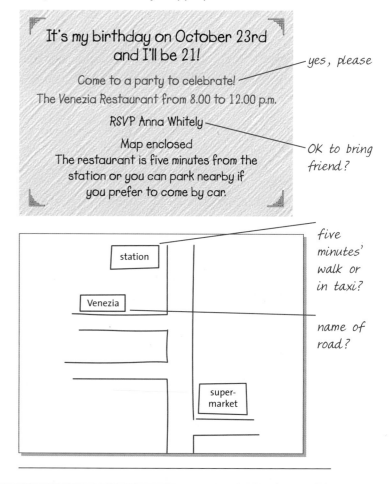

It's my birthday on October 23rd and I'll be 21!

Come to a party to celebrate! — *yes, please*
The Venezia Restaurant from 8.00 to 12.00 p.m.

RSVP Anna Whitely

Map enclosed
The restaurant is five minutes from the station or you can park nearby if you prefer to come by car. — *OK to bring friend?*

station

Venezia — *five minutes' walk or in taxi?*

super-market — *name of road?*

---

3 This is the email that Anna received. It would receive very low marks in the exam. Discuss with a partner what the main problems with this answer are. Then work together to rewrite it in a more appropriate way.

From: Sara Mikati
Cc:
Subject: Birthday meal

Dear Anna,

I'm writing with reference to the invitation you sent me on September 4th. I'm really greatful you asked to me and I'm pleased to come.
I am extremely greatful if you could tell me name of road restaurant is in. I will have friend staying with me. She is nice. I bring her.
I look forward to see you in near future.

Kisses

Corpus spot

Here are some of the most frequent spelling mistakes made by FCE candidates. Correct each word.

a accomodation
b advertisment
c wich
d belive
e becouse
f beggining
g confortable
h bycicle
i convinient
j embarrasing
k expecially
l recived
m beatiful
n comunicate
o sincerly

4 Read the advertisement and the notes you have made. Then write an email in 120–150 words to your friend Pat. You must persuade Pat and your other friends to come with you on the weekend.

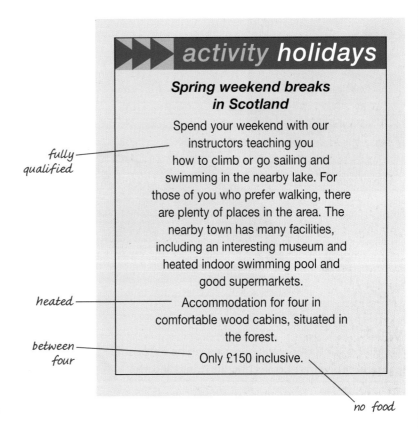

activity holidays

Spring weekend breaks in Scotland

Spend your weekend with our instructors teaching you how to climb or go sailing and swimming in the nearby lake. For those of you who prefer walking, there are plenty of places in the area. The nearby town has many facilities, including an interesting museum and heated indoor swimming pool and good supermarkets.

fully qualified

heated

Accommodation for four in comfortable wood cabins, situated in the forest.

between four

Only £150 inclusive.

no food

5 Write an email. You must use grammatically correct sentences with accurate spelling and punctuation in a style appropriate for the situation.

Remember, you want your friend to go with you so you need to be persuasive. Make sure you read both the advertisement and your notes carefully. Make sure any negative points are countered with positive ones. You need to sound enthusiastic and make this friend feel he/she is really wanted on this holiday.

EXAMPLE: *I know you really like swimming and that's one of the reasons I think you would enjoy this holiday. Don't worry about Scotland being cold, as the accommodation is heated and very comfortable.*

1 Here are two pairs of photographs showing various hobbies. Look at the first pair with another student. Decide who will be Student A and who Student B. Then read your instructions. Student A can also refer to the notes below.

2 Look at the second pair of photographs and change roles. Student A should listen carefully to what Student B says. Remember to keep talking for up to a minute.

Student A
Compare and contrast the pictures, describing the possible benefits and problems of collecting the things shown.

Fossils – very old! Books and equipment needed (hammer, etc.) to find your own. Dangerous? Travel to good places. Educational?

Football items – lots available. Expensive! Takes up a lot of space? What would friends think of this hobby?

Student B
When Student A has finished, say which hobby you would find more interesting, and why.

Student B
Compare and contrast the pictures, describing the main differences between these two hobbies. (about 1 minute)
Student A
Say which hobby appeals to you more, and why. (20 seconds)

Exam spot

In Part 2 of Paper 5, each candidate has to take a 'long turn', speaking for about a minute. Listen carefully while the other candidate is speaking, as you will have to make a brief comment afterwards.

Now carry out the speaking task. Student A should try to keep talking for about a minute and then Student B should talk for a maximum of 20 seconds. Time yourselves.

Did Student B manage to talk for a full minute? Suggest other ideas if necessary.

3 How many hobbies can you think of which involve collecting or making something? Work in two teams: the collectors and the creators. See who can produce the longer list! Then, in pairs, decide on the four most interesting hobbies from the two lists, giving your reasons why. You can agree to disagree!

Listening

4 🎧 You are going to hear eight short extracts to do with hobbies. For questions 1–8 choose the best answer (A, B or C). You will hear each extract twice. Compare your answers with another student.

1 You hear a man giving a talk about his hobby. Where does he find his best fossils?
   A at shops   B on beaches   C up cliffs

2 You overhear this conversation in a café. What sort of postcards is the woman keen to collect?
   A ones that are in good condition
   B ones from the 1930s
   C ones with a printed message

3 You hear a woman talking on the radio. Why were the wooden objects she describes unusual?
   A They were painted with beautiful designs.
   B They were made from different types of wood.
   C They were carved from a single piece.

4 You hear this radio interview. Who suggested the boy took up slot-car racing?
   A his father   B his friend   C his cousin

5 You hear part of a radio programme. Which kind of beads does the girl have most of?
   A glass   B wooden   C plastic

6 You overhear a man talking on the phone. Who is he talking to?
   A an assistant at a shop selling kits
   B a journalist working for a magazine
   C a member of staff at a factory

7 You hear a girl being interviewed about her hobby. Why does she paint pebbles?
   A to remind her of her holidays
   B to improve her art technique
   C to make some pocket money

8 You will hear a man talking on the radio. How does he spend his weekends?
   A pretending to be a soldier
   B studying a history course
   C producing different plays

5 In pairs, decide which of these hobbies would interest you **least**, explaining why. Report your views to the class.

6 In listening extracts 2, 3 and 6, *look* was used as in a–d below. Five more uses are given in e–i. Check their meanings before answering questions 1–9 below.

   a look for   f look at
   b on the lookout   g look into
   c the look of   h Look out!
   d Now look here!   i look up to
   e look after

1 Who might **look at**
   A teeth   B a passport   C a burst pipe?

2 What are you planning to do if you are **looking for**
   A a needle   B a saucepan   C a dictionary?

3 Who might be **on the lookout** for
   A a missing yacht   B murder clues
   C tax savings?

4 Describe **the look of**
   A leather   B thick mud   C concrete.

5 Who **looks after**
   A patients   B rose bushes   C local residents?

6 Continue the statement **Now look here** …, as if you are arguing with
   A a bank manager   B a young child
   C a journalist.

7 What might you discover if you **looked into**
   A a kitchen cupboard   B your friend's eyes
   C deep space (with a telescope!)?

8 Why might someone shout **Look out!** at you, if you were
   A driving   B swimming in the sea
   C walking under a ladder?

9 Who might these people **look up to**?
   A a six-year-old boy   B a first-year student
   C a trainee cook

17·2

Relative clauses

1 Look at the pair of sentences a and b, then answer questions 1 and 2 for each of them.

   a The children who were tired went straight to bed.
   b The children, who were tired, went straight to bed.

   1 Were all the children tired?
   2 Did all the children go to bed?

   Which sentence contains a defining relative clause? Which has a non-defining clause in it?

   G ⋯⋗ page 204

   Explain the difference in meaning between c and d.

   c It was getting late, so we decided to stay at the first hotel which had a pool.
   d It was getting late, so we decided to stay at the first hotel, which had a pool.

2 Here are two examples of relative clauses from the listening extracts. Which sentence has a defining relative clause and which has a non-defining one?

   a Jamie Eagle, who is the outright winner of today's slot-car racing, is with me now.
   b I'm on the lookout for older ones that have text on the picture.

   Identify the relative clause in each of these examples, underline the relative pronoun used, and decide whether the clause is defining (D) or non-defining (N).

   c Looking at the stamps, they're older than you say, which is brilliant.
   d I knew someone once who had an absolute passion for making things out of wood.
   e It was my cousin who's to blame.
   f Jenny Braintree, whose bedroom I'm sitting in right now, has a rather unusual hobby.
   g I'm trying to paint a scene from every country in the world, most of which I haven't been to.
   h The group that puts on these events was only formed about four months ago.

3 What relative pronoun has been left out in this example? Insert it in the correct place.

   Here are those cards I bought for you in Oxford.

Omission of the relative pronoun is quite common in spoken English, but can only be done when it is the object of a defining relative clause. So, for example, you could not leave out the word *that* in example *h*.

Decide what relative pronouns have been left out of these sentences and underline the defining clause in each.

   a The picture I wanted to buy had already been sold.
   b She was the teacher I really looked up to.
   c The thing I can't stand about Harry is his odd socks!
   d That boy you met at John's party plays tennis.
   e The hotel we stayed at had luxurious bathrooms.

4 The last example could be rewritten like this:

   The hotel <u>where</u> we stayed had luxurious bathrooms.

   You can use *where*, *when* and *why* in defining relative clauses after nouns to do with place, time and reason. Again, in spoken English, *when* and *why* are sometimes omitted. Here are two examples from 17.1.

   1987 was the year I found the most.
   That's not the reason she's mad at me though.

   In non-defining clauses, these words cannot be omitted.

   Insert *where*, *when* or another relative pronoun into these non-defining clauses.

   a The writer Iain Banks was born in Fife, Scotland, ... he still lives.
   b The earthquake happened shortly before dawn, ... most people were asleep.
   c Aidan, ... lives in our road, plays the double bass.
   d They sent an information booklet, ... was really helpful.
   e I went to the Body Shop, ... they had that make-up, but they had sold out.

5 For questions 1–12, read the text opposite and think of the word which best fits each gap. Use only one word in each gap. There is an example at the beginning (0).

A PASSION FOR BOTTLES

Hobbies (0) ...*can*... so easily take over your life, can't they? They make demands on your time and, even (1) .... seriously, they sometimes invade your living space. One friend (2) .... mine is haunted by the desire to collect bottles. This passion, (3) .... started quite by chance, has now reached an absurd stage, (4) .... he has literally had to rebuild his house to accommodate the 3,429 (at the last count) assorted exhibits. There are a few collectors' items, such (5) .... an example of the very first Coca-Cola design, a hand-painted wine bottle (6) .... the 1920s, and about fifty rather attractive perfume bottles in (7) .... colour, shape and size you could imagine. However, the overwhelming majority of his bottles are very ordinary and (8) .... to have been taken away for recycling long (9) .... The reason he has hung on to them for all of this time is (10) .... at all clear, although I suppose that's true of all obsessive hobbies. Just think, (11) .... only my friend had chosen bottle tops, his collection (12) .... only fill three drawers at most!

Pronunciation *Contrastive stress*

6 🎧 In two of the listening extracts in 17.1, where a person was being interviewed, there are examples of contrastive stress. In each case, the interviewer makes a factual error, which the interviewee corrects. Listen to the stress patterns used by the interviewee in these examples.

Interviewer	Did he know what he was doing when he persuaded you to take up such a time-consuming hobby?
Jamie	Er, actually, it was <u>me</u> who persuaded <u>him</u> – he's only been racing this year.
Interviewer	Jenny, you took up this hobby four years ago and …
Jenny	Er … it was four <u>months</u> ago, in fact.

7 🎧 Now listen to these short exchanges. In pairs, underline the words that are stressed by each second speaker. Read the dialogue again with your partner, who should check whether you have stressed the right words.

a Would you like a coffee?
No, thanks – it stops me sleeping. I wouldn't mind a cold drink though.
b I'm going to wear my red dress to the interview.
Oh no, red's much too bright. I'd wear your blue one – with the grey jacket.

c Hello, Jan? Listen, I've been waiting outside the cinema but no one's turned up.
The others said they'd meet you inside, didn't they?
d Why is it always my turn to empty the dishwasher?
It isn't. I did it yesterday – and I cleaned the cooker, too.

8 In pairs, read these short exchanges aloud, taking turns to respond to each suggestion with an alternative plan. Stress any word in bold and your new idea each time.

a Let's go and play tennis – it's not too cold, is it?
It's **freezing**! I think we should …
b Why not stay in and do your homework this evening?
Not **again**! I'd much rather …
c Paint your room yellow – it would look really good.
Ugh! Yellow's too …
d You know, you could have that magazine sent to you every month.
But it's so **expensive**. I think I'll just …
e Brian's the one who's interested in model cars.
No he isn't, that's …
f Here's the CD I bought in town. It was only £12.99.
£12.99? I've seen it for …

Exam folder 9

Paper 4 Part 4
Multiple choice

In this part of the Listening paper there are seven questions. Each question has three options (**A**, **B** or **C**). You must choose the correct option. The questions follow the order of the information in the conversation.

🎧 You will hear an interview with Rebecca Laing, who lives on an island. For questions 1–7, choose the best answer (A, B or C).

___

1 Rebecca says that nowadays most people on the island

  A were born there.
  B live near the harbour.
  C are fishermen.   `1`

2 What does Rebecca do for a living now?

  A She's an English teacher.
  B She's a computer programmer.
  C She's an editor.   `2`

3 Rebecca says the kind of people who want to live on the island

  A enjoy their independence.
  B must be prepared to accept the disadvantages.
  C don't have children.   `3`

4 Rebecca believes the island community needs to

  A attract a range of new industries.
  B encourage more people to live there.
  C be cautious about any new plans.   `4`

5 Rebecca thinks that the inhabitants of the island

  A suffer from traditional thinking.
  B should try to attract more tourists.
  C put wildlife first.   `5`

6 How did Rebecca feel when the hotel plans fell through?

  A relieved
  B disappointed
  C surprised   `6`

7 What does Rebecca dislike about living on the island?

  A her neighbours knowing what she's doing
  B sometimes feeling quite lonely
  C the number of disagreements that arise   `7`

What's in a book?

1 Look at the illustration and decide what it represents. Whereabouts in the world might this be?

2 You are going to read an extract from *The Old Man and the Sea* by Ernest Hemingway. First, read these brief reviews of the book. What do you learn about the book from them?

> Not only the finest short story that Hemingway has ever written, but one of the finest written by anyone.

> Every word is meaningful and there is not a word too many.

> The writing is as tight, and at the same time as cleverly played out, as the line on which the old man plays the fish.

Exam spot

The text in Part 1 of Paper 1 is sometimes an extract from a novel. There may well be words which you don't know, but these are unlikely to be tested, so don't panic!

3 Now skim the text below quickly, to get an idea of the scene that is being described.

The old man rubbed the cramped hand against his trousers and tried to ease the fingers. But the hand would not open. Maybe it will open with the sun, he thought. He looked across the sea and knew how alone he was now. The clouds were building up for the trade wind and he looked ahead and saw a flight of wild ducks against the sky over the water, and he knew that no man was ever alone on the sea. 5

He thought of how some men feared being out of sight of land in a small boat and knew they were right in months of sudden bad weather. But now they were in hurricane months and, when there are no hurricanes, the weather of these months is the best of all the year. If there is a hurricane you always see the signs of it in the sky for days ahead, if you are at sea. They do not see it ashore because they do not 10 know what to look for, he thought. But we have no hurricane coming now. He looked at the sky and saw the white cumulus clouds built like friendly piles of ice cream and high above were the thin feathers of the cirrus against the high September sky. 'Better weather for me than for you, fish,' he said.

His left hand was still cramped, but he was unknotting it slowly. I hate a cramp, 15 he thought. It is a treachery of one's own body and it humiliates oneself especially when one is alone. If the boy were here he could rub it for me and loosen it down from the forearm, he thought. But it will loosen up. Then, with his right hand he felt the difference in the pull of the line. As he leaned against the line and slapped his left hand hard and fast against his thigh he saw **it** slanting slowly upward. 'He's 20 coming up,' he said. 'Come on hand. Please come on.'

The line rose slowly and steadily and then the surface of the ocean bulged ahead of the boat and the fish came out. He came out unendingly and water poured from his sides. He was bright in the sun and his head and back were dark purple and in the sun the stripes on his sides showed wide and a light lavender. His sword was as 25 long as a baseball bat and he rose full-length from the water and then re-entered it, smoothly, like a diver and the old man saw the great blade of his tail go under and the line started to race out.

He is a great fish and I must convince him, he thought. I must never let him learn his strength nor what he could do if he made his run. If I were him I would 30 put in everything now and go until something broke. But, thank God, they are not as intelligent as we who kill them; although they are more noble and more able.

The old man had seen many great fish. He had seen many that weighed more than a thousand pounds and he had caught two of that size in his life, but never alone. Now alone, and out of sight of land, he was fast to the biggest fish he had 35 ever seen and bigger than he had ever heard of, and his left hand was still as tight as the gripped claws of an eagle.

It will uncramp though, he thought. Surely it will uncramp to help my right hand. There are three things that are brothers: the fish and my two hands. It must uncramp. It is unworthy of it to be cramped. The fish had slowed again and was 40 going at his usual pace.

I wonder why he jumped, the old man thought. He jumped almost as though to show me how big he was. I know now, anyway, he thought. I wish I could show him what sort of man I am. But then he would see my cramped hand. Let him think I am more man than I am and I will be so. 45

4 Read through the questions below and then read the text through again, more carefully this time. Then, in pairs, identify the parts of the text that relate to each question. Work out the correct answers together and decide why the other options are wrong.

1 How did the old man feel about being out at sea?
  A He enjoyed it because he had time to himself.
  B He didn't mind as there were creatures around him.
  C He realised how dangerous his work was.
  D He wasn't happy at being out of sight of land.

2 Why was he sure the weather would stay fair?
  A It was not the right time of year for hurricanes.
  B Bad weather had not been forecast ashore.
  C He could see no trace of an approaching hurricane.
  D There are more fish during good weather.

3 What does 'it' refer to in line 20?
  A his boat   **C** his hand
  B the line   **D** the fish

4 What does the old man worry about after seeing the fish?
  A The fish is too powerful for his boat.
  B He isn't as clever as the fish.
  C He doesn't have enough line.
  D The fish could escape if it swam fast.

5 What does the writer mean when he says the old man was 'fast to the biggest fish he had ever seen' in line 35?
  A He was joined to the fish by his line.
  B He was attracted by such a big fish.

C He was chasing the fish in his boat.
D He was surprised to see the fish's size.

6 The old man didn't want the fish to see that he was
  A alone in the boat.
  B so small.
  C too tired.
  D in some difficulty.

5 The extract described the fish *coming up* and *going under*. Can *come* and *go* both be combined with the following particles? Make phrasal verbs and use these in a suitable form in the sentences below.

	after
come	in for
go	out
	through
	without
	up against

a The novelist has .... a lot of criticism on his latest book.
b I don't mind .... most things, but I do need coffee.
c Let's .... the passage together to check on any difficult vocabulary.
d The dog .... the burglars but wasn't fast enough to catch them.
e We .... a major problem when we moved – the sofa was too wide and it wouldn't .... the new doorway.
f Those yellow roses have .... very early this year.
g I don't usually .... detective novels, but this one's really good.
h After all you've .... , you must be exhausted!
i When the tide .... , we did a guided reef walk and saw some wonderful shells and starfish.
j My blood went cold, as I noticed a dark figure with a hunched back, who was .... the fog towards us.

6 Finish this paragraph about the extract you have just read by giving some description of the old man's left hand.

In this part of the book, the writer keeps referring to the old man's left hand, which won't move. He mentions the hand so often in order to make sure the reader understands the serious difficulty the old man is up against. I imagine the hand looks like ...

18·2

enough, too, very, so, such

1 Identify the books shown, choosing from these types.

science fiction	biography	
short stories	thriller	non-fiction
historical novel	play	western

2 🎧 You will hear five people talking about books they have enjoyed. Match the books in the picture to the five speakers. There is one extra which you do not need.

Speaker 1 ☐ 1
Speaker 2 ☐ 2
Speaker 3 ☐ 3
Speaker 4 ☐ 4
Speaker 5 ☐ 5

Corpus spot

Be careful with word order when using *enough* – the *Cambridge Learner Corpus* shows FCE candidates often make mistakes with this.

> We were **lucky enough** to meet some famous writers. NOT We were ~~enough lucky~~ to meet some famous writers.

3 Read this article about the role of the book today, ignoring the missing words. Does the writer believe that the book has a future? Why?/Why not?

For questions 1–12, think of the word which best fits each gap. Use only one word in each group. There is an example at the beginning (0).

The book in the 21st century

How many times in (0) ..the.. last hundred years or so have people talked of the imminent death of the book? Films were an early threat, because they were so effective at telling stories in a visual way. Next there was radio, (1) .... swept into the mid-twentieth century and provided such alternatives to books (2) .... drama, documentaries and discussions. When television arrived, many people believed that it (3) .... finish the book off. Nowadays, (4) .... the threat by TV, the book is thought to be endangered by computers and the Internet, and by other technological attractions, too.

Surely there are now enough reasons (5) .... the book ought to be dead, (6) .... at least very badly injured. If so, why does it not show proper respect for these reportedly (7) .... literate times and die out? There is clearly more than a single answer to this question. Firstly, we have more leisure time than we (8) .... to, and people are generally living longer, which means there is more time to do more (including reading books). As (9) .... as this, there is the strength of the book as a tradition. We are all too dismissive of traditions in our modern world, but they can have a very strong pull (10) .... us. Added to this, the book is such a practical tool: it doesn't cost too (11) ...., it is usually small enough to carry around, and it can easily (12) .... revisited. We will never go without books, because they have served us so well for so long.

4 Find all the examples of the following words in the article and study the ways in which they are used. There are 14 examples in all. Then match the examples to the statements a–k. There is one extra statement which you do not need.

enough

a used before an uncountable noun or a countable noun in its plural form to say that there is as much of something as is needed

b used after an adjective or adverb to say that someone or something has as much of a quality as is needed

c used after an adverb in certain expressions for emphasis

too

d used in front of an adjective or adverb to say that there is more of something than is acceptable or desirable

e used after a piece of information, to emphasise its importance

very

f used to give emphasis to an adjective or adverb

so

g used to emphasise an adjective or adverb

h used to indicate that an amount is approximate

i used in a conditional clause

such

j used to give an example of something

k used to emphasise an adjective in a noun group

Now compare some of these examples. What are the differences in usage between the two words in brackets?

b and d (enough/too)
d and f (too/very)
f and g (very/so)
g and k (so/such)

G ⋯⟫ **page 205**

5 Insert *enough* into each of these sentences in the correct place.

a Surely you've had time to finish the exercise?
b The room wasn't large to hold everyone.
c There weren't books to go round, so we had to share.
d I had had of other people's problems, so I left work early.

e The course was cancelled as not people enrolled for it.
f – 'How much money do you have on you?'
 – 'I've got to pay for the cinema and buy us supper after.'
g 'But that's quite about me! What about you?'
h 'Funnily, I'm reading one of his books at the moment too.'

6 Complete the second sentence so that it has a similar meaning to the first sentence, using the word given. Do not change the word given. You must use between two and five words, including the word given.

1 The weather was too cold for us to go out.
 such
 It was .... didn't go out.
2 I'm sorry there's not enough time to explain.
 too
 I'm sorry there's .... you an explanation.
3 Why not turn professional, as you are such a good swimmer?
 so
 You swim .... turn professional.

4 Barry really knows how to get other people involved.
 very
 Barry .... other people involved.
5 I make all my clothes by hand so it's very time-consuming.
 such
 It .... time because my clothes are all hand-made.
6 Provided this is the case, your money will be refunded.
 so
 If .... will be given.

Writing folder 9

The set book

Exam spot

In Question 5 of Paper 2, there is a choice of two tasks, at least one of which will be an essay. The other task might be an article, report, review or letter. Although you must make reference to the book or short story you have read in your answer, you should avoid giving a lengthy description of what happens in the book. This is not asked for and may well be seen as irrelevant to the question that has been asked. If you include irrelevance, a low mark will be awarded. Remember to read the question carefully, decide exactly what is required, and plan your answer before you start writing.

1 Read this essay and correct the twenty spelling and punctuation errors.

The book 'Marcovaldo', by Italo Calvino, is actually a series of twenty short storys, all conteining the same charakter, Marcovaldo. He lives with his large family in an unamed city in Northern Italy. Each story is set, in a diffrent season: there are five stories about living in the city in summer, and so on. Many aspects of modern life are described, such as advertiseing and pollution of the enviroment, but the book is not completly true to life. This is perhaps it's greatest strength. It has a unique mixtur of realistic events and bizare ones, which often take the reader by suprise. One particluar story features the publicity campains of rival soap powder manufacturers. Marcovaldos' children and their frends collect hundreds of free cartons of washing powder, which they hope to sell to people in the neigbourhood. In the end, they have to get rid of everything quickly and so throw the cartons into the River. The story closes with a memmorable description of soap bubbles being blown over the city, their whiteness competing with the black factory smoke. Black wins.

2 Does the essay in exercise 1 answer the following question? How could it be improved?

How true to life is *Marcovaldo*?

Write an essay, discussing this question.

3 Now think about *The Old Man and the Sea*. How true to life is it? Look again at the extract on page 114 and think about how it could be used to illustrate an essay. Then read the notes. What else could you mention from the extract to support the view that this book is very true to life? Think about where the scene takes place and what is described apart from the old man.

> Introduce book briefly and give my opinion on how true to life it is (= very!)
>
> Mention part where old man gets fish on his line (mustn't describe story in detail here)
>
> Discuss character of old man – believable – strong, has great determination in spite of age, but has physical problems (mention writer's focus on hand in this scene)
>
> Add something else here?
>
> Include a conclusion

4 The notes talk about the old man's *determination.* Here are some other nouns that are useful to the set book question. Sort them into the two basic categories below, using a dictionary if necessary. Do any apply to both characters and events?

> personality   atmosphere   mood   incident
> qualities   defects   adventure   reputation
> episode   temper   risk   attitude   climate
> sympathy   impact   humiliation
> determination   surroundings

Characters	Events

5 Say which nouns in exercise 4 collocate with the adjectives below. For example, you can talk about *great determination* but not *small determination.*

> important   serious   great   enormous
> deep   small   minor   unimportant
> narrow   shallow   good   positive
> interesting   strong   attractive   bad
> weak   negative   difficult   dangerous
> final   concluding   closing   last

6 Remember to address the topic of the question in your opening paragraph. Notice how this has been done in the opening paragraph for question A below.

A How likeable is the main character in *The Old Man and the Sea*? Write an essay explaining your views.

> In 'The Old Man and the Sea', the old man, who is the main character, shows great determination. Although he is old and suffers a lot of physical pain, he is mentally strong. For this reason, he is extremely likeable and the reader has deep sympathy with him from the start. When he goes through the final humiliation of seeing the fish he has successfully caught being torn apart by sharks, we feel enormous sadness for him.

7 Now write a similar opening paragraph for question B, using the extract in Unit 18 as the part of the book you will refer to. Include some of the adjective–noun collocations in your answer.

B Several memorable events take place in *The Old Man and the Sea.* Write an essay, saying which part of the book you find the most memorable and why.

8 Choose which question you will answer, A or B. Finish the essay in 120–180 words.

Topic review

1 Together with a partner read these sentences and discuss which are true for you, giving more details. Try to use as much of the vocabulary and language from the units you have just studied as you can.

   a Although I like to read at night, sometimes I'm just too tired to stay awake.

   b I have never considered being a vegetarian.

   c I don't do enough to save the planet.

   d I'd rather have an interesting job than a large salary.

   e There was one teacher that I had at school who I just couldn't stand.

   f My teachers told me that I would never do well after I left school.

   g I think that more men have hobbies than women.

   h I don't have enough time to read books.

   i I admit that I could have worked harder at school.

   j My cooking is so bad that no one will eat it.

Vocabulary

2 For questions 1–12, read the text below and decide which answer (A, B, C or D), best fits each gap. There is an example at the beginning (0).

Example:

0 **A** made   **B** done   **C** got   **D** had

0	A	B	C	D

KITCHEN STAR

Peter White has (0) .... such a great success of his new restaurant 'Tastes' that he has just received a second star. The fourteen-table restaurant is fully booked every evening this year, and two receptionists are on full-time duty to ensure the business (1) .... smoothly. Not only is he fulfilling a lifelong ambition, he is also (2) .... more than he ever dreamt possible – he's just bought a new Ferrari to add to his (3) ....

However, life hasn't always been so easy for Peter. He (4) .... in Northern Ireland, in a family which, although poor, always (5) .... on eating well and they never went without. After doing a (6) .... at catering college, and (7) .... his exams with distinction, he moved to London to work in one of the city's (8) .... restaurants. On his first day Peter remembers two things – the smell of baking bread and the chef throwing a pan of sauce at him because he hadn't (9) .... it enough! Peter (10) .... that he doesn't treat his own (11) .... in such a manner, (12) .... he does admit to regular shouting and bursts of anger!

1	**A** runs	**B** happens	**C** flows	**D** moves
2	**A** taking	**B** gaining	**C** winning	**D** earning
3	**A** collection	**B** store	**C** set	**D** group
4	**A** brought up	**B** put up	**C** grew up	**D** showed up
5	**A** promised	**B** insisted	**C** accepted	**D** maintained
6	**A** training	**B** work	**C** course	**D** lecture
7	**A** passing	**B** succeeding	**C** graduating	**D** qualifying
8	**A** head	**B** peak	**C** top	**D** lead
9	**A** stirred	**B** chopped	**C** grated	**D** turned
10	**A** tells	**B** claims	**C** denies	**D** speaks
11	**A** crew	**B** troop	**C** staff	**D** band
12	**A** despite	**B** because	**C** even	**D** although

Grammar

3 Correct the following sentences.

a There are too much traffic in our town.

b I have so a lot of the work to do, I don't know where to start.

c The Netherlands and the Austria are both countries in the European Union.

d Her house, which roof is thatched, is twelfth century.

e John plays piano and the football, whereas his brother prefers playing the chess.

f Let me give you an advice – don't go on a travel without checking whether you need any visa or not.

g That shop has been standing on that corner for ten years.

h There's a man over there which has been watching us for about half an hour.

i I lived in Las Vegas for ten years and I am still finding it exciting.

j By this time next year I will taught since twenty years.

k He asked me where was the police station.

l I saw a bit of lightning when I was out in the garden.

m Have you got information enough to object about the factory noise?

n He's the one to whom I gave the book to.

o My eldest son who lives in Paris is a physicist.

4 Complete the sentence beginnings in A with suitable endings in B.

EXAMPLE: 1 *He apologised + e for overcooking the meat.*

A

1 He apologised

2 She denied

3 The chef claimed

4 The customer insisted

5 My neighbour warned

6 Next time you come I promise

7 The waiter urged

B

a me that the restaurant was expensive.

b to make you a cake.

c overcharging them for the coffee.

d on seeing the kitchen.

e for overcooking the meat.

f them to try the chocolate ice-cream.

g he hadn't forgotten to order the eggs.

Phrasal verbs

5 Complete the following crossword using ordinary verbs to replace the phrasal verbs in bold. There is an example to help you.

Across

1 What does the 'F' in his initials **stand for**? (9)

2 The Titanic **went down** in 1912. (4)

3 I've never been able to **add up** very well. (5)

4 It's hard to **put by** any money if you're on a low salary. (4)

5 I need to **draw up** a timetable for revision before I do an exam. (7)

6 I've **hung on to** all my old toys, and not given them away. (4)

7 Mr Jones **brought up** the question of parking at the meeting. (6)

8 People's hobbies sometimes **take over** their lives. (7)

Down

9 I need to **sort out** my desk, it's a bit of a mess. (8)

10 I think you need to **look into** the deal carefully before buying a second-hand car. (7)

11 A role model is someone you **look up to**. (7)

12 **Chop up** the onion into small pieces. (3)

13 What sort of hobby should I **take up**? (5)

14 **Face up to** the fact that your work is poor. (8)

15 The police **went after** the bank robbers. (6)

16 The rollercoaster ride made him **throw up**. (5)

17 I must **come up with** some new recipe ideas. (7)

19·1 An apple a day ...

Modals 3: Advice and suggestion

1 How healthy are you? Read through this questionnaire and decide which is the best answer for you.

1 How often do you get a good 8 hours' sleep?

A Every night – and I prefer 9 or 10 hours.
B Not often – I don't need much sleep.
C I find it hard to sleep.

2 How often do you do any exercise?

A once a week
B every day
C hardly ever

3 What do you usually have for lunch?
A a large meal
B salad or sandwiches
C nothing

4 When did you last have a cold?
A I usually have one or two a year.
B I can't remember.
C I get them all the time.

5 How many cups of tea or coffee do you drink a day?
A No more than 3
B I don't drink anything with caffeine in it
C 4–14

6 You have had a few headaches recently. Do you
A go straight to the doctor?
B take an aspirin or paracetamol?
C hope they will go away?

7 Do you think it's necessary to add salt to your food?
A sometimes
B never
C always

8 Which is true for you?
A I've given up smoking.
B I've never smoked.
C I smoke about 5 cigarettes or more a day.

9 Which is true for you?
A I think I'm really fit and healthy.
B I think illness is all in the mind.
C I worry about my health.

How did you score?

Mostly As
You are fairly healthy and have a good attitude to life. You should try to watch what you eat a little more and if I were you I'd try to do a little more exercise. Too much work and not enough play isn't good for you! I think it's about time you thought about your diet.

Mostly Bs
You are obviously in the peak of condition! I recommend you relax, as you ought to get some rest even if you don't need much sleep. Overdoing things can lead to illness! Why don't you try doing more reading, or go on holiday – or have you ever thought of playing a musical instrument?

Mostly Cs
Oh dear! It's time you took a good look at your lifestyle. Missing meals and not getting enough sleep and exercise are very bad for you. My advice to you is to start right away – you'd better book a place in the gym. I also suggest cutting down on coffee and drinking more water and fruit juice. Too much caffeine will keep you awake!

Do you agree with what is said about you? Compare your answers with a partner.

2 Reread the 'How did you score?' section and underline the verbs and phrases which are used to express advice and suggestion. One has been done for you in A – *You should try* is an example of advice. Make a special note of the construction which follows the verb or expression.

EXAMPLE: *'should' + infinitive without 'to'*

Look at the following problems and, with a partner, take it in turns to give appropriate advice and make suggestions. Try to vary the verbs and phrases you use.

EXAMPLE: *I can't stop sneezing.*
ADVICE: *If I were you, I'd take a cold shower.*
How about putting your head over a bowl of hot water?

a I can't stop hiccuping.
b I woke up covered in spots this morning.
c I can't sleep at night.
d I worry about my health all the time.
e I think I've broken my wrist.
f I'm going on holiday to a tropical country.
g I'm going to faint.
h I keep getting bitten by mosquitoes.
i I've put on so much weight recently.
j I've burnt my hand.

3 The expressions *It's time …*, *It's about time …*, and *It's high time …* are used to express strong feelings about something that hasn't been done or about something that should happen very soon.

*I think it's about time **you thought** about your diet a bit more.*
*It's time **you took** a good look at your lifestyle.*
*It's high time **you ate** less chocolate.*

Corpus spot

The *Cambridge Learner Corpus* shows that FCE candidates often forget to use the past simple with these expressions.

It's about time I **joined** a serious riding club.
NOT It's about time I ~~join~~ a serious riding club.

When you are talking generally it is possible to use the infinitive, but only after *It's time* and *It's about time*, not after *It's high time*.

It's time to go home now. (All of us including the speaker)
It's time you/he/she/we/I/they/Peter went home now. (Referring to specific people)

What would you say to a friend in these situations?

EXAMPLE: *Your friend's hair is too long.*
It's about time you went to the hairdresser's.
It's time you had a haircut.

a He smokes 40 a day.
b She drives everywhere.
c She watches TV for 6 hours a day.
d He lost his job six months ago.
e He likes eating chips.
f He's been living with his parents for 30 years.
g Her coat has holes in it.
h He never buys you a drink.
i She's always borrowing the newspaper from you.
j He's always late for work.
k Her car is always breaking down.

G ⋯◦ page 205

4 Can you name the parts of the body the arrows are pointing to?

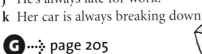

5 Which of the items in B would you do if the following in A happened to you?

EXAMPLE: *If I broke my arm, I'd wear a sling.*

A	B
If I	*I'd*
broke my leg	take an aspirin
had a headache	have stitches
cut my knee badly	go to bed
grazed my elbow	take some cough
sprained my ankle	syrup/mixture
had flu	put a bandage on it
had a cough	get an elastoplast/a plaster/a Band-Aid
	have it put in plaster

Phrases with *on*

6 In the questionnaire on health, the phrase *on holiday* was used. Look at the following expressions with *on* and then complete the sentences with a suitable expression.

on sale	on purpose	on duty
on time	on business	on foot
on fire	on the whole	on holiday

EXAMPLE: Unfortunately, I was in Paris *on business* rather than *on holiday*.

a As my gym is quite near to where I live, I always go there ....
b When I opened the oven I saw, to my horror, that the cakes were ....
c Honestly, the way my boss talks, anybody would think I broke my leg ....
d Joe can't come to the party as he has to be .... at the hospital.
e Why is it you can never be .... for anything?
f .... I prefer jogging to cycling.
g There was a wonderful new exercise bike .... at my local sports shop.

Listening

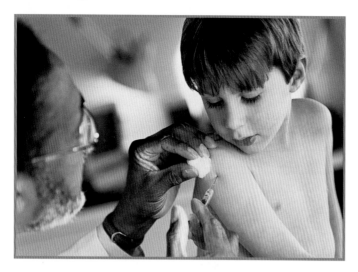

1 How do you think the patients in the photos feel at this moment? What differences do you think there are in the types of treatment being given?

2 Acupuncture is used in Chinese medicine. It consists of needles made of steel being inserted into the skin. Have you ever tried it?

3 Would you ever try a different type of medicine to the one you normally have?

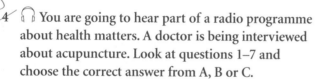

4 You are going to hear part of a radio programme about health matters. A doctor is being interviewed about acupuncture. Look at questions 1–7 and choose the correct answer from A, B or C.

1 What do we find out about Dr Carpenter's time in Hong Kong?
   A She was there to study acupuncture.
   B She practised acupuncture while she was there.
   C She enjoyed seeing a different approach to medicine.

2 Patients who she recommends for acupuncture
   A should have a blood test done first.
   B are able to choose an acupuncturist themselves.
   C need to go on a waiting list.

3 What does she say happens if you have a problem with backache?
   A You spend some time answering questions.
   B You have a needle inserted into the area which hurts.
   C You are given advice about changing your lifestyle.

4 What does she say happens after a treatment?
   A You usually feel better.
   B You might feel tired.
   C You have to go to bed.

5 She says people who have acupuncture complain of pain when the needle
   A is put in.   C is taken out.
   B is in position.

6 What does Dr Carpenter say about acupuncture?
   A It works whether you believe in it or not.
   B It's best to keep an open mind.
   C A negative attitude will stop it working.

7 In 1971 acupuncture received a great deal of publicity because an American reporter
   A went to China to investigate its use there.
   B was given some acupuncture treatment in China.
   C talked to patients who'd had operations without anaesthetic.

Grammar extra

'to have their chests X-rayed'
'to have a blood test done'

What do you think the difference is between
a to do a blood test
b to have a blood test done

You have a blood test done in a hospital.
You can also say 'to get a blood test done'.

Why do you go to the following places?
a a dry cleaner's
b a hairdresser's
c a garage
d a dressmaker
e a tailor
f a manicurist
g a jeweller
h a dentist
i a furniture maker

G ⋯⟶ page 205

Pronunciation

5 🎧 Listen to these words from the interview. What do they have in common?

конечность   однако   хотя

> | limb | though | knee | wrist |

Can you add two or three more words to each of the words below?

a knowledge   d fasten   g walk
b climb   e foreign   h palm
c wrinkle   f although

Vocabulary spot

List words with silent letters in your vocabulary notebook and look at them again before the Paper 5 Speaking test.

6 Look at the picture. Have you ever tried yoga? Why? / Why not? For questions 1–12, read the text below and decide which answer (A, B, C or D) best fits each gap. There is an example at the beginning (0).

Example:

O A taken **B** lasted **C** spent **D** passed

> | O | <u>A</u> | B | C | D |

7 Look at the sentences, or parts of sentences, below. They are all from the interview. Change the word in capitals into the right part of speech. Make sure you spell the word correctly.

a You're a great .... (BELIEF) in Chinese medicine, aren't you?
b We referred patients to .... (SPECIALISE) at the local hospital for .... (TREAT).
c When I was a .... (MEDICINE) student, …
d I saw how .... (EFFECT) acupuncture could be.
e He will insert needles in .... (VARY) parts of your body.
f Some areas are more .... (SENSE) than others.
g Acupuncture has been used .... (SUCCEED) on cats.
h He felt no pain during or after the .... (OPERATE).

Yoga

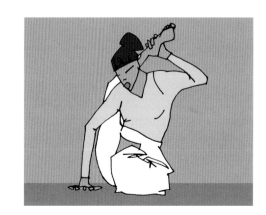

Yoga is one of the most ancient forms of exercise, originating in India 5000 years ago. Yoga has (0) ..... many years to become recognised world-wide, (1) ..... recently, much more attention has been (2) ..... to it because of the ways in which it can benefit health. Yoga can be practised by anyone, at any age, (3) ..... any physical condition, (4) ..... on physical needs. For example, athletes and dancers can practise it to restore their energy and to improve stamina; executives to give a much needed (5) ..... to their overworked minds; children to improve their memory and concentration.

It's a good idea to (6) ..... with a doctor first if you've suffered from any type of (7) ..... . None of the exercises should cause you any pain, but it's best to start slowly at first. The best (8) ..... to practise is either in the morning or in the evening. Beginners (9) ..... it easier in the evening (10) ..... the body is more supple. *гибки*

Contrary to what many people believe, you do not need to practise an hour of yoga (11) ..... day. Just taking ten to fifteen minutes out of your schedule can (12) ..... to be extremely helpful.

1	**A** although	**B** whereas	**C** if	**D** unless
2	**A** put	**B** paid	**C** allowed	**D** provided
3	**A** at	**B** in	**C** of	**D** on
4	**A** according	**B** matching	**C** fitting	**D** depending
5	**A** pause	**B** break	**C** interval	**D** interruption
6	**A** see	**B** check	**C** control	**D** call
7	**A** hurt	**B** ache	**C** injury	**D** scratch
8	**A** make	**B** do	**C** result	**D** cause
9	**A** find	**B** discover	**C** notice	**D** recognise
10	**A** though	**B** when	**C** until	**D** despite
11	**A** each	**B** all	**C** either	**D** several
12	**A** demonstrate	**B** prove	**C** show	**D** turn

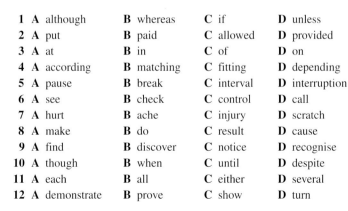

Reading skills for FCE

You will need to develop efficient reading strategies for the FCE Reading Paper. Useful skills include:

- using the rubric and the title and any sub-title to give you background information
- skimming the text to get an overall impression of what it is about
- scanning to locate specifically required information – in this case the particular examination questions; for more on this see the specific Exam Folders – 11 (multiple choice), 12 (gapped text) and 13 (multiple matching).
- understanding reference words such as *it*, *ones*, *this* and *that* and the way that the text is structured.

Background information

Look at the text opposite. What do the title, sub-title and photos tell you about what you are going to read?

Skimming

The FCE Reading Paper is made up of three texts each about 550–700 words long and is approximately 2000 words overall. You will need to answer 30 questions in one hour so you will probably have to increase your reading speed. The average person should be able to read up to 300 words per minute.

The text opposite has about 580 words. Read it and time yourself. Don't worry about words you don't know. Which of the following sums up the text best?

A The problems of working together on a project.
B How the Wheelers came to write guidebooks.
C Making sure a guidebook is accurate.

Reference

Every text has a structure. Recognising the way in which a text has been organised will help you to understand it better. In order to understand the text, it is necessary to understand how the sentences are related. Words like *it*, *this*, *here*, etc. refer to other parts of the text. You will need to understand these connections or links.

What do the following words refer to in the text?

a they (*line 8*)   e It (*line 28*)   i that (*line 56*)
b it (*line 11*)   f them (*line 31*)   j them (*line 61*)
c they (*line 12*)   g that (*line 47*)   k there (*line 62*)
d that (*line 21*)   h it (*line 48*)   l this (*line 63*)

Text structure

1 The writer is using *one* in line 23 in order not to repeat a word. What word is it?
2 Look at paragraph 1. There is a comparison here. Which words show you this?
3 In paragraph 6 there is a sentence beginning *Secondly* ... to mark a second point being made. What was the first point made?
4 What is the purpose of the *However, ...* at the beginning of paragraph 7? Other words which show a relationship between sentences are *for example, as a consequence of this, furthermore, in spite of this*, etc.
5 What word does the writer use in paragraph 3 to avoid repeating *guidebooks*? A writer will often use synonyms or near-synonyms to avoid repetition – for example: *apple/fruit*; *amount/sum*.

Paraphrasing

Being able to spot paraphrases is a very useful skill when tackling the Reading paper, especially for the multiple choice and multiple-matching questions. Find paraphrases of the following words and phrases in the text. (They are all in text order.)

a difficult to identify exactly
b you do everything the guidebook tells you to
c unquestionably
d to travel without any luxuries
e to become more mature
f the guidebooks have been the subject of some debate

Can you think of a different way of saying the following (without looking in a dictionary):

g they lied   j to set off
h accurate   k a blog
i dictated   l to make your way

Guide to the Planet

It all began with their account of a van journey to Australia in 1972. Now there are Lonely Planet guidebooks to some 200 destinations worldwide, and founders Tony and Maureen Wheeler are multi-millionaires.

Tony Wheeler is the man behind the *Lonely Planet* guidebooks; books which are loved and hated in equal measure. It's hard to pin down why they provoke such violent emotion; once it was simply
10 because they lied – you'd turn up for the weekly Wednesday ferry to find that actually it goes on Tuesdays. Nowadays they are carefully researched, the information is generally true, and the maps are accurate.

No, it's something about the way they take you over – you become a slave to the guidebook. Arrive in a place and out comes the book: Places to Stay, Things to See, Getting Around, Places to Eat – all of which is undeniably useful, but you end up
20 living a life dictated by Wheeler, and that life might not be right for you. On top of that they're boring to read, the pictures are terrible, and everyone else has got one too, so instead of being the independent traveller you thought you were, you end up being just another tourist.

It's not entirely fair to blame only Tony. His wife Maureen, who runs the company with him, is equally to blame. It all started in 1972 when, bored with Britain, they set off for Australia. They arrived
30 in Sydney three months later with 27 cents between them. Tony sold his camera, then sat down and wrote about the trip. They put the pages together and took it around the local bookshops and one of the bookshops sold thousands of copies.

More than thirty years on, *Lonely Planet* has, quite literally, taken over the world. Their 430-odd guidebooks, which sell millions every year, cover nearly everywhere and there are phrasebooks, atlases, walking guides, not to mention the website,
40 the podcasts and Tony Wheeler's own blog. Not surprisingly, the Wheelers have replaced their van with a red Ferrari.

I met them for lunch. Tony is small with glasses – more like a geography teacher than a traveller. Maureen admits they don't rough it like they once did. 'I don't want to spend all night on a train in India. I've been there and done that, I don't need to keep doing it.'

So what do they think about travel in general? 'My children have travelled all over the world so they're 50 aware of a lot of things,' says Maureen and Tony agrees. 'It helps you grow up a lot, just knowing how other people live and what happens in their countries. Secondly, being on your own, having to make your way from one place to the next and work out how you do that, gives you a self-sufficiency that I think is very important.'

However, there has been controversy surrounding the guidebooks. There are those who say that by encouraging people to go places they're destroying 60 them – an accusation they both deny, claiming that people would go there anyway. They admit that none of this is bad for business. 'All the publicity sold our books.'

After lunch, Maureen is flying back to Australia to do a bit of business and Tony is off for a bit of travelling. He's bought himself maps, guidebooks, a new one-man tent, and he's going to walk across Corsica, on his own.

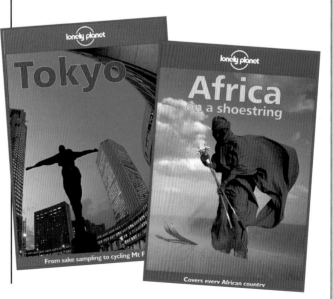

No place to hide

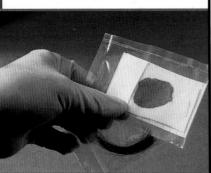

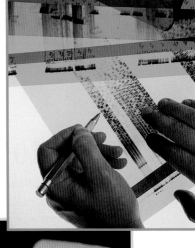

Exam spot

Part 3 of Paper 5 is a 'shared task', where you must have a discussion with the other candidate and decide together on a solution to the task. Remember to allow your partner time to give his/her opinion. Don't keep interrupting with your ideas.

1 Read and complete the task below.

Look at the five photographs of clues in a police case. Discuss which two clues are the most reliable, giving reasons for your choice. You have about three minutes to do this. It is not necessary to agree with each other, but make sure you have completed the task and not spent too much time on one point.

2 In Part 4 of Paper 5, you are encouraged to broaden and discuss further the topic introduced in Part 3. Discuss the following questions together.

  a What do you think are the causes of crime? (e.g. unemployment)
  b Do DVDs and TV help to cause more crime? Why?/Why not?
  c Should life imprisonment mean 'life'?
  d Is prison really the answer to crime?

3 Look at the vocabulary below. These are all words and phrases that you will see in the article you are going to read. Fill the gaps in the sentences with the word or phrase which fits best. (You may have to change the form of the verb.) Remember to use your English–English dictionary to help you.

to cover your tracks	a forensic scientist
the suspect	genetic code
to prove	evidence
guilty	to take someone to court

  a My sister studied to be a doctor but then decided she wanted to change careers and become .... working alongside the police.
  b It's up to the prosecution .... you committed a crime.
  c Psychologists believe you can tell if someone is .... by their body language.
  d Everyone has a completely different .... unless they are identical twins.
  e When the police have enough .... they will arrest ....
  f It is virtually impossible nowadays .... completely when you've committed a crime – there is always something that will give you away.
  g If you are caught drinking and driving you will be .... and fined.

4 You are going to read an article about detecting crime. Seven sentences have been removed from the article. Choose from the sentences A–H the one which fits each gap (1–7). There is one extra sentence which you do not need to use.

5 The following pronouns are in bold in the article. What do they refer to?

a line 8 – They
b line 15 – they
c line 20 – it
d line 24 – it

A In that time, many new scientific research methods have been developed, although the traditional way of dusting surfaces for fingerprints is still used most of the time.

B The human body is composed of millions of microscopic cells.

C However, a footprint may only suggest that someone was there.

D On the other hand, certain scientists specialise in gathering evidence from the scene of the crime.

E As it sweeps across doors, walls and furniture, any fingerprints present glow because they are fluorescent.

F As people find new ways to cover their tracks, scientists develop new techniques for linking suspects with their crimes and proving if they are guilty or innocent.

G A tuft of hair or spots of blood or saliva can be used too.

H If these traces of evidence can be found, they may provide the proof needed to bring the criminal to justice – that is, take them to court.

The Professionals

When it comes to fighting crime, it is science which is king. Sherlock Holmes was right to spend his time examining every footprint and strand of hair in his search for the criminal. Today, though, things have moved on and
5 scientists have a wider range of techniques at their disposal.

Modern scientists believe that it is impossible for someone to commit a crime without leaving something behind or taking something away with them. [1] **They** may take the form of fingerprints, hairs, and fibres from clothing, tiny
10 traces of chemicals, documents, bullets or fragments of glass. This evidence is collected and studied by forensic scientists.

Science is applied to crime-fighting now more than ever before. [2] In addition, old techniques are constantly
15 being improved so that **they** can be applied to smaller and smaller traces of materials.

Not all evidence carries the same weight of proof. A fingerprint offers definite identification of a person's presence at the scene of a crime. [3] Even if an item
20 does not offer enough proof to stand up in a court of law, **it** can still assist the police in focusing their enquiries in a certain direction.

Fingerprints have been used to help identify criminals for almost 100 years. [4] In most cases **it** works very well, but sometimes, different methods are needed. 25

Forensic scientists can now use a small portable laser to look for fingerprints. The scientist 'paints' the scene of the crime with the laser beam. [5]

An even more recent technique is called DNA profiling. [6] Each contains a unique code, the genetic code that 30 determines what we look like and how we develop. The code takes the form of long strings of molecules called DNA, and no two people have identical DNA unless they are identical twins. A technique for reading genetic codes was developed in the 1980s. DNA profiling, or genetic fingerprinting, was 35 rapidly taken up by the police and forensic scientists as a way of linking suspected criminals with their crimes.

The process of making a DNA profile may begin with a scrap of stained clothing found at the scene of the crime. [7] With a good sample that is rich in DNA, the chance of two 40 people producing the same genetic fingerprint is only one in 2.7 million, which is good enough for a court of law.

Gerunds and infinitives 2

Listening

1 🎧 Before you listen to the recording, read through the questions and make sure you understand them. You are going to hear a man talking about a daring escape from Alcatraz, the prison in the United States, which had a notorious reputation. Take notes while you are listening and then in pairs discuss the answers to the questions. What do you think happened to the men eventually?

a What happened at 9.30 pm?
b How long was Morris in jail for?
c What did some men prefer to do in the evenings?
d What did Morris do when he heard about the missing fan motor?
e Why did he buy an accordion?
f Why did they need a vacuum cleaner?
g How were they going to leave the island?
h What did they remember on the roof of the jail?
i What did the guard do?
j What happened in the end?

2 Look at the extracts from the story.

a Everyone had to stop talking.
b He stopped to listen.

c He tried picking at the concrete.
d … others [liked] to try to learn to play a musical instrument.

What's the difference in meaning between *stop* and *try* + gerund, and *stop* and *try* + infinitive?

Corpus spot

The *Cambridge Learner Corpus* shows that FCE candidates often make mistakes with the use of *stop* + infinitive and *stop* + gerund.

It's time you stopped **working** so hard.
NOT It's time you stopped ~~to work~~ so hard.

3 In Unit 7 you looked at which verb or expression took a gerund and which took an infinitive. However, there are some verbs that can take both.

1 **No change in meaning**
start, begin, continue

2 **A slight change in meaning**
like, prefer, hate, love

3 **A change in meaning**
try, stop, regret, remember, forget, mean, go on

Complete these sentences with the right form of the verb.

a The householder tried .... (fit) a burglar alarm to the house to deter thieves.

b I remember .... (read) about that kidnapping case in the papers some years ago.

c I regret .... (inform) you that your car tax has expired.

d Selling my car will mean .... (walk) home in the dark every night.

e I'm sure Peter didn't mean .... (hurt) the little girl – he only pushed her.

f I wasn't shoplifting – I just forgot .... (pay) for the scarf.

g I regret not .... (tell) the police about my suspicions.

h Although he'd been arrested for drunk driving he continued .... (drink and drive) just the same.

i I like .... (keep) an eye on my neighbours' houses when they are away.

j The policeman talked about robbery in general and then he went on .... (talk) about sentencing.

k I was mugged as I stopped .... (do up) my shoelace.

l Susan tried .... (run) after the pickpocket but although she's a good runner she couldn't catch him.

4 This exercise revises the work done on gerunds and infinitives in this unit and Unit 7. Complete the leaflet with the correct form of the verb in brackets.

Personal Possessions

A thief only needs a moment (1) .... (make off) with your valuables. Your coat hung up in a restaurant, your briefcase beside your chair, even your cheque book and cheque card left on the table while you pay the bill ... all are vulnerable if you look away for a second. So try (2) .... (be) careful at all times. Carry your wallet in an inside pocket, preferably one it is possible (3) .... (fasten), not your back pocket. If someone bumps into you in a crowd, it's worth (4) .... (check) (5) .... (see) that you still have your purse. Try (6) .... (avoid) (7) .... (carry) large amounts of cash. When on holiday abroad remember (8) .... (take) travellers' cheques. If your credit card is stolen, tell the Card Company immediately. If you delay (9) .... (report) the loss, it could (10) .... (lead) to a crime being committed in your name. Never let anyone (11) .... (know) your PIN number and remember (12) .... (sign) any new plastic cards you receive. In a car, keep your handbag or briefcase out of sight. If you have the windows open a thief may reach in when you stop (13) .... (turn) at a junction. Remember that the best way to minimise any risk is (14) .... (take) sensible precautions.

G ···⟩ page 205

Writing folder 10

Stories 2

In Writing folder 3 you saw how to approach the short story question in Part 2 of Paper 2. Remember to include the sentence you are given which either begins or ends the story.

1   Look at this question and the sample answer that follows. Discuss with a partner which of the endings A, B or C would have the best chance of winning the competition and say why.

Your teacher has asked you to write a story for an international magazine. The story must **begin** with the following sentence:

I couldn't believe my eyes when I opened the front door.

Write your **story**.

I couldn't believe my eyes when I opened the front door. When I had left home that morning the house had been clean and tidy. Now, everything was lying on the floor in a terrible mess. There were books on the carpet and all the drawers in my desk had been opened and the papers scattered round the room. I realised at once that I had been burgled. I rushed to the telephone to call the police. They told me to keep calm and not to touch anything.
I decided to take a look round to see what had been stolen. The TV was still there and so was the video. I went into my bedroom and that seemed to be completely untouched. The mess was only in the sitting room. I couldn't understand why, especially as nothing was missing.

A

Suddenly, the telephone rang. I picked it up. A voice said, 'Let this be a warning to you!' It was a woman's voice, and it made my blood run cold. I was now really scared. I didn't know what she could be talking about. I tried to dial the police again, but my hand was shaking so much I wasn't able to. Just then there was a ring at the front door.

B

I decided to make a cup of coffee while I was waiting for the police to arrive. Then they rang the doorbell and came in. They spent half an hour looking at the mess and told me that there had been a lot of burglaries in the neighbourhood recently. I felt very unhappy.

C

Suddenly, there was a knock on the door and my sister was standing there with her little boy, Tom. 'Oh, dear,' she exclaimed. 'Yes,' I said, 'isn't it terrible? I've called the police and they are on their way.' Tom suddenly threw himself into my arms. 'I'm sorry,' he said. 'It was me, it was me!'

разбросанны

2 It is very important when you are writing a story to keep in the right tense. Make the necessary changes to the verbs in brackets in the following story. What does the writer do at the end that might lose marks in the exam? This story has to end with the sentence:

For Joe, life at the office would never seem stressful again!

'I can't believe this (1) .... (happen) to me,' Joe thought. He (2) .... (arrive) at the tiny island only hours before and now he (3) .... (find) himself lying on the deck of a small fishing boat. 'What (4) .... (I/go) to do,' he (5) .... (think).
He (6) .... (look) forward to coming to the island for months. Anne, his cousin, (7) .... (come) the year before and (8) .... (tell) him how wonderful it (9) .... (be). 'It (10) .... (have) got everything you (11) .... (need) for a complete rest, away from the stresses of everyday life,' she (12) .... (say).
At this moment Joe (13) .... (want) to strangle her. 'Why (14) .... (I/decide) to follow her advice?' he asked himself. He (15) .... (know) no one on the island and (16) .... (have) no idea why he (17) .... (kidnap). Then he (18) .... (hear) footsteps coming. It (19) .... (be) a man, about fifty years old with short, black hair and a beard. He (20) .... (wear) a sort of uniform – brown shorts, a blue shirt and tie.
'We (21) .... (decide) to let you go,' the man (22) .... (say). 'A case of mistaken identity,' he (23) .... (continue). 'We (24) .... (be) sorry and (25) .... (hope) you (26) .... (enjoy) the rest of your holiday.' With that, he (27) .... (untie) me and pushed me off the boat. Luckily, I (28) .... (not have) far to swim to the shore. For Joe, life at the office would never seem stressful again!

3 Now discuss with a partner how you could change the parts of the story that are in the different colours.

the place
the person
the ending

Try to think of interesting alternatives and then tell the rest of the class what you have written.

4 Now do this writing task.

You have been asked to write a short story for your college magazine. The story must end with the following sentence:

Sam could hear no one following him, and realised that he was safe at last.

Write your **story** in 120–180 words.

With a partner, think of some ideas for the story.

a The people in the story – how will you describe them?
b The place where the story happens – what is it like?
c The action – how will you describe what happens?

Advice

- Remember to check the spelling, punctuation and grammar.
- Count the number of words you have written.
- Try to keep within 20 words of the upper limit.
- Get used to judging how many lines of your handwriting will make 180 words.

To have and have not

1 Look at the pictures above. Which things do you see as necessities – things you couldn't live without – and which as optional luxuries? Explain your reasons to another student.

2 What things do you like to treat yourself to every week? Do you ever buy something you don't really need on impulse?

Listening

3 🎧 You are going to hear five speakers talking about small luxuries they regularly pay for. Decide what each speaker values most about the thing they spend their money on, choosing from A–F. There is one extra letter which you do not need to use.

A the personal convenience of it

B the improvement to his/her surroundings   Speaker 1   [1]

C the feeling of privacy it gives   Speaker 2   [2]

D the entertainment it provides him/her   Speaker 3   [3]

E the professional care involved   Speaker 4   [4]

F the benefit to him/her physically   Speaker 5   [5]

4 🎧 Listen again to check your answers. Do you consider all five things as luxuries? Why?/Why not?

Phrasal verbs with *cut*

5 Look at these phrasal verbs with *cut* and read the examples from the recordings.

| cut across | cut back (on) | cut down (on) |
| cut in | cut off | cut out |

I wouldn't dream of cutting back on this …
I cut down on what I ate – and cut out cigarettes entirely.

What are the differences in meaning here, if any? Do these phrasal verbs have any other meanings?

In what contexts could the three other phrasal verbs with *cut* be used?

Choose the most suitable phrasal verbs with *cut* to complete the sentences below.

a After James announced his resignation, the department .... him .... of all their meetings.

b Let's .... the fields – it's much quicker than the road.

c You'll have to .... your composition – it's double the word limit!

d The interviewer tried to ask another question, but the angry politician .... again.

e Serious flooding has .... several villages, although the Red Cross is planning to drop emergency supplies by helicopter.

f The second engine .... and the plane began to lose height.

g I've had real problems with the phone today – that's twice now I've been .... !

h Despite record company profits, the research budget has been .... by 50%.

Vocabulary

6 🎧 In the listening extracts there are various words and phrases to do with money. Listen again and note them down under the headings below. The number in brackets tells you how many phrases there are. There are two examples.

Phrases to describe good value (3)
a small price to pay

Words/phrases about having money (4)
steady income

Nouns to do with cost (5)

Adjectives to describe being badly-off (4)

7 The example in 6 talks of a *steady* income. You can also say a *steady* job or describe 'progress' in this way, but you cannot use *steady* to describe some other things. So, for example, you would not say a 'steady river', because the words do not collocate.

Which noun in each set below does **not** collocate with the adjective given in italics?

a	account	charge	increase	path	*steep*
b	fit	road	schedule	spot	*tight*
c	cash	key	thought	time	*spare*
d	air	break	ideas	start	*fresh*
e	belt	hands	place	side	*safe*
f	film	girl	square	wasp	*delightful*
g	flavour	mood	report	swing	*full*
h	belief	confusion	horror	lack	*utter*

8 Now use some of these phrases to complete the story below.

Would you have done the same? Why?/Why not?

Last month I went to Italy on business. Despite being on a
(1) .... during the trip, I had a little bit of
(2) .... on the final afternoon, so I decided to have
a walk and get some **(3)** .... Even though the sun
was shining, I took an umbrella, to be on the **(4)** ....
I strolled through some quiet streets and then walked up a **(5)** ....
.... This eventually came out on a **(6)** .... ,
where a flower market was in **(7)** .... I decided to
buy some roses to take home and took out my last 50 euro note. To my
(8) .... , a sudden gust of wind blew the money out
of my hand. I watched it flutter across the square and saw roughly where it
landed. I rushed over, and, looking down, I could see that the note had fallen
through an iron grill in the gutter. Fortunately,
I had my umbrella and managed to push its
spike through the grill, although it was a very
(9) ....! At the
third attempt, I speared my much-needed
euros. Putting it in a very **(10)** ....
.... (my inside pocket), I went
straight back to the hotel, got my luggage
and found a taxi to take me to the airport,
so I never did buy those roses.

21·2

Clauses

When you are writing in English, don't use too many short, simple sentences. Instead, make longer sentences which contain more than one clause and are connected by well-chosen linking words. This shows an advanced level of writing and also avoids repetition. Earlier in this course you have practised conditional clauses (Unit 6) and relative clauses (Unit 17). Here are some more types of clause.

уступительные предлоги

Concessive clauses

1   Look at these examples from 21.1 and explain the function of the underlined words in the sentences.

   a   He was always carrying an armful of flowers, <u>even though</u> sometimes he'd only been away for a couple of days.

   b   We can usually decide on our order quite quickly, <u>even if</u> we still argue over some things!

   c   <u>Despite</u> being hard-up, I would still try to buy flowers.

   d   <u>While</u> not exactly loaded, I can afford it.

What is the difference between examples a and b and examples c and d?

Could the word *although* be used instead of the underlined words, without changing the meaning? If so, would you need to make any grammatical changes?

Several other words in English are used in clauses of this type.

 page 206

Corpus spot

Be careful when using *despite* – the *Cambridge Learner Corpus* shows FCE candidates often make mistakes with this word. Compare *in spite of* in this example.

> So, **despite** its disadvantages, a mobile phone is very useful. OR
> So, **in spite of** its disadvantages, a mobile phone is very useful.

NOT So, ~~despite of~~ its disadvantages, a mobile phone is very useful.

---

2   Correct any errors in these sentences.

   a   I always forget something when I go to the supermarket, despite of making a list.

   b   Even department stores claim to sell most things, I prefer using specialist shops whenever possible.

   c   Sainsbury's has gone into in-store banking, whereas that Iceland, the frozen food store, is developing its home delivery service.

   d   In spite of they want increased sales, some shops refuse to open on Sundays.

   e   I'm usually happy with the clothes I bring home, even they have been bought on impulse.

   f   The supermarket chain Tesco has found that more men are buying babycare products, although they usually picking up beer at the same time.

3   For questions 1–12, read the article below and think of the word which best fits each gap. Use only one word in each gap. Then underline the concessive clauses.

When penniless student Faye Pattison checked her bank account recently, she was surprised to find a very healthy balance …

I'm a typical student, struggling to make ends meet with a part-time job. One day I was checking my bank balance at the cashpoint machine, just in case my wages had already (**1**) .... paid in. Up came all these zeros! My first reaction was panic as I thought I was overdrawn, (**2**) .... I soon realised that my account was actually in credit (**3**) .... a massive amount. I knew the money wasn't mine so I went into the bank and told them they had made a mistake. Apparently, one number was keyed wrongly so the money ended up in my account.

Two weeks later I checked my balance again, so as to be sure they had sorted it out. Up popped £500,000! I felt (**4**) .... a lottery winner without the ticket. When I told the bank (**5**) .... time, they said that because their computers were down I would have to leave (**6**) .... with them. (**7**) .... though they had now made two mistakes with my account, within the week the sum had doubled!

4   With a partner, discuss whether you would have behaved differently from Faye if this had happened to you. Think about her action at each stage and say what you would have done.

Purpose, reason and result clauses

5   In the article about Faye there are a number of these clauses. For example:

I was checking my balance at the cashpoint machine, *just in case my wages had been paid in.* (Purpose)

They said that *because their computers were down,* I would have to leave it with them. (Reason)

One number was keyed wrongly *so the money ended up in my account.* (Result)

Find other clauses like this in the article. Which other words like *just in case, because* and *so* are used?

G ···⟩ page 206

I now had a balance of over a million. I was falling about laughing at the cashpoint: the people behind (**8**) .... have thought I was on drugs or something. At this point I gave (**9**) .... on my local branch and contacted head office, in order to sort the matter out (**10**) .... and for all.

Eventually, the £1,000,000 was debited from my account but the following day £300 appeared, (**11**) .... was the interest earned on the million. (**12**) .... the fact that the money wasn't mine, the bank said I could keep it! I'm spending it on a trip to Turkey.

6   Join the following sentences together using the words in brackets, making any other changes necessary.

a   Supermarkets give their customers loyalty cards. They want more information about what people buy. (so as to)

b   There weren't many stalls at the market yesterday. Yesterday was a public holiday. (because)

c   Some daily newspapers cut their prices. They want a bigger circulation. (in order to)

d   I like filling the house with flowers. I buy a lot of flowers. (since)

e   Harrods can charge a lot. Harrods is seen as a very exclusive shop. (so)

f   I went to London. I bought a special present for Ellen. (to)

g   It's always worth trying clothes on before you buy them. Clothes can be too tight. (in case)

h   Some supermarkets create the smell of freshly-baked bread. This is to make a good impression on their customers. (so that)

7   Complete the second sentence so that it has a similar meaning to the first sentence, using the word given. **Do not change the word given. You must use between two and five words, including the word given.**

1   Although it was cold last weekend, the store reported record sales of garden equipment.
despite
The store reported record sales of garden equipment .... last weekend.

2   Keep the receipt as it mightn't fit you.
case
Keep the receipt just .... fit you.

3   You usually find what you need in a smaller shop, although you pay more than at a supermarket.
if
Smaller shops usually have what you need,
....
more than a supermarket does.

4   Supermarkets have chocolate on sale at check-outs, because impulse buying of it is common.
since
Chocolate is sold at supermarket check-outs .... bought on impulse.

5   Saunas are popular in Sweden but not in Britain.
whereas
Many Swedish people enjoy Saunas
.... not.

Exam folder 11

Paper 1 Part 1 Multiple choice

In this part of the Reading paper you are tested on a detailed understanding of the text. There might also be the following type of questions:

- a question which tests global understanding – What is a suitable title for the text?
- a question which tests the meaning of a word or phrase from the context – What does the writer mean by x in line z?
- a question which tests reference – What does 'it' refer to in line q?

Advice

- Skim the text to get a general idea of what it is about.
- All the questions, except for the global one, are in order so you can concentrate on each part of the text at a time. The global question will come at the end, but you need to make sure you take **the whole text** into account when you answer it.
- Some of the choices may be true but do not answer the question. Other choices may seem very plausible and even contain elements of the same vocabulary, but do not answer the question correctly.
- The reference question may refer either forwards or backwards so check carefully on either side of the pronoun to see what it refers to.
- As you read, underline the part of the text which you think contains the answer.

You are going to read an extract from a newspaper article. For questions 1–8, choose the answer (A, B, C or D) which you think fits best according to the text.

1 What is the problem the writer has at the beginning of her holiday?
   A The weather is not good enough for painting.
   B She's brought the wrong materials with her.
   C There are no animals to paint.
   D She can't reproduce the exact colours.

2 The writer hid her work because
   A she believed Royale paints better.
   B it wasn't good enough to sell.
   C she thought it would disappoint Royale.
   D it was only a quick sketch.

3 What does the writer mean by the phrase 'what I am up to' in lines 37–38?
   A What I am painting.   C What I can teach him.
   B What I will give him.   D What I might do.

4 What does the writer say about her previous painting holiday?
   A She preferred the teacher she had had then.
   B The landscape was more familiar to her.
   C Her technique had improved much faster.
   D She had been able to complete a number of paintings.

5 The writer says that Susan Scott-Thomas
   A looks at things in a different way from her.
   B is a very capable person.
   C is not as good at cooking as her.
   D was a solicitor before going to Africa.

6 What does 'it' refer to in line 82?
   A the holiday   C the colour and shape
   B the country   D the finished painting

7 What is a suitable title for the article?
   A An unsuccessful holiday
   B An artist goes to Zimbabwe
   C Learning to work with others
   D Travelling in a different country

8 What is the writer's purpose in writing this text?
   A To encourage people to take up painting as a hobby.
   B To persuade people to visit Zimbabwe.
   C To describe how she combines her hobby with a holiday.
   D To criticise the organisers of her African holiday.

BY THE MIDDLE OF THE SECOND DAY I KNOW I'M IN TROUBLE. In front of me the land stretches up and away towards a distant hill, and into the space, between that summit and me, is crowded one of the most vivid concentrations of colour I have ever seen. It starts with the trees. The wet season is only a few weeks off and, almost as if they can smell the coming rains, they have put out their leaves. They are no ordinary green and the dry grasses beneath them are ablaze with golds, browns and reds. I want to recreate this scene with watercolours. Although I can make a try at it with words, trying to paint it in my sketch book is another matter altogether. I've already made one attempt: a series of zigzags in orange and red, with bluish trees placed across them, which now lies face down in the grass beside me.

I've put it there because the last thing I want right now is for someone else to come along and look at it. A young man called Royale walks up the hill. Royale is a sculptor, and, with several other local men, produces pieces of work in the local stone. Recently, and quite suddenly, this work, and that of several other local co-operatives, has acquired an international reputation. I certainly don't want a man capable of such things looking at my own awful brush-strokes. So I put my foot, as casually as I can, on the finished painting beside me and we resume the conversation started earlier in the day.

I want to talk to Royale about his life here. He, however, is only interested in what I am up to. To begin with, it seems that he considers me a fellow artist, and for a moment I find myself staring into the depths of embarrassment. But when he asks me, 'What is painting like?' I realise that this professional artist has never painted anything in his life before. He just wants a go with my colours.

When I signed up for this holiday, I was hoping for an experience like the one I had had four years earlier in Wales. That was my first painting holiday, and I loved it. Two things made it great. First was the teacher, a man called Robin, who showed me that what is important about drawing and painting is not the finished article but the process of completing it. The second element of that week was the place. I grew up in places like that, and I connected with it immediately. But it was stupid of me to think that I could reproduce the experience down here, deep in the Southern Hemisphere. Zimbabwe is not a part of me, nor I of it. Trying to draw it for the first time, from a standing start, is like trying to start a conversation in Swahili.

There were compensations. The holiday was wonderfully organised by a friend of mine – Susan Scott-Thomas. Admittedly, there are some rather large differences between us – she's extremely wealthy and she inherited a farm in Africa when she was in her mid-twenties, and instead of taking the easy option of becoming a solicitor and staying in London, she came out to reclaim the land and rebuild the decaying farmhouse. In the process, she learnt how to lay foundations and make clay bricks. All of which she did while I was just about mastering making sauce for pasta.

Even my disastrous painting didn't detract from enjoying the holiday. Painting really forces you to look at things, to consider their shape and colour. And even if it is a disaster, that process of looking and thinking and transferring those thoughts into movements of your hand leaves an imprint of what you have seen. By the end of the week I have still not produced anything to hang on my walls, although there is a drawing of a local schoolboy of which I am rather fond, not because it is much good, but because it was so challenging to do.

A little night music

Speaking

1 Look at these two pictures and discuss their similarities and differences.

2 🎧 Now listen to the recording, which is an example of Paper 5, Part 2. One student will talk about the pictures for about a minute. Then another student will talk briefly at the end. How do their views differ?

3 🎧 Listen to the recording again and tick any vocabulary you hear in the sets below.

Perform	Performers	Performance
play	musician	concert
take part	band	recital
improvise	orchestra	gig
participate	pianist	festival
join in	conductor	rehearsal
sing a solo	choir	show

Explain the differences in meaning of the words in the 'Performance' column.

4 Do you prefer to listen to music or to take part? What types of music do you enjoy? What do you dislike?

5 This article about a piano recital appeared in the *English Language Bangkok Post*. Skim the main text to get an idea of what the article is about. What do you think happened to Myron Kropp?

6 Now go through the main text again, underlining words and phrases that may help you to predict the content of each gap. Look out for linkers too. Time yourself as you do this.

A RATHER STICKY

The recital by American pianist Myron Kropp, which took place yesterday evening in the chamber music room of the Erawan Hotel, can only be described as one of the most interesting experiences in a very long time. It was Mr Kropp's first appearance in Bangkok. [1] Deceptively frail-
5 looking, with thin, sandy hair and a yellowish complexion, the man who has repopularised Johann Sebastian Bach approached the Baldwin Concert Grand Piano, bowed to the audience and placed himself upon the stool.

It is appropriate to say at this point that Mr Kropp, unlike many pianists, is
10 not happy about this form of seating. Due to the screw-type design, pianists often find themselves turning sideways during the most expressive parts of a performance. [2] Sadly, he returned without one. Having settled himself as best he could, the performance got underway.

Although a fine instrument, the Baldwin Concert Grand needs constant
15 attention, particularly in a climate such as Bangkok's. [3] This is doubly true when the instrument is as old as the one provided in the Erawan Hotel yesterday, where the D in the second octave proved particularly troublesome. During the 'raging storm' section of the D-minor Toccata and Fugue, Mr Kropp must be praised for putting up with it.

20 However, by the time the 'storm' was past and he was into the Prelude and Fugue in D major, in which the second octave D plays a major role, Mr Kropp's patience was wearing thin. Several concert-goers later questioned whether the awkward D key justified some of what was heard coming from the stage during softer passages of the Fugue. [4] He suggested
25 that the workman who had greased the music stool might have done better to use some of the grease on the D key.

The stool itself had more than enough grease on it. During one passage, in which the music and the 'lyrics' were both particularly violent, Mr Kropp was turned completely round. This meant that whereas before his remarks
30 had been aimed largely at the piano, to his surprise and that of those in the room, he found himself swearing at the audience. [5] Unfortunately, laughter is contagious, and many people joined in. Once the audience had regained its composure, Mr Kropp appeared somewhat shaken.

CONCERT

возвращаться

Nevertheless, he bravely swivelled himself back into position and, leaving the D major Fugue unfinished, went on to the Fantasia and Fugue in G minor. Why the G key in the third octave chose that particular moment to start sticking is a mystery. Mr Kropp did not help matters when he began to kick the lower half of the piano, causing the right front leg to buckle slightly inward, and leaving the entire instrument leaning at an angle. [6]   *бицирь*

улом

It was with a sigh of relief therefore that the audience saw Mr Kropp slowly rise from his stool and leave the stage. A few men in the back of the room began clapping and when Mr Kropp returned a moment later, it seemed he was responding to this applause. Apparently, however, he had left to fetch a red-handled fire axe, which was hung back stage in case of fire. [7]   At first it seemed that he was merely trying to make it tilt at the same angle as the right one, though when the piano collapsed with a great crash, it became obvious that Mr Kropp had no intention of going on with the concert. It took six people to disarm him and he was eventually dragged off the stage.

35

40

45

50

Exam spot

When you scan the sentences, don't worry about filling the gaps in text order. Think about what information you are looking for. If you recognise where the content of a sentence fits, go to that part of the text first.

7 Scan sentences A–H and decide where they fit. Check that the extra sentence doesn't fit anywhere.

A In the humidity, the felts that separate the white keys from the black ones tend to swell, causing keys to stick occasionally.

B The person who began to snigger at this point deserves to be severely reprimanded for his behaviour.

C There was a slight delay for this reason, as Mr Kropp left the stage, apparently in search of a bench.

D A gasp went up from the audience, for if it had actually fallen, several of Mr Kropp's toes would surely have been broken.

E As he was a true professional, Mr Kropp carried on unmoved, but the audience began to doubt his ability to weather the storm.

F Mr Kropp began to chop at the left leg of the piano with it.

G The room went quiet as he entered, dressed in formal black evening-wear.

H One member of the audience sent his children out of the room because of this bad language.

8 Explain the meaning of the underlined words and phrases from the article. The line number is given in brackets.

a Deceptively frail-looking (lines 4–5)
b during the most expressive parts (line 11)
c Having settled himself as best he could (lines 12–13)
d Mr Kropp's patience was wearing thin (lines 21–22)
e the awkward D key (line 23)
f the audience regained its composure (lines 32–33)
g deserves to be severely reprimanded (sentence B)
h to weather the storm (sentence E)

Complex sentences

1 To make his writing more interesting and to improve its cohesion, the writer of the article in 22.1 started sentences in various different ways. Look at these examples a–h and match them to descriptions 1–8.

 a Deceptively frail-looking, with thin, sandy hair and a yellowish complexion, …

 b It is appropriate to say at this point that …

 c Due to the screw-type design, …

 d Having settled himself as best he could, …

 e Although a fine instrument, the Baldwin Concert Grand …

 f This is doubly true when …

 g As he was a true professional, …

 h Why the G key in the third octave chose that particular moment to start sticking …

 1 linking to previous sentence
 2 prepositional phrase
 3 adjectival phrase
 4 concessive clause *уступительный*
 5 reason clause
 6 -ing clause
 7 rhetorical question
 8 emphasising new information

2 Read part of an FCE answer on the topic of live music, taken from the *Cambridge Learner Corpus*. Identify the underlined clauses and explain why they make the writing effective.

I really enjoy going to places in which you can see a good concert. When I listen to live music, I always have a special feeling of having fun and relaxing at the same time. Sometimes, when I really like the music I am listening to, I forget the real world and start dreaming. Although I like almost everything about music, if I can choose between a classical concert and a blues concert I am going to choose the second one. Seeing blues or soul bands in concert is one of the things that I really enjoy.

Which adverb is used three times? To avoid this, what other adverbs could be used instead?

3 Now rewrite the following sentences a–g in a similar way, using the patterns 1–8 in exercise 1 and producing a single complex sentence. The first word of each sentence and the pattern required is given in brackets.

EXAMPLE: *I don't know who it was that started a slow hand-clap. Immediately everyone joined in. (Who 7)*
Who it was that started a slow hand-clap I don't know, but immediately, everyone joined in.

 a It was late. We decided not to stay for the final band. (As 5)

 b The cello, which has been beautifully made by hand and is reddish brown in colour, has an excellent sound. (Beautifully 3)

 c Ellen learnt the recorder for three years. Then she went on to the flute. (Having 6)

 d The trumpeter is technically brilliant. However, his playing has no feeling. (Despite 4)

 e The conductor made a mistake. The soloist had to miss out a whole verse. (Due 2)

 f (Previous sentence: Mick Jagger often sings flat.) You notice that he sings flat especially in recordings of live concerts. (This 1)

 g The Squier is a low-priced guitar. It sounds very similar to a proper Stratocaster. (Although 4)

4 Expand these notes into complex sentences, using the linkers given and adding punctuation and any other words necessary. An example is given.

EXAMPLE: *What/rubber chicken/doing/stage/mystery/ gig started/although/realised later/Zappa hurled/drummer*
What a rubber chicken was doing on the stage was a mystery before the gig started, although we realised later, when Zappa hurled it at the drummer!

 a Due/delay/band's arrival/ insisted/refund/tickets *инверсия*

 b Since/last train/eleven thirty/ sadly/miss/performance

 c Despite/unwell/singer/decided/ not cancel/although/shortened

 d Instead/what/printed/ programme/pianist improvised/ over 40 mins

 e An oboe/suitable tone/even if/ underused/jazz instrument

 f As/violinist/stage fright/rarely/ performances/large audiences

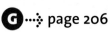 

G ⋯⟩ page 206

Three of its most famous music directors participated: Solti, Barenboim and Kubelik. Immediately before the concert, a celebration dinner was held for special donors. At an event like this, it is customary to give diners a small gift, so each person was presented with an attractive alarm clock, gift-wrapped. Why some of the clocks were put in their boxes with the alarm switched on is a mystery, but this was the case. It is appropriate to remind the reader that the dinner guests went straight on to the concert, armed with these ticking timebombs! However, after the interval more and more alarms were going off, so the concert had to be temporarily stopped and an announcement made. As the clocks were inside boxes and gift-wrapped, nobody in the audience had realised what the problem was. The rest of the evening then proceeded without incident.

5   Sentences a–d all belong in the paragraph opposite. Which sentence should come at the very beginning of this paragraph?

Insert the three remaining sentences into the text, to make one cohesive paragraph.

a During the first half there were few problems, with only an occasional beep being heard.

b Although for the wrong reason, the Chicago Symphony Orchestra's Centennial concert was a memorable event.

c Once the laughter had died down, they were instructed to take their gifts outside to the lobby.

d There were some 400 of these, each paying at least $500 for the privilege of attending.

6   For questions 1–12, read the text and decide which answer (A, B, C or D) best fits each gap. There is an example at the beginning (0).

Example:

0   A remains   **B** keeps   **C** stays   **D** continues

0	A	B	C	D

G ···⟩ page 206

G ···⟩ page 206

GEORGE GERSHWIN

George Gershwin, who was born in Brooklyn in 1898, (**0**) ...... one of the world's most popular composers today. He lived and worked in the perfect era for his unique talent to (**1**) .... It was at a time when the Jazz Age coincided with composers like Berg, as well as the first Broadway musicals. Although a gifted pianist, he had only (**2**) ..... reading skills in music, but due to his regular attendance at concerts, he was able to (**3**) ..... up his own repertoire. In 1924, Gershwin worked with his brother Ira on a musical comedy called *Lady Be Good*. This proved to be a successful (**4**) ...... that continued for the rest of his life.

George Gershwin was determined to (**5**) ..... an impression as a serious composer, which he also achieved in 1924. At its New York premiere, one of his most famous (**6**) ....., *Rhapsody in Blue*, received (**7**) ..... applause from an audience that included musical celebrities such as the Russian composers Rachmaninov and Stravinsky. Gershwin (**8**) ..... this success with innovative orchestral works such as *An American in Paris* and, in 1935, the memorable opera *Porgy and Bess*.

No one has been able to match Gershwin's ability to write original works that (**9**) ..... the boundaries of jazz, opera and classical music and his (**10**) ..... on modern music has been enormous. It is appropriate to (**11**) ..... that he made the American composer a respectable (**12**) ..... around the world, at a time when very little American music was being performed. Sadly, Gershwin died at the early age of 38.

1	**A** become	**B** develop	**C** result	**D** invent
2	**A** key	**B** plain	**C** basic	**D** easy
3	**A** grow	**B** pull	**C** move	**D** build
4	**A** company	**B** teamwork	**C** pair	**D** partnership
5	**A** make	**B** get	**C** put	**D** take
6	**A** writings	**B** exercises	**C** designs	**D** compositions
7	**A** hot	**B** wild	**C** deep	**D** full
8	**A** brought	**B** followed	**C** adopted	**D** led
9	**A** enter	**B** split	**C** cross	**D** carry
10	**A** power	**B** direction	**C** control	**D** influence
11	**A** join	**B** mix	**C** add	**D** link
12	**A** figure	**B** body	**C** human	**D** character

Writing folder 11

Reports

In Part 2 of Paper 2 you may be asked to write a report. This will involve the presentation of mainly factual information, with suggestions or a recommendation. Any report needs to be clearly organised with an introduction and conclusion. Headings usually help to signpost the content. Reports are often written in an impersonal style, using the passive.

1 Read the following exam question and its answer. Then rewrite the answer, making the improvements suggested in a–d.

  a What would you add at the beginning and end of the report?
  b How could the highlighted headings be improved?
  c Why are the underlined parts of the answer inappropriate to a report? How could the passive be used to address this?
  d Where you see the symbol §, use a conjunction to join the two sentences together, making any other changes necessary.

Every year, you help at a local music festival, which takes place outdoors over one weekend. The organisers want to improve the festival and have asked you to write a short report. You should comment on the facilities that were available at this year's festival and make recommendations for next year.

Write your **report**.

<u>Dear</u> Organisers

Here is my report ....

The place in town where you hold the festival

The site this year was disappointing, mainly because it wasn't large enough. There was some car parking. § Many people had to park over two kilometres away.

Eating

There was some choice of catering at the site. § Very little vegetarian food was offered. Also, <u>my friends and I</u> had to go to one end of the field for food and <u>then we ran over to</u> the opposite end for a drink. <u>This drove us nuts!</u>

The programme

People seemed to enjoy the performances. § Each band should be allowed more time on stage.

The cost

Several members of the audience thought the tickets were unusually cheap. § The price could be raised next year. <u>This would help us, wouldn't it?</u>

Recommendations

<u>You need</u> a bigger site and better-organised catering – <u>some changes to the timing of the event too.</u> ....

....

151 words

2 You could be asked to write a report about shopping facilities in your town. If so, you should think carefully about the group of 'shoppers' you are writing the report for. This is different from the target reader of the report, who will be specified – for example, the festival organisers in the last question, or your boss at the tourist office.

For each target group below, decide which types of shopping it would be suitable to focus on, choosing from a–j. Some will be used more than once. Remember to consider the advantages or disadvantages given in brackets and to recommend things that are realistic in the time allowed.

TARGET GROUP
1 American exchange students on a limited budget
2 Elderly tourists visiting as a group one weekend
3 Business people spending a free hour after their appointments
4 Families camping outside the town for a week

a an exclusive gift shop (in the main square)
b a large toyshop (limited parking)
c a central stationery shop (open late)
d the Saturday crafts market (very colourful)
e a discount computer warehouse (plenty of parking)
f a sports equipment store (good value)
g a supermarket on the edge of town (massive)
h a music store (very noisy)
i the university bookshop (discounts available)
j an art gallery (includes a coffee shop)

3 Now read this exam question.

Some British students are on an exchange programme at your college for a month. The college has asked you to write a report on local shopping facilities for the teacher who is in charge of the group. You should give advice on best value for money, including areas such as food, study materials and souvenirs.

Write your **report**.

Plan what you are going to write, starting with the ideas in 2. Remember that you are writing to the teacher, not the students, so your report should be fairly formal. Try to use some of the vocabulary on money and shopping from Unit 21.

Unexpected events

1   In pairs, discuss the photographs. How does each photograph make you feel? Would you be more worried about one of the events than the others? Why?/Why not?

Which set of words goes with which photograph?

a a bolt, a storm, thunder, a flash   **c** lava, ash, an eruption, gases
b to be stranded, torrential rain   **d** a tremor, cracks, to tremble

Listening

2   You are going to hear an interview with a woman, Liz, who together with her friend, Dave, had a horrific experience when they were camping. For questions 1–10, complete the sentences.

Dave thought at first that the cloud was the result of a	1
Liz says that what she saw was different from a	2
Liz thought it was odd because it was completely	3
The heat melted the [4] of the coffee pot.	
Dave and Liz tried at first to reach	5
Dave and Liz had been protected in the hole by	6
Dave and Liz put their [7] round their heads to help them to breathe.	
It was hard to walk because of the depth of the	8
There was an awful smell similar to	9
Liz now regrets not having a [10] with them.	

Pronunciation

3   Listen again to part of the interview.

Interviewer: I expect you were very frightened by then, weren't you?
Liz: Frightened! I was absolutely petrified, and so was Dave.

Notice how Liz's voice rises on 'frightened' and falls on 'petrified'.
Now you do the same.

EXAMPLE:
Student A: I expect the weather was very cold, wasn't it?
Student B: Cold! It was absolutely freezing!

a weather – cold/freezing   **f** salary – large/enormous
b water – hot/boiling   **g** sister – clever/brilliant
c film – bad/awful   **h** TV play – long/never-ending
d food – good/delicious   **i** book – interesting/fascinating
e hotel room – small/tiny   **j** you – angry/furious

Phrasal verbs with *off*

4 Match these phrasal verbs you heard in the
interview with their meaning.

1 It gave off a terrible smell. — removed
2 We took off our shirts. — began the journey
3 When we set off it was — produced
difficult to breathe.

Now complete the following sentences, choosing
a phrasal verb that means the same as the word
or words in brackets. Make sure you use the correct
tense.

pay off	come off	break off	call off
put off	put off	wear off	drop off
write off	run off		

EXAMPLE: *Don't (postpone) what you have to do
today until tomorrow.*

ANSWER: *Don't put off what you have to do today
until tomorrow.*

a He (end suddenly) what he was saying in order
to open the door.

b The Prime Minister's visit to Australia has been
(cancelled) because of the floods at home.

c Anne decided to (request by letter) for the
information pack advertised on the TV.

d The gold coating on the medal eventually
(disappeared) with time.

e If I won the lottery, the first thing I would do is
to (settle) my debts.

f I hope you won't be (discouraged from) seeing
the film just because I didn't enjoy it.

g Mr Roberts asked his secretary to (duplicate) a
copy of the invoice for me.

h The play was so boring it was all I could do to
stop myself from (falling asleep).

i I hope the plans for the new dam to prevent
future floods (succeed).

5 For questions 1–12, read the text below and think
of the word which best fits each gap. Use only one
word in each gap. There is an example at the
beginning (0).

An Unchanging Planet?

If you think of Earth (0) ..as.. a stable and unchanging
planet, think again. Nearly five billion years after it was
first formed, the Earth is still developing – (1) ....
alarming ways. Unlike earthquakes that strike (2) ....
warning, volcanoes build up (3) .... months and are
usually easier to predict. But their spectacular climax is
no (4) .... devastating. A volcano can erupt in many
different ways and it can spill out a variety of materials.
Mild eruptions spurt gas, steam and hot water and are
(5) .... geysers. Larger volcanoes shoot out ash and
large chunks of hot rock into (6) .... atmosphere, and
enormous fountains of glowing red hot lava that flow
(7) .... the sides of the volcano. This liquid lava quickly
thickens into a steaming sticky carpet (8) .... can travel
150 km before it stops and turns solid. Lava floods
(9) .... fire to and destroy (10) .... that stands in their
way. Famously, in AD 79, the Roman city of Pompeii
(11) .... covered in lava and ash, preserving buildings
and some of their contents to (12) .... day.

I wish / If only

1   Look at these examples from 23.1. Both *a* and *b* are wishes for the present and *c* is a wish for the past.

   a … apart from wishing I were somewhere else!
   b If only we could get in the tent, we'd be safe.
   c I wish now that we'd taken a radio with us.

   • When talking about the present or the future you need to use a past tense after *wish* and *if only*.
   • When referring to the past you must use the past perfect tense.

2   In the recording, Liz says that she wished she'd taken a radio. What other things do you think she wished for after the eruption? In groups, suggest five other things Liz might have said.

   EXAMPLE: *I wish we had chosen a different place to camp.*

   Tell your class about things that you regret doing or not doing in the past.

   > *I wish I hadn't gone to that boring party.*

   > *If only I had worked harder for the exam.*

3   When Liz says 'if only we could get in the tent, we'd be safe' she is saying what she felt at that particular moment.

   Now write down ten things that you wish for right at this moment. Compare your sentences with a partner.

   EXAMPLES:
   I wish I was/were on a beach instead of in class.
   I wish I could give up smoking.

   You can't say: *I wish I would/He wishes he would/They wish they would,* etc. This is because *wish … would* is usually used to express willingness, unwillingness, insistence and refusal.

4   After *wish* and *if only, would* can be used to complain about or criticise a person or situation.

   EXAMPLES:
   I wish it would stop raining. – It's raining at the moment and I want it to stop.
   If only my neighbour would be quiet. – She's making a lot of noise at the moment.
   I wish he would stop smoking. – The smoke is getting in my eyes.

   Is there anything bothering you at the moment? Write down a few examples using *would*.

5   *Wish* is often confused with *hope*.

   I hope I see you soon.
   I wish I could see you soon.

   Hope usually takes a present tense with a future meaning. When we use *hope* we usually don't know or can't tell the outcome, whereas with *wish* we do know the facts and they are the opposite of what we want.

   Decide on the correct alternative in the following sentences.

   a I hope / wish the rain stops soon.
   b I hope / wish you can come to my party.
   c I hope / wish I could speak Arabic.
   d I hope / wish Peter would finish writing his book.
   e I hope / wish I had remembered to bring the sleeping bags.

Corpus spot

Correct the errors that FCE candidates have made with *wish* and *hope* in these sentences from the *Cambridge Learner Corpus*.

   a I wish I win the trip!
   b I wish I can come back one day.
   c I wish I had know it two days ago.
   d I wish we can find some new form of energy.
   e I wish you agree with me.
   f I wish I would have more money.
   g If only he stopped smoking.
   h I hope the bus would come.

6 Here are some other expressions followed by the past tense.

a *as if / as though*
It wasn't like a smoke cloud, it was as if it were alive – it wasn't alive.
What is the difference between:
You talk as if / as though you were an expert on disasters!
You talk as if / as though you are an expert on disasters.

b *would rather*
This takes an infinitive without 'to' or a past tense.
I'd rather not tell you what really happened.
I'd rather you didn't ask me about the experience.
(Don't confuse *I'd rather* and *I'd better* (= *I had better*) – they mean different things.)

Say what you *would rather do* **in each situation.**

EXAMPLE: *Would you like to go camping?*
– I'd rather stay in a hotel.
– I'd rather we stayed in a hotel.

a Would you like to come with us for a pizza?
b Would you like to study engineering?
c Would you like to travel to the Moon?
d Would you like me to teach you Latin?
e Would you like me to buy you an iPod?

7 For the following questions, complete the second sentence so that it has a similar meaning to the first sentence, using the word given. **Do not change the word given.** You must use between two and five words, including the word given.

1 I regret not taking the park ranger's advice.
taken
I .... the park ranger's advice.
2 I think it's better for the children to stay inside in bad weather.
rather
I .... inside in bad weather.
3 What a pity we didn't see any wildlife on our trip.
only
If .... wildlife on our trip.
4 I don't like living in an earthquake zone.
wish
I .... somewhere else.
5 Don't walk so fast, I can't keep up with you!
wish
I .... walk so fast, I can't keep up with you!

6 I'd prefer you not to repeat what I've just told you.
rather
I .... repeat what I've just told you.

G ⋯⟶ page 207

Vocabulary

8 Liz and Dave had to 'unroll' their trousers to empty out the ash that had collected in them.

What sort of things do you:

a untie
b unbutton
c undo
d unwrap
e uncover
f unearth
g unfasten
h untangle
i unwind

EXAMPLE: *unzip – your trousers, a dress*

9 Fill in the missing letters for these weather words.

a The Mid-West states of the USA suffer from T _ _ _ _ D _ _ _.
b Last winter we had huge S _ _ _ D _ _ _ T S and had to dig our way out of the house.
c The meteorological office have issued a G _ _ _ W _ _ _ _ _ G to all shipping.
d The weather F _ _ _ C _ _ _ for tomorrow is quite good.
e The sky's a bit O _ _ _ _ _ _ T this morning.
f I got caught in a S _ _ _ _ _ and got soaked to the skin.
g H _ _ _ _ _ _ _ _ S are usually found in the Caribbean.
h Global warming has led to D R _ _ _ _ T conditions in parts of the world.
i Britain is famous for being D _ _ _, while parts of India are often H _ _ _ _.

Exam folder 12

Paper 1 Part 2 Gapped text

This part of the Reading paper requires you to read a text from which seven sentences have been removed, and then choose the correct sentences to fill in the gaps. There is always one extra sentence which you don't need.

Although there are fewer questions in this part than in Part 3, like Part 1, each question is 'double-weighted', that is, it is worth two marks instead of one. Part 2 is a difficult task and you must allow enough time for it.

Complete the exam task below using the steps in the Advice box. Try to keep to the suggested timings.

Advice

- Read the skeleton text quickly, in order to get an idea of what the text is about.   3 mins
- Underline key words in the text, to predict what a gap might contain. Look for linking and reference words too.   5 mins
- Scan the missing sentences for matching information and note down likely answers.   5 mins
- Read through the whole text with your answers in place, to check that it all makes sense.   3 mins
- Make sure that the extra sentence does not fit anywhere.   2 mins

You are going to read a magazine article about intelligence. Seven sentences have been removed from the article. Choose from the sentences A–H the one which fits each gap (1–7). There is one extra sentence which you do not need to use.

What makes intelligent?

The days when all you needed to make a living was sufficient physical strength to bring in the harvest are long gone. To survive today you need to be educated to rocket scientist level just to program a DVD recorder, make sense of a public transport timetable, or follow a complicated plot on TV. In short, what you have in your head has never been more important.

But what exactly is intelligence? Are there ways of getting smarter, or are you stuck with what you were born with? There aren't any easy answers. Despite the progress that has been made in genetics and psychology, human intelligence has remained one of the most controversial areas of modern science. `1`

Robert Plomin of the Institute of Psychiatry in London and his colleagues in the US have been looking into genetic make-up.

From their research, they have established that a slightly different gene is more common in those with a high IQ. Plomin analysed DNA from two groups of 51 children aged between six and 15. What he found was that the first group had an IQ of 136, putting them in the top 5% of the population, while the other group had an average IQ of 103. An analysis of their genes revealed that 32% of children in the higher group had the gene in question, while only 16% in the second group did.

`2`   He suggests that there are probably many genes that contribute to intelligence, rather than just one.

If you were born with a full set of intelligence-enhancing genes, then you'd expect to be very clever indeed. But just how important are genes in intelligence? Most of the early research depended on measuring the IQs of identical twins who had grown up separately. The argument was that if intelligence was 100% inherited, both twins would have the same IQ, no matter how different their backgrounds. `3`

someone

Since it is difficult to find many who have been separated at birth, recent studies have concentrated on adopted children instead. One does suggest that adopted children become increasingly like their biological parents as they get older.

In the past, the idea that intelligence is mainly inherited became an excuse for prejudice and discrimination. The concept of IQ itself was first developed a century ago by French psychologist Alfred Binet. [4] IQ measures something called general intelligence, testing word and number skills, as well as spatial ability.

Several studies have shown a strong link between IQ and career success, although some psychologists remain unconvinced about this. [5] 'The people with the highest IQs are not usually the ones who do best in their careers, but there's a big business out there with occupational psychologists offering all kinds of selection tests for companies. They won't go away because there's a lot of money to be made. But intelligence is not like temperature, and you cannot measure it in the same way. It's much more complicated than that.'

Many psychologists now believe that when it comes to intelligence, IQ isn't everything. Many alternative views have been put forward recently. [6] This offers a much broader view than the IQ theory, including creativity and communication skills as relevant factors in intelligence.

Tony Buzan, brain expert and author of *Master your Memory*, is enthusiastic about this belief, arguing that true geniuses do indeed appear to combine high levels of each type of intelligence. [7] At the same time, Buzan believes that everyone can develop their intelligence, if only they take the trouble to exercise their brain. Perhaps there's hope for us all!

A This may seem remote from everyday concerns, but does illustrate what the human brain is capable of.

B One example is the idea of 'multiple intelligences', which was developed in the 1980s by Harvard psychologist Howard Gardner.

C The tests were meant to select bright but socially-disadvantaged children, to ensure that they got a good education.

D Until now, that is, for the discovery of a gene linked to intelligence has made the experts think again.

E He lists Alexander the Great, Pablo Picasso and Albert Einstein as examples.

F Professor Michael Rowe, who has written a book called *Genius Explained*, is one of these.

G However, there is a lot more research to be done, and Plomin himself is cautious at this early stage.

H On the other hand, if differences in their IQs were found, this would point to background or environmental factors.

Priceless or worthless?

1 Discuss the two paintings and decide which one you like best and why. If you were very rich, would you spend any money on works of art? Do you have a favourite artist or sculptor? Describe in detail a work of art you admire.

2 Read this title and opening paragraph. Decide what you think the article is going to be about.

A New Genius?

The artist had some difficulty pointing out the features of his 3-metre-wide painting, which had just been sold for $19,000 to an adoring crowd at the opening night in Beverly Hills – perhaps because he is only 1 m 40 cms tall.

3 Now read through the whole article and answer the questions which follow.

THE ART WORLD'S LATEST CHILD PRODIGY, ten-year-old Beso Kazaishvili from the Republic of Georgia, looked resplendent in traditional costume: a belted cream wool tunic with sewn-in gunpowder tubes and a sinister curved dagger. He was 'very happy' about the sale but emphasised: 'Money is not everything.'
5

Beso has burst upon the art scene two years after the Romanian-born Alexandra Nechita was hailed as a genius at the age of ten. She has now made $10 million from her paintings. Her family has moved from a cramped bungalow by a Los Angeles freeway to a $1 million mansion. Alexandra began in California and made
10 a successful European tour. Beso began with some success in London, where his family stayed with the Georgian ambassador, and he is now touring the United States. His work is mostly in oils of human figures and faces, executed in a lively way in bright, sometimes almost garish, colours. Many tell stories with
15 symbolic themes of good and evil, death and time, and all are executed remarkably quickly. Ink drawings, which sold for £200 in London, are fetching up to $3,000 in Beverly Hills, where they are very highly thought of.

Beso and Alexandra are managed by the Californian art publisher
20 Ben Valenty. Beso has signed a contract in the 'mid-six figures'. Mr Valenty always takes half but pays all expenses. It is good money for both sides – Beso's sales hit $30,000 in an hour in the USA. Cynics like myself may question a second genius
25 arriving so soon, but Mr Valenty argues that there are probably half a dozen or more in the world. He adds: 'No sooner had I discovered Alexandra than parents from all over the world began sending me their kids' work. Yet none measured up to Beso, and I went to see him. Lightning can strike twice. Beso's work is deeper. After Alexandra the door is open. People believe a child's
30 art is worthy of serious consideration, so Beso won't meet the earlier scepticism. I believe he's a genius, and I'm prepared for the verdict of time.'

Mr Valenty and his colleague Rick Lombardo, a television producer preparing a documentary on child prodigies, cheerfully
35 admit that sales of the children's works are market driven. 'If Beso makes $19,000 in half an hour, it's because people want his work. Dozens of other youngsters haven't made that mark. Well, that's the market. Who knows what will happen next?'

Beso's parents, Badri an engineer, and Irma, a schoolteacher,
40 believe their son's work was influenced by Georgia's civil war of 1993–1995. They were often without water and electricity, and food was scarce. Short of money to buy paper, Beso made a drawing on the blank side of a card from his mother's stockings packet. 'That one is priceless and not for sale,' said Mr Valenty,
45 who acknowledges that Beso's 'story' helps sales. 'He's not like other kids,' Mr Lombardo says. 'He's structured. Sure, he'll watch television, play baseball, do his homework, but then start painting. He's never distracted from that. We're only just beginning to find out about these kids. Nobody studied **it** before.
50 Who knows what Picasso was like at 11? We don't know.'

1 Beso and Alexandra both
   A come from the same country in Europe.
   B are American citizens now.
   C paint similar kinds of pictures.
   D have an unusual gift.

2 What do we find out about Beso's painting?
   A He enjoys doing portraits.
   B He spends time getting the details right.
   C He prefers using subtle colours.
   D He uses ideas from famous fairytales.

3 What does Mr Valenty say about child artists?
   A He knows at least six possible geniuses at the moment.
   B He wants to meet as many as possible.
   C He believes that their work will be easier to sell in the future.
   D Their work improves as they get older.

4 What do you think 'measured up to' means in line 28?
   A had the same height
   B was the same standard
   C was the same age
   D had the same experience

5 What does Mr Valenty say about the money that Beso earns?
   A Beso could earn a lot more when he is older.
   B It's hard to put a price on Beso's works.
   C Beso only earns what people are prepared to pay.
   D It's crazy for people to pay so much for a child's work.

6 What do we find out about Beso from the article?
   A His only interest is painting.
   B He is a good student.
   C He is surprised that he is making so much money.
   D He loves being in the USA.

7 What does 'it' in line 50 refer to?
   A the subject of young artists
   B the particular style of painting
   C the way Picasso painted when young
   D how history can affect young people

8 How do you think the writer feels about Beso and his paintings?
   A He was impressed by how good the paintings are.
   B He isn't sure that Beso is really as good as Alexandra.
   C He's not convinced about child geniuses.
   D He thinks that money is Beso's real motive.

4 What do you think about Beso and his new career? Is it possible to put a price on a work of art?

Vocabulary *Collocations*

5 Look at this example from the article.

She has now <u>made $10 million</u> from her paintings.

The collocation is 'to make money'.
Can you match each verb in A with a word or phrase in B? Some are used more than once.

A	B
break	a conversation
sit	a promise
get	20 kilometres to the litre
spend	a look
taste	an expression
keep	still
have	a fortune
do	awake
wear	funny
	a secret
	a week
	a holiday
	better

6 🎧 You will hear people talking in three different situations. For questions 1–3, choose the best answer (A, B or C).

1 You overhear a conversation in a café. What does the woman say about seeing the Mona Lisa?
   A It hadn't been worthwhile.
   B She got to see some other good paintings too.
   C She went too early in the morning.

2 You overhear this man talking on the phone. What does he say about his choice of painting?
   A It makes his office look brighter.
   B It is appropriate for his position in the company.
   C It is worth more than the ones his colleagues have.

3 You overhear this woman speaking about the first night of an exhibition she recently attended. Why was the artist unhappy?
   A He hadn't sold enough paintings.
   B Few people attended the exhibition.
   C One of his favourite paintings had been bought.

24·2

Adverbs and word order

1 Read the following information about adverbs.

> Adverbs are usually formed by adding *-ly* to an adjective. However, some words ending in *-ly* are adjectives and have no adverb.
>
> *friendly, lonely, lovely, ugly, silly*
>
> If you want to use these words as adverbs you need to add 'in a … way'.
>
> > *He held out his hand in a friendly way.*
>
> • Some adverbs keep the same form as the adjective.
>   *She walks fast.*
>   *She is a fast walker.*
>   *He works hard.*
>   *He is a hard worker.*
> • Some adverbs have two forms, with a difference in meaning.
>   *She works hard.* (a great deal)
>   *She hardly does any work.* (almost no work)
>   *I came home late yesterday.* (not on time)
>   *Have you seen Peter lately?* (recently)

Adverb or adjective? Complete these sentences by using a word or phrase based on the word in capitals. Some sentences do not need to be changed.

a He seemed to be a very SILLY person.
b He drives quite GOOD for someone with so little experience.
c The gallery owner shook my hand FRIENDLY.
d I think Picasso painted GOOD pictures than Braque.
e Don't paint so FAST, you'll make a mess of it.
f Women painters were often GOOD than men, it's just they are less GOOD known.
g She draws CAREFUL than anyone else in the class.
h If you painted a little INTERESTING, people might buy more of your paintings.
i A painter's life can be very LONELY.
j Luckily my art teacher's drawing was BAD than mine.
k I've eaten HARD any dinner.
l Your hem isn't very STRAIGHT.

G ⋯⟫ page 207

2 Read the information about adverbs and word order.

| never   seldom   rarely   hardly   no sooner |

These adverbs can be put in the normal adverbial position. However, if they are put at the beginning of a sentence, the word order must be changed – this is called 'inversion'. This is because the subject and verb are 'inverted', that is, the word order is changed so that it looks like a question. It is done to give greater emphasis.

No sooner had I discovered Alexandra than parents all over the world began sending me their kids' work.

I had no sooner discovered Alexandra, than parents all over the world began sending me their kids' work.

Corpus spot

The *Cambridge Learner Corpus* shows that FCE candidates often have problems with adverbs and word order.

> I like Van Gogh very much.
> NOT ~~I like very much~~ Van Gogh.

Correct the mistakes that FCE candidates have made with word order in these sentences.

a I yesterday visited an art gallery in London.
b My mother goes often to the shops.
c Never I have seen a house like that.
d She drew quickly the cat.
e Zoos can be sometimes nice.
f Only I will be able to travel in July.
g Peter shook politely her hand.
h Always there is a queue for the cinema.
i He hardly can sleep at night.
j She hard works in an office.
k I never have been to Paris.

Vocabulary *Words often confused*

3 The article about Beso talked about a work of art being 'priceless'. This means that you can't buy it because it is so valuable: it has no price.
In the following sentences there are two words or phrases which are often confused by students. Decide which one is correct, then write another sentence to show how the other word or phrase is used.

a My sister spent so long talking on the phone every day that *at the end / in the end* my parents bought her a mobile phone.

b My next door neighbour's help has been *invaluable / priceless* while my mother was in hospital.

c You don't see many people smoking *nowadays / actually*.

d Prices of impressionist paintings have *raised / risen* a great deal in the last few years.

e *Lie / lay* down on the bed and have a rest.

f *Tell / say* me the story about how you met Monet.

g My mother is an excellent *cook / cooker*.

h The bank in town was *stolen / robbed* this morning.

i I *damaged / injured* the piano when I tried to move it.

j The watch I got for my birthday was very *priceless / valuable*.

k My friend was very *sympathetic / friendly* when I broke my arm.

l Jean is so *sensible / sensitive* that she cries whenever she watches a sad film.

4 Read the text below. Use the word given in capitals at the end of some of the lines to form a word that fits in the gap in the same line. There is an example at the beginning (0).

Example: 0 TALENTED

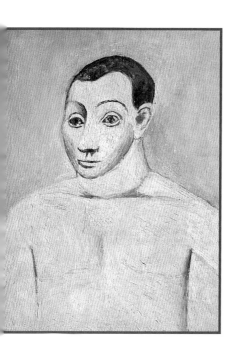

PABLO PICASSO

Pablo Picasso was born in Spain on October 25, 1881. He showed

himself to be a (0) .... artist as a child and when he was **TALENT**

19 he went to Paris to paint. He experimented with (1) .... styles, **DIFFER**

for a time painting sad subjects in shades of blue. During a

happier time, he used reds and pinks to paint more (2) .... **CHEER**

subjects such as dancers and (3) .... in circuses. **PERFORM**

   It did not take Picasso long to become (4) .... , but he was **SUCCEED**

constantly looking for new (5) .... He became interested in **INSPIRE**

African masks, particularly in the simple but very (6) .... way **EXPRESS**

 that they distorted the human face. He saw that it was possible

to build up an image using simple lines and angular shapes. This

was the beginning of cubism. Even though his cubist pictures are

(7) .... we still understand what they are meant to be about. **REALIST**

   In 1937 Picasso created one of his most (8) .... **FAME**

paintings – *Guernica*, a protest against an air raid on a

Basque village. In *Guernica*, Picasso used (9) .... forms that **SYMBOL**

are (10) .... found in his later works – things like a dying horse **REPEAT**

or weeping woman. *Guernica* now hangs in the Prado Museum.

Writing folder 12

Articles 2

In Part 2 of Paper 2 you might be asked to write a description of a place, a person or an object as part of the task.

1   Look at this exam question.

You see this notice in an international arts magazine and decide to write to them.

Write your **article**.

Look carefully at this painting and then read through a student's answer to the question.

My favourite painting is of a woman, a servant in a large house and it was painted about 1660 in Holland by Vermeer Van Delft. The young woman is a cook and is quite tall and I'd say fairly strong, probably as a result of having to carry heavy objects from an early age. I would say she is about 18 or 19 years old. She's wearing a white cap or scarf, which completely covers her hair, a yellow blouse, which buttons at the front, a blue apron and an orange floor-length skirt. This painting gives you a good idea of what ordinary working women wore in the seventeenth century.

The girl seems fairly happy and is concentrating very hard on what she is doing. I think she probably enjoys her job and her life, even though it is likely to be quite hard. Perhaps she already knows who her husband will be and is looking forward to getting married – the only option open to a young girl in those days. I find this an interesting painting because it isn't of someone rich or famous, but of an ordinary person going about her daily tasks. Although she isn't dressed in silks and lace she is, in her own way, rather beautiful.

Now think about what information the answer has given you about the cook and her life. Which of these titles would be best for this article?

A
Everyday life in the seventeenth century

B
A painting is as good as a photograph

C
Bringing the past to life

2 Look again at the painting of the cook and complete this short paragraph which describes the room she is in. Join the words together – you must keep them in the same order. You may need to add some words.

EXAMPLE: *The room she / probably / kitchen / house. The room she is standing in is probably the kitchen of the house.*

The walls / bare / painted white. There / window / wall / basket / hanging / it. the window / there / table / basket / bread, / bowl / milk, / cakes. Jug / milk / bowl / make / brown pottery. There / blue and white tiles / wall / joins / floor. floor / box / containing / pot / handle.

3 Look at this exam question.

You see this competition in an international nature and science magazine and decide to enter it.

EARTH MATTERS MAGAZINE
❋ **Have you ever been caught in severe weather conditions?**
❋ **Write and tell us where you were and what you did.**
We will print the six best articles we receive and the writers will get a year's subscription to the magazine.

Write your **article.**

4 How many synonyms can you think of for the following words? Use your dictionary to help you.

a big	**e** hot	**i** pretty
b small	**f** cold	**j** bad
c rich	**g** fat	
d poor	**h** thin	

Advice
- Make a plan – Remember there are two parts to this question.
- Think of a title.
- Use your own experience, or what you have read or seen on TV or heard about.
- Think about what kind of person reads the magazine.
- Try not to repeat yourself, especially when you use adjectives.

Units 19–24 Revision

Topic review

1 Answer these questions, giving your own opinions.

a What should someone do to lose weight?

b When should you tell someone it's time for them to leave a party?

c Even if someone has committed a crime, is prison the best form of punishment?

d Would you rather spend your money on entertainment or clothes?

e Is there a luxury you regret not having?

f Do you ever wish you were famous?

g What do you hope to do after you have passed FCE?

h What would you do if you were stranded in a storm?

i How often do you go to art exhibitions?

j Are modern painters and sculptors exceptionally talented professionals or totally worthless con artists?

Vocabulary

2 Read the statements or questions and choose the best option, A, B or C.

1 You have been out in the wind and your hair looks a mess. Should you
 A untie it? **B** unwind it? **C** untangle it?

2 If you give away your friend's secret even though you agreed not to, have you
 A broken a promise? **B** kept your word?
 C spent a fortune?

3 Which performer would you not see at a classical recital?
 A a violinist **B** a cellist **C** a bass guitarist

4 You are driving in torrential rain and a tree falls across the road 200 metres in front of you. Are you in danger of being
 A cut down? **B** cut off? **C** cut out?

5 While a photograph is being taken of you, should you keep
 A quiet? **B** calm? **C** still?

6 If you have a steady income but enjoy paying everyone's expenses, are you likely to be
 A tight? **B** broke? **C** loaded?

7 What should you do about a large debt?
 A pay it off **B** break it off **C** call it off

8 It's about time you found a glass of water. Are you
 A fainting? **B** hiccuping? **C** sneezing?

3 The twenty words below have all appeared in Units 19–24. Decide what they are with the help of the information given and then use one from each set to complete the sentences a–e.

- two verbs to do with illness or injury:
 1 S P _ A _ _
 2 C _ _ _ H

- three words to do with volcanoes:
 3 E _ U _ _
 4 _ _ H
 5 L _ _ _

- four musical instruments:
 6 O _ _ _
 7 _ I _ _ O
 8 _ U I _ _ _
 9 _ L _ _ E

- five serious crimes:
 10 _ _ P _
 11 F _ _ _ D
 12 _ _ G G _ _ _
 13 _ _ S _ _
 14 _ I J _ _ K _ _ _

- six adjectives to describe works of art:
 15 W _ _ _ H _ E _ S
 16 _ X _ _ _ S _ I V _
 17 _ R _ C _ _ _ _ S
 18 _ _ L _ _ B L _
 19 G _ _ I S H
 20 S Y _ _ O _ _ C

a She picked up the shiny silver .... and began to play her favourite piece.

b A flow of .... that is one metre thick would probably take more than two days to cool and become solid.

c If only that painting weren't so .... ! I would rather look at softer colours.

d It is very easy to .... your ankle when running to the back of the court for a difficult ball.

e Firemen found a half-full can of petrol near the incident, so .... seemed a certainty.

Grammar

4 Read the text below and think of the word which best fits each gap. Use only one word in each gap. There is an example at the beginning (0).

How to make a small fortune

Have you ever wished you had some savings to fall back (0) ....on..........? Perhaps you already have something put aside for a rainy day, but if (1) ...., here are some unusual ways to make a pile (2) .... cash. Look critically at your old toys. Very (3) .... remain in a condition that is good (4) .... for them to be sold, (5) .... that a pre-1950, well-looked-after teddy bear can be worth (6) .... to £2,000. Musical instruments can also raise (7) .... large sum, sometimes unexpectedly. Hazel Morgan hadn't played her violin for more (8) .... forty years, so she decided to sell (9) .... To her surprise, the violin itself was valued (10) .... £2,500 and the bow, despite (11) .... in bad condition, was expected to fetch even more. Fine wines can also be highly profitable, and even (12) .... your investment doesn't prove as big an earner as you hoped, you can still enjoy drinking the wine!

Urban decay, suburban hell

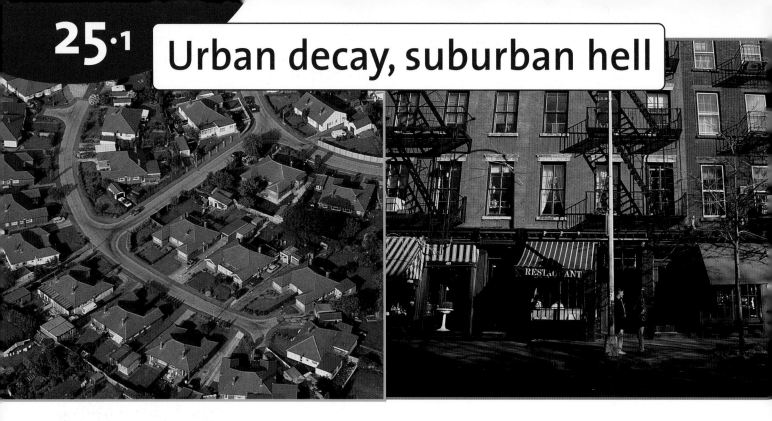

1 Compare and contrast these two pictures, and talk about the advantages and disadvantages of living in each city area. You can use some of the words below to help you.

Neighbourhood:
peaceful, quiet, calm/noisy, polluted, dangerous deprived, derelict, run-down/regenerated, improved

Buildings:
low-rise/high-rise spacious/cramped

Amenities:
entertainment centre, multiplex cinema, mall, pedestrian/shopping precinct, out-of-town shopping

Services:
litter/refuse collection, maintenance, street-lighting

Transport:
congestion, traffic jam, parking restrictions

Listening

2 🎧 You will hear an extract from a radio programme called *Challenge the expert*. Listen to the introduction to decide what profession the expert is in.

3 🎧 Read the sentences below before you listen, to predict what you might hear. Then listen and complete the sentences.

Julia explains that some 1960s architecture came about because of
[1] .

Today, [2] regulations are stricter than they were in the past.

Julia used to live in a [3] as a child, in a poor part of Bristol.

The [4] used for new buildings have improved since the 1960s.

Julia mentions [5] as an example of an environmental requirement for new buildings in Britain.

When explaining what she sees as a problem today, Julia refers to the [6] as 'urban sprawl'.

Some city centre shops have shut because of [7] facilities.

Julia believes that architects should design [8] for city centres.

In a multi-use building, there might be [9] downstairs.

People are unhappy about damage to their health caused by [10] in cities.

4 🎧 Compare your answers with another student. Then listen again to check.

5 🎧 These words with *up* all occurred in the recording. Match them to 1–5. Do you know any other words with *up*-?

a	uprooted	1	maintenance
b	upheld	2	expensive
c	upkeep	3	made to leave
d	upmarket	4	advantage
e	upside	5	supported

6 Explain what you think each speaker meant by the following statements. Do you agree with them?

a Lack of consultation over new buildings is rarely an issue with the public.

b City expansion isn't very good news for the countryside either.

c What I believe in is the regeneration of our city centres.

d Living in the city has to become a healthier and more acceptable option.

Speaking

Exam spot

Turn-taking skills are important, especially in Part 4 of the Speaking Test, where there is a three-way discussion involving both candidates and the examiner. This Part lasts 4 minutes and each candidate needs to have adequate opportunities to speak, which means being sensitive to the other people in the conversation.

7 Say whether the purpose of these turn-taking expressions is

i   to involve someone in the discussion
ii   to encourage someone to be quiet
iii to support what someone is saying

a You clearly know a lot about this, but let's move on.

b Would you say that this is true in your case?

c I believe your own view is slightly different?

d Come on, you're talking rubbish!

e Well, I have to admit you have a point.

f I'm going to say something here.

g What do you think?

h Absolutely, I couldn't agree more.

Do you consider any of these rude or offensive? In what other ways can a speaker or listener direct a conversation?

8 Now practise these turn-taking skills. Get into groups of four to discuss the following statements. For each statement, one person in the group should stay silent and time how long each of the others speaks for.

- There are both good and bad examples of modern architecture.
- Living conditions in our cities have got worse.
- City centres should be traffic-free.
- Urban sprawl is a serious threat to nature.

Mixed conditionals

1 Look at these two quotes from the recording in 25.1, which are examples of mixed conditionals. Explain what tenses are used and why.

If we were meant to live up in the sky, we would have been born with wings!
If 60s architecture hadn't happened, we would be making similar mistakes today.

In both examples, the second and third conditional forms are mixed.

2 You can use a mixed conditional to talk about a past action affecting a present situation, as in the second example above. Finish these mixed conditional sentences in a suitable way.

EXAMPLE: If we had bought that house, we
would be short of money now.

a If people hadn't objected to the plans, the building …
b If Tom had remembered to book a table at the restaurant, we …
c If I hadn't seen that programme, I …
d If we had set off earlier, we …
e If she hadn't answered the advert, she …

3 You can also use mixed conditionals to talk about how a different present situation would have affected a past situation, as in this example:

If the city centre was traffic-free, the council wouldn't have needed to build all these car parks.

Finish these sentences in a similar way, using the ideas in brackets.

a If high-rise buildings were of better quality, more people (choose to live in them in the first place)
b If there weren't so many distractions, you (tidy up your bedroom by now)
c If the suburbs were smaller, local taxes (be so high for the last 20 years)
d If the supermarket was open 24 hours, I (go out at 3 am this morning to buy you some paracetamol)

G···❯ page 207

4 Imagine a city with no advantages to it whatsoever. Discuss the impact of these problems.

- no refuse collection
- no shops
- no bus service
- no police

EXAMPLE: *If there was no refuse collection service, rubbish would pile up on the streets and there might be rats.*

5 Read the article about the architect Sir Norman Foster. For questions 1–12, decide which answer, A, B, C or D, best fits each space. There is an example at the beginning (0).

Example:

0 **A** chose   **B** fixed   **C** dealt   **D** wished

| 0 | <u>A</u> | B | C | D |

The grand designer

When asked to select his favourite building, Sir Norman Foster (0) ..... a Jumbo jet. His own buildings frequently (1) ..... materials and technology developed by the aerospace industry. Perhaps his most (2) ..... building is the Hongkong and Shanghai Bank, a massive construction of three linked towers 41 (3) ..... high. His most ambitious European (4) ..... has been the reconstruction of the Reichstag as the new German parliament building. He has also built a metro (5) ..... in Bilbao, and two space-age communications towers in Barcelona and Santiago de Compostela.

Foster (6) ..... in the vertical city, an architect's dream that began a hundred years ago and is still (7) ..... to be fully realised. He says that the city is in a continuous process of renewal; if buildings cannot (8) ..... to social or technological change, then unless they are outstanding, they should be replaced. It's all about (9) ..... the past and the future.

One of Foster's recent (10) ..... has been to re-design part of a famous London landmark, Trafalgar Square. Aiming to (11) ..... pollution and improve safety by re-routing traffic away from the north side of the square, he has created an impressive pedestrian (12) ..... in front of the National Gallery and transformed Trafalgar Square into a truly grand urban space.

полуграм

1	**A** lend	**B** fetch	**C** borrow	**D** bring
2	**A** famous	**B** known	**C** understood	**D** common
3	**A** flights	**B** levels	**C** storeys	**D** stages
4	**A** activity	**B** project	**C** occupation	**D** post
5	**A** method	**B** plan	**C** routine	**D** system
6	**A** believes	**B** hopes	**C** relies	**D** depends
7	**A** standing	**B** expecting	**C** waiting	**D** resting
8	**A** alter *изменить*	**B** adap	**C** fit *оденибать*	**D** match
9	**A** steadying	**B** settling	**C** estimating	**D** balancing
10	**A** trials	**B** challenges	**C** questions	**D** attempts
11	**A** reduce	**B** shorten	**C** dilute *разбав лять*	**D** lower
12	**A** site	**B** district	**C** region	**D** area

6 There are a number of words containing the prefix *re-* in the article, such as *renewal* and *re-routing*. Make new words from the ones below, using the same prefix. Sometimes, words with different parts of speech can be made. Use some of the words to complete sentences a–d.

consider	construct	generate
open	possess	write

a The old industrial city of Duisberg has been .... and now has new, cleaner industries right in its centre, alongside schools and housing.

b Following extensive fire damage, the timber framed buildings have now been fully .... in their original style.

c The city council's .... of the enquiry into noise pollution has been supported by local residents.

d Anyone who has left the city for the suburbs should .... their move, particularly in the light of how far rents have fallen in the centre.

Exam folder 13

Paper 1 Part 3 Multiple matching

This part of the Reading paper focuses on your ability to retrieve specific information from a text.
You are given 15 questions and you must find the answers either in a group of texts or in one
which has been divided into sections.

Advice

- Look at the title and any information you are
  given about the text or texts. Skim the texts very
  quickly to find out what they are about. Do not
  worry about vocabulary that you aren't familiar
  with. For this particular passage see how quickly
  you can find out what Raquel, David, Martin
  and Dick do for a living.
- Read through the questions carefully.
- You are looking for specific information to
  answer the questions, so you need to scan the
  texts rather than read them in detail.
- When you find the answer in a text, underline
  it and put the question number next to it (a
  highlighting pen is quite useful for this).
- Don't spend too much time looking for the
  answer to a question. Leave it until the end and
  go on to the next question.
- When you've finished the easy questions, go back
  and have another go at the difficult ones.
  If you still don't know – guess. Never leave a
  blank on your answer sheet.
- If there are more than four texts, you sometimes
  have more than one answer to find to a question.
  When this happens you can answer in any order.

Many of the questions ask you to locate words and
phrases that mean the same as the ones used in the
question. Sometimes more than one person talks about
the same subject, and you need to decide which one
really answers the question.

Now read the exam question. If you need any help,
look at these clues:

1 The key word here is 'important'. Remember that as
   you look through the texts.
2 What examples of modern technology can you
   think of? Now the phrase is 'working with' which
   narrows down the text.
3 Two texts talk about money. What sort of words do
   they use? Which one talks of 'a drop'?
4 What do you think 'at a moment's notice' means?
5 All of the people in the texts have done other jobs
   before. However, only one person did two jobs 'at
   the same time'. Which one?
6 Another way of saying 'has a good relationship
   with'?
7 Find a phrasal verb that means 'freedom of choice'.
8 What does an 'aspect' mean here?
9 Are you an early riser?
10 In a play a 'role' means a 'part'. Here it means a 'job'.
11 Look back at Unit 5 if you don't know what
   'claustrophobia' means.
12 Key word is 'hard'.
13 If you don't plan, then something happens by …
14 'Assistance' means …?
15 You need to find the word that means 'boring' in
   the text.

You are going to read a magazine article about people who have dream jobs. For questions **1–15**, choose from the people (**A–D**). The people may be chosen more than once.

Which person

says their job was more important than it appears?	1
dislikes working with modern technology?	2
took a drop in salary in order to do the job?	3
often has to travel at a moment's notice?	4
used to do two jobs simultaneously?	5
has a good relationship with their employer?	6
says they believe in freedom of choice?	7
doesn't enjoy one aspect of the job?	8

says they aren't an early riser?	9
now has another role to play?	10
suffers from claustrophobia?	11
finds their job hard?	12
didn't plan to do this job?	13
needs assistance with their work?	14
has to do some very boring duties?	15

It's a tough job?

Chris Arnow asks people with dream jobs if they're as wonderful as they seem.

A Raquel Graham

Raquel Graham rings from the taxi taking her to the airport. She can't make our appointment tomorrow because her boss wants her to be in Los Angeles instead. When you're personal assistant to a pop star, you're expected to jet around the world at the drop of a hat. Raquel loves her job and gets on well with her boss.

There's just one minor problem – she can't stand flying. 'On a nine-hour trip to California I usually take sleeping tablets to help calm me down,' she admits. Her worst experience was being on Concorde. 'It seemed so shut in with those tiny windows.'

Offices in Manchester and London occupy her when she comes down to earth. There's some mundane paper work to get through – organising the diary, sitting in on meetings with solicitors and accountants, sorting out itineraries and making yet more travel arrangements.

She didn't train for the job. A chance meeting with the manager of a pop group led to the offer of work behind the scenes. Five years later she was in the right place at the right time when her boss needed a PA.

B David Brown

David Brown has been an accountant and a golf caddy, a man who carries a golfer's bags. On the whole, he preferred the golf. Well, so would you if golf was your passion. There were drawbacks however. A small flat fee is on offer, plus a percentage of the winnings. The average earnings are between £25,000 and £35,000 and much of that will go on travel and hotels.

He was 31 when he first caddied for the golfer, Greg Norman. 'You're not just carrying bags. You're offering advice, pitting your knowledge against the elements and trying to read the course.'

His accountancy skills were recently recognised by European Tour Productions when they made him statistical data administrator. From cards brought in by the caddies, he compiles and analyses the statistics of each day's play. The results are sought after by television commentators, golfing magazines, and the golfers themselves.

C Martin Fern

Martin Fern is the editor of the 'Food and Drink' pages of a daily newspaper and one of his less difficult tasks is to sample what's on offer in the finest restaurants. What does he think about restaurants that charge exorbitant prices? 'For those who can afford it, it's up to them,' he says. 'I'd rather spend £120 on a meal I'll remember for the rest of my life than buy a microwave.'

It was his talent as a cook that led to the offer of a food column from a friend who happened to edit a Saturday Review. For Martin, at the time creative director of an advertising agency, it was a useful secondary income. He was 42 when another newspaper rang to offer a full-time job. 'It meant a 50 per cent cut in guaranteed income,' he says. 'But it was a chance to convert my passion into a profession.'

He still does all the cooking at home and tries to keep his waistline under control by cycling a couple of miles to the nearest tube station.

D Dick Prince

'I started writing children's stories about twenty years ago,' says Dick Prince, one of Britain's most popular children's writers. 'Before that, I had always loved words and enjoyed using them, but my writing had mainly been verse. Then I had this idea for a story. I had been a farmer, and knew the problem of chickens being killed by a fox. So I wrote a kind of role reversal story called The Fox Busters, which became my first published children's story.'

Where do his ideas come from? 'Well, it's not easy, I have to work at them,' he says. 'That is what I usually do in the mornings. I'm not up with the dawn, I'm afraid. After lunch, I spend another couple of hours typing out the morning's scribbling – all of which I do with one finger on an old portable typewriter rather than on one of those awful word processors.

I get between fifty and a hundred letters a week and that is the part about being a writer that I enjoy the most. I do try to answer them all, but nowadays I have some secretarial help.'

Getting around

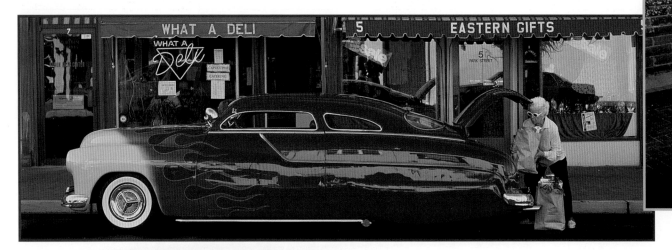

1   How important is the car to you? Could you live without one? Describe the role of the car in your way of life.

2   🎧 Listen to these short extracts, where five different people give their opinions on this subject.

Which speaker
- finds it necessary to use the car every day?
- would prefer not to travel by car at all?
- claims to be a car enthusiast?

3   You are going to read a magazine article where four people talk about driving. For questions 1–15, choose from the people (A–D). The people may be chosen more than once.

Which person

chose a car that disappointed a family member?	1
couldn't really afford their chosen car?	2
enjoys driving while listening to music?	3
has never bought their own car?	4
used to imagine driving somewhere fast at night?	5
spends a lot of money on petrol?	6
had to consider the size of the car before buying it?	7
qualified as a car driver in order to compete?	8
complains about their car?	9
had an accident in their car?	10
gives someone close to them a regular lift?	11
remembers one night-time occasion that was special?	12
knows a lot of information about certain cars?	13
gets positive comments from other road users?	14
would like to drive something different?	15

A   I dreamt about having the car I drive now when I was at school and almost ruined myself financially to buy it! When I first got it, it had a really loud sound system, and I reversed into a brand-new car because I couldn't hear the horn beeping at me to stop. It has lots of speakers and there's nothing better than driving through the city with all my favourite tunes blasting out. My best moment was when I was at the Glastonbury pop festival and drove it up the hill there after dark. The whole of the site below was blinking with lights and it was a fantastic moment. On the downside, it isn't comfortable on long journeys, and it drinks fuel like a fish. I've got a pair of tiny red, black and green boxing gloves hanging from the mirror. Now that I'm a father, pressure has been put on me to get rid of it. I won't go that far but I do have a Punto now, as the family car.

B   As a child, I used to love memorising facts and few delighted me as much as those about cars. I can still produce all sorts of trivia about 0-60 acceleration times, top speeds, and the engine sizes of all the fastest and most exciting cars. I'm very fond of car magazines because of that and I go through as many as I can get my hands on! Whenever I visit Britain, I pick some up and enjoy the deliciously technical writing and wonderful shots of car interiors – all those dials! If I couldn't get to sleep as a teenager, I'd pretend to be doing a long journey in the dark in an open-top sports car. But do you know what I currently drive? A VW estate with a small engine. It won't do; I must change my life.

устойчивый, поддерживаемый

4 How <u>sustainable</u> is it for people to have their own cars? Should private road users pay more for using the roads than they currently do? Why? / Why not?

C I haven't always had four wheels and, in fact, I only learned to drive a car three years ago. I passed my test quite quickly after that and was lucky enough to be given my car – a Mazda sports – as a present. It's very <u>quick off the mark</u>. I really switched to cars instead of bikes in order to join Formula Women, an organisation that's been set up to encourage more women to go into racing. I love the challenge of it all and I know my biking days have helped me to find the best racing line on the track. I've been doing really well recently. Dad comes to all my races and likes to <u>get the crowd behind me</u>! Mum used to worry about the danger involved but she's okay about it now, and she thinks I'm a good road user. Once a week I come and collect her in the Mazda and we go off to do the out-of-town shopping bit together.

D My mum was almost in tears when I said I was going to buy the Mini. I'd previously owned an open-top Audi, which she loved being driven around in, but I felt it was time to downsize. I must admit I felt some sadness, knowing I wouldn't be able to drive with the wind whipping through my hair. But I soon <u>got attached</u> to the Mini. When I went for a test drive in one to see if it was really suitable, I realised that they are actually very roomy. Even my husband can fit in it and he's incredibly tall. It's faster than you'd think and I've already received three points on my licence for speeding, unfortunately. Everyone seems to have a great affection for Minis. Drivers always nod and some even start chatting about the car when I'm stopped at traffic lights. My favourite journey is driving home each evening during spring and autumn just as the light starts to fade.

Vocabulary *get*

5 Each of the articles about cars contains a phrase with *get*. Underline them and match them to their meanings, choosing from a–h. Then think of other phrases with *get* for the remaining meanings.

a escape from a routine
b win support for   *c*
c communicate something
d become fond of   *d*
e obtain something   *B*
f sell something unwanted   *A*
g make no progress
h hurry up

Grammar extra

Look at these examples.

Nowhere is increasing traffic more noticeable than in the countryside.

Not only did Matt fail to notice he was speeding, he also went through a red light!

What is the reason for starting sentences like this?
Rewrite the following sentences in the same way, using the words in bold first and paying attention to word order. In examples *c* and *f*, you have to add an extra word.

a There has **not only** been a huge increase in the number of private cars on the roads – more goods are now transported by lorry too.
b We can **no longer** depend on the unlimited use of our cars.
c Brendan **not only** rides a bike to work – he also uses it to travel longer distances.
d The government should **in no way** weaken its transport policy.
e Members of the public are **seldom** willing to walk to work, especially if it's raining.
f Cars **not only** pollute the air but they endanger people's lives too.

Relative pronouns

1 First, reread the notes in the Grammar folder for Unit 17, which dealt with relative clauses.

Now look at the sentences 1–4 opposite and answer questions a and b about each one.

a Is the information introduced by the relative pronoun essential or additional?
b What does the relative pronoun refer to?

Which of these relative pronouns does not always refer to people?

1 Richard Simmons, who is chairman of the Commission, summarises the current position.
2 Visitors who come to the countryside to get away from it all are unpleasantly surprised.
3 It is essential that the people for whom the plans are being developed are fully involved.
4 Nowhere is increasing traffic more noticeable than in the countryside, whose pure air and green fields are now seriously under threat.

who or *whom*?

2 In informal English, it is always safe to use *who* as both subject and object. However, in formal written English, *whom* is the object form, often used with a preposition, as in the example in 1.

Rewrite the following sentences using *whom*, adding commas where necessary and making any other changes.

EXAMPLE: The man they had given all their money to took a one-way flight to Rio.

The man to *whom they had given all their money took a one-way flight to Rio.*

a I went with Wetherby on several expeditions and he was always the perfect gentleman.
Wetherby, with ....
b The ranchers that cowboys worked for expected them to spend at least 12 hours a day on horseback.
The ranchers for ....
c The ancient Greeks believed in Apollo, who was supposed to ride a chariot of flame across the sky.
Apollo, in ....
d Rollerblading is seen as a quick way of getting around and teenagers often take unnecessary risks in traffic.
Teenagers, to ....

whose

3 You use the relative pronoun *whose* to talk about something belonging to a person or thing, as in the example from the article.

How many different means of transport do you know of? Identify what is being described in a–g, selecting the appropriate picture and giving the English word.

EXAMPLE: *A fast boat whose fins enable it to travel above the surface of the water.* (1) hydrofoil

a A type of aircraft whose large blades rotate to allow it to hover in the air. ....
b A four-legged animal whose back has one or two humps. ....
c A narrow boat, usually for one person, whose hull is made of fibreglass or wood. ....
d A large vehicle whose skirts inflate to allow it to travel across land or water. ....
e A type of ship whose main purpose is to move secretly underwater. ....
f A bicycle whose twin seats allow two people to ride it. ....
g A South American animal whose hair is very thick. ....

4 Join the two sentences in a–f, using *whose*.

EXAMPLE: *Johnson is going to sail around the world alone. His yacht is sponsored by a leading British firm.*

Johnson, whose yacht is sponsored by a leading British firm, is going to sail around the world alone.

a The Regent's Canal in London runs between Camden and Islington. Its towpath is increasingly used by cyclists.

b This new jetski has a top speed of over 100 kph. Its seating accommodates four people easily.

c The hot air balloon was designed by the Montgolfier brothers. Its first flight was made in 1783.

d From 1983 to 1987, the number of cars and trucks in the United States increased by 20.1 million. The population in that period grew by only 9.2 million.

e The Brox, a new four-wheel cycle trailer, is being trialled by the Royal Mail. It has seven gears to allow it to go up hills, and even steps, easily.

f The American space shuttle can be used again and again. It has heat-proof tiles to allow it to re-enter the earth's atmosphere safely.

G ⋯⋗ page 207

5 Below are several words for parts of different means of transport. Put them into the correct columns. Sometimes, words can go into more than one column. Explain why.

bonnet   boot   brake   cab   cabin
dashboard   exhaust   flap   funnel   gearbox
hull   indicator   jet engine   mast   oar
paddle   porthole   propeller   radiator   rudder
steering wheel   tyre   undercarriage   windscreen

Cars, trucks	Boats, ships	Aircraft

6 Now use *whose* to describe problems with some of these things, choosing a suitable adjective from the ones below.

bent   broken   faulty   flat
jammed   missing   stuck

The canoe, whose paddle was bent, was difficult to steer.

7 For questions 1–12, read the article below and think of the word which best fits each gap. Use only one word in each gap. There is an example at the beginning (0).

RECORD-BREAKING CYCLIST

Forty-four years on the road and over half a million kilometres have given Heinz Stücke (0) .....a..... philosophical outlook on life. Within hours of getting off the ferry from France in Portsmouth on Monday night, the bicycle (1) .... has been his constant companion since 1962 was stolen. But he's not bitter. 'I trust everybody,' he says, 'because (2) .... you didn't, you just wouldn't go around the world.' In fact, his bike was returned to him little (3) .... than 36 hours after the theft. After the media attention it received, the thief (4) .... have realised that this was (5) .... ordinary bike and would be too (6) .... trouble.

It all started in the small town of Hövelhof in Germany, in the late 1950s, (7) .... Heinz was a metal work apprentice. 'I hated it,' he remembers. 'I was 14 and getting up at 5.40 (8) .... morning to catch the train to work.' He started planning a journey by bike around the world and, once he was 20, finally got (9) .... from it all. But did he ever imagine (10) .... a young man that he would still be (11) .... the road at the age of 66? Maybe not, but then Heinz, (12) .... epic journey has put him into the *Guinness Book of Records*, is truly special.

Writing folder 13

Essays 2

See also Writing folder 4, Essays 1, which dealt with organisation and linkers.

1 The essay below is a poor attempt! Read it and try to decide which statement it addresses: A, B or C.

   A Not enough is being done to encourage people to leave their cars at home.
   B Cycling is a cheap and enjoyable alternative to the car.
   C Traffic congestion threatens our health and the government must develop new policies urgently.

Advice

- Answer the question – do not wander off the topic.
- Write in paragraphs – start a new one every time you go on to a different idea.
- Use suitable linkers – but do not overuse them!
- Present a balanced argument, if the question asks for this, but make sure that your own opinion is stated.
- Write in a consistently neutral or formal style.

There is a lot of truth in this statement. Nowadays there are more and more cars on the roads, causing traffic congestion in city centres and outside, too. This clearly endangers our health. If we're driving, the stress of waiting in a traffic jam is, oh god, unbearable. As walkers or cyclists we're put at risk by motorists, whose only concern is to get where they want to be fast. I think cycling is healthier because you have to make an effort and it's exercise. It is less expensive, because you don't have to buy petrol or pay for many repairs. A car, on the other hand, goes wrong and as I don't understand how it works, mine has to be fixed at the garage. Although I don't have one myself, I think it would be fun to use, why not, and it might be quicker than the car. You can choose different routes that avoid the main roads and follow beautiful places, like canals or rivers. Yes, it is definitely better than driving.

2 The five points in the Advice section are important to remember when writing an essay. Has the writer done any of them? Underline the parts of the essay that could be improved.

3 Here are some useful neutral phrases, which could be used in an essay.

The key to solving/reducing/dealing with … is …
One of the biggest questions/challenges/problems in the short-term will be …
It is essential/vital/important that …

Which of the following ideas (a–j) would be relevant as part of an answer to statement A in exercise 1? Expand these ideas using one of the three phrases above, and including a reason.

a tax motorists more
b improve public transport
c give cyclists free helmets
d restrict parking in cities
e build more motorways
f set lower speed limits
g put up petrol prices
h ban car advertising
i develop solar-powered cars
j issue driving permits for use on certain days

EXAMPLE: *It is essential that motorists are taxed more, so that their cars become a less attractive option.*

4 Statement C includes a time indicator, *urgently*. There is often some reference to time in an essay task.

Some of the phrases below are used in jumbled sentences a–c. Reorder these sentences, adding commas where necessary.

> in the short-term/medium-term/long-term
> within the next five years/our lifetime
> urgent/ immediate/instant action
> of major importance/high priority/the utmost urgency

EXAMPLE: *which cannot be justified / take urgent action / the government should / to cancel new road-building*
The government should take urgent action to cancel new road-building, which cannot be justified.

a whose exhaust fumes / is the introduction of tighter laws / cause greater pollution / on older vehicles / of high priority
b to consult the public / in the short-term / whose concerns have never been fully aired / it is essential
c is needed / while in the medium-term / to reduce the volume of cars / instant action / in our cities / alternative forms of transport / further research should be done on

5 Now answer this exam question, in 120–180 words.

You have had a class discussion on transport. Now your teacher has asked you to write an essay, giving your opinion on the following statement.

The key to solving traffic problems is a better public transport system.

Write your **essay**.

Material girl

Listening

1 🎧 Before you listen write down everything you know about Madonna and share the information with the rest of the class.

Now listen to a student journalist called Jonas Day being interviewed about Madonna. As you listen, make notes about Madonna on the following:

> Born:
> Place:
> Family:
> Education:

2 🎧 Listen again. Write down the word or phrase which the speakers use when they are:

taking charge of the conversation
correcting some information
changing subject
apologising
partly agreeing
making a generalisation
giving some information which may not be reliable
thinking
explaining

3 Work with a partner for this activity. Try to use some of the words and phrases you heard in the interview.

One of you is A and the other B. B chooses a famous person and A then interviews B to find out more information about the person B has chosen. When you run out of things to say, swap roles.

EXAMPLE:
Student A: *So, William Shakespeare, I believe you were born in London?*
Student B: *Actually in a place called Stratford-upon-Avon.*
Student A: *Okay, right, now can you tell me a little bit about your career?*

4 🎧 Listen to the rest of the interview with Jonas about his article on Madonna.

For questions 1–7, choose the best answer (A, B or C).

1 One surprising thing about Madonna is that she
  A prefers making records to films.
  B has extensive business interests.
  C is unconcerned about media attention.

2 How did Madonna get into the pop music business?
  A She worked in New York clubs.
  B She wrote to record producers.
  C She found out about the people in control.

3 She wanted to have Michael Jackson's manager because
  A he only looked after one pop star.
  B she admired what he'd done for Michael Jackson.
  C she wanted to be more famous than Michael Jackson.

4 According to Jonas, Madonna's main quality is her
  A cleverness.   B ability.   C persistence.

5 What does Jonas say about Madonna's acting career?
   A It has been disappointing so far.
   B It has been more profitable than singing.
   C She has upset too many people for it to succeed.

6 Jonas says that in the nineties Madonna
   A had better luck with her films than her records.
   B preferred singing with other people.
   C tried to widen her business interests.

7 Jonas thinks Madonna will succeed because she
   A is determined.
   B is still producing great songs.
   C challenges people to think.

Pronunciation *Intonation patterns*

5 🎧 Listen again to Jonas talking about Madonna.

Anyway, she did ballet, singing and piano lessons.

Notice how his voice goes **up** when he says *ballet* and *singing* and **down** when he says *piano lessons*.

Now you do the same.
One person in the class says:
I've been to Moscow.
The next student says:
I've been to Moscow and Washington.
The next student says:
I've been to Moscow, Washington and London.

Continue round the class, adding new places and making sure that you get your intonation right.

6 🎧 Now listen to the interviewer.

'A scholarship?'

He sounds surprised and so his voice goes **up**.
Now you do the same in groups of four.

A I saw Stephen cycling to school this morning.
B Stephen?
C Cycling?
D This morning?

Now make up sentences of your own and the others show surprise at what you've said.

7 🎧 Listen to the interviewer again.

What about her family?

When he asks a question beginning with *Wh-* or *How*, then his voice goes down at the end.

In pairs, practise asking and answering these questions.

Where do you live?
What do you do?
When were you born?
How do you get to work?

Think of some more *Wh-* questions you can ask your partner.

If you didn't hear the question properly you can repeat it using a different intonation pattern. In this case your voice goes up at the end. Normally you insert 'did you say' in the question.

🎧 **Where** did you say you live?
What did you say you do?

Now you do the same.

8 🎧 In English our voices rise and fall to show interest or friendliness. When this does not happen, the speaker can appear indifferent or even rude. Often it's not **what** we say, it's **how** we say it that's important.

Listen to this man speaking and decide if he's being friendly or not.

a It's over there.
b Make me a cup of coffee.
c Thank you.
d Hello.
e Excuse me.
f See you soon.

Revision of tenses

1 What are the differences in meaning between *a* and *b*?

1 a I believe Madonna has asked you to write about her.
 b I believe Madonna asked you to write about her.
2 a She sees quite well without glasses.
 b She is seeing her manager this afternoon.
3 a He agreed when he saw her.
 b He agreed when he had seen her.
4 a She was making an album when she met her producer.
 b She made an album when she met her producer.
5 a She believed her life to be totally under control.
 b She had believed her life to be totally under control.
6 a Her records haven't done very well.
 b Her records haven't been doing very well.
7 a It will probably sell 20 million copies.
 b It is going to sell 20 million copies.

2 Match the two parts of these sentences so that every sentence is correct and makes sense.

1 I've been waiting for you	**a** before.
2 I went to the cinema	**b** over 100 years ago.
3 I didn't have breakfast	**c** for the time being.
4 My grandfather was born	**d** last night.
5 He has given up buying CDs	**e** for two years.
6 I haven't done my homework	**f** this morning.
7 I go clubbing	**g** recently.
8 She got married	**h** yet.
9 I haven't had a holiday	**i** once a month.
10 I think I've heard this record	**j** since three o'clock.

Corpus spot

The *Cambridge Learner Corpus* shows that FCE candidates often have problems with the present perfect tense.

 I **have been** listening to pop music since I was eight years old.
 NOT I ~~am~~ listening to pop music since I was eight years old.

 The pop festival **was** held last weekend.
 NOT The pop festival ~~has been~~ held last weekend.

3 Put these sentences into the correct tense. Sometimes there is more than one possibility.

a Where .... (you born)?
b I .... (fly) to Hong Kong tomorrow.
c I .... (play) football when President Kennedy .... (shoot).
d I .... (go) phone you, but I lost your number.
e Shakespeare .... (be) the greatest English playwright.
f It was the first time I .... (go) to the theatre.
g It is the first time I .... (hear) that record.
h After the film .... (finish), everyone clapped.
i I wonder who .... (make) more money – Michael Jackson or Madonna?
j I .... (try) to explain how to do it for the past ten minutes!
k This time next week I .... (sit) on a ride in Disneyland.
l What time do you think the plane .... (arrive)?
m He arrived at the party late because he .... (work).
n Madonna .... (produce) some great records recently.
o I .... (not see) you for ages. What .... (you do)?
p This time last week I .... (be) in New York.
q Where you .... (live) before you .... (move) here?

G ····∴ page 207

Vocabulary

4 🎧 Listen to the whole interview again and complete these sentences with the phrasal verbs and expressions that you hear.

a I guess she didn't want to .... the moment of stardom .... any longer.

b I'm afraid I never .... of that story.

c Right, OK, now tell us how her career ....

d Especially when she married Sean Penn – the newspapers really .... her ....

e She said at the time that what they said in the newspapers .... her ....

f Also she .... a lot of people's .... with her desire to shock.

g I think she's very good at ....

h She's the type who will get on whatever she .... *разрушать*

Rewrite the sentences using one of the alternative words or phrases from the box below.

> decide to do   postpone   begin
> criticise   upset   communicate
> astonish   find out the truth

5 In pairs, ask and answer these questions. Use an English–English dictionary to help you.

a Do you ever put off doing things? If yes, which sort of things?

b Have you ever put someone's back up? If yes, how?

c Would you be put out if someone told you your English accent wasn't very good?

d What would put you off buying a Porsche?

e Do you put anything by for a rainy day?

f Have you ever read a book you couldn't put down?

g What sort of things do your family do that you can't put up with?

h Would you be able to put someone up if they came to visit you?

6 For questions 1–10, read the text below. Use the word given in capitals at the end of some of the lines to form a word that fits in the gap in the same line. There is an example at the beginning (0).

Example: 0 ENGLISH

SINGING AND ENGLISH

Standard **(0)** .... is independent of accent.	**ENGLAND**
As long as you use Standard English words and Standard English **(1)** .... forms, you're	**GRAMMAR**
still speaking Standard English. However, singing disrupts **(2)** .... patterns to some	**SPEAK**
(3) .... People usually sing more slowly than	**EXTEND**
they speak and so the tempo is disrupted. As the **(4)** .... must hit the notes, in key, so the	**SONG**
ordinary intonation patterns are **(5)** .... obscured.	**LARGE**
Other **(6)** .... of accent are clearly not	**CHARACTER**
destroyed. You can usually tell the **(7)**	**DIFFERENT**
between someone from England and an American singing because the latter pronounces all the 'R's. That being said, there does appear to	
be a **(8)** .... for many pop and jazz stars,	**TEND**
(9) .... opera stars for example, to make	**LIKE**
some **(10)** .... in their singing style towards	**ADJUST**
some kind of mid-Atlantic compromise, not quite either British or American.	

объясн *регулировать* *приспосабливать*

7 Make nouns from these verbs which you heard in the listening.

to associate	to act (two forms)
to believe (two forms)	to die
to know	to announce (two forms)
to manage (two forms)	to operate (two forms)
to decide	to choose

Make adjectives from these nouns which you heard in the listening.

occasions	intelligence
a responsibility	talent
fame	a success
determination	harm

Exam folder 14

Paper 5 Speaking

The Speaking Test is an opportunity to demonstrate your level of English. Don't be too worried about making mistakes – you are not only assessed on your accuracy, but on your range of grammar and vocabulary, your pronunciation, and your ability to communicate with other people in discussion.

Advice

- Try to be relaxed and cheerful – it will take less than 15 minutes!
- Ask the examiner if you are unclear about an instruction.
- Don't be afraid to spend a few seconds thinking, in order to plan what you are going to say.
- Give detailed answers in Part 1, rather than answering the examiner's questions in a single word.
- Listen carefully to the other candidate's long turn in Part 2, so that you can make a comment when asked.
- Keep going during your own long turn, remembering to compare and contrast, rather than describe an individual picture.
- Be sensitive to the other candidate in Part 3 and use turn-taking skills to ensure you both work towards completion of the task.
- Interact both with the other candidate and the examiner in Part 4. Here, you have the chance to broaden the discussion, so take the initiative and show them what you know.

Now put all the advice into practice in this complete Speaking Test.

Part 1: Answer these questions.

How do you like to spend your free time?
Do you go shopping because you have to, or because you enjoy it?
What kind of music do you prefer to listen to?
Can you describe a work of art that is special for you?

Part 2: Look at these pictures, which show a famous person.

Student A: Compare and contrast these pictures, saying what sort of lifestyle you would want to have if you were famous.
Student B: Talk briefly about how your life differs from that of a famous person.

Now look at these pictures, which show two different parts of the world.

Student A: Compare and contrast these pictures, saying which place you think would be more difficult to live in, and why.
Student B: Comment briefly on which place you would prefer.

Part 3: Look at the picture together.
It shows a living room which doesn't have enough furniture in it. Talk about the problems with the room and decide together on which *three* things you would buy to improve it.

Part 4: Now discuss these questions.
How important is it for a room to be comfortable?
Which of your possessions are particularly special to you?
Is it useful to have a computer at home? Why?/Why not?
Will more people work from home in the future? Why?/Why not?
What are the advantages and disadvantages of having an office at home?

Sense and sensitivity

1 In pairs talk about these questions.

  a Which of the rooms above do you prefer? Why?
  b What's your favourite colour? Why?
  c What colour do you dislike? How does it make you feel?
  d What colour do you think is best for
    a bedroom?   a bathroom?
    a kitchen?   a living room?
  e If you are not sure exactly what the name of a colour is in English you can say, for example, that the curtains are 'light' or 'dark' blue, or 'bluish'. What shade is:
    sky blue?   off white?
    navy blue?   pea green?
    deep blue?

f Match the colours on the left with the feelings on the right.

red	jealousy
blue	cowardice
green	depression
yellow	anger

g Would the answers be the same in your country?

Reading

2 You are going to read an article about people who have a very strange gift. Seven sentences have been removed from the article. Choose from the sentences A–H the one which fits each gap (1–7). There is one extra sentence which you do not need to use.

Listening to colour

Colour has a deep impact on each and every one of us. In both offices and factories, shops and homes, the management of colour is used to improve the environment. Apparently, green helps people relax, whereas red is good for getting people to talk and produce ideas. However, too much colour can have a different effect from the one intended – excess red brings out our aggression, for example, while too much green makes staff lazy.

In the early part of the twentieth century Rudolf Steiner studied these effects of colour on individuals. He developed a theory from which he produced colour schemes for a learning environment. [1] The younger ones had pink/red, while the older ones had yellow/green.

Although learning to integrate information from different senses is vital, for the majority of people sight, touch, taste, smell and hearing are fundamentally separate. [2]

This idea of sensory unity is a very old one. The ancient Greek philosopher Aristotle argued that the five senses were drawn together by a 'common sense' located in the heart. [3]

In more modern times, many individuals have reported experiencing what is normally felt through one sense via another, and have described occasions when experiences of one sense also trigger experiences of another. [4] One such, the physicist Sir Isaac Newton, wrote that, for him, each note of the musical scale corresponded to a particular colour of the spectrum: when he saw a colour, he sometimes heard the note. And the philosopher John Locke reported the case of a blind man who claimed that he had had a revelation of what the colour scarlet looked like when he heard the sound of a trumpet for the first time.

More recent studies include the case of a girl who associated colours with the notes of bird song. There was also a boy who felt pressure sensations in his teeth when cold compresses were applied to his arms. [5] When their tutor asked them to draw what they 'saw' when they heard a note

rise and fall on a clarinet, their images included lips, lines and triangles. One even drew a house nestling amid hills.

The author Vladimir Nabokov was once interviewed for a magazine article. [6] Interestingly, he stated that his wife and son both have the gift of colour hearing and that their son's colours sometimes appear to be a mix of those of his parents. For example, the letter M for him was pink, and to his wife it was blue and in their son they found it to be purple.

In his autobiography, he remembered the time when he was seven years old. He was using old black and white alphabet blocks to build a tower, while his mother was watching. [7] It turned out that she could also see the letters in different colours and that she also heard musical notes in colour.

This gift for seeing letters or hearing music in colour is not yet understood. There are probably more people out there who have the gift, but feel embarrassed or awkward about admitting it.

3 In small groups answer the following questions about some of the words and phrases in the article. Use an English–English dictionary to help you.

a What's another way of saying 'a deep impact'?
b What is a 'colour scheme'?
c What do we call people … who can't see?
    … who can't hear?
d Do you know another word for 'fundamentally'?
e What is an 'anecdote'?
f What's the difference between a biography and an autobiography?
g What colour is scarlet?

Phrasal verbs

4 Replace the phrasal verb with *out* with the correct form of one of the verbs or verb phrases in the box.

It turned out that she could also see the letters in different colours.
… excess red brings out our aggression

to turn out = to transpire
to bring out = to emphasise

| solve | produce | put a line through |
| bloom | prolong | last | distinguish | lose |

EXAMPLE: *The men broke out of the gaol in the night.*
The men escaped from the gaol in the night.

a Her work was a mess because she kept crossing things out.
b The flowers are all coming out, now that it's spring.
c He drew out the speech until it was time to go home.
d They held out for two months on very little food.
e In the fog it was just about possible to make out the cliff edge.
f I was late so I missed out on the chance to be in the choir.
g After spending a long time thinking about it, I finally worked out the maths problem.
h They turn out plastic bags at that factory.

A Among a group of college students it was found that more than 13 per cent consciously summoned up images of colour when they were listening to music, claiming that this made the experience more enjoyable.
B The scheme of colours that he recommended for each age group was intended to reflect a child's stage of development.
C Later we see that the anatomical drawings of Leonardo da Vinci reflect the 15th century belief that the senses have a common mechanism.
D Furthermore, as each child develops, he or she learns to use all the senses co-operatively. What the child learns from one sense can be transferred to another.
E He told the reporter the story of his 'rather freakish gift of seeing letters in colour'.
F Many respected scholars have reported the linking of the senses, known as *synaesthesia*.
G He casually remarked to her that the colours of the letters were all wrong.
H Yet there is evidence, some anecdotal, some more scientific, to suggest that they are, in fact, linked.

G rammar extra
Verbs and adjectives followed by prepositions

Complete these sentences with a preposition from the box. A preposition can be used more than once.

listening to music
embarrassed about admitting it

| from | for | away | with | on |
| to | in | about | | |

a I prevented her .... throwing the old table ....
b I congratulated them .... their marriage.
c Throw the ball .... me!
d We need a government we can believe ....
e I agreed .... everything my mother said.
f He apologised .... kicking the ball into my garden.
g I'm fairly keen .... canoeing.
h You can't compare musicians like the Beatles .... Mozart.
i The teacher was very annoyed .... me .... losing my textbook.
j I don't object .... people smoking so long as it isn't in restaurants.
k I'm worried .... doing my music exams.
l Could you explain this word .... me, please?
m I don't think this drink is very different .... that one.

28·2

Number and concord   concord

Corpus spot

The *Cambridge Learner Corpus* shows that FCE candidates often have problems with agreement.

She is one of my **friends** at school.
NOT She is one of my ~~friend~~ at school.

Everybody **has** a mobile phone.
NOT Everybody ~~have~~ a mobile phone.

I think you **are** working too hard.
NOT I think you ~~is~~ working too hard.

1 Complete these sentences with either a singular or plural form of the verb in brackets. You will also need to decide which tense to use – sometimes there is more than one possibility.

a No one .... (have) a black and white TV any more.
b One of the boys at school .... (play) football very well.
c Everybody .... (watch) international sporting events, like the World Cup.
d The majority of politicians .... (believe) they are doing the right thing.
e Every advertiser .... (want) to sell as much of their product as possible.
f The police .... (be) trained to deal with crowd violence.
g Go straight along this road until you come to a crossroads which .... (have) a hotel on one corner.
h My family .... (be) extremely artistic.
i You'll find the scissors .... (be) in the drawer.
j Five pounds .... (not seem) very much money these days.
k Neither my brother nor my husband .... (enjoy) golf.
l The United States .... (form) in 1792.
m More than one pop group .... (find) success too difficult to handle.
n A group of us .... (go) to France on a camping holiday every year.
o Neither of the doctors .... (be) available.
p Neither child .... (like) ice-cream very much.
q Politics .... (be) something I've always been interested in.
r Forty kilometres .... (be) too far for me to cycle in a day.

G ···▷ page 207

2 Put the words in the box below in the right section A or B (some of the words can go in both sections).

A Words which take a singular verb
B Words which take a plural verb

each	every	a group of	all
none	neither	either	both
staff	no one	one of	
the majority of		everybody	
more than one		the police	
people	the news		sunglasses
jeans	a series		

3 What is the difference between this pair of sentences?

a My family are not very good at posing for photos.
b The family nowadays is much smaller than it used to be.

Do you know any other words which follow the same rule?

G ···▷ page 207

180 UNIT 28

4 Complete these sentences using *each, every, both, none, either, neither* or *all.*

a Those apples are thirty-five pence ....

b He sings .... of the time he is in the car.

c .... of my parents speak English better than I do.

d – Which of these three cars do you prefer?
– .... of them.

e I bought two hats last week, but haven't worn .... of them.

f – Do you want a cheese or a chicken sandwich?
– ...., I'm on a diet.

g .... mother worries about her children.

h .... side of the garden had flowerbeds.

i She took quite a few photos but .... looked any good.

j .... time I see my grandmother she gives me roses.

k I tried to phone Jane two or three times, but .... time there was no answer.

Listening

5 🎧 Listen to this journalist talking about hair colour and the effect it can have on personality. For questions 1–6, complete the sentences.

1 New research has found that brunettes are sensible and ....
2 Dyed blondes are apparently less concerned about ....
3 People dye their hair blonde as a sign of ....
4 A personality test was done on .... who had dyed their hair.
5 One red-haired actress was called .... at school.
6 Peter Jameson believes that stereotyping also affects men and causes ....

6 For questions 1–12, read the text below and think of the word which best fits each gap. Use only one word in each gap. There is an example at the beginning (0).

Example: 0 OF

Colour in the workplace

Companies study and make use (**0**) .... our colour associations and preferences in (**1**) .... to sell us their products. The packaging, for example, relies heavily (**2**) .... colour, both to carry information and to make the product appear more attractive. Sugar (**3**) .... sold in packets coloured in bluey-pinks and blue because, unlike colours (**4**) .... as green and brown, these colours are associated with sweetness.

In the same way, in experiments with washing powders, (**5**) .... colour of the packet has (**6**) .... shown to have a profound influence on choice. Even (**7**) .... the powder in three sample packets – coloured yellow, blue and yellow-blue – was the same, customers thought the powder in the yellow packet was too strong, that in the blue packet too weak. The most popular powder was in the yellow-blue packet. In similar research, coffee in a brown can was thought too strong and in a red can too rich, in a blue can not mild (**8**) .... , and in a yellow can too weak – although the coffee was the same in all of (**9**) ....

It's a fact that fast-food outlets are often decorated in reds, yellow and whites. Red is a colour (**10**) .... can make a restaurant seem warm and inviting. Yellow, together with white, emphasises cleanliness. Together they create a place (**11**) .... customers can relax and enjoy their food but do (**12**) .... linger too long.

Writing folder 14

Applications 2

1 Look at this advertisement and decide what information you should include in your letter of application.

WANTED

FAMILY TO SPEND A MONTH ON A DESERT ISLAND

IPK Magazines is looking for a family who would be willing to spend a whole month by themselves on a desert island.

Write and tell us
- ◆ *why you think your family would be suitable*
- ◆ *what qualities you think would be particularly useful*
- ◆ *any special experience anyone in your family has*

Contact Dave O'Hare

2 Now read this letter of application. Correct any grammar, punctuation, spelling or vocabulary mistakes that you find in the letter.

Dear Mr O'Hare;
    I saw your advertisement for a family to spend a month on a dessert island and I would like suggest my own family. My family is six persons – my parents, myself (I have 22 years), my two sisters (12 and 16), and my brother (8). We are coming from Iceland. My father is doctor and my mother is sports teacher. I study Economical course on the university, and my brother and sisters are still studing at school.
    I think we would really enjoy to spend a month by our own, as we all get on very good with each other. We aren't the kind of person wich watches TV all day or needs to be entertain all time. We are a sociable and sympathetic family who is capable of taking care themself.
    The last year we spent a month in the mountains camping on ourselves wich was useful experience for being on a dessert island. As my father is doctor he can take care of some emergencies that would happen. My mother is very interesting in sport and we are all very fit and in a good condition. I learnt fish two years ago and I have a good knowledge of wich plants are good eating and wich poisonous.
    I wish you will consider my aplication and look forward to hear from you.
Yours faithfully
Magnus Baldursson

3 Read this advertisement and then look at the plan below.

WANTED

Judges for the Most Interesting Hobby competition

Do you have a hobby?

Do you think you could join a panel to judge other people's hobbies?

Write and tell us about

- your hobby
- why you think you would make a good judge
- any relevant experience you have

Write to Mr P. Crispin

Planning a formal letter

Remember NO address needed!
Beginning and Ending? Dear Who?, Yours?
Good first sentence!
Important points
1 ?
2 ?
3 ?
My hobby - stamp collecting
Useful vocabulary
1 to collect, a collection, an album, to swap stamps, first day covers and ?
2 my personal qualities - (be positive) - enthusiastic, fair, polite, tactful, energetic and ?
3 competitors, a panel of judges, to make a decision, to choose a winner, to decide between, and ?

4 Here is the application that the student wrote, based on the plan. Complete the gaps with a verb from the box below using the correct tense.

try	hold	make	write
see	help	criticise	ask
consider	collect	know	
enjoy			

Dear Mr Crispin,

I (1) .... your advertisement for people to judge the Most Interesting Hobby competition. I am a 24-year-old Norwegian boy and I (2) .... stamps for the past ten years. I (3) .... it may seem like a boring hobby to some people, but I really (4) .... it. I have eight stamp albums to keep my collection in and collecting stamps (5) .... me to find out more about the world. I also practise my English as I have pen friends all over the world and we (6) .... to each other in English.

I think I (7) .... a good judge of other people's hobbies because I'm so enthusiastic about my own. I (8) .... to be tactful and fair, because it is so easy to hurt someone's feelings if you (9) .... something as personal as a person's hobby.

I (10) .... to be a judge when I was at school. We (11) .... an art competition and four of us students had to judge the best picture. We had to spend a long time discussing who to pick and it was very difficult to choose between the best ones!

I do hope you (12) .... my application and I look forward to hearing from you in the near future.

Yours sincerely,

Ole Olafson

5 Write **a letter plan and the letter of application** for either:

a the family on the desert island
   or
b a judge in the hobby competition.

29.1 Newshounds

1 What do you think these headlines are about? Is it fair to talk about people in this way? Give examples of recent stories where the press has invaded people's privacy.

SOAP STAR'S SHOPLIFTING SHAME

Footballer turns wife-beater
★ shock pics on page 5 ★

Boss stands down after bribery charge

MINISTER'S TEENAGE SON IN DRUGS SCANDAL

Judge's secret love nest

2 Describe what is happening in this photo and say who is involved, choosing from the people listed below.

> agent   bodyguard   cameraman   editor
> journalist   manager   paparazzo   star

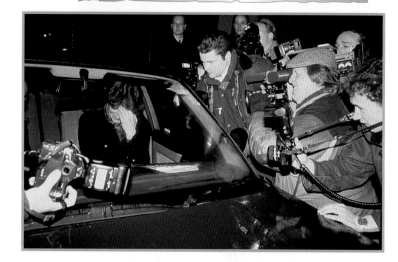

3 🎧 You are going to hear five speakers talking about a newspaper story which involves a teenage girl and a rock band. For questions 1–5, decide which of the opinions A–F each speaker expresses. Use the letters only once. There is one extra letter which you do not need to use.

A Journalists create scandal that is only remembered in the short-term.
B Journalists should check their information more carefully than they do.
C Journalists are insensitive towards the people they deal with.
D Journalists have an obligation to inform their readers of the facts.
E Journalists concentrate their efforts on people who are well-known.
F Journalists have to invent things to get a good story.

Speaker 1 [   ] 1
Speaker 2 [   ] 2
Speaker 3 [   ] 3
Speaker 4 [   ] 4
Speaker 5 [   ] 5

4 🎧 Listen to the five speakers again and tick all the idioms you hear, noting which speaker (1–5) said them. Explain what you think the idioms mean, by referring back to the people and events in the news story.

> break new ground
> have a change of tune
> flavour of the month
> get sick to the back teeth with
> go to someone's head
> be in the public eye
> keep a low profile
> out of the blue
> put a brave face on something
> the rest is history
> a three-day wonder
> turn something on its head

5   What do you think the newspaper actually printed? Look at these three headlines then discuss ideas in groups, using the information in the recording and your own imagination.

PARENTS' AGONY AS ONLY DAUGHTER RUNS AWAY WITH ROCK STAR

BLONDE SCHOOLGIRL HELD ON BAND'S YACHT AGAINST HER WILL

BAD BOYS OF ROCK ARE AT IT AGAIN – WILD PARTY EXCLUSIVE

6   Read this article from a few years ago about tabloid reporting on the royal family. For questions 1–12, decide which answer (A, B, C or D) best fits each gap. There is an example at the beginning (0).

Example:

0	**A** turned	**B** put	**C** set	**D** moved

0	<u>A</u>	B	C	D

Royal press coverage

Royal reporting has been (0) ..... on its head recently. On Thursday July 9, *The Sun* newspaper had a 'world exclusive' headlined 'Camilla meets Wills', (1) ..... how William, the son of the Prince of Wales, had finally met his father's close friend, Camilla Parker Bowles, later to become his wife. The article was full of the details that would (2) ..... any reader of its truth. A week later, *The Sun* (3) ..... about a 'royal world exclusive' under the headline 'Prince Charles writes in The Sun'. This was accurate, strangely enough, (4) ..... to a letter with Charles's signature on page four. It stated how grateful he was to *Sun* readers for helping to (5) ..... money for a Nepalese hostel. Exactly a week later came yet another 'world exclusive': 'When Harry met Cammi'. This story (6) ..... that Camilla, in an 'historic encounter', had now met Prince Harry, Charles's younger son.

The Express, a rival newspaper to *The Sun*, (7) ..... a story about Charles's deputy private secretary Mark Bolland, which described him being (8) ..... 'out on the town with one of *The Sun*'s female executives.' To outraged competitors like *The Express*, it was (9) ..... what was going on. Charles's press team were cosying up to the very newspaper which had (10) ..... him such pain with its years of intrusive reporting. In other words, *The Sun* was getting leaks from his own (11) ..... . This change of heart towards the media may be down to Mark Bolland himself, who is the son of a former bricklayer and was (12) ..... at a comprehensive school. He and the establishment are as different as chalk and cheese.

1	**A** speaking	**B** talking	**C** explaining	**D** insisting
2	**A** conclude	**B** prove	**C** fulfil	**D** convince
3	**A** boasted	**B** applauded	**C** congratulated	**D** greeted
4	**A** sending	**B** referring	**C** bringing	**D** pointing
5	**A** develop	**B** grow	**C** raise	**D** lift
6	**A** demanded	**B** believed	**C** requested	**D** claimed
7	**A** directed	**B** spread	**C** stood	**D** ran
8	**A** looked	**B** regarded	**C** spotted	**D** realised
9	**A** actual	**B** obvious	**C** certain	**D** sure
10	**A** produced	**B** created	**C** resulted	**D** caused
11	**A** office	**B** company	**C** business	**D** party
12	**A** instructed	**B** learned	**C** educated	**D** studied

English idioms

Do not attempt to change any of the vocabulary in an English idiom. Similar idioms in your own language may use a different word – for example, in one Swedish idiom, you say you have a chicken in your throat, whereas in the English one, it's a frog!

Be careful when you use idioms in your own writing. They are effective if used *сдато* sparingly, but the writing becomes unnatural if too many are included. See Writing folder 15 for more information.

Parts of the body

1 Many common idioms contain a part of the body, like the ones used in 29.1, for example *a change of heart*. It's usually quite easy to work out the meaning of these idioms. Start by thinking of the literal meaning of the words, even forming a picture in your head, like the ones above.

In this way, match idioms 1–20 to meanings a–t.

eye

1	see eye to eye with someone	a	ignore
2	raise your eyebrows	b	agree
3	cast your eye over something	c	surprise
4	turn a blind eye to something	d	check

head

5	turn something on its head	e	panic
6	get your head round something	f	survive
7	keep your head above water	g	change
8	lose your head	h	understand

hand

9	have a hand in something	i	be in control
10	be given a free hand	j	refuse responsibility
11	have the upper hand	k	make the decisions
12	wash your hands of something	l	help create

feet

13	find your feet	m	reject
14	have your feet on the ground	n	become anxious
15	get cold feet	o	gain confidence
16	vote with your feet	p	be sensible

fingers

17	put your finger on something	q	be unsuccessful
18	get your fingers burned	r	accuse
19	keep your fingers crossed	s	identify
20	point the finger at someone	t	hope for good news

Common verbs in idioms

2 You know the meaning of the verbs used below, but can you work out the meaning of the idioms? Check in a dictionary if necessary.

break new ground	get your act together
make your mark	take somewhere by storm
get to grips with something	put your oar in
come out of your shell	catch someone off guard
tighten your belt	go out of the window
keep a low profile	put something on ice

3 Decide which idiom you would use for the situations a–k and include it in a suitable sentence, changing pronouns and tenses where necessary.

EXAMPLE: *Company executives were advised to make budget cuts because of a shortfall in profits.*
Company executives were advised to tighten their belts because of a shortfall in profits.

a The paparazzi managed to surprise them unexpectedly in their hideaway cottage.

b The government has delayed many of its proposals for new road development.

c She forgot all her promises to her parents about studying hard when she met Danny.

d The software uses an innovative technique that requires much less memory.

e Some town councils have dealt seriously with traffic problems.

f Kevin has done a lot in his new job in a short period of time.

g The British film *Control* went down very well in Cannes.

h The argumentative politician could not resist adding his views.

i John hid in the back row of the cinema, hoping he wouldn't be seen by his teacher.

j On the first day at a new school, children are very nervous, but they soon begin to open up.

k Caroline's always letting people down – she really needs to improve her behaviour.

Idioms and prepositions

4 Many common idioms, including some of the ones above, feature a preposition. Choose the correct preposition from the ones below to fill the gaps in a–m and suggest what these idioms mean.

at	for	in	off
on	out	to	with

a the icing .... the cake

b .... full swing

c .... a nutshell

d .... the count

e shocked .... the core

f .... a loose end

g .... a tight corner

h .... a limb

i economical .... the truth

j thin .... the ground

k .... loggerheads .... someone

l pie .... the sky

m quick .... the mark

5 Select one of the idioms above to illustrate cartoons 1–4. Now use the remaining idioms in a–h.

EXAMPLE: *I've had some lovely presents, but this one is truly* the icing on the cake .

a Tickets for Rachid Taha's concert next month are very ....

b I'm going to go .... and say that Italy will win the World Cup.

c Faye's always having ridiculous ideas – they're all .... !

d If you're .... , why not come round and see us this evening?

e To put the problem .... , my boss wants to fire me.

f The press was really .... and there was full coverage of the scandal the next day.

g Politicians can be rather .... , preferring not to give any bad news.

h I was .... by what Gerry said, as I had absolutely no idea of what had been going on.

Exam folder 15

Paper 2 Writing

In the Writing paper you will have 1 hour 20 minutes to answer two questions. Make sure you use the time well, planning each answer, and leaving a few minutes at the end to check what you have written. Remember that you can write slightly more in your Part 2 answer.

1   Read the exam question below.

You have had a class discussion on the media. Now you have to write an essay, giving your opinion on the following statement.

Newspapers used to carry real news, but their main role today is to shock and entertain us.

Write your **essay**.

2   The answer opposite could be improved in a number of ways, some of which are given in the teacher's notes. Read through the answer and the notes. Then make the changes suggested and add any improvements of your own. Your final answer should be 180 words long.

Advice

- Read each question carefully, underlining key words.
- Make a quick paragraph plan for each answer.
- Write legibly and leave a line between paragraphs.
- Don't copy out phrases from the question – you must use your own words as far as possible.
- Try to use a variety of structures and a range of vocabulary.
- Check you have included all four points in Part 1.
- Choose a Part 2 question that you know something about, and use your imagination if you run out of ideas.
- Write at least 120 words for each answer.
- Don't include irrelevant information in Part 1, but try to expand the points with ideas of your own.
- Aim to write 180 words in Part 2, for a fully developed answer.
- Make sure you write in a consistent style, that is appropriate for the target reader.
- Correct any spelling or grammatical errors clearly.

Where is the introduction?
Very unclear beginning

Join the ideas in the
first three sentences
to make one complex
sentence.

I think it depends which newspapers you read. Some of

them still report the news. Others don't do it much. I

think it's important for any newspaper to report what (had)

happened, but people like to read other things too. I think

it's good to expose scandal occasionally. Famous people

are in the public eye and they cannot turn a blind eye

to this.

Incorrect
tense

Develop your ideas
here – give an
example of what you
mean re scandal.

Lose the second idiom – very unnatural. You haven't commented on
newspapers 'entertaining us' (see question) – add something on this.

Who does 'their'
refer to? Avoid
the repetition here.

I don't think it's (their) main role though. (Their) main role

Check spelling

is to inform and this means (writting) reports on current

Expand your
ideas on
television news.

news and events. I think television can do this too, but

with a newspaper it's not the same. You have time to read

and think about it. That's what I think.

116 words

Very sudden end – summarise your
views in a final paragraph.
You have used 'think' seven times!
Reword in different ways.

30·1 Anything for a laugh

1 Say what the word 'funny' means to you. Then compare and contrast the types of comedy shown in the pictures, and explain which you would rather see and why. Talk for about a minute each.

2 You are going to read four 'urban myths'. These are modern-day stories, usually humorous, which people enjoy telling each other at parties or at the pub. First, read questions 1–15.

In which urban myth does someone

need to withdraw money?	1
have an injured pet?	2
appear unconcerned?	3
mistake a person for a criminal?	4
have urgent treatment?	5
have a conversation in an elevator?	6
go to a restaurant?	7
intend to use public transport?	8
disobey a request?	9
have to make a hard decision?	10
break the rules?	11
try to hide something?	12
give a person the sack?	13
receive an apology?	14
have something taken from them?	15

A A woman was looking forward to an important dinner party, where her guests would include her husband's new boss. She wanted to serve a really special meal, so she bought a whole salmon, which she cooked and prepared beautifully. The dinner party started well, and the woman received many compliments about the starters she served. At a suitable moment, she slipped out to get the fish from the kitchen, where she found a rather horrifying sight: her cat was sitting on the work surface, tucking into the fish with gusto. She shooed the cat away and, in a state of total panic, hastily disguised the damage with some carefully-placed slices of lemon and cucumber. Then she took the salmon through, to gasps of admiration. However, when the woman went to the kitchen to make the coffee, she found her cat writhing around on the floor in agony. Convinced that the salmon was to blame, the poor woman went back in to tell her guests the truth. They all rushed off to hospital to have their stomachs pumped. The woman had only just returned home when the doorbell rang. It was the milkman, who explained that he was just calling to see if the cat was all right. Apparently, he'd dropped a metal milk crate on its head that morning.

B A young man had been out for the evening in central London. When the pubs closed, he went to Charing Cross station to catch his train home, but then decided he would rather have something to eat first. Checking his pocket, he found he only had about £5. It was a difficult choice: go home or get a quarterpounder with all the trimmings. Then he remembered he had his cash card, so all was well. He bought himself a burger, which he had already started to eat when he reached the cashpoint machine. He put in his card, set the snack down next to the keypad, punched in his numbers and waited for the cash to come out. Instead, the screen flashed up: 'Sorry, you have used the wrong number. Do you wish to try again?' A bit nervous, he keyed in another number. Again the message appeared. He was convinced that the first number was right, so he keyed it in carefully. No sooner had he finished than a message came up, saying his card had been retained. This was not the only thing he lost, either, for the glass shield came down, locking away his delicious burger.

3 Now scan the four texts for the answers, ignoring the underlined words. Compare your answers with another student.

4 Which do you think is the funniest of the four urban myths? Are any of them not funny at all, in your view? Explain your reasons to another student.

5 You may not know the underlined words, but still have been able to answer the questions. Try to work out their meaning now by looking at the surrounding context. Then use some of them in a–h.

a They sensed movement in the trees and suddenly, a huge bear .... in front of them.
b It was West's favourite role in Shakespeare and he played the part ....
c Take that .... look off your face – it's me in disguise!
d Rafter .... the ball in the air badly and, apologising to his opponent, decided not to play the serve.
e Jane's father .... everyone .... , so that she could get some rest.
f Their large wedding, which had .... , cost a fortune.
g We .... the cost of Gregor's meal between us, as it was his birthday.
h The TV news showed thousands of villagers .... their homes.

6  Listen to another urban myth about driving. Then retell the story.

C An English couple who were driving around America were spending a few days in New York. They'd had some great evenings out on the town, including a show on Broadway and an Italian meal on the Lower East Side. They'd been a bit anxious at first, having seen all those violent shoot-'em-up cop shows on TV, but by the final evening, they were really enjoying themselves. They drove back to the hotel, parked in the basement car park, and waited for the lift up to reception. It was quite dark and rather scary. Suddenly, a huge man with a Rottweiler <u>loomed</u> out of the shadows. The lift came and the couple hurried in, followed by the man and his dog. As the doors closed, the man shouted 'Get down, lady'. Rather than put up a fight, the petrified couple <u>tossed</u> all their money at him and threw themselves on the floor. When the lift arrived, they scrambled to their feet and ran out in a panic. To their surprise, when they checked out the next day the receptionist explained that a man had already <u>settled</u> their bill, and handed them an envelope. Inside was all the money they'd given the 'mugger', and a note saying: 'I'm real sorry about scaring you yesterday, and I hope paying your bill has made up for your <u>ordeal</u>. By the way, Lady is the name of my dog …'

D One day at his Mirror Group headquarters in London, Robert Maxwell, who lived in the luxurious <u>penthouse</u> flat at the top, was coming down in the lift. At the next floor he was joined by a young <u>lad</u> in a <u>scruffy</u> suit, who happened to be smoking. Maxwell was furious to find one of his employees ignoring the company's no-smoking policy. The lad was promptly told to <u>extinguish</u> the cigarette, but paid no attention, and indeed started <u>blowing</u> smoke in Maxwell's face. Maxwell angrily insisted that he put it out immediately. 'No way,' said the lad, and carried on puffing. At this, Maxwell demanded to know how much the lad earned a week. On being told £200, he took £400 in cash from his pocket and handed it to the <u>bewildered</u> lad, saying, 'I'm giving you two weeks' notice. You're fired! Get out of my offices now.' 'Don't worry, mate,' said the lad, <u>fleeing</u> through the lift doors with his wad of cash, 'I'm going – I work for Telecom anyway!'

Grammar extra
rather

Look at these examples from the five urban myths and then answer questions a–c below.

1 So, rather than standing around waiting at the garage, he went off to the local pub …
2 Rather shaken, the man drove off the motorway …
3 … but then decided he would rather have something to eat first.
4 It was quite dark and rather scary.

a In which example could you use 'instead of'? Which word apart from 'rather' would you also have to omit?
b In which example is 'rather' used to mean 'prefer'? Which word has to be used as well? What word could be added to these words to give the opposite meaning?
c In which two examples is 'rather' used in the same way? What similar word is also used in one of these examples?

Turn to the Grammar folder for a summary of the uses of *rather*.

G ⋯⟩ page 208

30·2

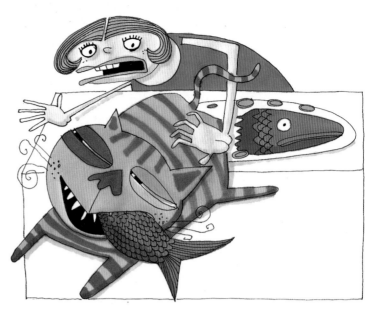

The grammar of phrasal verbs

1 Look at these examples from 30.1. First, say which two contain intransitive phrasal verbs (verbs which have no object). Then, look carefully at the word order used with the remaining phrasal verbs. Can the position of the object be changed in any of the examples? If so, give the alternative word order.

EXAMPLE: She shooed the cat away. ✓
          She shooed away the cat.

a A woman was looking forward to an important dinner party.
b She slipped out to get the fish from the kitchen.
c He set the snack down next to the keypad.
d He keyed it in carefully.
e No sooner had he finished than a message came up.
f Rather than put up a fight, the petrified couple …
g I hope paying your bill has made up for your ordeal.
h Maxwell insisted that he put it out immediately.
i They offered to clean the car up.
j I've just ploughed into a herd of cows with my lorry.

Which of these general rules are true, in your view? Use the examples a–j to back up your opinions.

1 When a phrasal verb is intransitive (has no object), the verb and the particle cannot be separated by other words.
2 When a noun is used as the object of a phrasal verb, it can always come before or after the particle.
3 When a pronoun is used as the object of a phrasal verb, it always comes before the particle.
4 In a three-part phrasal verb, the object cannot come between the two particles.

2 With some phrasal verbs, the particular meaning alters the rule on word order. Compare these examples. In which ones is it possible to change the word order?

a He put a sign up to show them the way.
b The soldiers put up fierce resistance to the attack.
c You shouldn't have kept the children up so late.
d Jenny couldn't keep up the payments on her flat.

3 Complete these sentences using the phrasal verb given in brackets in a suitable tense, and including a suitable noun or pronoun.

EXAMPLE: I *turned the car round*
          and headed home, with my foot on the accelerator all the way! (turn round)

a Please .... – you've watched far too much already. (turn off)
b Sooner or later you'll have to tell me the truth, so let's ....,
shall we? (get over with)
c It was getting foggy, but they ....
.... in
the distance, which had its lights on. (make out)
d That story ....
driving in an open car for life! (put off)
e While we were living in Sweden, we ....
....
quite well. (pick up)
f If there are any words you don't understand,
.... in a
dictionary. (look up)
g Why don't we ....?
It'll be warmer down on the sand. (make for)
h Everyone ...., who
really appreciated their support. (get behind)
i I've just ....
to that question! (work out)
j You really should ....,
you know – they're really fattening.
(cut down on)

G ⋯▸ page 208

4 Match the first lines (1–15) and second lines (a–o) of these jokes. Then take a vote to decide on the three funniest ones, giving reasons for your choices.

1 What do you call someone who hangs around with musicians?
2 Every time I drink coffee I get a stabbing pain in my left eye.
3 When a man has a birthday he takes the day off.
4 What's the definition of a modern artist?
5 I ended up as the teacher's pet.
6 What's the best way to make the landlord paint your apartment?
7 Did you start out as an actor?
8 What's the best way to stay out of the army?
9 Why did you wake me up? It's still dark.
10 My brother and I are inseparable.
11 What are you doing in my tree, young lad?
12 A Hollywood couple have finally worked out their divorce settlement.
13 Would you please open up the piano?
14 Old pickpockets never die.
15 What would you do if you were in my shoes?

a One of your apples fell down and I'm putting it back.
b No, as a little boy.
c Clean them up.
d She couldn't afford a dog.
e In fact, it takes six people to pull us apart.
f I can't – the keys are inside.
g Take the spoon out of the cup.
h Join the navy.
i Someone who tosses paint on a canvas, wipes it off with a cloth and sells the cloth.
j A drummer.
k Well, open your eyes!
l Now they can get married.
m Move out.
n They just steal away.
o When a woman has one, she takes a year off.

5 Read this biography of Jim Carrey. For questions 1–12, fill each gap with one word only. There is an example at the beginning (0).

Example: o MUCH

A funny man with a funny face

Jim Carrey's humour is very **(0)** .... his own brand. It is often slapstick, sometimes a **(1)** .... tasteless, but always hilarious. Carrey, who was born in 1962, believes that his sense of humour developed **(2)** .... his teenage years. This was his way of dealing **(3)** .... a difficult period in his life. His father had lost his job and Carrey junior had to earn money and study **(4)** .... the same time. He took a job **(5)** .... a janitor and somehow managed to fit the schooling in too.

When he was only 15, Carrey performed live at Yuk Yuks, a famous club in Toronto. He later moved to Los Angeles to tour the club circuit there. From 1990, he starred regularly in the TV sketch show In Living Color, **(6)** .... one of the many characters he played was Fire Marshall Bill, who always went **(7)** .... in smoke! Sadly, this character finally had to **(8)** .... laid to rest because of complaints that his fire act might have a bad influence on children.

Carrey's first feature film was Ace Ventura: Pet Detective, one of 1994's **(9)** .... popular films. The Mask, his next film, was the perfect vehicle **(10)** .... his oddball humour and was hugely successful. Other films **(11)** .... then have included Batman Forever and The Truman Show. His current salary **(12)** .... estimated at around $20 million per film.

Writing folder 15

Transactional letters and emails 3

1 In one type of transactional letter, you have to correct facts (see also Writing folder 4). Read this article and the notes made on it. Decide on the four main points that need to be covered in a letter to the editor.

NO GREAT LAUGHS AT FESTIVAL OF FUN!

The comedy on offer at this year's Festival of Fun has been very disappointing indeed. I cannot think of a single performance that has been memorable, in contrast to last year's wonderful line-up of stars from stage and screen. It seems that the organisers have tightened their belts considerably this year, selecting unknown and second-rate acts on the cheap!

I can! eg Larry Hatfield on Fri pm?

There have been just too many dull and predictable performances: the pathetic slapstick routines of Forbes and Company, the very unfunny stand-up comedian Linda Ritson, whose jokes were very thin on the ground, and the dreadful comedy duo Holmes and Watson, who were clearly under-rehearsed.

it's called improvisation!!!

Saturday's audience was shocked to the core by Ted Grainger's rude and offensive jokes. To make him top of the bill was a big mistake and it was interesting to see how many people voted with their feet soon after he came on stage.

what's wrong with political jokes?

This year's event was a total disaster. Let's hope the organisers get their own act together next year!

not true (summarise my impression)

2 Now read this sample answer. Apart from the opening paragraph, it is a well-written letter. However, it has missed out a content point. Which point has been omitted?

Dear Editor

I want to point the finger on the reporter who wrote the article about the Festival of Fun, which breaks new ground, published in yesterday's Daily News. The article raised my eyebrows and I couldn't get your head round it. Your reporter has been economical of the truth and I don't see eye by eye with him.

For a start, the reporter says there were no memorable performances. Perhaps he was absent on Friday evening, when some excellent acts were on offer. The well-known comedian Larry Hatfield, for example, was superb. преувеличение

Your reporter described Ted Grainger's witty political humour as 'offensive', but the majority of the audience found him very entertaining and I didn't notice many people walking out, either!

It cannot be called a disaster. In a nutshell, the organisers have done a brilliant job this year and will, I'm sure, do the same again next year.

Yours faithfully
Izzy Edwards

3 What is wrong with the first paragraph of the letter? Edit the paragraph to improve it, and make it shorter.

4 If you use idioms in a piece of writing, remember these things.

- Be careful to use the correct pronoun.
- Make sure the tense fits the sentence.
- Check any preposition used is correct.
- Don't include too many idioms together!

5 Now do this similar Part 1 task.

You see this newspaper article about a concert which you enjoyed recently. You decide to write to the editor, correcting the facts and giving your own point of view.

**GOOD SOUND SYSTEM –
SHAME ABOUT THE BANDS!**

Last night's annual *Talentspot* concert at the Juniper Theatre was a huge disappointment. None of the bands who performed there were worth watching. An excellent sound system was provided by the theatre, too, so the performers had no excuse. If this is the best local bands can do, I would rather stay at home and listen to CDs!

paper should support local music?

First on stage was the group *Acid Rain*, whose twenty-minute set was appalling. The microphone used by the singer was of poor quality – I couldn't make out any of the words she sang. Next came *Dingbats*, who couldn't even agree on what to play – the bass player was at loggerheads with the lead guitarist for much of the time! ᔕᴏᴧᏰᴀᴡ

not their fault (as reporter says earlier!)

part of their act! played very well, especially...

Down and out, the final act, is exactly how I felt by the end of the evening. This second-rate group performed an unambitious collection of songs, supported by a useless drummer and a guitarist who knew a total of three chords! I hope the organisers wash their hands of this embarrassing event next year!

no! – should definitely happen again (say why)

Write a **letter** of between 120 and 150 words in an appropriate style.
Do not include any postal addresses.

Units 25–30 Revision

Topic review

1 **Together with a partner read these sentences and discuss which are true for you, giving more details. Try to use as much as possible of the vocabulary and language from the units you have just studied.**

   a If I had learnt English when I was very young, I would be fluent now.
   b I could never put up with being famous.
   c I think that four or five families should share a car between them rather than having one each.
   d I would rather watch a comedy programme than the news.
   e I enjoy reading newspaper stories about people whose problems are different from mine.
   f I raise my eyebrows when I hear some kinds of jokes.
   g My family lives in a low-rise apartment, near a shopping precinct.
   h I would wear clothes in colours that didn't suit me, if they were fashionable.
   i If I were rich and famous, I would definitely employ a bodyguard.
   j I have never got cold feet about anything.

Grammar

2 **Complete the second sentence so that it has a similar meaning to the first sentence, using the word given. Do not change the word given. You must use between two and five words, including the word given.**

   1 I'm not happy when people park outside my house.
      object
      I ....
      outside my house.
   2 Traffic is worse in my town than it is anywhere else.
      as
      Nowhere ....
      as it is in my town.

3 I had never bought a flat before.
   first
   This was the .... a
   flat.
4 'I'm terribly sorry I laughed at your new hairstyle,' he said to her.
   apologised
   He ....
   new hairstyle.
5 I can't tolerate people who never consider other people's feelings.
   up
   I won't ....
   who never consider other people's feelings.
6 I have read neither the Sunday Express nor the Sunday Times.
   either
   I ....
   the Sunday Express or the Sunday Times.
7 I'm sorry but there aren't any seats left.
   all
   I'm afraid ....
   been taken.
8 London is the city in the United Kingdom with the largest population.
   people
   More ....
   in any other city in the United Kingdom.

3 **Correct the following sentences. One sentence does not need correcting.**

   a Just cross up the words you spell wrongly in your essay.
   b That's the man whom I sold the house to.
   c I'd rather prefer a blue car to a red one.
   d Please turn off it at once – you're making too much noise.
   e The police is available twenty-four hours a day.
   f Neither my father nor my mother has blond hair.
   g It's the first time I had been to the Paris Motor Show.
   h I am believing in the trustworthiness of our police force.

i The office block had been standing on this street for more than a decade when they decided to demolish it.

j What time do you think the train is arriving?

k Seldom we see new ideas on saving energy.

l The building which roof had been blown off by the gales is on the next street.

m If we all share a car to work, then the motorways wouldn't have been necessary.

Vocabulary

Idioms and expressions

4 Complete the sentences with one of the words in the box.

eye	keep	end	tune	ice	feet
eyebrows		hands			

a She'll soon change her .... when she realises people have stopped going to her films.

b I've been at a loose .... all summer, now that I've got no studying to do.

c If I became famous, then I think I'd prefer to .... a low profile.

d My father got so fed up with my brother's laziness that he washed his .... of him.

e We can't afford a new car at the moment so we've decided to put that particular plan on ....

f It took me some time to find my .... when I arrived in Tokyo.

g The dress she turned up to the wedding in raised a few ...., I can tell you!

h It must be very difficult for people in the public .... to get any peace and quiet.

Phrasal verb story

5 Complete the story with the right form of a phrasal verb from the box.

end up	take aback	call up	bring in
put off	miss out on	work out	take on

If the Royal Marines had drummed one thing into Sergeant Ken Murgatroyd during his twenty-two years of service, it was the importance of seizing opportunities. After he left the Royal Marines, his new job in telesales involved (1) .... computer companies. However, one morning he rang the direct line of Neil Corbould, a senior assistant to the film director Steven Spielberg, by mistake. Within minutes Mr Murgatroyd had been (2) .... for a leading role in the war film *Saving Private Ryan*.

No one was more (3) .... than Mr Murgatroyd. Mr Spielberg needed to (4) .... someone who could (5) .... how to make the scenes as realistic as possible. Mr Murgatroyd, who was one of the navy's foremost authorities on landing manoeuvres, was perfect.

'I hadn't even heard of the film when they gave me the job. I was trying to sell an Internet database, when I pressed a wrong button and (6) .... talking to Spielberg's assistant. I told him I had made a mistake, but out of curiosity asked him what kind of work he did. When he told me, I thought, I can help with that.'

Working with celebrities didn't (7) .... Mr Murgatroyd at all. 'In fact, I found all the Hollywood types very pleasant. I don't think they had ever worked with someone like me before. I wouldn't have wanted to (8) .... an opportunity like that.'

Grammar folder

Unit 1
Comparison

There are various ways of making comparisons in English.

1 Comparative and superlative adjectives

Regular adjectives of one syllable have forms like these:

Adjective	Comparative	Superlative
young	young**er**	(the) young**est**
large	larg**er**	(the) larg**est**
slim	slim**mer**	(the) slim**mest**

Note that if an adjective ends in a single vowel and consonant (not *w*), the final letter is doubled, as in *slim* above. Some common examples are:
sad, big, thin, fat, hot, wet.

Two-syllable adjectives ending in a consonant followed by the letter *y* are formed like this:

Adjective	Comparative	Superlative
dirty	dirt**ier**	(the) dirt**iest**

Some common examples are:
angry, busy, easy, funny, happy, heavy, silly, tiny.

Most other two-syllable adjectives and all longer adjectives form their comparative and superlative forms like this:

Adjective	Comparative	Superlative
careful	**more** careful	(the) **most** careful
casual	**more** casual	(the) **most** casual
outrageous	**more** outrageous	(the) **most** outrageous

Some common two-syllable adjectives have both forms:

Adjective	Comparative	Superlative
simple	simpl**er** *OR*	(the) simpl**est** *OR*
	more simple	(the) **most** simple

Other examples are:
clever, common, cruel, gentle, likely, narrow, pleasant, polite.

Irregular adjectives have the following forms:

Adjective	Comparative	Superlative
good	better	(the) best
bad	worse	(the) worst
far	farther/ further	(the) farthest/ furthest
old	older/ elder	(the) oldest/ eldest

2 Adverbs of degree

These adverbs of degree can be used in front of comparative adjectives:
a bit, a good deal, a great deal, a little, a lot, much, rather, slightly.
This T-shirt is a bit cheaper than the others because it's last year's design.
Helen is much more intelligent than the rest of the group.

These adverbs of degree can be used in front of superlative adjectives:
by far, easily, much, quite.
You're easily the cleverest person I know!

3 not as … as

This structure is used to compare two things or people. A less common form is *not so … as*.
Sally is not as tall as her brother.
Most adverbs have regular comparative and superlative forms, where *more* and *most* are added to the verb, like this:
seriously   more seriously   most seriously
A few adverbs are irregular:
well   better   best
badly   worse   worst
The irregular adverbs far and old have the same form as their related adjectives.

Unit 2
Adverbs

Most regular adverbs are formed by adding *-ly* to a related adjective:
quick → quickly, endless → endlessly
Adjectives ending in double *ll* just add *y*:
full → fully
However, there are sometimes spelling changes when an adverb is formed in this way:
-le becomes *-ly*: gentle → gently, remarkable → remarkably
-y becomes *-ily*: easy → easily, cosy → cosily
-ic becomes *-ically*: tragic → tragically, automatic → automatically
-ue becomes *-uly*: true → truly

Some irregular adverbs do not end in *-ly*:
fast, hard, late, well.

The adverbs *hardly* and *lately* have different meanings from *hard* and *late*:
I worked hard on the project all day.
I hardly had time to stop for a coffee all day.

I finished the work late in the evening.
I've put in some long hours at work lately.

Review of present tenses

Uses of present simple tense

- Permanent situations
  Most people access the Internet for information.
- Habitual situations
  I check my emails twice a day.
- In time clauses
  Once you finish your work, give me a ring.
  We usually play tennis until it gets dark.
- In zero conditionals
  If you use all seven letters in the board game Scrabble, you get fifty extra points.
  Steam forms when water boils.

Uses of present continuous tense

- Temporary situations
  I'm living at home until I find my own flat.
- Developing situations
  Traffic is becoming heavier and heavier.
- Events happening now
  Sit still while I'm talking to you!
- Events in the near future
  Tim's leaving for Hanover next week.

See Unit 10, Review of future tenses (page 202), for further information about the present simple and present continuous tenses.

Stative verbs are not normally used in continuous tenses. The commonest of these are:
admire   be   believe   belong   consist   dislike   doubt
fit   forget   guess   hate   hear   imagine   include
keep   know   like   love   mean   prefer   realise
recognise   remember   seem   smell   sound   suppose
taste   understand   want   wish

I keep forgetting to pay the phone bill.
We wish we could be with you right now.

Unit 3
Modals 1: Obligation, necessity and permission

Strong obligation   *must* and *have to, have got to* (Informal)

Present and future   *must*   *have to*   *have got to*
Past   *had to*

1   ***must***
    Must is used to talk about strong obligations in the present and future that are imposed by the speaker.
    You must brush your teeth before you go to bed.
    I must arrange to have my windows cleaned.
    (It is also used to talk about laws: *Drivers must obey traffic signals.*)

2   ***have to/have got to***
    Have to/have got to are used to talk about strong obligations in the present and future that are not imposed by the speaker.
    I've got to do some homework tonight. (My teacher says so.)
    If in doubt whether to use *must* or *have to*, use *have to*. Do not use *I've to*, which is incorrect.

3   ***had to***
    Had to is used to talk about past and reported obligations:
    I had to help on the farm when I was young.
    We were told we had to get a visa before we left on holiday.
    There are also other ways to express obligation:
    to make someone do something
    to be compulsory

Weak obligation   *should, ought to*

Present and Future   *should do*   *ought to do*
Past   *should have done*
                                      ought to have done

There is no difference in meaning between *should* and *ought to*.
You ought to/should write home more frequently.
In the past *should have done* and *ought to have done* are often used for criticism or regret, because an action didn't happen:
We should have bought/ought to have bought your sister a card for her birthday.

There is no difference in meaning in the following uses.

Lack of obligation   *needn't*
                      doesn't/don't need to
                      doesn't/don't have to

Present and future   *needn't*   *don't need to*
                            don't have to
She doesn't need to/needn't come to the meeting if she doesn't want to.
You don't have to wear a uniform at our school.

The following past uses express different meanings.

Past   *didn't have to*
              needn't have done
              didn't need to do

Needn't have done is used when something is done but it was unnecessary:
I went to the bank but I needn't have done as I had some money in my coat pocket.
Didn't need to is used when doing something is not necessary:
I didn't need to have an injection to go to the USA.

You can also use the expression *to be optional* to express lack of obligation:
Going to lectures was optional at my university.

Asking for and giving permission   *can   could   may*

Can is the more usual way of asking for and giving permission.
Could is a bit more polite and *may* is quite formal:
Can/may/could I borrow your bike?
Yes, you can/may.

Other ways of asking for and giving permission are:
to allow someone to do
to permit someone to do
to let someone do

Prohibition   *mustn't   can't*

Present and future   *mustn't*   *can't*
Past   *was not to*   *couldn't*

Mustn't and *can't* are used when something is forbidden:
You mustn't cross the road without looking.
Elizabeth can't go out this evening – her father says so.

Other verbs which can be used are:
to forbid someone to do something
to ban someone from doing something
to not allow someone to do something
to not permit someone to do something
to not let someone do something.

It is also possible to use an imperative: *Don't cycle on the pavement!*

Unit 4
as and *like*

(See also grammar summary in Unit 4)

Like can be used as a preposition and is followed by a noun (*like a house*), a pronoun (*like it*), or a gerund (*like swimming*). It is used to give a comparison:
Your house is like our house/ours. (Is similar to ours.)
My bed is so hard it's like sleeping on the ground.

As can be used as a preposition to tell you what job or function a person or thing has:
As a chef, I have to cook one hundred meals a day.
I used the tin as a cup to drink out of.

Please note these other uses of *as* and *like*.
It's like living in a palace, living in your house. (It's not a palace.)
As a palace, Windsor is very impressive. (It is a palace.)

As is used in prepositional phrases:
At my school, as at most schools, pupils were expected to respect their teachers.

Some verbs can be followed by an object and *as*:
He is known as a generous person.
I don't regard learning a language as optional.

Like and *such as* can be used to mean 'for example':
I enjoy films like/such as thrillers.
I dislike sports such as/like skiing.

As can be a conjunction and is followed by a subject and verb:
She cut up the vegetables as I had taught her. (In the way I had taught her.)

In British English it is becoming more common to hear *like* followed by a subject and verb. *Like* followed by a subject and verb is acceptable in American English:
I don't speak like he does.

Unit 5
Table of common irregular verbs

INFINITIVE	PAST TENSE	PAST PARTICIPLE
become	became	(has/had) become
bet	bet	bet
burst	burst	burst
buy	bought	bought
creep	crept	crept
cut	cut	cut
draw	drew	drawn
drive	drove	driven
eat	ate	eaten
feel	felt	felt
find	found	found
get	got	got
hear	heard	heard
hold	held	held
hit	hit	hit
keep	kept	kept
know	knew	known
leave	left	left
lose	lost	lost
put	put	put
run	ran	run
say	said	said
see	saw	seen
send	sent	sent
set	set	set
shake	shook	shaken
shut	shut	shut
sink	sank	sunk
speak	spoke	spoken
spend	spent	spent
swim	swam	swum
take	took	taken
tell	told	told
think	thought	thought
weep	wept	wept

Review of past tenses
Past simple

This is used to talk about events in the past which:
- occurred at a particular time
  The Titanic sank in 1912.
  I drove back from London last night.
  This indicates a completed action in the past with a fixed time phrase.
- happened regularly
  Matthew spent most weekends at tennis tournaments.
  She burst into tears every time she heard his name.
  Note that *would* and *used to* are also used to talk about the past in this way – this is dealt with in Unit 8 (page 201).

Past continuous

This is used to talk about events in the past which:
- had a longer duration than another action
  I was cutting up vegetables in the kitchen when I heard it on the six o'clock news.
- were temporary
  Norwich were losing two-nil, with only five minutes to go.

  It is also used to set the scene in a story: *The sun was shining when the old man set off from the cottage.*

Present perfect

This is used to talk about events or a period of time which:
- started in the past but are still true or are still continuing
  We've lived here for eight years.
  Ellen has eaten no meat since she was six.
- happened in the past but have an effect in the present
  They've cancelled tonight's concert so we'll have to do something else.
  I've heard from Iain again.

Past perfect

This is used to talk about events which:
- happened earlier than something else
  Ken sat in the dark miserably and thought about what he had said to his girlfriend.
  Once I had finished my exams, I started clubbing again.

  Note that the past perfect needs to be used when it is important to show a time difference.

  Unit 14 deals with the perfect tenses in more detail (page 203).

Unit 6
Adverbs of frequency

always, never, often, normally, seldom, sometimes, usually
These adverbs describe how often an event happens. They go in different places in a sentence, as follows:
- after the verb *be*
  The post is always late on Saturdays.
- before the verb in simple present or past tenses
  I normally start work at nine.
  We usually swam in the local pool, but we sometimes went to a different one further away.
- after the first auxiliary verb in other tenses
  I'll never forget his look of absolute horror.
  Helen has seldom seen her mother.
- at the beginning of the sentence for emphasis
  Sometimes we walked home along the river.
  Never had I felt so alone.
  (Units 24 and 26 deal with inversion.)

Conditionals with *if*

These are normally used to talk about possible events and the effects of them. There are four main types:
- Zero conditional
  Not a true conditional, as the events described both happen.
  If I stay up late, I feel awful the next day.
  When the moon passes between the earth and the sun, there is an eclipse.
  If/When + present tense | present tense
- First conditional
  Used to talk about likely events in the future if something happens.
  If I pass FCE, I'll have a big party!
  If you don't stop talking, I'll send you to the head teacher.
  If + present tense | future tense *will*
- Second conditional
  Used to talk about unlikely or impossible situations.
  If I won the lottery, I'd give all the money to Oxfam.
  People might behave differently if they had the chance to repeat their lives.
  If + past tense | *would, could, might*
- Third conditional
  Used to speculate about the past.
  If we'd had more money, we'd have gone to the States last year.
  If you'd told me the truth in the first place, I wouldn't have asked the teacher.

If Tom had taken his guitar, he could have played with the band that night.
If + past perfect | would have, could have, might have + past participle
(Unit 25 deals with mixed conditionals.)

Unit 7
Gerunds and infinitives 1
The gerund

The gerund is a verb which is used as a noun. It can be the subject of a clause or sentence: *Climbing the hill took them all day*, or the object: *I consider learning to save to be an essential part of growing up.*

You use the gerund after certain verbs and expressions, especially those expressing liking/disliking:
I don't mind getting up early in the morning.

Common examples:
like   love   enjoy   adore   fancy   feel like   detest
hate   loathe   can't stand   dislike   don't mind   finish
avoid   give up   keep   suggest   consider   miss
imagine   it's not worth   it's/there's no use
there's no point (in)

A Gerunds are used after all prepositions except for *to*
(Some exceptions to this rule are: *to look forward to doing, to object to doing, to get used to doing.*)
On hearing the news, she burst into tears.

B After adjective and preposition combinations
Steven is fantastic at cooking Thai food.

Common examples:
good/wonderful/fantastic/bad/awful/ terrible at
happy/pleased/glad/anxious/sad/worried about
afraid/frightened/scared/terrified of
interested in
keen on
capable of
proud of

A common use is with the noun *difficulty* (to have difficulty in).

C After verb and preposition combinations
I don't approve of people drinking and driving.

Common examples:
insist on   approve of   apologise for
consist of   believe in   succeed in
accuse someone of   congratulate someone on

D After phrasal verbs
I gave up playing tennis when I hurt my knee.

The infinitive

A The infinitive is used after certain verbs
I learnt to speak Spanish in Valencia.

Common examples:
afford   agree   ask   choose   help   hope   want
intend   pretend   promise   expect   prefer   used

B After certain adjectives
I was surprised to see him at the party.

Common examples:
difficult   possible   happy   certain   simple

C After verbs which follow the pattern verb + someone + *to do* + something
I asked her to open the window.

Common examples:
encourage   permit   allow   persuade   teach   force

D To express purpose
I went to the shops to get some bread.

E The infinitive without *to*
This is also used after modal auxiliaries (*can, must*), after *let, had better* and *would rather*. *Make* has no *to* in the active, but adds *to* in the passive:
I made him go to school /He was made to go to school.

Unit 8
used to and *would*

Used to and *would* express habitual actions in the past.

1 *Used to* is followed by the infinitive and is used for actions which no longer happen. It is used for permanent situations as well as habitual actions.
I used to have a tricycle when I was five years old.
John used to have long hair before he joined the army.

The negative is *didn't use to.*
I didn't use to go abroad for my holidays before I won the lottery.

2 *Would* is used for past habitual actions which were repeated. *Would* takes an infinitive without *to.*
I would get up for work at seven, then get the bus at seven-thirty.

3 *Get/Be used to doing* means to be or to get accustomed to. It can be used with all tenses and is always followed by a gerund (an *-ing* word).

Unit 9
Modals 2: Speculation and deduction

● *could, might, may* are used to speculate about something the speaker or writer is unsure about:
It could be a sea eagle, though the feathers look too dark.
That star you're looking at might in fact be Jupiter.
The answer may be to readvertise the job.

● *must* is used to indicate certainty:
That car must be doing over 50 mph at least!
It must be possible to make a booking on the Internet.

● *can't/cannot* and *couldn't/could not* are also used to indicate certainty, in relation to impossible ideas and situations:
It can't be her birthday – she had a party in August.
You cannot be serious!
They couldn't possibly be here before lunchtime.

● *couldn't/could not* can also be used in questions, sometimes with possibly, to speculate about something:
It couldn't possibly be a case of mistaken identity, could it?
Couldn't it be a computer error?

● *could have, might have, may have* are used to express uncertainty about something in the past:
It could have been Greg you saw on the bus – he often catches the 206.
The dinosaurs might have survived without the meteor impact.
I think I may have met you before.

● *couldn't have/can't have* is used to express certainty that something in the past was impossible or didn't happen:
He couldn't have damaged your bike – he was with me all evening.
It can't have been raining, as the path is completely dry.

- *must have* is used to express near-certainty about something in the past:
  It must have been cold that winter.
  Jan must have arrived home by now.

Order of adjectives
Opinion adjectives always come before descriptive adjectives:
the brilliant French film 'Le Bossu'
an appalling old brown tracksuit
Descriptive adjectives generally follow this order:
size shape age colour nationality material
a small oval brooch
the young American film star
It is unusual to have four or more adjectives together –
a separate phrase is more commonly used:
a slim-cut black leather jacket with a classic Italian look

Unit 10
Review of future tenses
There are many ways of talking about the future in English. Sometimes, more than one tense is possible, with no change of meaning.

The future simple tense *shall/will* can be used for:
- future plans
  I'll give you a ring sometime.
- definite future events
  Our representative will meet you at the airport.
- predictions based on general beliefs
  Mass space travel will soon become possible.
- offers or promises relating to the future
  I'll prepare some salads for the party.
  I'll do my homework after this episode of the Simpsons.

  Remember that the future simple is also used in the first conditional (page 200).

The 'going to' future can be used for:
- future plans, particularly if they are likely to happen soon
  I'm going to clear out the kitchen cupboards at the weekend.
- intentions
  James says he's going to work harder.
- predictions based on facts or events in the present
  It's going to snow tonight.

The present continuous tense can be used for:
- imminent future events
  I'm having a meeting with Charlotte at two o'clock.
- definite future arrangements
  Johnny's starting school next September.

The present simple can be used for:
- events based on a timetable or known date
  The plane leaves at 09.45.
  'Twelfth Night' opens on Saturday at the Arts Theatre.
- future intentions
  NASA plans to send further rockets to Mars.
- definite planned events
  The new pool is due to open in April.

The future continuous tense is used to indicate certainty, when we are thinking ahead to a certain point in the future:
Tom will be sharing an office with Fran.

The future perfect simple is used to refer to events that have not yet happened but will definitely do so at a given time. This tense also conveys the idea of completion at some point in the future:
This time next year I'll have finished my course.
Space tourism will have become a reality by 2010.

The future perfect continuous tense is used to indicate duration:
At the end of June, Henry will have been working here for sixteen years.

Unit 11
Past and present: participles
The past participles *bored, interested, thrilled*, etc. are used when we want to talk about how people feel:
I was thrilled when I received her birthday invitation.

The present participles *boring, interesting, thrilling*, etc. are used to describe what causes the feeling:
The film was so boring that I fell asleep.

Unit 12
The passive
The passive is used:
1 When the action is more important than the person doing it:
  The film is loaded into the camera automatically.
2 When we don't know who did something:
  The camera was put together in a factory.
3 Very frequently, in reporting the news, scientific writing and other kinds of writing where we are more interested in events and processes than in the person doing the action:
  A factory was set alight during the weekend and two million pounds' worth of damage was caused.

Formation of the passive
The passive is formed with the verb *to be* and the past participle of a transitive verb. For modals it is formed with the modal + *be* + past participle.
Get can sometimes be used informally instead of *be*.
It is used with all tenses except for the present perfect continuous and the future continuous.
Compare these sentences:
A *George Eastman invented the Kodak camera.*
B *The Kodak camera was invented by George Eastman.*

Sentence A is active and follows the pattern of Subject (George Eastman), Verb (invented) and Object (the Kodak camera).
Sentence B is passive and the pattern is Subject (the Kodak Camera), Verb (was invented) and Agent (by George Eastman).
Sometimes there are two objects:
My uncle gave me some money for my birthday.
It is more common to say:
I was given some money by my uncle.
rather than
Some money was given to me by my uncle.

The agent *by*
It is sometimes unnecessary to include the agent – if for example we don't know who did something or it is obvious from the context of the sentence who did it:
She was arrested for speeding. (It's obviously going to be by a policeman so it's not necessary to include it.)

The infinitive
For sentences where the situation is in the present and need to have an impersonal sentence you can use the passive form of the verb plus the infinitive:
The President is believed to be in contact with the astronauts.
In the past we use the passive plus the past infinitive:
He is said to have poisoned his opponents in order to gain power.

Unit 13
Reporting

When direct speech is reported, it becomes indirect speech. There is usually a change of tense in the indirect speech, which is called 'backshift':

'I want to go home straightaway,' said Jennifer.
Jennifer said that she wanted to go home straightaway.

'Can I show you my stamp collection?' asked Billy.
Billy asked if he could show me his stamp collection.

'After Robert left primary school, he grew up very quickly,' said his mother.
Robert's mother said that after he had left primary school, he had grown up very quickly.

When something is reported that is a general truth, there is often no tense change:

'Girls' exam results are generally better than boys',' the head teacher admitted.
The head teacher admitted that girls' exam results are generally better than boys'.

There are a number of different reporting verbs in English. Here is a list of common ones, showing the structures they can take:

accuse + of + -ing
Mary accused Nick of deliberately forgetting to tell her.
admit + to (optional) + -ing; + that (optional)
The company admitted to selling banned products.
I admit that I was to blame.
apologise + for + -ing
James apologised for being late.
argue + for + -ing; that (optional)
The department argued convincingly for having extra staff.
Sally argued that it was unnecessary to delay the expedition.
claim + that (optional)
Newspapers are claiming that Mr Blair was told in advance.
deny + that (optional); + -ing
He denied his part in the crime.
Kirsty denied hiding the files.
explain + that (optional)
Geoff explained that there was no more money available.
insist + on + -ing; + that (optional)
The children insisted on staying up late.
Keith insisted that the project was too difficult.
promise + that (optional); + to + infinitive
Mum promised she would pick me up at 4 pm.
Jackie has promised to look after the cats while we're away.
refuse + to + infinitive
The MP has refused to comment on these rumours.
say + that (optional); in passive, 'is said' + to + infinitive
People said that the flames were visible ten miles away.
The CD is said to include many new songs.
suggest + that (optional); + -ing
Vera suggested that they should seek sponsorship for the exhibition.
Hugh suggested contacting everyone by phone.
urge + to + infinitive
Owen urged them to keep calm.
warn + that (optional); + to + infinitive
His sister warned us that he might not come.
The police warned people not to use that part of the motorway.

Unit 14

Perfect tenses

See other units for information about:
- the present perfect tense, the past perfect simple tense (Unit 5)
- the future perfect simple and continuous tenses (Unit 10)

Present perfect continuous tense

This is used to emphasise the duration of a recent or ongoing event:
Lars has been talking about his own experience – does anyone share his views?
I've been learning Italian for six years.

Past perfect continuous tense

This is used to emphasise the duration of a past event:
I'd been working for the same company for twelve years and it was time to move on.

all/the whole

All is used with plural nouns and cannot be used on its own with a singular noun. You cannot say *All company is moving*; instead you say *The whole company is moving*.

The whole is not used with plurals. You cannot say *The whole businesses are affected by computerisation.* Instead you say *All businesses are affected by computerisation.*

Note that it is possible to say *Whole businesses are affected …* without the definite article, but this gives a change of meaning: you are now referring to each individual business.

Possessive pronouns are also used with *whole*:
Your whole career has been ruined.

You can use *of the* with both *all* and *the whole*:
All of us were sad to leave.
The whole of the world is watching the event.

Unit 15

Countable and uncountable nouns

1 A noun can either be countable or uncountable. Uncountable nouns cannot be made plural, and they only have one form. They take a singular verb. Uncountable nouns are often the names of things or substances or abstract ideas which cannot be counted.
   Examples of common uncountable nouns:
   accommodation, traffic, news, bread, milk, wine, information, advice, electricity

2 Some nouns can be countable and uncountable and have a difference in meaning:
a *Her hair is very long.* Uncountable noun meaning the hair on her head.
b *There's a hair in this sandwich!* Countable noun.

a *Coffee grows in Brazil.* Uncountable noun for the product.
b *Would you like to come round for a coffee?* Countable noun meaning 'a cup of coffee'.

a *I haven't got enough paper left to finish this composition.* Uncountable noun.
b *Run out and buy me a paper will you?* Countable noun meaning a newspaper.

3 Uncountable nouns can be limited by using a countable expression. *A bit* or *a piece* are often used with uncountable nouns, although it is usually better to use a more specific expression.
   a piece/slice of cake
   a clap of thunder
   an item of news
   a loaf of bread

4 Determiners can be used with countable and uncountable nouns.
   Singular countable nouns can use *a/an* and *the*.
   A new table was delivered this morning.
   The man next door is a chef.

Uncountable nouns	Countable plurals
how much	how many
a lot of	a lot of
lots of	lots of
little	few
a little	a few
some/any/no	several
the	some/any/no
plenty of	the
a large amount of	plenty of
a great deal of	a large number of

5 There is an important difference in meaning between *a few/few* and *a little/little*:
  a I've seen little improvement in your work recently.
  b I've seen a little improvement in your work recently.
  a is considerably more negative than b in tone.
  Compare:
  a There were few people at the meeting. (It was disappointing because not many people were there)
  b There were a few people at the meeting. (There weren't many people there, but there is no suggestion that more were expected).

some/any/no

In general we use *some* in positive sentences and *any* in negative sentences and questions:
I bought some new CDs this morning.
Did you get any bread at the supermarket?
I haven't had any breakfast this morning.

However, *some* is also used in questions when we offer something to someone:
Would you like some cake?

Also when we expect the answer to be 'yes':
(In a tourist office) *Do you have some information about the museum?*

Any is often used to show we don't have a preference:
You can take me to see any film at the cinema – I don't mind which.

When you use *no*, *nothing* or *nobody/no one* you use a positive verb:
I saw nobody when I went swimming this morning.

Unit 16
The article

1 We use the indefinite article *a/an* before a singular, countable noun. It is used when we are talking about something in general or when it is mentioned for the first time:
I saw a man outside the bank selling watches.
A pet can be a good companion for the elderly.
It is also used for jobs:
My aunt is a doctor.

2 The definite article *the* is used in the following ways:
  a When something has been referred to before or is common knowledge:
  I wouldn't buy a watch from the man standing outside the bank.
  b When there is only one of something:
  the Earth, the Sydney Opera House.
  c With rivers, seas, oceans, mountains, regions, national groups and countries which are groups of states:
  the United States, the Netherlands, the Atlantic, the Himalayas, the Irish
  d With buildings:
  I'm going to the prison to visit a prisoner.
  He's in the office at the moment.

  e With species:
  the cat, the polar bear
  f With superlatives:
  the biggest tower in the world, the greatest sportsperson, the most important question
  g With musical instruments:
  I play the piano.
  h When talking specifically about something:
  The life of an airline pilot is hard.

3 There is no article:
  a With most streets (except for *the High Street*), countries, single mountains, towns, cities (except for *The Hague*), lakes:
  Austria, Mont Blanc, Tokyo
  b When talking about sports:
  I play football well.
  c When a noun is used generally:
  Life is hard.
  d With illnesses:
  She's off school with chickenpox.

4 Expressions
  You go *to prison* if you have been found guilty of a crime. You go *to hospital* if you are ill.
  You go *to the prison* or *to the hospital* to visit someone there or to work.
  Other expressions which don't take an article include:
  to go to bed, to have lunch, dinner, breakfast, to go on holiday, to go to work, in October, to hold office, etc.

Unit 17
Relative clauses

There are two types of relative clause: **defining** and **non-defining**. A defining relative clause gives essential information about the subject of the sentence. A non-defining relative clause gives additional but non-essential information. In other words, this information could be omitted without affecting the sense of the sentence:
The girl who is studying to become a vet is called Sarah.
Sarah, who is 20, is studying to become a vet.
As these examples show, punctuation is used in non-defining clauses but is absent from defining clauses. It is very important to use commas accurately in relative clauses, as inaccurate use may change the meaning of the sentence:
The sports facilities which are not in regular use will be sold.
The sports facilities, which are not in regular use, will be sold.
In the first example, only the sports facilities which are not being used will be sold, whereas in the second example, all the facilities will be sold, as none are being used.

Relative pronouns

In defining relative clauses, you can use:
- *who* or *that* when talking about people
  The boy who is playing is county champion.
  The teacher that I met is Head of Maths.
- *which* or *that* when talking about things
  Colours which can be worn are black, navy and grey.
  The book that I recommend costs £8.50.

The relative pronoun can be left out when it is the object of the sentence, as in the second example of each pair above. It must be included when it is the subject of the sentence.

In non-defining clauses, you use:
- *who* when talking about people
  Ned, who plays the violin, is living above a music shop.
- *which* when talking about things
  The new brand of shampoo, which is selling well, contains only natural ingredients.

That cannot be used, because there is no linking of the clauses, unlike in sentences containing a defining relative clause.

See also Unit 26 for information about the relative pronouns *whom* and *whose* in defining and non-defining clauses (page 207).

Instead of using a relative pronoun, *where*, *when* or *why* can be used after a noun. It is possible to omit *when* and *why* in defining relative clauses as in the following examples:
The hotel where we stayed had a beautiful garden.
Christmas is the time when many people start thinking about their next holiday.
That's the reason why she's so upset.
In non-defining relative clauses, *when* and *why* cannot be omitted:
I moved to London in 1975, when I started teaching.

Unit 18
enough, too, very, so, such
The word *enough* can be used:

- after an adjective or adverb
  The room wasn't large enough to hold everyone.
  You haven't worked hard enough this term.
- before an uncountable or plural countable noun
  The car has enough space for five people and their luggage.
  There are not enough girls doing science subjects.
- as a pronoun
  Enough has been made of this in all the papers.
- with a modifying adverb
  There is hardly enough memory in the computer.
- with certain adverbs for emphasis
  Funnily enough, we heard from him only last week.

too and *very*
These words are often confused. Here are the main uses.

- each can be used in front of an adjective or adverb, but *too* indicates an excessive amount of something, whereas *very* is just an intensifier:
  It is too cold in winter for many plants to survive.
  It is very cold in winter but a few plants do manage to survive.
- *too* can be used to show that two things or people have something in common:
  Dictionaries are useful at school and in the home too.
  You're Swedish too, aren't you?
  Note that here *too* always comes at the end of a clause.
- *too* can be used for emphasis:
  Computers are much more powerful than they were, and less expensive too.
- *too* can be used with a quantifier:
  There are too many loose ends to this story.
  A lot of people earn too little money to pay tax.

so and *such*
These words are also confused sometimes. The main uses are:
- both can be used for emphasis and to express the same idea, but in different grammatical structures.
  It rained so much that most of the area was flooded.
  There was such a lot of rain that most of the area was flooded.
- *such* is used with *as* in giving an example of something
  Dairy ingredients such as cheese and milk are best avoided.
  See also Unit 21 for uses of *so* and *such* in purpose, reason and result clauses (page 206).

Unit 19
Modals 3: Advice and suggestion
Giving advice

You should	try to watch what you eat.
You ought	to get some rest.
You'd better	book a place in the gym.
If I were you,	I'd try to do more exercise.
My advice to you is	to go to the doctor's.

Making a suggestion

I suggest	(that) you (should) cut down on coffee.
	cutting down on coffee.
I recommend	(that) you (should) relax a little more.
	relaxing.
	you to relax.
What about/How about	doing some reading?
Why don't you try	doing some reading?
Have you thought of	playing a musical instrument?

It's time …, It's about time …, It's high time …
After these phrases we use the past simple tense, even when we are talking about the present or the future:
It's time you went to bed.   You need to go to bed now.

It is also possible to use an infinitive with *to* after *It's time* if we are speaking in general terms rather than to particular people:
It's time to go.   Everybody needs to go now.

to have/get something done
Compare: | *I cut my hair.* | I did it myself.
| *I had my hair cut.* | Someone else did it for me.
A *have* + object + past participle
B *get* + object + past participle
Both of these forms are used, but B is more informal than A.

Unit 20
Gerunds and infinitives 2
Some verbs can be followed by both a gerund and an infinitive. Depending on the verb, this can result in a change in meaning.

No change in meaning
Verbs such as *start, begin, continue, attempt, intend, be accustomed to, be committed to, can't bear.*
These can be used with either a gerund or an infinitive with no real change in meaning:
The audience started to clap when the performance finished.
The audience started clapping when the performance finished.

Slight change in meaning
Verbs such as *like, prefer, hate, love.*
Compare:
I like swimming. | In general.
I like to swim in the morning. | Talking about a habit.

Note that in American English, the infinitive is used more often than the gerund for both meanings.

After *would like, would prefer, would hate* and *would love* an infinitive is used for a particular occasion or event:

Would you like to dance?

A change in meaning

Verbs such as *try, stop, regret, remember, forget, mean, go on.*

Try

I tried to open the window, but it was stuck. I couldn't do it as it was too difficult.
It was hot, so I tried opening the window. I did it as an experiment to see if some fresh air would help.

Stop

I stopped the car to get some petrol. Purpose.
I stopped going to that garage when they put their prices up. I didn't go there any more.

Regret

I regret to tell you that we have no more rooms available. Giving bad news.
I regret not making more friends when I was at school. For past events.

Remember and forget

I remember/never forget going to New York by Concorde when I was quite small. This happened in the past.
I must remember/mustn't forget to buy a newspaper while I'm out shopping. Events that still haven't happened.

Mean

I mean to work hard at university. Intention.
It will mean going to the library more often. Involve/this is the result.

Go on

When I've finished shopping, I think I'll go on to see a film. A change of activity.
Please don't stop, go on showing us your photos. Continue.

Unit 21
Concessive clauses

These are used in English to give contrasting information to the information in the main part of the sentence.
James insisted on playing in the match, despite feeling ill.
A number of different conjunctions can be used in front of the concessive clause:
although   despite   even if   even though
in spite of   much as   though   whereas   while
Much as and *whereas* are less commonly used and occur mainly in formal written English.
I prefer to buy free-range eggs, even though they are more expensive.
Although we were very tired, we watched the whole of the play.

Sometimes it is possible to reduce the concessive clause by leaving out the main verb. So, in the second example, you could say:
Although very tired, we watched the whole of the play.
You should only do this when the concessive clause refers to the subject of the main clause. So, for example, you would not say:
Although very boring, we watched the whole of the play.

Remember that *despite* and *in spite of* cannot be followed by a main verb. You cannot say:
Despite he was late, John had another cup of coffee.
Both can be followed by a gerund or a noun:
In spite of being late, John had another cup of coffee.
Despite the time, John had another cup of coffee.
You can add *the fact that* and follow this by a verb clause:
Despite the fact that he was late, John had another cup of coffee.

Purpose, reason and result clauses

A purpose clause explains information given in the main clause:
I looked the meaning up in a dictionary to see if I was right.
The conjunctions used at the front of a purpose clause are:
because   in case   just in case   so   so as to
so that   in order to   in order that   to

A reason clause also explains information in the main clause, for example why something happened:
At midnight, we could still see perfectly well, because there was a full moon.
The conjunctions used are:
as   because   for   since

A result clause explains the effect of a situation or action that is mentioned in the main clause:
The dress was very expensive, so I didn't buy it.
The conjunctions used are:
so   so … that   such   such … that
That can often be omitted:
I've had such a lot of bills (that) I can't afford a holiday.
See Unit 18 (page 205) for other uses of *so* and *such*.

Unit 22
Complex sentences

Here are more examples of some of the complex sentence types covered in the unit.
Prepositional phrase
Besides jazz and hip-hop, I also enjoy baroque chamber music.
Adjectival phrase
Elegantly dressed in red velvet, the pianist adjusted the stool and began to play.

Concessive clause
Despite the fact that he is world-famous, Keith Gregory earns relatively little from his live performances.
Reason clause
Mark turned the amp up fully, so as to be heard at the back of the hall.
-ing clause
Having played together for more than eighteen years, the quartet rarely disagree on interpretation.

Rhetorical question
How he ever managed to carry that tuba round as a child, I'll never know.

Unit 23
Intensifiers
Gradable adjectives

A gradable adjective is one which can be used in the comparative, such as *sad (sadder)*. You can use *very* to make it stronger:
I was very happy when my friends held a surprise party for me.

Non-gradable adjectives

These are extreme or absolute adjectives such as *gorgeous, fantastic, marvellous*. You can use *absolutely* or *really* to intensify them:
The weather yesterday was absolutely gorgeous.

I wish/If only

Talking about the past – things you regret doing/not doing:
Wish/If only + past perfect
I wish I hadn't been so rude to my mother last night.

Talking about the present – things that haven't come true now and things that might come true in the future:
Wish/If only + past simple
I wish I were/was lying on a beach somewhere instead of being here.
I wish I could speak Japanese.
Both *were* and *was* are acceptable but *were* is more formal.

Talking about irritating habits – things which are annoying you:
Wish/If only + would
He wishes his daughter would wear smarter clothes.

as if/as though

Both *as if* and *as though* mean the same.
To talk about 'unreal' situations you use the past tense after both *as if* and *as though*:
He looks as if he's tired. He is tired.
He looks as if he was/were exhausted. He isn't.

would rather

Would rather + past simple is used to talk about the present or future:
I'd rather you didn't go to the disco tonight.

Would rather + past perfect is used to talk about the past:
She'd rather they had gone to an Italian restaurant.

Would rather + infinitive without to is used to talk generally about the present and future:
The government would rather not give out too many benefits to young people.
Do not confuse this phrase with *had better*, which means 'should'.

Unit 24
Adverbs and word order
At the beginning, usually for emphasis

- Time adverbs – *tomorrow, yesterday evening* – can go at the beginning or the end of a sentence.
  Tomorrow I'm going swimming.
  We had a curry last night.

- Most negative adverbs can be placed at the beginning of a sentence but the word order changes as a result. This is called inversion.
  seldom, never, rarely, under no circumstances, no sooner, hardly.
  Never have I seen such a wonderful sunset!
  Notice the change in word order. The meaning is the same as '*I have never seen such a wonderful sunset*', but the inversion gives the sentence more emphasis.

- Adverbs of frequency – *sometimes, often*, etc.– can start a sentence for emphasis, but they usually go between the subject and the verb. There is no inversion after them.
  Sometimes I go shopping after work.

- Adverbs of manner – *suddenly, quietly*, etc. – can start a sentence for emphasis.
  Quietly she stepped into the cellar.

- Adverbs of opinion – *actually, surprisingly*, etc. – are often placed at the beginning of a sentence for emphasis.
  Actually, I'm older than you think.

In the middle

- Adverbs of frequency – *sometimes, often, always, usually*, etc. – are placed:
  before the verb in simple sentences – *We often play tennis.*
  after the first auxiliary verb – *I have always been fond of chocolate.*
  after the verb 'to be' – *I am never ill.*

- Adverbs of degree – *almost, very, quite* – are placed before the word they modify:
  It was very dark outside.

- Adverbs of manner – *suddenly, quietly*, etc.
  They suddenly appeared from behind the wall.
- Adverbs of opinion – *obviously, stupidly*, etc.
  I obviously forgot to tell you where I would be.

End position

Adverbs of Manner (*How*), Place (*Where*) and Time (*When*) usually go in the end position. Never place one of these adverbs between a verb and its object. You cannot say *They gave generously the present.*
If there are two or three adverbs of manner, place and time they are placed in this order:
Manner – Place – Time
Valerie behaved badly at her aunt's yesterday.

Unit 25
Mixed conditionals
- *If* + past tense (second form) with *would(n't)/might(n't)/could(n't)/should(n't)* (third form):
  If I weren't so busy all the time, I could have come along.
  Used when a change in a present situation would have affected a past situation.

- *If* + past perfect tense (third form) with *would(n't)/might(n't)/could(n't)/should(n't)* + infinitive (second form):
  If you had told me about the skiing trip, I would be there with you now!
  Used when a change in a past situation would have caused a different present situation.

Unit 26
Relative pronouns
See also Unit 17 on relative clauses (page 204).

who or whom?

Both pronouns are used in relative clauses. *Whom* is a formal word, which can only be used as the object of a verb or with a preposition:
Ruth Gresham, who cannot sell her house as a result of this new rail route, says she will seek compensation.
The people for whom this new housing development is planned are unhappy about the lack of public transport.

whose

This pronoun is used to refer to both people and things:
Professor Newton, whose latest book on urban sprawl has had excellent reviews, will open the conference.
This revolutionary new car, whose energy comes from solar panels, is expected to go into production shortly.

Unit 27
Refer to the sections for Units 2 (present tenses), 5 (past tenses), 10 (future tenses) and 14 (perfect tenses).

Unit 28
Number and concord
Singular verbs

The following all take a singular verb:
crossroads, headquarters, series, news
Thirty kilometres *is a long way to go.*
Four pounds *isn't enough to buy a meal with.*
More than one *voter is going to be disappointed.*
One of *my friends is from Russia.*

The United States is governed from Capitol Hill.
Your **hair** is too long. *(and all **uncountable nouns**)*
Athletics has become very popular in schools. (**politics, mathematics**)
Every house has its own garage.
Everybody/everyone in the room agrees more housing should be built.
No one likes eating blue food.

Plural verbs

The following all take a plural verb: *нребносильки*
jeans, scissors, the police, sunglasses, premises, stairs, clothes
A group of girls were dancing in the disco.
The majority of people I know don't smoke.
A lot of builders try to cut corners.
A number of people had to stand at the concert.
All of us believe in freedom of speech.
Both of the students were late handing in their homework.

The following take either a singular or a plural verb – usually a singular verb is more formal:

Family, staff, team, government, committee, firm, public
Neither the Prime Minister nor his Deputy has/have replied to the ultimatum.
None of us is/are going to the party.
Each of them eats/eat an apple a day.

Unit 30
Uses of *rather*

- Used as an adverb, in the same way as *quite*:
  Eddie Izzard's humour is rather surreal at times – elephants on skis, that sort of thing.
  Some comedians are quite direct and indeed rather rude to their audiences.

- Used with *would* to mean *prefer*:
  I'd rather go to a live show than watch a video.
  John says he'd rather not come with us, as he's very tired.

- Used as a prepositional phrase to contrast two things or situations:
  The jokes were about society in general rather than being purely political.
  Rather than stay at home watching TV, he got changed and went off to the party.

- *Rather* can also be used as an adverb immediately before a verb of thought or feeling, to express an opinion politely:
  I rather think his recent success has gone to his head.
  I rather like your hair cut short.

The grammar of phrasal verbs

Phrasal verbs consist of a main verb and a particle (which is an adverb or a preposition).

- When used intransitively (that is, without an object), the verb and particle of a phrasal verb cannot be separated:
  The engine cut out and they drifted on the waves.

- When the particle is an adverb, transitive phrasal verbs can either be separated or followed by a noun as object; they are always separated by a pronoun as object.
  He keyed the number in carefully.
  He keyed in the number carefully.
  He keyed it in carefully.

  Could you set the drinks down on that table?
  Could you set down the drinks on that table?
  Could you set them down on that table?

- When the particle is a preposition, no separation is possible:
  The lorry ploughed into a barrier.
  My older sister keeps getting at me!

- For three-part phrasal verbs, no separation is possible:
  The sparkling blue sea more than made up for their difficult journey.
  I was really looking forward to that concert – what a shame it's been cancelled.

Self-study folder

The following pages contain all the answers to the exercises, sample answers for the writing tasks, the recording scripts, and lots of additional notes, including useful background information on the texts and topics. The *Map of Objective First Certificate Student's Book* on pages 2–5 gives full details of the language and exam skills covered in each unit. The *Content of the First Certificate Examination* on pages 6–7 provides information about the exam, with links to the relevant Exam folder or Writing folder.

Unit 1

1.1 pages 8–9

1

> **Suggested answer**
> Generally, I prefer to wear casual clothes like jeans and T-shirts. If I have to attend a meeting, I'll put on a smart suit, but I don't feel very comfortable in it. I wouldn't be seen dead in a tie!

2 Further topic vocabulary:

Clothes: jeans, jacket, T-shirt, polo shirt
Footwear: trainers, boots, sandals
Jewellery: earrings, necklace, ring
Headgear: hat, baseball cap
Materials: cotton, silk, polyester, suede, fur
Hairstyle: straight, shaved, loose, tied back
Appearance: casual, untidy, scruffy, fashionable

3

> **Suggested answers**
> **1a** This guy is casually dressed. He's wearing a bright pink T-shirt, a pair of jeans, and trainers. He's got a watch on his left arm.
> **1b** The man must be a biker, because he's holding a helmet and is dressed in biking leathers and boots. His dark blue T-shirt has some sort of design on the front. He's got really long hair.
> **2a** The girl seems quite fashion-conscious. She's wearing a short denim skirt and a fake fur jacket. She's got a pink silk scarf and a pink top. She's wearing black boots and leopard skin tights. She's got long dark hair.
> **2b** This girl prefers to dress down. She's in jeans and a v-neck, striped top, and she's wearing flat leather shoes. Her naturally blonde hair is tied back.
> **3a** The man is probably in his work clothes. He's wearing a dark double-breasted suit, a white shirt and a

> patterned silk tie. He's wearing black shoes. He's got a short beard.
> **3b** This guy looks quite stylish, in a casual sort of way. He's wearing a black jacket, a black sweater and jeans. He's got dark hair and he also has a very short beard.
> **4a** The woman could be going to a wedding, as she seems to be quite smartly dressed. She's wearing a white dress and a black jacket and she has a matching bag, shoes, and hat. Her outfit is expensive-looking.
> **4b** This woman obviously likes wearing loose, comfortable clothes. She's in a long, multi-coloured dress with a fringe at the hem and has a black shawl over her shoulders. She's got a handmade beaded bag and is wearing loads of jewellery, including a silver bracelet, earrings and a necklace. She's got flattish black sandals.

7

> **Answers**
> Speaker 2 – 2a   Speaker 3 – 1a   Speaker 4 – 4b
> Speaker 5 – 3a

The underlined parts of the recording script confirm the answers.

Speaker 2: I started working this year, so I'm able to get new clothes more regularly than before, when I had to save up for months. I buy a lot, I must confess. My mum thinks I should cut down a bit on what I spend, but my image is really important to me: if someone sees me in something once, I don't like to go out in it again – well, not for a while, in any case. I <u>like to wear bright colours</u> and always dress up when I go clubbing. I buy a big range of styles and I do try to keep up with the latest fashions. <u>Sometimes the things are a bit outrageous</u>!

Speaker 3: Shopping for clothes isn't really my scene, if you know what I mean. I don't really mind what I wear, to tell you the truth. I'm the least fashion-conscious person I know! I suppose if anything I favour the casual look. <u>I've got two pairs of jeans and I wear them mostly, with a T-shirt</u> or something. I have got one favourite top, which a girlfriend gave me. It's red and it's got a sort of abstract design printed in navy blue on the back. She said she gave it to me so I would always stand out in a crowd!

Speaker 4: My clothes <u>have to be comfortable, make me feel relaxed</u> as soon as I slip them on. I often put together outfits from stuff I find in street markets – they're less expensive that way. Second-hand clothes can be real bargains, and usually, they've hardly been worn! I'll change the look of my clothes quite frequently, you know, sew in a new piece of material, swap buttons, dye something a different colour, just for a change. I make a lot of my own jewellery too.

Speaker 5: My friends take far less trouble with clothes than I do – sometimes they wear the tattiest things ever! As my job involves dealing with people, I have to make an effort to look good all the time. I like to present a classy, sophisticated image. I go shopping for clothes about once a month, though if I see something by chance, I'm quite likely to go for it there and then. I think I've got good taste and I very rarely make a mistake when I buy clothes. I did take a jacket back last week, but that was because it was badly tailored.

8 The speaker is given in brackets in the answers.

> **Answers**
> **a** stand out (3) **b** put together (4) **c** take back (5)
> **d** dress up (2) **e** save up (2) **f** cut down on (2)
> **g** slip on (4) **h** go out (2) **i** keep up with (2)

Corpus spot

The authors of *Objective First Certificate* have referred extensively to the *Cambridge Learner Corpus*, an electronic collection of Cambridge ESOL candidates' scripts from all over the world. Currently containing more than 27 million words of data, around 3 million words of recent candidate writing are added to the *Cambridge Learner Corpus* each year. This unique resource has given the authors a more accurate and fully up-to-date picture of what FCE candidates can and can't do, and this research has informed the Second Edition of *Objective First Certificate*.

9 Read the Corpus spot. It is good to use phrasal verbs in an informal letter (but not in a formal one).

> **Answers**
> **1** went out **2** slipped on **3** dressed up
> **4** put together **5** stood out **6** keep up with

1.2 pages 10–11

1 The picture shows the finale of a Vivienne Westwood fashion show.

> **B**ackground information
>
> Some other famous British designers are Paul Smith (mentioned in 1.1 Listening), Helen Storey and Stella McCartney. Donna Karan is an American designer.

2 You have probably been taught all the basic structures by now. *Objective First Certificate* will review these structures using an 'inductive' approach, which means that you will be asked to work out grammar rules for yourself, by looking at examples. The *Grammar folder* on pages 198–208 gives important information about the grammar covered in each unit, with more examples.

> **Answers**
> • Single syllable adjectives add *-er/-est*; longer adjectives use *more/the most*
> • Some two-syllable adjectives, e.g. *common, likely, narrow, pleasant, simple, stupid*
> • Adjectives ending in a single vowel and consonant double the consonant (*slim → slimmer*); adjectives ending in *-y* change to *-ier/-iest*.

Corpus spot

> **Answers**
> **a** What are **the best** clothes to wear at the camp?
> **b** He is **more famous** than all the others in the film.
> **c** You look more tired and **thinner**.
> **d** I would like to buy a **much better** one.
> **e** It's now **easier** to get there.
> **f** This is even **worse** than before.

3 You need to be careful with spelling when making some comparative and superlative forms, for example adjectives ending in 'y' become *-ier/-iest*; some adjectives double their final consonant.

> **Answers**
>
> | | |
> |---|---|
> | larger | the largest |
> | thinner | the thinnest |
> | dirtier | the dirtiest |
> | more/less casual | the most/least casual |
> | | the most/least outrageous |
> | better | the best |
> | worse | the worst |
> | farther/further | the farthest/furthest |

4

> **Answers**
> **a** larger **b** the most outrageous / the brightest
> **c** more casual **d** the dirtiest **e** thinner
> **f** the furthest/farthest **g** brighter **h** better

Grammar extra

> **Answers**
> a a bit; much
> b a great deal/a bit; much
>   (*much* can be used with both comparative and
>   superlative adjectives)

5   The structure *not so … as* is less common in everyday
    English.

> **Suggested answer**
> The Beetle is not as sexy as the Ferrari, but it's more
> practical, as it's got a roof rack for carrying extra luggage
> – and surfboards!

6

> **Answers**
> more commonly; less strictly; more readily

7   This exercise is an exam task (Paper 3 Part 4, Key word
    transformations). The task is introduced in Exam folder
    1, which follows Unit 1.

> **Answers**
> 1 were cheaper/less expensive   2 the most talented
> designers   3 as old as   4 is a lot quicker/faster than
> 5 the least expensive of / less expensive than   6 more
> elegantly dressed than   7 as straight as it
> 8 less smartly when

Exam folder 1

Paper 3 Part 4 pages 12–13

1   There are two marks available for each question, so even
    if you cannot produce the whole answer, you can still
    get a mark if one element is accurate.

2   Remember that you cannot change the key word.

3   Use the advice when you do the transformations in the
    next exercise.

4

> **Answers**
> 1 told Sally about a new   2 took it back
> 3 make an effort   4 were not / weren't as fast as
> 5 do not / don't dress up   6 much more easily if / when
> 7 far the best writer / author   8 highly priced that

Unit 2

2.1 pages 14–15

1

> **Suggested answer**
> I disagree with this statement. I enjoy playing computer
> games with my friends, so it isn't anti-social, and we're
> quite normal people, not nerds!

2   The main views expressed by Dr Griffiths are:

● Computer games can have a positive effect on people:
  building relationships, improving social skills, increasing
  self-esteem.
● They are being used to help children with behavioural
  problems.
● They give people a way of releasing their aggression in a
  non-destructive way.
● Therapists use them to win the confidence of children
  under their care.

Interviewer: I have here with me now Dr Mark Griffiths,
senior lecturer in psychology at Nottingham Trent
University. In a recent article for the journal *Education
and Health* he says some rather surprising things about
computer games … or video games, to call them by their
other name. Dr Griffiths, computer games get a lot of bad
publicity, but you don't see them quite so negatively, do
you?

Dr Griffiths: Indeed not. The trend in society is to label
computer games as mindless and antisocial. But there is
another side to the argument, because computer games
actually help some people to develop relationships and
improve their social skills … They make people feel
better about themselves, too.

Interviewer: Yes, and you mention in your article that
therapists are using computer games to help children
with problems … children who are perhaps aggressive …
but don't most people think that computer games make
people more aggressive? Some of these games are very
violent, aren't they?

Dr Griffiths: That's true, but you see the aggressive content
of these games doesn't seem to have a negative effect. In
fact, games like this actually allow the players to release
their own aggression in a non-destructive way, so they can
work positively on anyone with problems. And of course,
introducing 'shoot-em-up' games at an early meeting
allows the therapists to get through to these kids … you
know, they win their confidence, their friendship even.

Interviewer: Well, that's good news … and your article is
called 'Video games: the good news' … Dr Griffiths, stay
with us and after this short break we can talk further
about your work …

3 Skimming and scanning skills are essential for Paper 1 Reading. The answers here come from the bottom of each article.

Answers
a 4 b 2 c 4 d 3

4

Suggested answers
1 This is a multi-level 'shoot-em-up' game with good music.
2 This game focuses on motorbike racing and you play against the computer.
3 This is an adventure game based on the sinking of the Titanic.
4 This is a stupid game with awful graphics, where you become a bird-headed robot.

5 The relevant words in each text are given in italics.

Answers
a clone b cliché c goes downhill d ammunition
e thrill f demanding g joyless h elaborate
i stomp around j at the mercy of

6 The *downside* of something is its disadvantage or less positive side. Compound nouns like this one are often formed from phrasal verbs.

The three used in connection with computers are:
upgrade (software/memory)
back-up (disk/system)
downloading (files/from the Internet)

7

Answers
a letdown b back-up c Downloading d set-up
e upturn f breakdown g upgrade h crackdown

Grammar extra

Answers
endless: regular: add -*ly*
tragic: add -*ally*

NB This applies to all adjectives ending in -*ic* apart from *public*, which becomes *publicly*.

remarkable: lose *le*; -*ly*
easy : lose *y*; add -*ily*
true: lose *e*; add -*ly*

a I didn't sleep much.
b I found it difficult to sleep.
c There have been a lot of good films recently.
d We arrived after the film had started.

Corpus spot

Answers
a **Unfortunately**, I'm quite busy at the moment.
b If I were you, I would **definitely** spend my evenings reading by the fireside.
c You just have to say your name and the computer opens the door **automatically**.
d Entering the restaurant, you **immediately** feel comfortable.
e We **really** started to work hard the morning before the show.
f You must adjust the laser **extremely** carefully to get it in the correct position.
g I would like more information, **especially** about accommodation.
h The computer **completely** takes hold of our lives.

2.2 pages 16–17

1 Completed statement

1 The present <u>simple</u> tense is used for permanent situations (examples <u>d</u> and <u>h</u>) or to talk about actions which are habitual or repeated (examples <u>a</u> and <u>c</u>). This tense is also used in time clauses introduced by words such as *until, once, as soon as*, <u>when</u> (example <u>a</u>). Note also that it is used in both parts of zero conditional sentences, as in this example and in example <u>e</u>.

On the other hand, the present <u>continuous</u> tense is used for temporary situations (example <u>b</u>), situations that are changing or developing (example <u>f</u>), and for events or actions happening now (example <u>g</u>).This tense can also be used to talk about the future (example <u>j</u>).

2 Three sentences are correct.

Answers
a ✓ b is selling (temporary) c ✓ d play (time clause)
e get (zero conditional) f ✓

3

Answers
a finish, get b are improving c is coming out
d flies, explodes, hit e are becoming f take g make
h crashes, lose, are working, save

4

Answers
1 is becoming 2 are creating / create 3 (are) updating / update 4 means 5 submits 6 is adding / adds
7 sounds 8 believes 9 is encouraging
10 is changing 11 find out 12 google
The extra verb is spend.

5

> **Suggested answers**
> a In my opinion, this is sometimes true of older people who have never learned how to use a computer. There are other reasons why some people hate computers though, for example the annoying habit they have of 'auto-correcting' what you key in!
> b Books are still a vital part of our lives, both in schools and colleges and for pleasure. It is still easier to put a book in your pocket!
> c The downside to the Internet is the huge amount of pornography it holds, which is harmful to children.
> d There may be a slight risk, if you sit at a computer for a long period of time – it can be bad for your eyes, or for your neck and back (though if you sit correctly, in a chair with proper support, this danger is minimised).
> e Some people even live a separate life in the virtual world by taking part in Internet-based games where they invent a completely new identity for themselves and live the life of that character online.

6

> **Answers**
> Positive: brilliant, elaborate, excellent, popular, sensational, sophisticated, terrific, tremendous
> Negative: appalling, demanding, joyless, useless

Writing folder 1

Informal letters and emails pages 18–19

In Paper 2 Writing, you must write in a register that is suitable for the task set. The Part 1 letter or email can be either formal or informal, depending on the reader and purpose. There is sometimes an informal letter or email in Part 2 of the paper, for example a letter giving advice to a friend.

1 The informal words and phrases are given below.

> **Answers**
> A – get-together, It's a pity …, terrific, Why not …?
> C – Anyway …, Well …, weird guy, at my place

In the exam, it is important to understand who you are writing to and why.

> **Answers**
> A – departmental secretary to staff in department; invitation to next get-together.
> B – department head to staff; report on the last meeting and a reminder about the next one.
> C – friend to friend; invitation to stay for a party.

2 The style clues are: 'Guess what?', 'splash out' (phrasal verb), 'I can't' (contraction), 'a bit more'.

3 In the exam, you will be assessed not only on accuracy, but on content, range of vocabulary and structure, organisation, register and format. The sample answer would score low marks due to this, as explained below.

> **Answers**
> ● failure to answer the question set (answer ends up talking about something different)
> ● inconsistent register (paragraphs 1 and 3)
> ● poor organisation: long middle paragraph with an absence of linkers
> ● language errors in middle paragraph.

> **Corrected and improved answer**
>
> Dear Frankie
>
> What brilliant news in your letter! Congratulations on passing the exam – and how nice to get some extra cash as a result.
>
> You say you can't decide whether to buy a computer game or some clothes. As you say, if you choose clothes, you'll need to save up more first. Clothes are not as cheap as computer games and I know you like really expensive designer outfits.
>
> The next question is, if you choose a computer game, which one? There are so many available – although, to my mind, they're all the same! Personally, I would spend the money on something else, but you've asked me for advice, so I'll try to help you. My brother says the new version of Sim City is very good, or you could get a sports game, perhaps one of the Madden ones? They've all got excellent graphics and they're not too expensive.
>
> Well, I hope you find these suggestions useful. Let me know what you end up buying.
>
> Love

4 Plan your letter, working through the ideas given under the C-L-O-S-E headings.

> **Answers**
> Informal expressions in 1–6:
> 1 Initial greetings: 1, 3
> 2 Congratulations: 1
> 3 Opinion: 2, 5
> 4 Advice/Suggestion: 1, 2, 4, 7
> 5 Linkers: 2, 3, 5, 6, 7
> 6 Endings: 1, 3, 4
> 7 Opening and closing a letter:
>
> Dear Jayne … Love (informal)
> Dear Sir … Yours faithfully (formal; use when the reader's name is not known)
> Dear Ms Jones … Yours sincerely (formal)

Sample answer

Dear Jan

Thanks for your letter and well done for passing that exam. Your parents sound much more generous than mine!

I'm not sure that you need any more computer games, do you? If I were you, I'd save up for a bit longer and then buy some clothes. In fact, why not get something special, like a new pair of boots or a coat? There are some lovely winter coats in the shops, and many of them are quite a bargain. Also, you said you needed a new coat last year – well, now's your chance.

I think a charcoal grey one would suit you really well, especially something stylish and well-cut. Make sure you choose wool, and find one with nice, deep pockets, to stuff all your bits and pieces in. I'd go for a longish one, below the knee or even full-length. Then you'll be nice and warm when the snow comes!

Let me know what you decide and have fun shopping.

Lots of love

Unit 3

3.1 pages 20–21

1 The picture on the left shows a walking or trekking holiday, which the girl appears to be doing on her own. In contrast, the picture on the right shows a crowded cruise ship.

2

Suggested answers
Student A
To enjoy high-altitude trekking, you need to be fit. If you're going to walk alone, you need to be self-sufficient and have first-aid and map-reading skills. On a cruise ship, you're more likely to be someone who enjoys taking it easy. You need to be able to get along with other people.

Student B
Trekking holiday: beautiful scenery, open spaces away from the crowds, clean air BUT lonely, possibly dangerous, heavy backpack (you need to carry everything with you). Cruise holiday: good weather, very relaxing, with swimming pool and other amenities BUT crowds of people, confined on board for most of the holiday, food might be terrible.

3

Suggested answer
I usually spend my holidays on an island like Sardinia or Corsica, because I love swimming and snorkelling.

4 Further topic vocabulary

Cruise: crew, cabin, deck, passenger, seasickness, on board
Trip: flight, crossing

5 The underlined parts of the recording script confirm the answers.

Answers
1 7 degrees 2 Explorer 3 under the bed 4 American
5 stormy 6 animals 7 research station 8 buildings
9 rubbish 10 wildlife

Interviewer: Good morning, everyone. Well, in the studio today we have Steve Jackson who's going to tell us about his recent trip to the Antarctic. So, Steve, what was it like? Did you freeze?

Steve: No, I didn't. The temperature was about seven degrees most days and I must say I found it quite comfortable. You should take warm clothes though and you really need a good windproof coat.

Interviewer: Now, tell us a bit about the ship you were on.

Steve: It was called the *Explorer*, and it was built only three years ago. The cabins are very small and at first I did wonder where I was going to put all my stuff. However, whoever designed the ship thought of just about everything a passenger would need and I eventually found plenty of cupboard space under the bed.

Interviewer: What were the other passengers like?

Steve: Oh, the atmosphere on board between the passengers was really great. The crew really tried to get everyone to mix. I was invited to eat with the expedition leader, he was American, on the first night, and then after that I sat at a different table for dinner every night, but you don't have to if you don't feel like it.

Interviewer: Did you get seasick at all?

Steve: Some of the passengers did – the weather can be stormy in the Antarctic. Of course there is a doctor on board and he gave anyone who needed it an injection for seasickness – luckily, I didn't need one and the others got over it pretty quickly once they'd had the injection.

Interviewer: I bet that was a relief! What's your best memory of the trip?

Steve: Well, that's hard to say, but probably it's of the animals we saw – whales, penguins and seals. One day we set off to a place called Cuverville Island, which is famous for its birds. There were ten of us in a tiny rubber boat – that was a bit hair-raising I can tell you! Anyway, once there we had to climb up a steep, icy hill, but the view from the top was terrific.

Interviewer: Did you come across any people apart from your fellow tourists?

Steve: Yes, a few of the scientists at a research station. They gave us coffee and biscuits one morning! There used to be a thriving fishing industry in this area at one time, but all that's left are some deserted buildings.

Interviewer: Did you feel guilty about disturbing such an untouched region?

Steve: Well, yes and no. Cruise ships <u>are not allowed to dump rubbish</u> or to go where they like, and they have to carry scientists to lead the excursions. Only small parties are permitted to land in one area at a time and <u>you've got to keep away from the wildlife</u>. So, all in all I felt that well-run trips, like this one, would do more good than harm. I also felt completely changed by the experience – it was like going to another world.

Interviewer: Well, thank you for telling us about your trip, Steve. Now next …

6

> **Suggested answer**
> I think small groups of tourists should be allowed to visit unspoilt parts of the world, but such tourism needs to be carefully controlled. I would certainly like to visit somewhere like the Antarctic, in order to see the different kinds of wildlife.

7

> **Answers**
> a **boats** – canoe, ferry, liner, yacht
> b **movement** – journey, flight, crossing, voyage
> c **seaside** – cliff, shore, coast, sand
> d **people** – courier, travel agent, holiday-makers, sightseers
> e **accommodation** – campsite, caravan, hotel, bed and breakfast

8 It is important to learn collocations like these, as they are often tested in the FCE exam.

> **Answers**
> take – a trip, a ship, a plane, a flight
> book – a trip, a hotel, a flight
> catch – a plane, a flight
> set – sail
> board – a ship, a plane, a flight
> get – a plane, a tan, a hotel, a flight
> go – skiing, sightseeing

9 Expressions with the verbs *do* and *make* are commonly confused. *Do* is often combined with actions, for example *do the washing up*, whereas *make* is commonly used for creating or constructing something, for example *make a cake, make a tree house*.

> **Answers**
> a do business with b do for a living c do military service d do the shopping e did me a favour
> f do my best, do my homework

10

> **Answers**
> RE<u>CENT</u> EXPE<u>DI</u>TION DE<u>SER</u>TED
> <u>TEM</u>PERATURE IN<u>JEC</u>TION UN<u>TOUCHED</u>
> <u>COM</u>FORTABLE <u>SCI</u>ENTISTS EX<u>CUR</u>SIONS
> <u>PAS</u>SENGER <u>BIS</u>CUITS PER<u>MIT</u>TED
> <u>AT</u>MOSPHERE <u>IN</u>DUSTRY EX<u>PE</u>RIENCE

11 The underlining shows where the stress occurs.

Travel Agent: Good morning, can I help you?
Customer: Yes, have you got any <u>bro</u>chures on <u>A</u>frica? I'm a keen pho<u>tog</u>rapher and I'd like to spend some time pho<u>tog</u>raphing the <u>an</u>imals.
Travel Agent: Well, we can offer you <u>var</u>ious <u>pack</u>age deals. What kind of accommo<u>da</u>tion would you prefer?
Customer: Oh, a good ho<u>tel</u>. I don't like to be un<u>com</u>fortable – I'm not the camping type.
Travel Agent: Well, I think we have <u>some</u>thing here to suit you. Let's see. We have two weeks in <u>Ken</u>ya. It looks very at<u>trac</u>tive, I don't think you'll be disap<u>poin</u>ted. They also guaran<u>tee</u> plenty of <u>wild</u>life.
Customer: That sounds good. Thanks. I'll take the <u>bro</u>chure and have a look at it tonight.

3.2 pages 22–23

1 There is more than one possible answer for 1.

> **Answers**
> a 6 b 2 c 5 d 3 and 1 e 1 f 4 g 1

2 Note that *must* is also used in a friendly way in conversation, for example *You must come to dinner sometime!*

> **Answers**
> a The speaker is telling him/herself to do something. (The obligation comes from the speaker.)
> b Someone else is telling the speaker what to do. (The obligation doesn't come from the speaker.)
> c Use of *must* for laws, notices and rules, where there is no choice of action.

Corpus spot

> **Answers**
> a You needn't worry about me.
> b Another thing, should I take my camera with me?
> c You mustn't smoke in this part of the restaurant; it's a no smoking area.
> d It will be nice when I am older.
> e We have to get to the exhibition early or we won't get a ticket.
> f You mustn't swim off the rocks because it's dangerous.

g My doctor says I need to give up smoking.
h Lisa has to buy a ticket before getting on the bus.
i I mustn't be late or I'll miss my plane.

4

Suggested answers
a I must tidy up the flat and I should do some washing, but I don't really want to. I have to meet my uncle at the airport on Saturday afternoon.
b I need to start thinking like an adult! I must work hard and prepare for my exams.
c I must buy a new outfit and I should try to find out what she would like as a wedding present.
d I have to get an identity card from security. I must introduce myself to some of the people in the other departments.
e I must give up work immediately! I need some dark glasses so I won't be recognised.
f I need to save up for driving lessons. I have to apply for a driving licence.

5

Answers
a allowed/permitted b can c let d permitted/allowed

6 The Grammar folder (page 199) explains the differences between *didn't need to do* and *needn't have done*.

7 Remember to use between two and five words including the key word. Contractions count as two words.

Answers
1 had to change 2 needn't have gone to
3 didn't let me go 4 aren't permitted to swim
5 should get health insurance 6 don't have to have/get

Grammar extra

Answers
a on b at c into d in e across f in g on
h on i into j off

Exam folder 2

Paper 3 Part 3 pages 24–25

1 Words can be made negative by putting a suitable prefix at the beginning.

Answers
a dissatisfied	g uncomfortable	m displeased
b irrelevant	h dishonest	n unrealistic
c impatient	i unpopular	o imperfect
d incomplete	j illegible	p irregular
e illegal	k inaccessible	q illiterate
f impossible	l irresponsible	

2 Remember that not all prefixes are negative.

Answers
a very small skirt b without stopping c to train again
d under the road e undo action f not cooked enough
g against/to stop freezing h very conservative
i to live longer than someone/something

mini = small *mini-cab, mini-bus*
non = not *non-smoker, non-stick*
re = again *re-grow, replace, redo*
sub = under *submarine, subtotal, substandard*
un = not/reversing action *unlock, untie, unable*
under = not enough *underfed, underwatered, undervalue*
anti = against *anti-government, anti-war, anti-smoking*
ultra = very *ultra-rightwing, ultra-clean*
out = more/external *outgrow, outnumber, outdoors*

3-7 These exercises summarise the different kinds of suffix.

Answers
3
a happiness b intelligence c approval d repetition
e information f popularity g friendship
h socialism i payment

4
a truth b success c death d height

5
a windy b attractive c hopeful/hopeless
d peaceful e edible/eatable

6
a widen b behave c sympathise d clarify

7
a hard b well c slowly d peacefully e fast
f truly/truthfully

8

Answers
0 noun – PUBLICATION 1 verb – PRODUCED
2 noun – YOUTH 3 adverb – EXTREMELY
4 adjective – SCIENTIFIC 5 adjective – RELIGIOUS
6 noun – SAFETY 7 adjective – SUCCESSFUL
8 noun – VARIETY 9 adjective – INACCURATE
10 adjective – IMPOSSIBLE

Unit 4

4.1 pages 26–27

1

> ### Background information
>
> An animal protection charity recently ran a poster campaign saying: *A dog is for life – not just for Christmas.* Keeping a pet is a long-term commitment, which many people don't realise.

Answers
2 b 3 b

2 There is no single right answer here.

Suggested answers
1 The elderly lady might prefer a budgerigar, which she could talk to. Budgies don't need much looking after, just some seed and water every few days.
2 A furry rabbit would be suitable for the little girl. She could feed it carrots.
3 If the couple are out at work all day, they should have a cat, which could come in and out of the house through a cat flap.
4 The little boy might like a white mouse, but I hope he would be kind to it!

3 The four pets have been to see an animal behaviourist – someone who recommends therapy for pets.

4 The four texts are from an article.

5 The relevant words in the text are given after each answer.

Suggested answers
1 B my neighbour reported me
2 D was immediately better / worked like a dream
3 A he bit me
4 D I'd got her as a puppy
5 A retraining me / the hardest job I've ever done
6 B needed a bit of company / living on my own
7 C wouldn't survive
8 A He had to learn that I was in charge
9 B she couldn't do anything for him
10 D there was nothing basically wrong with her
11 C buy him fresh prawns and salmon

6

Suggested answers
a I'd buy that device called an Aboistop, which sounds as if it works.
b I'd consult an animal behaviourist.
c I'd ban the cat from the living room.
d I'd do nothing, as I like a quiet life.

7

Answers
a organisation b tricky c advertisement
d arguments e successful f aggressive
g excessive h reputable

4.2 pages 28–29

1 *As* and *like* are commonly confused at FCE level. See the Corpus spot.

2

Answers
a The strange man looked like a burglar.
b I know it sounds foolish, but I want to buy a tiger.
c You can work full-time in my shop.
d The new shopping centre is very big – it's like an airport terminal.
e She could play the piano just like a professional.
f He went to the fancy dress party dressed as a gorilla.
g Pete regarded his cat as a member of the family.

3 Use compound adjectives in your writing to describe people and things, as this will show the examiner your range of language.

Answers
a
1 animals in general
2 a tiger which eats people (not just men!)
3 a blue-eyed, long-haired, bad-tempered cat
4 a two-toed, scaly-backed animal

c
1 You'd sit in a car.
2 If you are hard-up, you don't have much money, so you may not be very happy.
3 You need to have a lot of money.
More examples: a phone-in programme, a pick-up truck, a standby flight, a takeaway meal

d
1 a fifty-kilometre journey
2 a twelve-year-old girl
3 a seventy-five-minute film
4 a thirty-five-thousand-pound car
5 a ten-second pause

4 The underlined parts of the recording script confirm the answers.

Answers
1 B 2 A 3 B

1

Man: Well, I've had him about six years now, and he's grown a bit in that time. He was only tiny when I first got him from the pet shop. People said I was mad keeping an animal like that in a small flat, but I haven't really had any problems. Cats are a bit of a problem sometimes, of course. They try to get in through an open window, but I haven't noticed him eat any. Then again I keep him well fed. Here, feel his <u>skin – it's lovely and smooth</u>, isn't it?

2

Woman 1: How are you getting on with that puppy you were given?

Woman 2: Oh, not too well I'm afraid. I have tried hard to be a good owner, taking it to the vet for injections and all the other things you need to see to regularly. The thing is that he's one of those types of dog that is always on the front page of the newspapers for <u>attacking children</u>. So even though he's as good as gold, I <u>have to make the time to take him out for runs in the countryside, just to avoid people</u>.

3

Man: We always seem to be taking the kids to zoos. It doesn't matter where we are on holiday we seem to end up there. They have a really great time – it doesn't seem to bother them that these poor creatures are miles away from their natural habitat. I guess nowadays zoos spend most of their time trying to breed endangered species, <u>but I always feel uncomfortable somehow and have this urge to unlock the cages</u>, even though the kids tell me zoos are doing a good job really.

5 Look up any words you don't know in an English–English dictionary. By doing this, you will learn about related forms and other meanings – for example, claw is both a noun and a verb. Here are its two definitions from the *Cambridge Learner's Dictionary*.

claw[1] /klɔː/ *noun* [C] one of the sharp, curved nails on the feet of some animals and birds.

claw[2] /klɔː/ *verb* [I, T] If a person or animal claws something, they try to get hold of it or damage it with their nails or claws. *He clawed at the rope, trying to free himself.*

> **Answers**
> 1 parrot – perch, squawk, claw, beak, feather, wing
> 2 cat – fur, paw, whiskers, claw, kitten, purr
> 3 dog – bark, paw, kennel, puppy
> 4 horse – hoof, stable, foal, mane, neigh

6

> **Answers**
> a behind the times   b time for lunch   c times as much
> d In time   e have a good time   f pass the time / kill time   g tell the time   h wasting time

Writing folder 2

Transactional letters and emails 1
pages 30–31

In the Part 1 letter or email, you must include all the content points given in the question. There are four points, some of which can be developed, using relevant ideas of your own.

1

> **Answers**
> 1 c correcting information
> 2 d giving information
> 3 a and b complaining and suggesting

2 It is very important to read the question carefully, so that you know exactly what you have to do. Underline key words and phrases on the question paper, to help you plan your answer.

3

> **Answers**
> ● You need to write a formal letter – it is to an airline rather than to someone you know.
> ● There is no name, so you begin *Dear Sir or Madam* and end *Yours faithfully*. Always give your reason for writing at the beginning of the letter. It is important always to be polite. **You lose marks if you are rude in any way.**
> ● This kind of letter is usually broken up into 2–3 paragraphs. It is important to use a variety of linking words, not just *and* and *but*. Other words include *although, nevertheless, however, moreover, finally, in conclusion,* etc.
> ● There are four important points in this letter (the first one is in the instructions):
>   ● late boarding
>   ● ask for a refund
>   ● rude staff
>   ● old movie
>   **Never leave out any points.**
> ● You can add information about the seats if you have enough words left.

4

> **Answers**
> b paragraphing   c length   g content points   i tone
> j linking words

Corrected and improved answer

Dear Sir

I am writing to complain about the flight to Florida that I made with your airline on June 12 this year. There were several problems and I feel you should offer me a partial refund.

To start with, we were three hours late boarding the plane, though no one was able to tell us why. Another problem was the air steward, who was very unhelpful. I had problems with my hand luggage, but she told me sharply that she was too busy to help me.

A further disappointment was the in-flight entertainment. There was only one film, which had already been shown on TV. I had been looking forward to seeing something new.

I hope you will consider my request favourably.

Yours faithfully

5   It is important to remain polite when writing a letter of complaint, and use formal register.

Answers
Formal – b, d, e, f, h, k

6

Answers
a Please reply   b For example   c and so on
d Please note   e Telephone   f Square, Avenue, Street,
Road   g Please turn over   h kilograms, kilometres
i numbers   j maximum, minimum   k Doctor
l Care of   m approximately   n continued   o minutes

7   The sample answer below contains no mistakes and would receive full marks in the examination. Note that you **never** need to include postal addresses in your answer.

Sample answer

Dear Sir or Madam,

I am writing to correct the information in an article in your newspaper, dated 10 November, about foreign students working on a local farm. I worked at the farm all summer and I enjoyed myself very much and made many good friends.

There were only 15 of us, not 30 as you said, and we came from many different countries. Moreover, we only worked in the mornings and we had the weekends off, so we had plenty of time to go sightseeing and relax. In addition, we were paid adequately – not much but enough, considering that we had free food and accommodation.

Our living accommodation was excellent. The farmer, Mr Stevens, had built modern, wooden cabins with good washing facilities – there were enough showers for us all and everything was spotlessly clean. I should know, as I helped to clean them every day!

I would be happy to go back and work for them again, and I know my friends would as well. There was a wonderful atmosphere and we had a great time.

Yours faithfully,

Unit 5

5.1 pages 32–33

1

Suggested answer
I get a bit tense walking home on my own after dark, especially if it's windy or the buildings look spooky. I don't like rats and I'm absolutely petrified of large spiders. I'm not very keen on snakes either.

4   The man was in a lift and spent over four hours there. The answers to 1–5 give the basic storyline.

Answers
1   to attend an interview for a job
2   early evening
3   from the 27th to between the 12th and 13th floors
4   He tried to press the emergency button and use the phone.
5   Most people had already left and it was four hours before the night porter realised he was there.

5   The underlined parts of the recording script confirm the answer, which is C. Other sequence words and phrases are given in italics.

I'd had this interview for a job, up on the twenty-seventh floor of a big office block. It was after six and a lot of people had already left. I got in the lift and pressed the button. *At first,* I noticed that it sort of shook but it started to go down. *Then* there was this horrible sound of twisting metal and it shuddered to a stop. I was stuck between the twelfth and thirteenth floors! To begin with, I was determined not to panic. There was an emergency button, which I pushed for ages. *Next,* I saw a phone, but when I lifted the receiver, it was dead. *At this point,* I completely went to pieces. I shouted and screamed, I hammered on the doors, but nobody helped. *Eventually,* I sank to the floor and wept like a child. *In the end,* it was a good four hours before the night porter realised what had happened and called the Fire Brigade. I've never been in one since.

6 The underlined parts of the recording script confirm the answers.

> **Answers**
> 2 C 3 B 4 B 5 A 6 B

2

It was late at night and I was in the living room watching television on my own. Funnily enough I was watching a horror movie – it wasn't very spooky though! Well, I thought I heard footsteps upstairs. So I turned off the TV, held my breath and listened. Someone was definitely moving around up above me. My first thought was – it's a burglar. And then, there was this horrific crash. I was scared stiff but I knew I had to go up there. I remember I picked up an umbrella – goodness knows what I would have done with it! Anyway, I crept up the stairs and the first thing I saw was a bookcase on its side, with hundreds of books on the floor. Then I heard this whimpering sound, coming from underneath the pile of books. It was the next door neighbour's cat! It was her footsteps I had heard. While I was putting away the books, I found something else. A live frog! It sort of jumped out at me. I tell you, <u>that was the really hair-raising part</u>!

3

Somehow I have to sort out their problem, this fear they have of flying. First we talk as a group, and one by one they tell me about particular times when they've flown and what happened. Nine times out of ten they describe regular, problem-free flights, <u>just like the hundreds I flew myself</u>. You see, most of their worries are only in their imagination. I also use drama and role play, to teach them how to deal with other people's fears, because through that they sometimes forget their own problem, or take it less seriously than before. Finally, but only if I think it's still necessary, we go up in a plane. My passenger is accompanied by an actor, who plays the part of the nervous first-time traveller. I sit a few rows behind and it's wonderful to watch my 'student' staying calm, offering advice to this stranger. I've never failed yet.

4

We were all living in a small house in the countryside at the time. The house was in the middle of nowhere and it was quite a long journey back from the university each evening, so I'd bought myself a small motorbike. Anyway, on one particular evening I was on my way home when a really thick fog came down. I didn't know where I was and I became very uneasy. I went on – rather slowly – but couldn't see anything I recognised. At one point the road curved round, but because of the fog I didn't see this and carried straight on ... and hit a wall. The impact threw me off the bike and I ended up underneath it, with my leg trapped. I screamed for help but of course there was no one about. I realised that I had to get up and carry on – or stay there all night. So I pulled myself out from under the bike, got back on and somehow arrived home, where my friends all took one look at me and <u>drove me off to casualty</u>. I needed seven stitches and they kept me in for observation.

5

Interviewer: Malcolm Jarvis, you have recently sailed single-handedly around the world. At one stage, you were shipwrecked all alone in the middle of the ocean, clinging on to your damaged yacht. Weren't you terrified?

MJ: Not at the time. I suppose I was too busy trying to survive.

Interviewer: You mean finding things to eat?

MJ: More basic than hunger! First, I had to get myself out of the sea. Sharks had been a problem there. I managed to pull myself back into the yacht but it had taken in a lot of water. So I spent a bit of time sorting that out.

Interviewer: And then were you able to keep yourself warm?

MJ: <u>Only for a while</u>. I wrapped myself in whatever I could find, including the sails, but by the second day <u>I was in a really bad way because I couldn't feel my fingers and toes</u>, they were completely numb. That was the most dreadful time. It was just as well they found me when they did.

6

We were all in the main room planning what to do that day. The others were looking at a map on the table, but I was standing by the back window. About six of them burst in, waving guns and shouting things in a dialect we didn't understand. <u>I knew they hadn't seen me</u> over by the open window. They grabbed John and Gary. Ruth rushed to the doorway but they got her too. In the meantime, I had managed to throw myself safely outside and had crawled underneath the house – because of the rainy season, all the houses there are raised above the ground on wooden stilts. I kept totally still. I remember watching a beetle on a leaf, staring at it and hoping that they wouldn't find me. Finally, when I realised that they'd gone, I ran inside and radioed for help. My friends weren't so lucky. They were held as hostages for over three months.

7 As you listen to the recording again, notice the use of the past perfect.

8

> **Answers**
> started   lifted   shouted
> The /ɪd/ ending follows the consonants *t* and *d*.

Grammar extra

The verb forms appear on page 200 of the Grammar folder. *Burst* has the same form throughout. Other verbs like this include *bet, cut, hit, put, set*.

5.2 pages 34–35

1

> **Answers**
> a PP b PS; PS c P d PC e PS; PP f PC; PS
> g PC; PC h PS; PP i PS; PP; PS j P

In e, h and i, the past simple and the past perfect are both used (the past perfect for an action further back in the past).
In f, the past continuous describes an action that happened over a longer time period than the second action, which happened at a specific moment.

2

> **Answers**
> 1 was walking 2 was blowing 3 was pouring
> 4 was 5 drove 6 stopped 7 curved 8 decided
> 9 was feeling 10 got 11 drove 12 happened
> 13 pulled up 14 waited 15 drew up 16 pulled away
> 17 was 18 stood 19 was coming down
> 20 was shaking 21 (was) wondering 22 came
> 23 was pushing 24 grabbed 25 made 26 went
> 27 was trying 28 heard

3 You must use the past perfect tense to make time differences clear.

> **Answers**
> a had spent; decided
> b told; had happened; explained; had found
> c had kept; thought; was

4

> **Sample answer**
> Eventually, the police forced the robbers to stop and arrested them. They had chased them all over town at high speed with their sirens blaring and blue lights flashing. The thieves had made their getaway in a red car, dressed in balaclavas and with the banknotes stuffed into a holdall. At the bank, the three robbers had worn masks to avoid being identified. They had held up the cashiers at gunpoint.

5

> **B**ackground information
>
> Raymond Chandler, author of *The Big Sleep*, was born in Chicago, but went to school in London. For most of his life, he lived in Southern California, which is where most of his novels are set. His most famous character is the private detective Philip Marlowe, who has been played in films by Humphrey Bogart, Robert Mitchum and Elliot Gould.

6 This exercise is an introduction to the 'open cloze', Paper 3 Part 2. Exam folder 3, on the following pages (36–37), focuses on this task.

> **Answers**
> 1 at 2 the 3 when 4 of 5 and 6 any 7 had
> 8 so 9 not 10 was 11 out 12 went

Most words tested here fall into the five grammatical categories given below. These areas are commonly tested in the open cloze task.

> **Answers**
> ARTICLE: the
> CONJUNCTIONS: and, because, so
> PREPOSITIONS: at, of, out
> QUANTIFIERS: any, some
> VERBS: had, has, was, went

Exam folder 3

Paper 3 Part 2 pages 36–37

1 'Balancing the risks' is the best title, as it looks at both sides of the question.

2

> **Answers**
> 1 spend 2 unless 3 a 4 at 5 few 6 if, though
> 7 who/that 8 than 9 although/whereas 10 out
> 11 In 12 such

Unit 6

6.1 pages 38–39

1 The article is about winning the lottery and describes someone who visits winners the day after their win (key words are 'winner's home', 'draw').

2 The article contains four gaps, with a sentence missing from each. This is an easy introduction to the gapped sentence task (Paper 1, Part 2). In the exam, seven sentences will be missing from the text.

3 The writer works for Camelot, the National Lottery in Britain, visiting jackpot winners.

> **B**ackground information
>
> The National Lottery started in November 1994. There are now two draws per week, on Wednesdays and Saturdays. Jackpot wins have been as big as £35.4 million (August 2007, won by a Scottish postal worker). The lottery is run by a private company, Camelot, with some of the profits being handed to the government for distribution to good causes.

4

> **Answers**
> C and D include a time reference (My initial visit; Then).
> 1C; 2A; 3B; 4D.
> B refers back to the previous paragraph.

Grammar extra

Be careful with word order when using adverbs of frequency.

> **Answers**
> usually   always   seldom   never   sometimes   often
>
> I usually arrive (line 1)   It's always a very crowded room (line 3)   ... they always say (line 7)
> They seldom bother to read it (line 12)
> I usually have to go over the same points (line 21)
> Winners often burst into tears (line 24)   I always go to the door (line 26)   They'll sometimes say (line 39)
> they never really expect to win (lines 44–45)
> They're often surprised (line 52)
>
> before; be; after; after
>
> **Suggested answers**
> a On Sundays, I always get up late, because I don't have to go to work.
> b I've never been frightened of spiders, which is why I don't mind picking them up.
> c When I was younger, I often enjoyed playing board games, but now I never get the time.
> d I'm never good at remembering people's names and this is often embarrassing at parties.
> e I sometimes wish I could win a lot of money, because then I would be able to do exactly what I want.

5

> **Answers**
> a They have forgotten what he told them, usually because of shock.
> b They can't sleep or eat properly.
> c He asks to take his jacket off and is offered a cup of tea.
> d On the Monday morning following their win.

6

> **Answers**
> a link   b deal with a problem successfully
> c making the right decisions   d say no
> e become public knowledge   f afraid of other people
> g unable to trust   h happening frequently
>
> The meaning of 'emotional panic' is explained in the rest of that sentence – they don't know how to react and they become worried about what is going to happen.

7

> **Suggested answer**
>
> Anyone winning a large prize will inevitably attract publicity. Even close friends of the winners will find it hard to refuse offers up to £10,000 for their story. The public is interested in stories about lottery winners.
>
> Pros: financial security, the chance to stop working, money to spend
> Cons: stress surrounding the publicity, losing friends, having to learn new skills, becoming suspicious of people
>
> I don't think the decision would be up to me – as the article says, it is impossible to remain anonymous and enjoy the money.

6.2 pages 40–41

1 These recordings are 'unscripted' – the four speakers just said what they wanted to, at natural speed. Don't worry if you don't understand every word. Listen out for the second conditional form *I'd/I would*, which will give you the answers.

> **Answers**
> Speaker 1 would have more homes and would eat better.
> Speaker 2 would spend all his time on a yacht in the sun.
> Speaker 3 would no longer be in debt and would own a massive house in the country.
> Speaker 4 would live in a warm climate and pay off debts.

1

I'd buy a Seychelles blue Bentley convertible. I'd buy a nice, fat house in Holland Park. I'd get a lovely, big house in the countryside. I'd buy a beautiful house in Spain, with swimming pool, palm trees, that sort of thing. I'd get a flat in Manhattan probably. Um ... I'd also have a permanent chef ... top of the range chef who could cook all different types of food, so I could have whatever food I wanted whenever I wanted it. I'd have my own personal masseur ...

2

I don't believe it when people say that if they won the lottery it wouldn't change their lives, because it would certainly change mine. Um, and I think I would just alter my life entirely. I love the sun and I hate English winters so I think I'd buy a yacht. And as I don't know anything about um ... sailing, I'd have to buy a crew as well. So, um, I'd ... I'd get this luxurious yacht and a very skilled crew – and probably a ... a ... a skilled cook – who would just take me all around the world going from hot spot to hot spot, so I could have a really great time.

3

Well, I know I'd have a problem with having all that money. I'd ... I think it is a problem really, in some ways, because you ... you'd have a sort of social responsibility and there are all kinds of people who you need to help, which I would want to do very much. Um, so of course I'd sort out my debts, my family's, but in the end I think what I'd do is buy – depending on how much money I had – buy a huge house, a really massive house somewhere in the country and just surround myself by all the people I want to be with, um and people who perhaps never had a chance to get out into the country at all.

4

Again depending on how many millions I won, um it would change what I would or wouldn't do with it. Frankly, if it was a lot, I mean five million upwards ... sort out my own debts, which God knows are bad enough, sort out the family's debts and then invest as much as possible and just try and live off the interest, keep it there, nice little nest egg, growing and growing and growing, developing, flowering bountifully, and holiday, get away, move, anywhere but cold Britain.

2

Answers
a 2 b 3 c 0 d 1

3

Answers
1 d 2 a 3 g 4 b 5 f 6 c 7 h 8 e

Corpus spot

Answers
a There will be no improvement in my tennis unless I ~~don't~~ get some training.
b correct
c People hardly ever use candlelight today unless there ~~isn't anything~~ is something wrong with the power supply.
d There isn't much to do in the city unless you have (got) friends.
e You must stop working so hard if you don't want to end up in hospital sooner or later.
f correct

5

Answers
Tense errors:
won't > wouldn't (be so unreliable)
hasn't > hadn't (run out of)
I'll find > I find
can't > couldn't
will > would OR didn't > don't
will get > gets (really angry)
will do > do
would pay > paid

1 If 2 unless 3 If 4 if 5 if 6 unless 7 if 8 unless 9 if 10 if

6

Suggested answers
a Unless I get up early tomorrow, I won't finish my essay.
b If I had enough money, I'd buy a Ferrari.
c My life would be a lot easier, if I cut down on my work.
d If I hadn't come to class today, I would have gone swimming.

7

Answers
a In fact b in case c in control d in time

Suggested answers
e Jenny rang us from a phone box, in a real panic – she had lost both sets of keys.
f I couldn't take the news in – Jess had already left for New York and wouldn't be coming back.
g Mike really has it in for his secretary – she can't seem to do anything right, according to him!

8

Answers
Nouns: experiment, trial, try, attempt
Verbs: received, accepted, gathered, welcomed
Prepositions: on, by, in, to
Adjectives: tiny, light, delicate, gentle
1 attempt 2 light 3 received 4 by

Writing folder 3

Stories 1 pages 42–43

In the story question you will be given a sentence, which you **must** include – you will lose marks if you omit it. You will also be told whether to put the sentence at the beginning or the end of your story. Read the question carefully, to find out about the content, and who the story should be about.

1

Answers
a There could possibly be some continuation of the third conditional structure (talking about what would have happened if he hadn't picked up the phone), but the story must focus on actual past events, mainly using the past simple.
b Because of this final sentence, the past perfect will be needed earlier in the narrative, along with the past simple and possibly past continuous.

2 The tenses used are the past perfect, the past continuous and the past simple.

3

> **Answers**
> **1** A **2** C **3** suspiciously **4** nervously/anxiously OR desperately **5** wildly OR nervously/anxiously

4 Try to use a variety of sentence openers when writing a story.

> **Answers**
> Order: g, e, b (Suddenly …), h (Without a second thought …), d, f, a (By now …), i (Eventually …), c (At first …)

5

> **Sample answer**
>
> As soon as he got out of the car, Martin felt uneasy. He was in the middle of nowhere, with only a few sheep for company. Why had he agreed to meet Martha and John so far away from the city? It had been Martha's idea to go for this picnic on a Scottish hillside. Now, in mid-November, the whole thing seemed completely crazy. To make matters worse, they were late. Or was he in the wrong place? Perhaps he had missed a turning, or misread their map. He felt more and more anxious, and sighed as he pictured his nice, warm flat in Edinburgh.
>
> Just then, he heard the unmistakable noise of Martha's Vespa and saw them climbing slowly up the hill. He recognised the little scooter immediately, as Martha had painted it bright pink. He shouted and waved, and soon they were there beside him. John gave Martin a big bear hug. "Happy birthday, mate," he said, "we've brought your birthday cake!" Martha grinned at them both and at that moment the sun came out. It was a truly memorable afternoon.

Units 1–6 Revision

pages 44–45

1

> **Suggested answers**
> **a** If I don't have to get up early, I prefer to stay in bed reading the paper.
> **b** For me, fast cars are irrelevant, as I can't drive. If I had some money, the first thing I would buy is a good camera.
> **c** Actually, the opposite is true for me – I'm not as good at Maths as I am at English.
> **d** I'm quite good at remembering things, especially my homework.

e I'm absolutely petrified of large spiders, even if they're not poisonous.
f I'm fairly tolerant of other people and I like to keep an open mind on everything.
g This is something I should do, but don't!
h I prefer my clothes to be comfortable and I don't spend a lot on clothes.
i Sometimes I enjoy playing computer games, but I soon get bored – but I can read a good book for hours.
j I don't like the idea of going on holiday with crowds of other people, so this statement is true for me.

2

> **Answers**
> **1** on **2** the **3** some **4** has **5** while/when **6** was **7** if **8** too **9** as/because **10** who **11** his **12** from

3

> **Answers**
> **a** save **b** ring/call/phone **c** dress **d** end **e** put **f** stand **g** sort **h** work **i** go **j** make **k** to cut down on **l** an upturn **m** you take back **n** to set off **o** to get over

4 Sometimes more than one answer is correct, as shown.

> **Answers**
> **1** are **2** seems **3** are **4** sees **5** has tried / has been trying **6** has done **7** has developed **8** is **9** puts / has put **10** has had **11** came **12** had never flown **13** had had **14** took **15** had never worried **16** announced **17** had **18** tried **19** overcame / had overcome **20** managed / had managed

5

> **Answers**
> **1** wouldn't go dancing unless **2** worst film I've ever **3** would have met you **4** aren't allowed to **5** more frightened of ghosts than **6** shouldn't have bought you **7** had (already) started **8** see to drive without

Unit 7

7.1 pages 46–47

1

Answers
a swimming goggles and hat b ski sticks and skis
c football d rugby ball e table tennis bats and ball
f ice skates g golf clubs and ball h shuttlecocks –
badminton i basket for basketball j squash racket
and ball k baseball bat l tennis racket and ball
m oars – rowing n volleyball

2

Suggested answers
a I can't stand watching wrestling.
b I really enjoy watching tennis and football.
c I'm keen on seeing Carlos Moya play, because he's so
  talented.
d I've taken up volleyball recently.
e I don't mind watching rugby in the rain, if I've got a
  good umbrella!
f I feel more like relaxing on holiday, so I only do
  watersports then.

3 Gerunds are verb forms which are used as nouns.

Answers
a adjective (the kind of rope)
b participle (past continuous tense)
c gerund (gerund – subject of sentence)

4

Answers
a 4 b 1 c 5 d 2 e 3

5 There is a list of common verbs which are followed by a
gerund on page 201 of the Grammar folder.

Answers
a in getting b of learning c on teaching
d for dropping e in doing f at swimming
g to playing

6

Answers
1 c 2 e 3 b 4 a 5 d 6 f, d

Corpus spot

Answers
a I suggest taking / we take the easier route.
b Do you want to go out with me?
c I'm used to sleeping in a tent.
d There's no point (in) playing today.
e I suggest (that) you go to the sports centre. / I suggest
  going to the sports centre.
f I like playing hockey.
g I recommend (that) you go there.
h I hope to hear from you soon.
i I am interested in applying for this job of personal
  trainer.
j I should give up swimming every morning.

7

Answers
1 climbing 2 tell 3 arriving 4 training 5 to assess
6 to make 7 to teach 8 mountaineering 9 to use
10 work 11 climbing 12 to sleep 13 Reaching
14 jumping 15 seeing 16 tell

8 Gerunds and infinitives are frequently tested in Paper 3
Part 4.

Answers
1 accused him of pushing
2 is too wet to
3 had difficulty in learning
4 advised me not to go / advised me against (going)
5 would rather go on

7.2 pages 48–49

1 The photos are of:

a – Ximena Restreop (Colombian runner)
b – Paolo Maldini (Italian footballer)
c – Tiger Woods (American golfer)
d – Michael Schumacher (German racing driver)
e – Venus Williams (American tennis player)

Suggested answers
a The greatest footballer of all time is the Dutch player
  Johann Cruyff, because he played total football.
b Some sports are less physical than others, but I'm not
  sure that this makes them any easier.
c I think sky-diving is dangerous, because your
  parachute might not open.
d No, I haven't!

2

> **Answers**
> bungee jumping (ground far away, jumps, attached to a rope)

3 The underlined parts of the recording script confirm the answers.

> **Answers**
> 1 E 2 A 3 D 4 C 5 F

Speaker 1: All of us in the office where I work love doing it, probably because <u>we're all desperate to get out of that 9-5 routine</u>. It's an expensive sport but we all joined a Dangerous Sports Club to help keep costs down. The first time I did it I really was frightened as the ground seemed so far away, but I said to myself that nothing would happen and I wasn't going to die. I did my first two jumps in Canada and then in London. Apparently, in Germany they're doing it without being attached to a rope but with just a net beneath. That could be pretty scary, couldn't it?

Speaker 2: About four years ago I was very ill and nearly died. Sometime later I was involved in a serious car crash. It made me realise how risky everyday life is, and it seemed to cure me of fear, so I said to myself <u>why not push things to the limit</u>? So, <u>I had a go at white-water rafting in the States and then moved on to other things</u>. It's been brilliant. I've done all sorts of things from abseiling down mountains to skydiving. The skydiving was the worst! Now I set myself challenges all the time, not that I've got anything to prove, it's just a personal thing really. I'm thinking of doing river sledging next.

Speaker 3: I took part in a trek to ski across the Arctic last year. It was probably the most dangerous thing I've ever done, but I'd do it again tomorrow. <u>I was conscious all the time that death was very near and in a strange way that made it seem more fun.</u> I cried in absolute terror sometimes, especially when the ice began to melt and great holes would suddenly appear just in front of me. It was the ultimate challenge for a skier like myself and I guess I'm not afraid of anything any more. In fact, I'm looking forward to skiing in the Antarctic next year!

Speaker 4: I've always enjoyed diving as it's quite an exciting sport, but last winter I had the ultimate experience of going shark-feeding in the Caribbean. The sharks were about three metres in length and obviously they are quite aggressive and can bite you, but if you put on the right protective clothing and take precautions <u>it's no more of a risk than driving fast motor cars. I must say I had more accidents when I went horse riding</u>. I did feel a bit nervous as I went over the side of the boat, after all, I've seen Jaws like everyone else! But I was never in any real danger.

Speaker 5: Some of my mates had started doing this free climbing – you know where you don't use ropes, only your hands and feet. I guess they needed to have a bit of excitement in their lives, didn't they? Me, I think I get enough from my job as a motorbike courier in London. Anyway, I went with them one weekend. It was terrifying and I was sure I'd end up lying in a hospital bed, but <u>I felt I had to do it, especially with them looking on</u>. There was no pressure from them, but you know how it is. Anyway, I did it and I have to say it gave me a real 'buzz'. I can understand why people go in for this type of thing now.

4

> **Answers**
> 1 bungee jumping
> 2 white-water rafting, abseiling, skydiving, river sledging (going down rapids on a small sledge)
> 3 skiing
> 4 diving, driving fast cars, horse riding
> 5 free climbing (without a rope or harness)

5

> **Answers**
> a 2 b 4 c 1 d 3 e 6 f 5

6 Read sentences a–k carefully, looking at the forms of the question tags.

7 Try writing out some of these questions – imagine you are interviewing a famous sports star!

8

> **Answers**
> a wouldn't you? b aren't I? c can you? d won't you?
> e don't they? f won't there? g will you?
> h haven't you? i don't you?

9

> **B**ackground information
>
> A personal trainer is a person who comes to your house to encourage you to work out or works with you individually at the gym. Many film stars employ a trainer so that they can exercise in private.

> **Answers**
> 1 famous 2 ensure 3 qualified 4 training
> 5 youth 6 demanding 7 movement 8 education
> 9 qualifications 10 freedom

10 The words are all adjectives.

> **Answers**
> a danger b fear/fright c risk d aggression
> e protection f nerve(s)/nervousness g terror
> h excitement

Exam folder 4

Paper 3 Part 1 pages 50-51

The Vocabulary spot on page 51 gives useful advice on organising new vocabulary.

Unit 8

8.1 pages 52–53

1

Suggested answer
In many ways, things have got better – people are generally paid more, there are proper health and safety rules, and working conditions have improved. However, in this digital age, there is far more pressure on working people than there used to be.

2 The top two pictures show commuters in New York and people in a village helping with the harvest.

The second two show an old woollen mill with a lot of workers and a car factory run by robots.

3

Background information

'Downshifting' is when people decide they don't want to carry on working in a large city or for a large company. Underlying this is the idea that quality of life is more important than money or prestige. They usually move out to the countryside for a better life.

4

Answers
1 C 2 B 3 D 4 A 5 B 6 C 7 D 8 C

Detailed explanation of questions 2–8:

2 The answer (B) is confirmed in the third paragraph, where it talks about 'radical changes in the employment market, where a job is no longer guaranteed'. A is likely but not stated. C is plausible, but the text talks about 'taking personal responsibility for your career', which is not the same as saying that people have to look hard for a job. D may be true but the text doesn't say this.

3 The answer (D) is found in the final sentence of paragraph five, where it says 'They both earned a large amount of money'. A is wrong because he worked in central London but lived in the suburbs. Neither B nor C is stated in the text.

4 A is the answer: 'I always wanted to have a farm here.' B is wrong because Daniel says: 'It's taken some getting used to'. C is wrong because he doesn't mention holidays abroad (nor does he say he misses having holidays). D is wrong because they took a year to make the decision.

5 The answer (B) is in the final two paragraphs. Daniel says 'I think it's made us stronger as a family, and the children are a lot happier'. Liz then says 'One thing I do like is being able to see more of my children'. A is ruled out by what Liz says at the end of the text, even though Daniel talks of the time taken to reach the decision to downshift. C is not stated, though Daniel talks about money. D cannot be true, as both Daniel and Liz express a downside to the move.

6 Here, the word 'tip' means a word of advice (C), and this is clear from the context, where Liz refers to other people.

7 To get to the answer (D), you need to understand the meaning of 'the same' earlier in the sentence. It is clear from this that Liz is referring to the whole move, or 'downshifting'.

8 The answer to this global question is (C). The second paragraph begins by mentioning this new trend, saying 'people are wondering what life is all about'. The third and fourth paragraphs also talk in terms of a social trend, of which Daniel and Liz are one example. A is ruled out as the text is fairly positive about downshifting. B is not true, as the text does not explain what to do. D is plausible but the text doesn't actually say this.

7

Answers
para 1 – volume, stuffed with, horrified   para 2 – single-minded pursuit   para 3 – approach, radical
para 4 – swapping   para 5 – suburbs   para 6 – run

8.2 pages 54–55

1 It is important to understand the differences between *would* and *used to*. Read the section in the Grammar folder on page 201.

Answers
a =1, b=3, c=2

2 Refer to the Corpus spot.

a used to be **b** correct **c** used to have **d** correct
e used to doing **f** used to working **g** correct **h** correct

3 The underlined parts of the recording script confirm the answers.

> **Answers**
> Speaker 1: window cleaner
> Speaker 2: dentist
> Speaker 3: pop singer
> Speaker 4: plumber / heating engineer
> Speaker 5: chef

Speaker 1: It was quite a good job, but I never got used to working at the top of a <u>ladder</u>. I've got <u>no head for heights</u> at all. <u>Cleaning the ones in those large tower blocks was the worst</u>. You also have to be careful not to look too closely as well. I often used to see things I shouldn't have done. People would forget I was outside and they would be inside having a big argument or having a bath.

Speaker 2: Well, life's much better now I don't spend my time listening to that <u>drill</u> going all day. It really got me down when people would arrive shaking with fear – I used to take it personally. The <u>anaesthetic</u> is so good these days that they really had nothing to be worried about. I'm running a bed and breakfast place in the country now. Much nicer, though not as well paid of course.

Speaker 3: Yeah, well it was great while it lasted. But look at me now – I look about twenty years older than I really am. We used to have to <u>travel overnight to a different gig each evening</u>. They used to put us up in good hotels but there were always one or two <u>fans</u> who managed to get through security and come looking for a souvenir. It wears you out after a while, you know.

Speaker 4: The best thing about it used to be people I'd meet. They would always be so pleased to see me. Well, wouldn't you be if you were <u>freezing</u> to death in the middle of winter? They'd be making me cups of coffee and offering me biscuits all day. They weren't so pleased <u>when they got the bill</u> though.

Speaker 5: It was the recession really that closed us down. We had a great <u>business</u> going and <u>we used to be full every time we opened</u>. There were great reviews in all the best newspapers and people would be queuing at the door. I suppose it couldn't last, though. I had <u>a team of six under me</u>, so all I had to do was <u>be creative all day</u> – great.

5

> **Answers**
> 1 captain, purser, steward, mate, chef, waiter
> 2 headteacher/principal, teacher, caretaker, secretary
> 3 matron, surgeon, doctor, nurse, porter, staff nurse, sister, consultant, specialist
> 4 manager, buyer, assistant, window dresser, accountant
> 5 manager, coach/trainer, cleaner, receptionist

6

> **Answers**
> a must   b take/eat/have   c being/going to be/will be
> d fetch/make   e received   f arrives/comes   g have
> h arrange for

7

> **Answers**
> a his guards   b my new boss   c your exams
> d being made redundant   e his new job   f much money
>
> **Answers**
> a escaped   b like   c pass   d recovered from
> e is making a success of   f manage

8

> **Answers**
> single-minded, long-hours, time-consuming, better-balanced

9 Use a dictionary to help you. For example, the *Cambridge Learner's Dictionary* has a very useful 15-page appendix on word building.

> **Answers**
> a to horrify, horror
> b to succeed, unsuccessful
> c energetic, energetically
> d nation/nationality, nationalise
> e unemployed, employ
> f responsible, irresponsible
> g decisive, to decide
> h commuter, commuting

Writing folder 4

Essays 1 pages 56–57

In the exam, essays are usually written for a teacher and generally ask you to give your opinions about a statement. Any essay requires careful organisation and you should make a plan before you start writing. Remember to include an introduction and conclusion, and use a suitable number of paragraphs.

1 This exercise focuses on organisation and linking.

> **Answers**
> 1 F   2 A   3 E   4 G   5 B   6 D   7 C

2

> **Answers**
> Paragraph 1 – F, A   Paragraph 2 – E, G, B   Paragraph 3 – D, C

3 The essay only uses the linkers *And*, *But* and *So*. It is better to avoid using these linkers at the beginning of a sentence – there are many other ones to choose from, as the box on page 57 shows.

> **Answers**
> **And** – *in addition, moreover*
> You can't use *as well as* in place of the first *And* because you're not joining two ideas which are the same. The subjects of the sentence are different.
>
> **And** – *in addition, moreover, as well as*
> You can use *as well as* in place of the second *And* but you would need to change the structure so that it reads:
> *As well as working about 35 hours a week, they have 4 weeks' holiday a year.*
> The subject in both is *people in my country*.
>
> **But** – *However,*
> Notice that after *However* you need to use a comma.
>
> **But** – *However, Nevertheless*
> In place of the second *But* you can't use *in contrast* or *on the other hand*. This is because no contrast is being offered in that sentence – just a comment on what is happening.
>
> **So** – *As a result*
> **So** – *Therefore*
> In place of the second *so* you can't use *as a result*. You are not giving a result, just concluding your ideas, whereas in the first sentence with *so* there is a result.

4 Note that after *Not only* …, the subject and verb have to come in reverse order (this is called 'inversion').

> **Answers**
> Not only is there very little heavy industry, but also most manufacturing is fully automated.
> Not only do they usually only work about 35 hours a week, but they also have four weeks' holiday a year.
> Not only are there fewer jobs, but also people are being made redundant.

5 Always begin a new paragraph if you are making a different point.

> **Answers**
> Paragraph 1: First of all – holiday a year.
> Paragraph 2: But in some countries – up until now.
> Paragraph 3: But things – too hard.

6 The sample answer below contains no mistakes and would receive a good mark in the examination, as it is well linked and suitably paragraphed.

> **Sample answer**
> It is said that stress causes more health problems nowadays than anything else. In my opinion, sport is a good way of reducing stress levels.

There is nothing better than calling in at a pool after a hectic day, where you can let your mind switch off completely. As well as swimming, visiting a gym is a good way to relax your body. However, it is important not to train too hard, as this could be dangerous for your heart.

On the other hand, sometimes sport is stressful in itself. In competitive games like football or basketball, there is pressure on each team member to play well. In this situation, you cannot relax. Nevertheless, even this kind of sport allows you to forget the day's problems, which will probably help to control stress.

In contrast to sport, there are gentler ways of relaxing, such as listening to music, going out with friends, or staying in with a good book. All of these activities will help to calm you down. Therefore, it is up to each individual to do what is right for him or her. Personally, I choose sport.

Unit 9

9.1 pages 58–59

1

> **Suggested answer**
> I think it must be for a holiday, or travel insurance. It can't be for food, because they always show the product. It could be advertising a TV programme – everyone's watching, so the place is empty.

The answer on page 83 can't be true! What will they think of next?

2 The speaker is certain – the words 'must be' and 'can't be' tell you this.

In the final example, when the sentence is read as a statement (with a full stop), the speaker is certain. As a question, the same sentence becomes a speculation. The use of 'possibly' changes: in the statement, it confirms the certainty, whereas in the question, it becomes a 'hedging' device – it shows uncertainty. The question would be improved with the addition of the question tag 'could it'.

These modal verbs may be useful when discussing the photos in Paper 5 Part 2.

3

> **B**ackground information
>
> The Cannes Film Festival is held every May–June in the south of France, where a parallel Advertising Film Festival is also held.

> **Answers**
> 3rd paragraph: can't be; Might it be; Could it be
> 4th paragraph: must have won; couldn't

4

> **Answers**
> a spoken commentary played over a film
> b a short, memorable tune, often with words, used to advertise a product
> c someone famous
> d decision
> e one particular make of product
> f clever

The use of the idiom 'missed the boat' in the title is appropriate, as it refers to the failure of Delvico Bates to meet the festival deadline, and also to the fact that the advert should have won. It is also a play on words, as Cannes is a port, where there are a lot of boats.

5 In examples a and b, the speaker is sure; in c, unsure.

6

> **Answers**
> 1 can't/couldn't (possibly) be 2 it must be
> 3 might be sung 4 must have had
> 5 must have been paid 6 couldn't/can't have been

7 Try to learn collocations in the way that the Vocabulary spot advises.

> **Answers**
> huge: variety, budget, market, picture
> high: budget, voice
> low: budget, voice
> deep: message, character, voice
> shallow: message, idea, character
> narrow: variety, market, picture, view (+ narrow ideas)
> wide: variety, market, picture

9.2 pages 60–61

1

> **Sample answer**
> There's one advert that keeps coming back on TV – it must be very successful, I suppose. It's for a 'd-i-y' product called *Ronseal*, which you paint onto wooden doors and fences to protect them. The actor looks like a normal person and he's dressed in casual clothes. At the end, he says to camera the now-famous words: 'does exactly what it says on the tin'. This is a no-nonsense advert, promoting an everyday product. I think it's really clever.

2

> **Answers**
> a, d, f and h are mentioned.

Part 1

Man: There's one car advert that opens with part of a song by Bjork – it must have cost a <u>fortune</u> to make, and it looks tremendous ...

Woman: I've seen that one. You're not sure what it's advertising to begin with, are you? A graceful silver vehicle moving through an unusual landscape ... it could be a spacecraft of the future. All very stylish. The trouble is, it's a bit of a let-down when you realise it's just another <u>car</u> advert!

Man: Yes, the beginning <u>is</u> a bit misleading ... It's funny, isn't it, sometimes the most effective ads are the really simple ones – you know, like a football manager sitting down at the breakfast table with his family, enjoying a particular cereal ...

Woman: ... he eats it so it <u>must</u> be good. And that actress from *Friends* advertising shampoo – Jennifer Aniston, wasn't it? You know, seeing famous people on screen can be a huge influence on us, we see them as ... well, as role models.

Man: Definitely. ... The ads they put on TV before the World Cup or the Olympics always use megastars, don't they?

Woman: Yeah, remember the one that had a <u>whole team</u> of top footballers from around the world! The special effects were incredible – the budget must have been <u>huge</u> ... all for <u>one</u> advert!

Man: But the company probably earned <u>millions</u> of dollars in increased sales, so for them it was worth it.

Grammar extra

The order cannot be changed because an opinion adjective (*graceful*) always comes first. Refer also to the Corpus spot.

> **Answers**
> Opinion adjectives: classic, sensational, popular, delicious
> Size: full-length, bite-sized
> Age: new
> Colour: navy
> Nationality: British
> Material: cotton, creamy

> **Answers**
> a a huge black dog b ✓ c the famous Italian singer
> d a large red apple e an elaborate square wooden box
> f a sophisticated new novel by a tremendous Scottish author

3 The stressed words are underlined in the recording script in exercise 2.

4 The underlined parts of the recording script confirm the answers.

> **Answers**
>
> **1** M **2** W **3** B **4** M **5** W

Part 2

Woman: There's one advert I really like, partly because it's brilliantly put together ...

Man: And it's for?

Woman: Bacardi – it's set on a tropical island somewhere in the Caribbean. And there's this radio DJ who's broadcasting in a studio and ...

Man: Oh, not Ray on Reef Radio?

Woman: You've seen it too!

Man: Yep. <u>Detest it, actually</u>. All about some friend of Ray's who's leaving for the mainland and how he's going to miss his wonderful life on the island ...

Woman: And you see what he's been up to – I adore the way the DJ, Ray, tells the storyline on air and you see flashbacks of the other guy ... Like 'I know you're going to miss the way they serve Bacardi around here' – and you see a girl throw a glassful in the friend's face! Such a striking image and <u>totally unexpected</u>.

Man: Mmm, <u>I suppose ads do work well when they contain something out of the ordinary</u> – I guess they stick in your mind that way.

Woman: <u>Right</u> ... and of course, the ending itself is unforgettable – quite spectacular, isn't it? Seeing the friend sailing away on the boat, listening to all this on his radio – and then, what does he do ...

Man: He dives off the deck and swims back to the island.

Woman: For another night on the town and a glass of ...

Man: Yes, yes ... You know, I must admit that although I personally loathe the ad, it sells the product pretty well. It's got the right ingredients – you know, exotic location, powerful images ...

Woman: So what didn't you like about it?

Man: The characters themselves, I think ... especially Ray!

Woman: But come on, the very fact that you remember him now means he made an impact on you ... which must mean that the ad has worked.

Man: <u>True enough</u> ... And what about you? You said it makes you laugh, is that why you like it so much?

Woman: That ... and the way it succeeds in telling a story in such a short time, I think that's quite clever, getting the message across like that. <u>The music's great, too</u>.

Man: But was it truly successful? I mean, did you dig into your pocket and buy a bottle?

Woman: Well, no... I don't drink spirits! I bet plenty of people were persuaded to rush out and buy some, though.

5

> **Answers**
>
> **a** very well made/edited
> **b** an unusual and memorable sight
> **c** you remember something and think about it again
> **d** the essential parts
> **e** interesting (and faraway) place
> **f** had an effect on
> **g** communicating
> **h** spend money

6

> **Possible answers**
>
> high-quality production, striking images, memorable in some way, uses famous people, catchy jingle

7 This is a Paper 5 Part 3 task, which candidates do together. If you are studying on your own, record your opinions on the billboards for practice, using the language you have learnt in this unit.

8 Here is some information about each billboard.

a Volkswagen Bora: the ad suggests that owners of the car will want to think up further reasons for taking long, time-consuming drives to inaccessible places, as driving the Bora is such a pleasurable experience.

b Vodafone: traffic cones on motorways and other busy roads are a major source of irritation to drivers. The ad shows a solution, by using the mobile phone to get advance warning.

c Electricity: the basset hound usually has a sad facial expression, with droopy ears and doleful eyes, and this is certainly the case in the left-hand image; however, the dog sitting in front of the loudspeaker on the right is animated, with ears raised.

d Dolphin: this ad for another mobile phone company suggests the many contexts where a mobile phone is useful or essential, and the slogan stresses the improved communication that results.

e Cable film: the ad is launching two new film channels available from a cable TV company. The double clipper board image reinforces this.

f Daily Telegraph: because this is a serious newspaper, the ad sticks to text rather than visual images, playing on the common saying 'It's easy to be wise after the event'.

Exam folder 5

Listening skills for FCE pages 62–63

1   This exam folder covers skills and strategies for Paper 4 Listening. There are similar Exam folders for Reading (Exam folder 10) and Writing (Exam folder 15).

Answers
1 C   2 A   3 (no recording)   4 B

Recording script

A

Interviewer: So, in spite of a high salary and a powerful position within the company, you took the decision to leave and start up on your own. Why was that?

Man: I'm often asked that question. People think the place I left must have been in trouble, but in fact sales were at a record high that year. I just felt I needed more freedom, the chance to produce things that I knew the market would buy.

Interviewer: But wasn't it stressful? You took a big risk.

Man: Indeed, but my previous role was equally demanding and pressured. I decided that if I was going to put in such long hours, at least it should benefit me directly.

B: I was getting so fed up. The calls would always come at just the wrong time, when I was cooking a meal or getting ready to go out. I used to say it was inconvenient but then they'd offer to ring back at another time. I also tried walking away from the phone but I'd come back five or ten minutes later and find them still there, reading from their script! In the end, I bought a new phone with a number display and now I only answer if I recognise the number of the caller.

C: Many campaigns use celebrities, either in person or as voice-overs, in order to link a product to fame and success. This one is very different, as it shows ordinary people and their daily lives. What's being targeted here is how to win the approval of others in the customer's social group. Sometimes this technique is used in a negative way, for example to suggest that if you don't use a certain product, you'll lose your friends. So, group acceptance is a powerful weapon.

2   Predicting topic vocabulary can be useful.

Answers
Words to do with an athletics event: jump prize race track

3

Answers
1 washing powder   2 lifestyle   3 unusual behaviour
4 puppies (and) kittens

Recording script

1 To support the suggestion that one product is better than its competitors, the existence of actual proof is often mentioned. In one case, involving the promotion of <u>washing powder</u>, reference was made to an unnamed university research project, which analysed shades of white.

2 It must be true that there are more advertisements focusing on our love of driving than on anything else. While the messages of freedom and mobility are always important, it is above all the aspect of <u>lifestyle</u> that is stressed in this particular one. We are supposed to believe that this car will take us to new places in society and change our role for ever.

3 Advertisers adopt different strategies as far as young people between the ages of 15 and 19 are concerned. For this population, it is not about conforming but about the complete opposite of that. Indeed, products for this age group are frequently connected with <u>unusual behaviour</u>, the kind that older people such as parents might well disapprove of.

4 Turning to mothers and fathers as consumers, advertisements targeting these people often reinforce the experience of bringing up a family. An advert that links its product to young children or even, interestingly enough, to <u>puppies</u> and <u>kittens</u>, will probably succeed because these images appeal directly to motherly or, perhaps less commonly, fatherly instincts.

5

Suggested answers	
Speaker	**Topic**
1	working while studying
2	city traffic and transport
3	public Internet access
4	the cost of watching live football
5	setting up a business in another country

Recording script

Speaker 1: I think every first-year student should do the same as I've done. My parents were both totally against me working part-time, but the way I saw it was that I had to earn some money in order to be able to enjoy myself at uni. I'm really pleased at how well it's worked out, my grades haven't suffered at all.

Speaker 2: Well, the situation's getting worse and worse. In fact, I believe the whole place is choking to death. In my opinion, the car parks outside the city should be free, with regular buses laid on to take people into the centre. We clearly can't go on like this.

Speaker 3: I'm really disappointed in the government's position on this. They seem to think that everyone has a computer in their home, when that's obviously not true. As I see it, there should be more hardware available in schools and public places, so that there really is online access for all.

Speaker 4: Yeah I'm very unhappy about it. This is the second time the club has put their ticket prices up in a year. I love football and I'm a big fan of this team, but I just can't afford to go to matches any more. I reckon they're losing loads of their true supporters.

Speaker 5: It's been really hard setting up the juice bar here. Before I opened, there was endless paperwork and because I didn't speak the language terribly well back then, I had to rely on other people too much. I guess if I could do it again, I'd go into business with a local person. To my mind, that's the best solution.

6

> **Answers**
> **a** I believe (2), I reckon (4), I guess (5)
> **b** pleased at (1), disappointed in (3), unhappy about (4)
> **c** the way I saw it (1), In my opinion (2), As I see it (3), To my mind (5)

7 Look out for paraphrase (different ways of saying the same thing) whenever you refer to a recording script.

> **Answers**
> Paraphrasing of key information:
> **1** biggest benefit > *main advantage, positive point, chief improvement*
> **A** seat more people > *accommodate ...*
> **B** continue > *go on*
> bad weather > *when it's raining*
> **C** growing conditions > *protect the grass*
>
> **2** problem > *difficulty, challenge (verb), headache, issue*
> **A** weight > *heaviness*
> **B** schedule > *complete on time*
> **C** increased cost > *gone over budget*
>
> **Answers**
> **1** B **2** C

Recording script

Interviewer: So, Peter, you've been one of a team of architects developing this state-of-the-art stadium. Can I ask you what you see as its main advantage over the existing facility?

Peter: Well of course there are many positive points. For a start, the stadium will accommodate an extra 800 people, which means an increase in ticket sales. However, the chief improvement over the original building is that the new one will have a movable roof, allowing matches to go on even when it's raining. There's also a minor benefit in that because the roof is transparent, it may help to protect the grass during winter.

Interviewer: I see. Well, this is all good news, but you are experiencing some difficulty on the project at present, aren't you?

Peter: That's true. Every large-scale project causes us a few headaches and this one is no different. At the start, we were challenged by the heaviness of the roof we had designed but we solved that problem fairly easily with a change of materials. What *is* an issue right now is that we've gone over budget and will need to make a few savings in the coming months, but I'm confident we can do that and still complete the project on time.

Unit 10

10.1 pages 64-65

1

> **Suggested answer**
> The picture on the left shows two astronauts walking over a red planet – it could be Mars. They appear to be going back to their vehicle and must have been exploring the surface. They're wearing helmets and have breathing apparatus, so there can't be much atmosphere. The picture on the right is a film still and those people are in deep sleep – stasis – apart from one man, who is checking on them.
>
> In 2001, a very rich businessman paid $20 million dollars to go up into space, so I think by 2050, more members of the public will have done this.

2

> **Suggested answers**
> I don't think I'll have a holiday in space, unless I win the lottery!
>
> There are many other things for national governments to spend taxes on, like health, education and crime prevention. However, I do think it's important for space exploration to be funded, because the world's population is growing rapidly and we will soon need to find somewhere else to go.
>
> Satellites are used for telecommunications, so I believe the technology will increase in importance.

3 This unit introduces the gapped sentence task, Paper 1 Part 2. Unit 6 looked at a simplified gapped sentence task.

4 Sentence A is the extra sentence which does not fit anywhere.

5

> **Answers**
> 1 D 2 G 3 B 4 H 5 F 6 C 7 E

6 There are two examples of negative prefixes in the words.

> **Answers**
> a re-usable b commercial c economics d delivery
> e efficiency f endlessly g irreversible h settlement
> i inappropriate j affordable

7

> **Sample answers**
> I think it's a good idea to encourage commercial development because then, governments won't have to invest so much tax-payers' money in space exploration.
>
> The benefits are more rapid progress and financial savings; one possible drawback would be the lack of control at government level.

10.2 pages 66–67

1

> **Answers**
> a future simple b *going to* future c future continuous d future perfect e *going to* future
> f (simple present – *plan to ...*) g (simple present – *is due to ...*)

2

> **Answers**
> 1 (prediction): a, b, c 2 (planned event): f, g
> 3 (event that has not yet happened): d
> 4 (intention): e

3

> **Answer**
> The present continuous is commonly used to refer to definite events in the near future.

4 Both examples use modal verbs to talk about future prediction – *might* is also used in this way.

5 The sentence contains reported speech. David Ashford's words were probably "Space tourism will begin ten years after people stop laughing at the concept." This is then reported as 'he said space tourism would begin …' Unit 13 will be looking at reported speech.

6

> **Answers**
> a will fall (not a continuous state)
> b won't be (prediction rather than definite truth)
> c may (prediction of possible future event)
> d will carry (future event + verb not tied to an end date)
> e am going to (definite plan in the near future; intention)
> f would (reported speech)
> g will be living (future truth)
> h will have been (anniversary has not yet happened)

7 One verb in the summary requires a passive form.

> **Answers**
> 1 will have risen
> 2 will have included
> 3 will have been filled
> 4 will have become
> 5 will have taken---

8 The underlined parts of the recording script confirm the answers.

> **Answers**
> Speakers 1 and 2 express negative views; Speaker 3 is positive.

Speaker 1: I find it quite scary actually. Films like Bladerunner could really come true. Imagine a city like Los Angeles in twenty years' time. I mean it's dangerous now, isn't it – remember the riots? People will be living in run-down buildings, too frightened to come out. Oil supplies will have run out, so there won't be any cars. And with global warming and El Niño, the climate is changing, so the lack of sunlight and pouring rain in the film may well be accurate ... what LA weather will be like.

Speaker 2: I'm reading one of his sci-fi ones at the moment. It all happens way off in the future, thousands of years from now. There are human-like characters, but they're a very sophisticated race – we'll never be as clever as them! They live for at least three hundred years and after that, they can choose to live on in a different state. And there's no poverty, no war ... For the human race, this seems completely unattainable – there will always be some country at war with another. I don't see a long-term future for the human race ... even if our planet survives in one piece, we'll have wiped each other out or something.

Speaker 3: Things may be different, but they won't necessarily be any worse. We'll just enter a new phase of our culture, our existence. We've always adapted ... I mean, think of the huge changes with the Industrial Revolution ... why should this be any different? And as for the eco-threat, we're going to have to deal with it somehow, aren't we? <u>I think we will</u>. I can't accept that the human race will cease to be. <u>Call me an optimist</u>, but that's what I feel ...

9   There are many fixed phrases with *at*, like *in* and *on*. It's good to learn these, as they are often tested in Paper 3.

> **Answers**
> 1 B   2 C   3 A   4 B

Writing folder 5

Articles 1   pages 68-69

In the real world, articles are usually read for pleasure or for information. They need to be clearly written and interesting to read. An unusual title leading on to a good opening paragraph encourages the reader to continue. In the exam, these features will impress the examiner!

1   All four titles are short and succeed in attracting the reader.

2   Paragraph B fails to pick up on the idea of a lifelong ambition. The other three link well to their titles.

> **Answers**
> **A** 3-2-1 Lift off!   **B** A lifelong ambition
> **C** Aliens are coming ...   **D** Is anybody there?

3   Look critically at your writing and try to improve what you have done. Varying your vocabulary like this will get you better marks in the exam.

> **Sample answer**
> (D, first stage)
> On some nights, I open my window and gaze at the stars. It's a wonderful thing to do. Sometimes I stay there for ages, wondering what the universe holds. It makes me feel humble. Space is a vast place. There are so many galaxies apart from our own – so there must be other life?
>
> **Answers**
> **a** adjectives   **b** noun phrase   **c** quantifiers   **d** adverbs
>
> **Sample answer**
> (D, second stage)
> On some beautiful, cloudless nights, I open my window and gaze at the twinkling stars. It's such a wonderful thing to do so I sometimes stay there for ages, wondering what the universe holds. It makes me feel very humble as space is a truly vast place. There are so many galaxies apart from our own – so there must surely be other forms of life?

4   The improvements suggested on page 69 show why the paragraph is a poor attempt.

> **Sample answer**
> (B)
> It has always been my dream to step on board a shiny, silver rocket and be launched into space. An article which I read recently said space travel may be possible for ordinary people soon. Wouldn't it be wonderful to be one of the first to go? I really hope that I am lucky enough to experience this.

5   In-flight magazines are designed to entertain, so the article shouldn't be too serious.

6

> **Answers**
> **a** Future forms of transport; destinations for holidays
> **b** More than one kind of transport should be mentioned
> **c** Given the type of magazine, it should be fairly lively and 'easy to read'
> **d** Probably four: an opening paragraph; one on transport; one on holidays; a final paragraph

7   The sample answer below contains no mistakes and would score top marks in the examination, as it is interesting to read, has a good title, and starts and ends well. Note the use of modal verbs to speculate about the future.

> **Sample answer**
>
> TRAVEL TO THE STARS
>
> You are probably reading this on board a jumbo jet, but imagine how you could be travelling and where you might be able to get to on holiday in fifty years' time!
>
> By then, planes could be seen as old-fashioned, with re-usable space rockets being used for holiday destinations instead. Or perhaps someone will have invented a completely new form of transport, capable of travelling faster than the speed of light?
>
> If that ever happens, we will be able to go wherever we want to on holiday – not just within our own solar system, but out to other parts of our galaxy, or even to another galaxy further away. A cheap weekend break might consist of a couple of nights on an orbiting space station, watching the world below.
>
> Just sit back in your seat, close your eyes, and dream of your future. Isn't it exciting!

Unit 11

11.1 pages 70-71

1 The photos (left to right) are of:

Hillary Clinton and her daughter Chelsea Clinton
Jerry Hall and her daughter Elizabeth Jagger
Martin Sheen and his son Charlie Sheen

3

> **Answers**
> - Did she go to the cinema? No. How do we know? Because she went to a film set, which is a place where a film is made.
> - Did she meet Harrison Ford? We don't know.
> - How did her parents treat her? Well, but they didn't spoil her.
> - Did she have any brothers and sisters? No.

4 The answer (B) comes from 'my mother arranged for me and a few friends to go to the film set to see him working on his latest film, as a treat for my birthday'.

5 The underlined parts of the recording script confirm the answers.

> **Answers**
> 2 B 3 C 4 B 5 A 6 C 7 B

Presenter: So, Hannah, what was it like growing up in Hollywood as an only child, and having such a famous mother?

Hannah: Well, I guess I was pretty privileged as I had things most other kids only dream about. For instance, when I was 14 I just loved Harrison Ford films, and my mother arranged for me and a few friends to go to the film set to see him working on his latest film, as a treat for my birthday. I don't think I was particularly spoilt though, even though I was an only child, and I didn't get into trouble like some of the kids I knew did.

Presenter: You, yourself, are an actress now. <u>Did she ever try to put you off acting?</u>

Hannah: <u>Not at all. Just the opposite.</u> She felt I should follow my feelings, I guess in the same way she had done when she was younger. My grandparents hadn't wanted her to take up acting you know, especially as she had to move from Europe to Hollywood. I don't think her family took her seriously at first and I think she was quite homesick and felt she could have done with a little more family support.

Presenter: Now, you look very like your mother, don't you?

Hannah: Oh, yes. My mouth, the shape of my face, my jaw line is my mother's. <u>My nose too, but only the tip of it, not the bridge</u> – that is unique, like no one else's in the family. My eyes, my forehead, my colouring, my height are different from my mother's but everyone tells me I look like her. When I say everybody, I mean everybody. People stop me in shops, on the subway, in the street.

Presenter: What does your mother say about this?

Hannah: <u>Well, we both looked in the mirror one day and came to the same conclusion – people exaggerate.</u> Then one day I went into a dress shop. I was alone except for another customer. <u>I thought to myself, 'She looks like my mother.'</u> Then I walked too close to her and crashed into a mirror – <u>the lady was me! I hadn't recognised myself!</u>

Presenter: What qualities do you think your mother possesses?

Hannah: Great physical energy. She used to walk fast, and when she wasn't acting she cleaned and organised the house perfectly. She loved acting more than cleaning; she loved acting most and above all. <u>It took me some time not to feel hurt by this.</u> I wanted to come first. When asked what was the most important thing in her life, she got real embarrassed and nervous, but my mother couldn't lie; she had to say 'acting'; though I know for our sake she wished she could say 'family'. She is terribly practical, and I am too. We consider it one of the greatest qualities in people. We give it the same status as intelligence. <u>Practicality is what made my mother advise me to learn to be an accountant. 'If you know how to do it, you know you'll never be cheated out of any money,' she says.</u> I didn't finish the course as I decided I wanted to act.

Presenter: Did she have any personal experience of being cheated out of money?

Hannah: Well, my mother has always been a very generous person to people she likes. I think another actor who she fell out with started the rumour that she is a bit stingy. She does say that I'm a bit extravagant.

Presenter: Now, you don't sound like your mother, do you?

Hannah: Oh no. <u>She still has a bit of an accent.</u> But her voice is definitely an actress's voice – the clearest speech, the most commanding delivery, and loud. The family used to tell her that she didn't need a phone, she could have just talked to us on the other side of town and we would have heard her. She justifies it with 'I picked it up in the theatre. My voice has to reach all the way to the last row.'

Presenter: Thank you for coming in today to talk to us Hannah and good luck in your new film which, I believe, is released on Tuesday?

Hannah: Yes, that's right. Thank you.

6

> **Answers**
> a privileged b homesick c unique
> d embarrassed and nervous e being practical
> f generous/stingy g loud/commanding

Grammar extra

Don't confuse these two uses of *like*:

What's she like?   Friendly and outgoing.
What does she like?   Cream cakes!

> **Answers**
> **A** tall, friendly, amusing
> **B** swimming, hamburgers, watching TV, photography

11.2 pages 72–73

1

> **Answers**
> **a** conceited **b** cheerful **c** optimistic **d** generous
> **e** sensible **f** considerate **g** unreliable **h** self-conscious
> **i** bad-tempered **j** amusing **k** aggressive **l** lazy
> **m** loyal **n** sociable

2 Read the Vocabulary spot and then revise negative prefixes if necessary (see Exam folder 2, page 24).

> **Answers**
> Positive = cheerful, optimistic, generous, sensible,
> considerate, amusing, loyal, sociable
> Negative = conceited, unreliable, self-conscious, bad-
> tempered, aggressive, lazy
>
> Opposites
> **a** modest **b** miserable **c** pessimistic **d** mean/stingy
> **e** irresponsible **f** inconsiderate **g** reliable/dependable
> **h** unselfconscious **i** good-tempered/easy-going
> **j** serious **k** peaceful/cowardly **l** energetic **m** disloyal
> **n** shy/introverted

3

> **Answers**
> **a** picked up **b** grew up **c** put them off **d** turns up
> **e** stood by **f** look on

4 These verbs are usually connected with our senses.

> **Suggested answers**
> **a** It sounds romantic/revolting, etc.
> **b** It smells salty.
> **c** It feels scary/quiet.
> **d** It tastes great/delicious.
> **e** It looks interesting/honest/tempting.
> **f** It feels good / expensive.

5

> **Answers**
> **a** adjective – delicious **b** adverb – gently
> **c** adjective – happy **d** adverb – carefully
> **e** adjective –loud/scary/terrifying
> **f** adjective – expensive **g** adverb – meaningfully
> **h** adverb – suddenly

6 Read the Corpus spot. -*ed* and -*ing* words are commonly confused at FCE level. Check these endings in your written work, using the information on page 202 of the Grammar folder.

> **Answers**
> It would mean Hannah was embarrassed by her mother.
> **1** the past participle -*ed*
> **2** the present participle -*ing*

7

> **Sample answers**
> **a** I am usually gripped by soap operas. Their plots are
> very gripping.
> **b** I am sometimes horrified by westerns. For example,
> the violence in Clint Eastwood's *Unforgiven* is really
> horrifying.

Exam folder 6

Paper 4 Part 1 pages 74–75

1 Underline key words in both the question and options, like the sample answers below.

> **Sample answers**
> **1** You hear this advertisement on the radio for a new
> magazine.
> Who is the magazine aimed at?
> **A** gardeners **B** cooks **C** climbers
>
> **2** As you leave the cinema, you overhear this conversation.
> What is the man's opinion of the film?
> **A** It is longer than necessary.
> **B** It has a weak storyline.
> **C** Its actors are disappointing.

2 The underlined parts of the recording script confirm the answers.

> **Answers**
> **1** A **2** C **3** C **4** B **5** C **6** A **7** B **8** A

1

If you enjoy spending time in the kitchen, you'll already know about our successful magazine *Taste!* In answer to readers' requests, we've introduced a sister magazine called *Dig*!, for everyone who enjoys being outdoors whatever the weather. It's full of tips to keep things looking at their best throughout the year and <u>includes a free packet of seeds</u> every month. Available now!

2

Woman: Well that was a long one, wasn't it?
Man: Was it? Seemed normal ...
Woman: No, no. That scene at the end should have been cut, if you ask me. I thought Jim Franklin was really good though.
Man: Hmm, <u>I've seen him do better ... and that co-star was a weak character, wasn't she?</u> What a shame – the book was absolutely gripping and they haven't changed anything, so you can't criticise the story.

3

Hello, is that the news desk of the Daily Times? Yes, I'm ringing with some information ... you see, <u>I'm a close friend of Heather Woods</u> ... last week's jackpot winner, that's right. I know she doesn't want any publicity but <u>if the price is right, I'm willing to give you a story.</u> I mean it's ridiculous, all that money and she's sitting there miserably! I could visit your office tomorrow ... or fax you something if you prefer. ... Okay, that sounds interesting, my number's 0181 ...

4

Interviewer: So, Duncan, you left a well-paid job in Glasgow to move to this beautiful island off the west coast of Scotland. Was it to escape the pressures of city life?
Duncan: Not really. I grew up in the countryside and I know only too well how quiet it can be – I go back to Glasgow regularly, in fact, to enjoy the fast pace again! The point is, I was trying to write a novel while I was working – you know, weekends, evenings – and I realised I couldn't do both. So I quit and <u>came here to cut costs</u> ... at the time I didn't even have a publisher's contract, so it was a risky move.

5

Receptionist: How may I help you, madam?
Woman: I was on the phone to you from my room just now and ...
Receptionist: Oh yes. There was something wrong with the phone ... Is there a problem with the room? You're in 203, aren't you?
Woman: Yes I am ... it's fine. I was actually <u>ringing about room service – it's taken over forty minutes</u> for them to bring me a simple sandwich and a cup of coffee. Well, <u>I was so appalled,</u> I decided to come down here, to have a word with you ...

6

Well, Grangewood–Trent United has finished one nil, after a match that was full of excitement. Grangewood took the lead with Bellamy's early goal, a wonderful return for him after his long absence with that broken leg. <u>A crowd of supporters rushed across to Bellamy</u> when the game was over, glad to see their hero back. The referee tried to stop them but in the end, it was the whole Grangewood team who walked off the pitch with their delighted fans.

7

Interviewer: I'm with Liam O'Neill, and we're surrounded by his latest range of swimwear that's caused a real sensation <u>here at the Clothes Show.</u> Liam, why do you think you've done so well this year?
Liam: It's unbelievable, isn't it? ... I dunno, it's kind of strange. The new stores have created a lot of interest throughout the country and I guess people wanted to come and see for themselves.
Interviewer: Liam, <u>your display</u> is most impressive – how did you move all that sand?
Liam: We had three lorries driving through the night to get here – it just wouldn't be right to launch swimwear without the beach!

8

I've started this astronomy course – two hours a week on a Monday evening. Every week the lecturer shows a short film ... we've seen one on the Hubble Space Telescope and another about the sun. It's useful, although I can't help thinking we could take the tapes away and do that bit at home. <u>We have to work out lots of calculations in class and I must say that it's terrific!</u> I thought it would be really hard work, but the time goes by really fast and there's always a break – not that the coffee is anything special! <u>I can't wait to get back to my sums!</u>

Unit 12

12.1 pages 76–77

1 There may be some words you don't know in the questionnaire. For example, what do 'viciously' and 'resignedly' mean in question 5? Use the advice in the Vocabulary spot and guess the meaning from the surrounding words *kick* and *walk away.*

2

> **Answers**
> a wooden/metal closures that cover something – in this case a window
> b something that came before
> c something over his face which disguises him
> d small
> e place everyone recognises
> f reasons

3 Skimming the text first is important.

Answers
1 A 2 C 3 B 4 D 5 E 6 C 7/8 C/D 9 E 10 B
11 A 12 B

Background information

Some inventions and the dates they were invented:

1902 – teddy bear
1910 – washing machine
1914 – bra
1928 – peanut butter
1935 – colour film
1947 – microwave oven

1951 – home computer
1959 – Barbie doll
1964 – fax machine
1970 – snowboard
1980 – inline skates

12.2 pages 78–79

1

Answers
a past simple passive
b active – past simple
c modal passive
d past perfect passive; past simple passive
e active – past perfect
f past simple passive

3 The passive is often used in newspaper articles like this one, where the action reported is more important than the people doing the action.

Answers
1 could be persuaded/encouraged
2 were encouraged/persuaded; have been encouraged/persuaded
3 were used
4 are (often) filled
5 can be talked into
6 are (being) supplied
7 are dissolved
8 can be dispersed/are dispersed
9 (can be) stored
10 will be issued/are going to be issued
11 is hoped
12 can be made up
13 are constantly being asked

4 Remember that *by* is used when a person or animal is involved, while *with* is used for objects.

Answers
a The kitchen floor was covered with mud.
b He was scratched by a cat.

c He was run over by a car. (someone was driving the car)
d The old house was smashed down by bulldozers. (someone was driving the bulldozer)
e The school is being rebuilt with a new type of brick.

5 It isn't necessary to use *by* when it can be understood from the meaning.

Answers
a by Spielberg. (It's important to know who the person was.)
b correct – (obviously by builders)
c –/by her uncle (usually you'd say who by, unless she'd been out of work for a while and actually getting the job was the important point)
d –/by his wife/by the Mafia
e – (unless a famous surgeon)
f deliberately/by children

Corpus spot

Answers
a The house was/is painted blue.
b The mobile was not answered.
c My laptop was bought for me two months ago.
d He was born in June.
e The meeting has been cancelled.

6

Answers
a In a canteen.
b Same or in any building or on public transport.
c Parking spaces or seats at a club. Somewhere where membership is important.
d On a parcel or packet of biscuits, etc.
e As a headline for a newspaper article.

7

Suggested answers
a My photo of the festival was used in last week's local newspaper – I was paid a fee for it!
b More work will be done from home, because of improvements in computer software and worsening traffic conditions.
c I'm not quite sure, but it starts with trees being cut down and transported to a mill, where wood pulp is produced and refined to make paper.
d My watch was made in Switzerland, the birthplace of many good watches!
e I was given some CDs, a new jumper and some credit for my mobile phone.

Answers
a John Lennon was killed in New York.
b Gunpowder was invented in China.
c The telephone is used by half a billion people.
d The tomb of Tutankhamun was discovered by Lord Caernarfon.
e Satellites were first sent into space in 1957.
f The Olympic Games will be held in London in 2012.
g Togas were worn by the Romans.
h Leather is made from cows.

9

Answers
1 object to their ideas
2 were those chemicals being mixed
3 was made to hand over
4 is supposed to be
5 was informed of his / my boss's
6 has been a decrease in

10

Answers
come – to a conclusion, into money, to a decision, apart
take – a seat, advantage of, offence, turns, notice of, apart, an interest
tell – a story, a lie, the difference, the time, apart, the truth
fall – asleep, in love, ill, apart

11 The underlined parts of the recording script give clues to the answers.

Answers
a the printing press   b penicillin (antibiotics)   c plastic
d the wheel

1 Around 1450 a man in Germany created a means of mass-production. In doing so, he gave the world a way of getting knowledge, and therefore power, out of the hands of the few and into the hands of the many. No other invention has done as much to make knowledge available. By 1500, nine million were in circulation – at least a thousand times more than there had been before when things had been done by hand.

2 This key breakthrough in medical history might never have happened had a scientist in London been more particular about keeping his laboratory clean. By leaving a glass plate coated with bacteria lying around, the scientist discovered something that has saved millions of lives round the world.

3 This cheap, light material was invented in the nineteenth century. It was first used to make cutlery handles – which unfortunately went up in flames rather easily. Not until

1910, with the advent of a tough, non-inflammable kind, did this invention really take off. Now we each throw away around 45 kg of this material each year in Britain alone, and the product has a bad image as a pollutant. The truth is, however, that in terms of total energy and resources they use, this product often turns out to be 'greener' than glass or paper.

4 Well, this invention is probably the most important ever invented. No one knows for certain where or when it came about, but it is perfectly designed for what it has to do. It is the mathematically optimal shape for minimising the amount of contact with other surfaces – leading to minimal friction and energy loss. Plus its surface has no edges, so it's good for smooth, repetitive motion.

Writing folder 6

Reviews pages 80–81

Reviews can be written in formal, neutral or informal register, but should be consistent throughout. Remember to include a balance of information and opinion.

Suggested answers
The Simpsons Movie
Good points: funny, exciting, cleverly written
Bad points: none!

2 The writer preferred film A.

3

Answers
1 frighteningly realistic
2 excellent acting skills
3 interesting locations
4 fascinating storyline
5 historical events
6 shocking violence
7 tremendous soundtrack

4

Answers
a I suggest (that) you see this film immediately.
b correct
c correct
d I would advise you not to miss this film.
e correct
f correct
g I can recommend this film to you.

5

Possible answers

a The film is directed by (Pedro Almodovar).
b This wonderful story is set (at the end of the eighteenth century).
c All of the costumes were designed by (students at art college).
d The main character is played by (the French actor Daniel Auteuil).
e The supporting cast have been chosen for (their dancing ability).
f Most of the music was composed by (Ennio Morricone).
g A subtitled version will be shown (in a few weeks' time).
h The screenplay has just been nominated for (an award).

7

Possible answers

comedy:	jokes, comedian, laughter, humour
documentary:	photography, wildlife, facts, interviews
game show:	quiz, questions, points, prize
reality show:	celebrities, relationships, lifestyle, conflict
soap opera:	drama, script, character, plot, story

8

Sample answer

One of my favourite shows on TV is the comedy series *Frasier,* starring Kelsey Grammer. Although new programmes are no longer being made of this long-running series, it is possible to watch regular repeats.

The key to the programme's success is the sensitive and humorous way in which it shows everyday life. Frasier hosts a radio phone-in show, assisted by his efficient producer Roz Doyle. The supporting cast includes his father Martin, a retired policeman, who lives with Frasier; Martin's amusing (and exceptionally well trained) dog Eddie; Frasier's younger brother Niles, who has gone through many disappointments in love and yet who finally ends up with the woman of his dreams, Daphne Moon; and Frasier's icy ex-wife Lilith and their son Freddy, who appear on the programme from time to time.

The series is set in Seattle and rarely strays far from this city. In fact, the two commonest locations are Frasier's apartment and his broadcasting room at the radio station. But the programmes are never dull! What makes this series so remarkable is its scripts, which are tightly written and contain some memorable jokes. I highly recommend this show.

(190 words)

Units 7–12 Revision

pages 82–83

1

Answers

1 in
2 although/though/while/whilst
3 For
4 must/would/might/could
5 be
6 used
7 All/Most
8 a
9 because/as/since
10 not
11 ones/ingredients
12 This/It

2

Suggested answers

a Five years ago, I used to be a fun-loving person and I would spend night after night clubbing, but last year I had a baby, so now I'm a stop-at-home mother who goes to bed early!
b Next weekend I'm going to go white-water rafting for the first time.
c You may not believe this, but I look identical to Hugh Grant, with lots of wavy hair and the same shaped nose.
d My parents must have been scared stiff when I used to run off on my own on busy streets at the age of two.
e I really loathe having piles of work waiting to be done.
f Some lessons were so boring that we used to fall asleep at our desks.
g I remember I couldn't stand vegetables, but my mother made me sit and finish every last pea on my plate!
h Definitely – and I'll have passed CAE too!
i I do enjoy watching adverts on TV, especially when they show something unexpected – like that snail race in the Guinness advert.
j If the Earth had been invaded by aliens, we'd all be taking trips to other planets with them by now.

3 The verbs are *get* and *take.*

Answers

a getting b gets c take d get e take f got
g take h took

4

> **Suggested answers**
> a 'Cunning' is the odd one out, because it means 'clever'. The other words all refer to something bad, like a frightening experience.
> b 'Campaign' refers to an advertising push, whereas the other words are elements of advertisements.
> c A 'plumber' is not employed at a hospital like the other three.
> d 'Fancy' means that you like someone or something, while the other verbs mean the opposite.
> e 'Shallow' describes a small volume, whereas the other adjectives refer to large dimensions.
> f A 'rink' is the only one made of ice!
> g 'Pretend' means that something isn't true, while the other verbs refer to future plans or expectations.
> h 'Extravagant' involves spending a lot of money, whereas the other adjectives refer to reasonable prices or costs.

5

> **Answers**
> ON
> a looked b get c insist
> OFF
> d take e work f put

6

> **Answers**
> A 4 (conclusion) B 2 C 3 (opening)

Unit 13

13.1 pages 84–85

1

> **Suggested answer**
> The classroom on the left looks more informal than the one on the right, where there are rows of desks facing the blackboard. Here, the children are wearing school uniform, while in the other classroom they seem to be allowed to wear what they choose. That classroom looks more welcoming, too, with a variety of things pinned on the walls. My own school was more like the one on the right. I had to wear a green uniform and had a desk just like the ones in the picture.

> **B**ackground information
>
> It is compulsory for children to attend school in Britain between the ages of 5 and 16. There are both state and private schools. State nursery education is offered to younger children and the government has promised more money for this; there is a growing private nursery sector.

2

> **Suggested answers**
> a My secondary school was fairly small by today's standards. There were around 450 students aged 11–18. It was in the centre of Bristol, in a 200-year-old building with beautiful gardens. There weren't many discipline problems and the atmosphere felt quite purposeful – you knew you were expected to work hard from day one.
> b There's one history teacher I remember particularly well. She was an excellent teacher and really brought history to life, but it's her appearance I remember so vividly. Her clothes were always colour-coordinated. One day she wore a navy blue suit with red stripes on the jacket collar and skirt, red shoes and handbag, blue stockings and bright red lipstick. For some reason that day she ended up with blue ink around her mouth – so everything about her was either red or blue, it looked so funny.
> c Although I'm not terribly good at painting, I really enjoyed spending time in the art room. It was at the top of some creaky old stairs and was a wonderfully light and airy room, where you could be as creative as you liked – the teacher was always encouraging, no matter how daft your ideas were.
> d There was one science teacher I didn't get on with at all. She seemed to have it in for me the whole time and, unlike the other science teachers, her lessons were really boring – everybody said so.

3

> **Answer**
> David said that he wanted to describe what had really happened. He had been inside the classroom during break and he had seen a group of his friends outside. He had gone over to the window and had tried to get their attention. He had waved at them but they hadn't seen him, so he had hammered on the window. He said he knew glass was/is* breakable but he hadn't thought. When his hand had gone through he had panicked. He hadn't been hurt and he had wanted to avoid getting into trouble, so he had put Simon's bag over the hole and had left the room. He said he was sorry he hadn't told anyone the truth until that moment.
>
> * because it is a fact that glass is breakable, the present tense can also be used here.

4

> **Answers**
> 1 T 2 T 3 F 4 F 5 T 6 T 7 F 8 T

The underlined parts of the recording script confirm the answers.

Interviewer: With me now are Sandra Wilson and Mike Tripp. Mike is owner of a successful new travel company *Just Trips* and Sandra works for him as Publicity Manager. They were actually in the same class at school, though at that time, they did *not* get on with each other! They met again by chance last year, when Sandra went for an interview at *Just Trips* and was surprised to find Mike across the table, asking *her* the questions. Sandra, when you were at school, did you think Mike would become successful like this?

Sandra: To be honest, no one thought Mike would get anywhere – he was the original under-achiever! That's why we didn't get on. My group of friends were quite hard-working, you know, we did all the homework, made an effort in class, but Mike was the complete opposite. He was bad news, actually.

Interviewer: Is this true Mike?

Mike: I'm afraid so. I wasn't the only one though. It was ... uncool for boys to work, a whole group of us were like that. I don't remember being especially horrible to Sandra ...

Sandra: Talk about a selective memory!

Interviewer: Why?

Sandra: Well, he would regularly do annoying things like stealing my ruler or hiding my books. You saw it as a big joke, I suppose, Mike?

Mike: Never thought about it. I can see now that I might have been a ... a bit of a nuisance.

Sandra: I've forgiven you though!

Interviewer: And you've done very well since, Mike ...

Mike: Yeah. I got on with my life. Um ... I don't really regret my behaviour back then – obviously I shouldn't have made trouble for you, Sandra – but for myself, it didn't matter ... I've done okay in spite of school.

Sandra: You have Mike, but there are lots of others in your gang who didn't make it.

Mike: Mmm ... I can think of one or two ... But I still think, if you know what you want out of life, you'll get there. I mean, look at me, I didn't pass many exams ... I even walked out of some, like science ... wrote my name at the top of the paper and thought, I can't do this ... oh, what the heck, the sun's shining, I'm off.

Sandra: Incredible. I was totally stressed out during exams, spent hours revising, and Mike managed to fail virtually everything and still be successful.

Interviewer: Should you have been more relaxed at school, Sandra?

Sandra: That's easy to say now. I had a lot of pressure on me to do well. My parents, my brothers ... all my family expected ... the best.

Mike: Same here. But my dad sort of looked beyond school. He knew I'd be okay – he'd left school himself at 14 and he always felt that I'd sort things out for myself, somehow.

Interviewer: And how did you get the company started? No careers advice from school, I imagine?

Mike: Careers teachers? They didn't have a clue! I got things started in a small way while I was still at school, actually – I used to help out in a local travel agency, buying and selling cheap tickets on the phone. In my final year, I sometimes spent my lunchtimes checking the Internet on the school computer. I found some good deals for flights, that I managed to sell on. Then, when I left school, my dad gave me a bit of money and I set up an office ... and it all ... like ... took off.

Interviewer: So school did help you a little ... or its facilities did?

Mike: Yeah ...

Interviewer: Okay, well we'll have to leave it there. One final thing, Mike. Why did Sandra get the job?

Mike: Oh, university education, languages, a good communicator – she's great, just what the company needed.

Sandra: All thanks to school, Mike.

5   The expression *didn't make it* here means that they didn't succeed in life, unlike Mike, who has done well. Look at these other common uses:
I'm sorry but I won't be able to make it to your party, as I'll be away.
Did your car make it home or did you have to call out the breakdown service?
I hope we make it to the hotel before it gets dark.

> **Answers**
> **a** made a start   **b** made use of   **c** made a profit
> **d** made a success of   **e** made an impression

6

> **Answers**
> **A** Tom Cruise   **B** Socrates   **C** Annie Lennox
> **D** Paul Gauguin   **E** Madonna   **F** Agatha Christie

7   Useful words and phrases for letters of application include:

gain experience, spend x years …, full-time career (A)
have (a) talent for, determination (B)
On leaving school …, find employment (C)
earn/make in a day (D)
work long hours (E)
take a position, unpaid assistant, qualify in, a sound knowledge of, extremely relevant (F)

13.2 pages 86–87

1   Read the section in the Grammar folder on page 203, if you have not already done so.

> **Answers**
> In *a*, there is 'backshift' in the reported statement. Greg's actual statement contained a present and a future tense; in reported speech, the present tense *can't* has become a past tense *couldn't* and *will* has become *would*.
>
> In *b*, there is similar backshift from the simple past to the past perfect in the reported statement.
>
> In *c*, the reported statement uses the present because the situation reported continues to be true.

2 Refer to the Corpus spot. Reporting verbs and their various structures are commonly tested in Paper 3 Part 4.

Answers
apologise + for + -ing
argue + for + -ing; argue + that
claim + that (optional)
deny + that (optional); deny + -ing
explain + that (optional)
insist + on + -ing; insist + that (optional)
promise + that (optional); promise + to + infinitive
refuse + to + infinitive
say + that (optional); in passive, 'is said' + to + infinitive
suggest + that (optional); suggest + -ing
urge + someone + to + infinitive; urge + that
warn + that (optional); + to + infinitive

3

Answers
a 3 **b** 4 **c** 1 **d** 2

4 Underline key words to help you predict content.

5

Answers
1 are **2** need **3** are affected
Speaker 1 C

Caller 1: I'm a retired head teacher and I want to make two points. First, I know from my own experience that teachers tend to be female ... and I believe we need to get more men into all our schools – boys need men around as role models, from an early age. My second point is linked to this. There is a growing problem of broken marriages and one-parent families, which affects all children but especially boys, because they usually end up living with their mothers and having less contact with their fathers. Men are so important to boys' development.

6 Notice how many different reporting verbs have been used in the suggested answers below.

Suggested answers

Caller 2: statment E
She said that when boys and girls start school, they are both keen to learn.
She complained that parents don't help boys at home.
She insisted that basic skills have to be introduced in the home.

Caller 3: statement A
He suggested discussing society rather than just schools.
He explained that as society has changed so much, boys don't have clear goals any more.
He claimed that girls, in contrast, have a lot to aim for.

Caller 4: statement F
She explained that girls' brains develop differently to boys' at a young age.
She warned that in Britain, education is too formal at the beginning.
She urged that nursery education should be extended to the age of six in Britain.

Caller 5: statement B
He insisted on the recent achievement by girls being a good thing.
He argued that this was not true ten years ago.
He suggested that this is part of more equal opportunities nowadays.

Caller 2: Well, I'm an infant teacher and I work with children from the age of four. Both boys and girls arrive at school interested and excited on day one. But I find during that first year that I can't get the parents of boys to help their children at home. They expect their boys to be out playing football after school, not sitting at home reading a book. Basic skills have to be introduced in the home and because the girls' parents do this, the girls race ahead. Then the boys feel they're failing, so they start mucking about, and things go from bad to worse.

Caller 3: Can I widen the topic beyond schools? Society has changed radically in the last twenty years and fathers are no longer the bread-winners, necessarily. Indeed, the average boy growing up now may see a lot of men on the dole ... and of course he's going to look at that and say, 'What's the point? There's no future for me.' Girls, on the other hand, now see lots of opportunities and they want to get out there and compete, get to the top. We haven't faced up to this, and yet it was obviously going to happen.

Caller 4: Picking up on what the infant teacher said, I've always understood the brain develops differently in boys and girls, so girls aged four develop quickly, whereas boys take longer to get going. For boys especially, I think we formalise education too soon in Britain. I can find no other examples in the world where formal teaching starts so early. I believe we should extend nursery education to the age of six, so that there is more time for play, for discovery ... and above all, language. Then by the age of six, boys would be ready for formal learning.

Caller 5: I think we should give credit to what has happened ... I mean, it's a success story for girls, isn't it? Okay, so girls are now achieving better results at school than boys ... well, that's great. It was not the case twenty years ago ... even ten years ago. For the last three years, more girls have gained university places than boys ... good for them. I think this is all part of the wider picture of equal opportunities and we should view it positively.

7

Answers
a tend (to be) **b** race ahead **c** mucking about
d bread-winners **e** faced up to **f** picking up on
g extend **h** give credit to

8 Here is some useful vocabulary for the discussion points. Check any words you don't know in a dictionary.

skills – academic/vocational
equal opportunities
role model
motivation (noun), motivate (verb), motivated (adj)
diligence (noun), diligent (adj)
attention span, attention deficit disorder
behavioural (problems)

Grammar extra

Answers
a why girls are/were gaining more university places.
b in what ways the situation had been different twenty years ago.
c if/whether things would get better in the future.
d if/whether British children should spend more time at nursery.
e why we hadn't faced up to this problem.

9

Answers
1 accused Charlie of putting   2 warned Johnny not to misbehave / warned Johnny to stop misbehaving
3 did you do   4 urged them not to fall
5 said she had not wasted   6 if/whether they had tidied up   7 apologised for forgetting   8 'll/will/shall see you tomorrow

Exam folder 7

Paper 4 Part 2 pages 88–89

Remember that you will never need to write more than three words. Don't waste time writing a full sentence.

1 Predicting what you might hear is useful preparation before you listen.

2 The underlined parts of the recording script confirm the answers.

Answers
1 Personal Assistant   2 typing   3 cookery course   4 Palace
5 two interviews   6 phone calls   7 chef's office   8 public
9 delicious food   10 cook

Interviewer: Good morning and welcome to the Food and Drink Show. In the studio today we have Christine Whitelaw who works as a <u>Personal Assistant</u> to the world famous chef Patrick Millar. Cristine has worked for him for the past 18 months and has loved every minute of it. Her boss has many interests ranging from a cookery

school for professionals and amateurs, to a catering service and a range of luxury food items. Christine's organisational skills have to be faultless as a result. She also considers a good memory, confident phone manner and <u>fast typing speeds</u> to be vital to her job. So Christine, how did you become PA to such an important figure in the food and drink industry?

Christine: Well, I always wanted to work in catering, so after leaving school I completed a year on a <u>cookery course</u> before spending another year at secretarial college. My first job came about following a visit to London. I went to lunch at the <u>Palace</u> Hotel and thought, 'I would really like to work here', so I wrote to see if they had any positions, and it just so happened they did.

Interviewer: That was a lucky break, wasn't it?

Christine: It certainly was. I worked as a PA to the executive director of the hotel group for more than three years before hearing that Patrick Millar was advertising for a new PA. I applied, had to go to <u>two interviews</u>, and got the job.

Interviewer: How does an ordinary day go?

Christine: I usually meet Patrick first of all to run through his diary and letters. If clients are expected for lunch, I may take them on a pre-lunch tour of the cookery school. It has a collection of 6,000 cookery books, which many people are keen to see. Then I take them to the restaurant. In the afternoons I usually do letters and make <u>phone calls</u>. I have an assistant to help me. Each day is fairly different, however. If Patrick is busy in the morning we sometimes have a working lunch together in the <u>chef's office</u>, never in the restaurant or kitchen.

Interviewer: Did you find your previous experience in the hotel business useful?

Christine: Yes, especially in learning how to deal with <u>the public</u>, both face to face and over the phone. One thing it didn't prepare me for was the long hours, as, nowadays, I often have to work until 7pm and then go on to a reception or function.

Interviewer: You often hear about how difficult these top chefs are to work for. Is Patrick very moody or do you get along well?

Christine: Oh, he's terrific and he involves me in most of the decision-making. The worst part of working for him is that I'm surrounded by <u>delicious food</u> all day. I try not to be tempted!

Interviewer: Can you cook yourself?

Christine: Well, I do enjoy cooking and I have tried a few things from his recipe books. However, I have no plans to work as a <u>cook</u>. The job I have combines everything I love: food, meeting people and being at someone's right hand.

Interviewer: Thank you, Christine, for coming in to talk to us today. Next week we'll be interviewing ...

Unit 14

14.1 pages 90–91

1 The jobs shown are a member of a Formula One technical support team (left) and a restorer of ancient pottery.

> **Suggested answer**
> Well, these are very different jobs – one in motor-racing and the other working in a museum or a university, maybe. Being a member of the technical support team, you'd have to be strong physically, able to work fast under pressure and as part of a team. On the other hand, restoring ancient pottery as the woman is doing is very specialised work. It takes a long time, so you need to be patient, have good eyesight and steady hands, and enjoy working on your own – be self-motivated.
>
> I'd like to do the job in motor-racing, rather than be shut away in a dusty old museum somewhere. It must be so exciting to work at a Grand Prix!

2

> **Answers**
> a insecure   b flexible   c concerned

3

> **Suggested answer**
> I feel fairly positive about these trends. As long as you don't expect to stay in one career for life, there are plenty of opportunities. However, you do need to keep your skills updated and be willing to be flexible. Another important change in the job market has been the shift away from manual work, which has happened because of automation. That's created some unemployment.

4 The part of the text that confirms each answer is given below.

1, 2	A, C	did homeopathy courses; took English and Law at night school
3	B	the takings will have overtaken my previous salary by next year
4	A	my income has reduced … my overheads are lower
5	E	the company eventually passed to me
6	A	foreign business trips
7, 8	B, E	My work is very sociable; deal with people … tailor-made for me
9	D	People who need certainty and structure would find my new life very difficult … made the right decision
10	C	it was three years before I felt I'd cracked the job
11, 12	B, D	Everything is based here in the house; I've set up the spare room as an office
13	D	I worked for three cabinet ministers
14, 15	B, E	I'm nothing like as tense as before; a huge responsibility and I worried constantly

5 Remember that negative prefixes are tested in Paper 3 Part 3.

> **Answers**
> a *Possible answers*: she had been doing the job for too long; her life felt empty outside work; she was getting fed up with the travelling.
> b *Possible answer*: if she doesn't earn enough!
> c When she was a salon apprentice.
> d It lacks a set routine and she has no regular income.
> e She might be seen as unable to work in a team.
> f Because a registrar has to deal sensitively with people and needs experience of life.

6

> **Answers**
> impractical, incapable, disorganised/unorganised, independent, unsuccessful, dishonest, disloyal, impatient

Grammar extra

All is a very common word in English and is used in many expressions. Try to use the ones given in your writing.

> **Answers**
> a had everything   b one bit
> c used with a superlative to emphasise
> d doing your very best, making the most effort possible
> e used to emphasise   f despite
> g on the whole; used to summarise
> h every type of person
>
> a all (of the)   b the whole (of the)   c The whole (of the)
> d all   e all/the whole; all of   f all (of the)

14.2 pages 92–93

1

> **Answers**
> Sentence *a* says that the person has sent no e-mails (neither in the past nor in the present). Sentence *b* only refers to the past and doesn't tell us whether the situation is still true. Sentence *c* tells us that the person started to send emails at some point in the past but before that time had never sent any. Sentence *d* forecasts a future situation at a certain time.
>
> a present perfect   b simple past
> c past perfect; simple past   d future perfect

2 All of these examples come from the article in 14.1.

3

Corpus spot

4 The skills mentioned are given below. Other useful skills or qualifications would be: effective communicator (1), degree in languages/translation and interpreting (2), good at selling (3), life-saving qualification (4), creative/imaginative (5).

Speaker 1: There's a big music festival in my town every summer. For the last three years, I've worked in the festival office, doing a whole range of things, from putting leaflets in envelopes to arranging hotel bookings for the various performers. I know I'm flexible – I've had to be – and I've definitely got commitment – I don't

mind working long hours as long as there's an end in sight! I really enjoy big events, too – the more people there are, the more enjoyable it is!

Speaker 2: I've always been keen on languages. My mother's from Quebec in Canada, so we speak both German and French at home. I've been learning English since I was twelve. By next summer, I'll have been learning it for over ten years, so I'm sure I'll be really fluent. I like dealing with people face to face and people say I've got quite a lot of talent for communication. I can think really fast which gives me a lot of confidence. Oh, and I'm a very positive person too!

Speaker 3: I've been working in The Gap since I left college last year. I think I dress well myself – that's important when you're in this sort of job. I know a lot about sports and leisure clothing, and I often get asked for advice when people are choosing what to buy. Once you've worked in a busy clothing store you can handle anything – I don't mind pressure, in fact it's usually a good thing – makes the day go more quickly.

Speaker 4: I'm having a year off between school and medical school. I've been doing part-time voluntary work in a hospital and I'm also going to evening classes to get a first-aid qualification. I've got lots of energy and I like to think I'm extremely fit. My boyfriend thinks I'm obsessed with sport, actually – I swim for a club and I play tennis or basketball whenever I get the chance. I'd like to specialise in sports medicine when I'm older.

Speaker 5: I did a one-year course in catering after leaving school, and since then I've been working alongside one of Edinburgh's top chefs. She's taught me so much – not just recipes and techniques, either. The most important thing I've learned is how to cope with working at speed. It can get very busy some evenings, but through her, I've developed ways of being better organised ... er ... staying in control when it gets really hot in the kitchen.

6 The article is written for office workers.

Writing folder 7

Applications 1 pages 94–95

Applications require formal register and a clear layout, with suitable paragraphing. You do not need to include postal addresses, even if they are given in the job advertisement on the question paper. Remember to say at the beginning why you are writing, quoting any reference number or title of the job. It is important to 'sell' yourself to the reader, explaining in detail why you are the right person.

1   Many of these words have already come up in Units 13 and 14.

Answers
motivated   committed   determined   cheerful
enthusiastic   energetic   organised   talented
skilled/skilful   confident

2   Skills and qualities include: cheerfulness, energy, self-confidence, fluency in English, some experience of bar/restaurant work.

3

Answers
Letter A has covered all the points.
Letter B has omitted to talk about his knowledge of English. The letter is thin on relevant experience and on the reason why he would like the job. It is also thin on personal qualities and what is said would probably irritate the reader. The letter is also inappropriately informal and its tone is too colloquial / chatty.

4

Corrected and improved letter

Dear Sir or Madam

I have seen your advertisement for restaurant and bar staff on your ZY cruise ships in the Mediterranean and would like to apply. I have travelled around the Mediterranean myself and find its history and culture fascinating. I'm sure I could share my knowledge with your on-board guests, as I am a fluent English speaker.

Although I haven't worked on a cruise ship before, I do have extensive experience of bar work and am able to mix a wide range of cocktails. I have also worked in a beach café, serving meals and snacks. I realise that your own restaurants will probably have a more formal atmosphere, but I am quick to learn new skills and would enjoy working in this type of restaurant.

I have lots of energy, so the idea of working long hours doesn't worry me. My previous employers have always found me cheerful, committed and honest. Finally, I think it is important to tell you that I have never suffered from seasickness.

I look forward to hearing from you soon.

Yours faithfully

Harry Lime

5   Make a paragraph plan before you start writing.

Sample answer

Dear Sir or Madam

I am writing to apply for the job of tour guide with Europewide Coach Tours, which was advertised in The Times last Saturday. I am just the person you are looking for.

I have been studying English for twelve years, so I am fluent. I recently spent three months in London, as part of my studies. I also speak French and a little German.

Although I know many parts of Europe well, I am always keen to visit new places and find out more about them. It would be good to share this knowledge with others.

People say I am a good communicator and I enjoy being with other people. I have a good sense of humour and plenty of energy.

In terms of relevant experience, I have spent the last two summers working as a guide, taking groups of foreign tourists on walking tours around our city. I therefore have a good understanding of the needs of visitors from other countries.

I hope you will consider my application favourably.

Yours faithfully

Unit 15

15.1   pages 96–97

1   The photos are of:

(left) one of the Pyramids and the outskirts of the city of Cairo
(top right) the Colosseum in Rome, surrounded by traffic
(bottom right) the Grand Canyon with a group of tourists

Suggested answer
I remember visiting Stonehenge, a circle of massive stones dating back 5000 years, which is situated in the county of Wiltshire. People had scrawled graffiti on the stones and there was litter everywhere. Now it's fenced off, which means the stones are protected, but you can't get up close to them any more.

Perhaps there should be stricter limits on the number of visitors to a site and more staff to keep an eye on them.

2   The underlined parts of the recording script show where the answers occur.

Answers
1 northwestern   2 1.6 km/kilometres   3 1919
4 5m/million   5 bus (service)   6 air pollution
7 water   8 seven/7 degrees   9 rapids   10 (seven/7 natural) wonders

Situated in the <u>northwestern</u> part of Arizona, the Grand Canyon is one of the natural wonders of the world. Contrary to popular belief, the Grand Canyon is not the longest, deepest, or widest canyon in the world. But it is accessible, and with little vegetation to hide it, it feels big. Nothing prepares you for that first sight of it. From the top it drops <u>1.6 kilometres</u> to the desert floor below. But however vast it seems, it is not big enough to support the millions of people who visit it every year.

When one section of the Grand Canyon was declared a national park in <u>1919</u>, three years after the creation of the National Park Service, visitor numbers were 44,000. Today, with <u>five million</u> visitors a year, the Park Service is finding it difficult to keep the Canyon accessible to the public and to safeguard it for future generations.

The pressures on the Grand Canyon National Park have forced the Park Service to draw up a management plan. One of the first problems it has tackled is that of the large number of visitors' cars. Options included the introduction of an electric <u>bus service</u> and a light railway system in and around Grand Canyon village.

Some of the other problems faced by the park are the result of things happening outside its boundaries. Take <u>air pollution</u>. On summer days, when there are southwesterly winds, the pollution blown in from Southern California can restrict the views over the Canyon.

Then, another of the big problems is the availability of <u>water</u> resources in the park, as, at present, there is a drought. The Park cannot draw water from the river but only from a spring on the north side of the canyon, using a pipeline. If this pipeline is damaged, then water has to be brought in by truck. This last happened in 1995 when floods caused a landslide, which destroyed the pipeline.

The Colorado River, which created the Canyon, looks wild but in fact, is managed intensely. Twenty-four kilometres upstream is the Glen Canyon Dam which has had a profound impact on the river. Now the river flow is about a tenth of what it was previously.

The Colorado used to reach temperatures of twenty-four degrees in summer. Today, it is a cold <u>seven degrees</u> all year as water release comes from deep within the reservoir. As a result, some species of fish have become extinct. In addition, the <u>rapids</u> are getting bigger, as the river is too weak to move the boulders washed out of the canyons downstream.

Visitors are proving to be powerful allies of the park. Those who once thought that the Grand Canyon was just an awesome hole in the ground soon learn that however big it is, its popularity is in danger of destroying the very qualities that made it one of the <u>seven natural wonders</u> in the world.

3

Answers
a throw away: rubbish, junk, litter
b use again: recycle, bottle bank, second-hand

4

Suggested answers
a We recycle newspapers and bottles, and compost vegetable waste.
b Fairly, although the washing machine and dishwasher are used every day.
c I am happy to walk or cycle short distances, up to say 10 km.
d Although I enjoy some meat, and love fish, I would be equally happy eating vegetarian food, which is delicious.
e Unprintable!

5

Answers

adjective	noun	adverb	verb
longest	length	lengthily	lengthen
weakest	weakness	weakly	weaken
deepest	depth	deeply	deepen
strongest	strength	strongly	strengthen
widest	width	widely	widen
shortest	shortness	shortly	shorten

Answers
1 products 2 surroundings 3 chemical 4 unwanted
5 poisonous 6 Unfortunately 7 Scientists
8 eventually 9 disappear

6

Answers
1.6 kilometres/kms   millions   1919   three years
44,000   5 million   1995   24 kilometres/kms   a tenth
24 degrees   7 degrees   7

7 Listen carefully to the recording and practise your pronunciation.

Measurement
thirteen kilometres
thirty centimetres
nought point five kilometres
two point five metres
one hundred and fifty-three kilos
one metre, fifty-three centimetres
a half
a quarter
two thirds
Dates
the first of May, eighteen ninety-nine
the third of August, two thousand
the twelfth of February, two thousand and four
the twenty-fifth of December, nineteen ninety
the fifteenth century
the fourth of the fifth, forty-five

Money
ten p or ten pence
one pound forty-five
fifty dollars
'0'
oh one two, three two three, double six, double seven, eight
three nil
forty love
zero or nought degrees Celsius
Telephone numbers
oh one two five six, three double one, three double nine
oh oh four four, three two four, double six seven, oh one two
Maths
two plus six equals eight
three minus two equals one
four times four equals sixteen
ten divided by two equals five
twenty per cent
three degrees
the square root of sixteen

15.2 pages 98-99

1   Read the Corpus spot. Always check your written work and remember that *advice, information, luggage* and *furniture* **never** have an 's', because they are uncountable.

> **Answers**
> **Countable** – country, meal, recommendation, journey, job, coin, storm, temperature, verb, vehicle, seat, hairstyle, suitcase, mountain, note
> Four words can be countable and uncountable:
> **lands** e.g. tribal lands rather than the idea of ground/soil
> **works** e.g. the works of Shakespeare rather than something you are employed to do
> **hairs** e.g. hairs on the body rather than hair on the head
> **travels** e.g. The Travels of Marco Polo rather than the concept of movement

2

> **Answers**
> a How many of the tourists actually realise the problems they cause?
> b Little of the soil can be used for cultivation now the trees have been cut down.
> c A large amount of equipment is needed to camp at the bottom of the Canyon.
> d Little luggage can be carried on the back of a donkey down the dirt tracks.
> e A large number of rainforests are being cut down every year.
> f The amount of traffic is causing too much congestion in major cities.
> g Many governments believe that nuclear power is the key to future energy problems.
> h The Park Ranger gave me a lot of/a great deal of good advice about camping in the national park.
> i Few people nowadays wear fur coats.

3

> **Answers**
> few mistakes – I'm good at English.
> a few mistakes – I'm quite good at English, but not perfect.
>
> little time – I'm really too busy.
> a little time – I do have some time but it's not very much.

Grammar extra

> **Answers**
> *Some* is used with an affirmative verb, for offers and if the answer to a question is going to be 'yes'.
> *No* is used with an affirmative verb to give a negative meaning.
> *Any* is used with a negative verb and in questions. Also when the answer to a question may be 'no'.

4

> **Answers**
> a shower of rain   a slice of cake   an item of clothing
> a glass of water   a clap of thunder   a pane of glass
> a ball of string   a flash of lightning   a crowd of people
> a bar of chocolate

5

> **Answers**
> a some; bars   b any/some; flashes
> c Some / A few / Many/Most/Lots; panes
> d hair   e some advice/information   f any coins
> g most/some; traffic

6

> **Answers**
> 1 some   2 few   3 ago   4 in   5 deal/amount
> 6 Although/Though   7 than   8 of/from
> 9 which/that   10 one   11 had   12 is

Exam folder 8

Paper 4 Part 3 pages 100–101

2

> **Answers**
> 2 E   3 C   4 F   5 A

The underlined parts of the recording script confirm the answers.

Speaker 2: I left school and moved to a college to take my final exams. It was the best decision I could have made. <u>At the college nobody seemed to care about homework and this really motivated me. I had to plan my work myself – there was no one to make you do it and no one to check up on what you'd done.</u> I was still dependent on my parents for money – but that was OK. I learned a lot about real life there – things like getting on with people and organising your time, which has been really useful now I'm working.

Speaker 3: When I left school I didn't have a particular career in mind so I decided to do Environmental Studies at university, mainly because I'd enjoyed geography at school. I didn't really like the course at university and I did think about leaving but instead I changed courses, which was easier than I expected. I think university was useful in that I learnt how to <u>live alone and how to budget, and as I'm an underpaid teacher now that really helps.</u>

Speaker 4: I had no difficulty choosing what I was going to do – my parents are both doctors and ever since I was small I also wanted to do that. They really encouraged me and I did well at school and got into a good medical school fairly easily. <u>It was surprisingly tough at medical school</u>, but I had some good friends and we pulled through together. I think the doubts only began to set in when I graduated and got my first job in a hospital. I began to wonder if I'd missed out because I'd been so focused on becoming a doctor. So now I'm doing some voluntary work in Africa which I'm really enjoying.

Speaker 5: I decided to take a year off after doing my last year at school. I'd had enough of revising and sitting in a library so I decided to go off to Australia for nine months and earn a bit of money. I've got relatives there who put me up when I first arrived and found me a job. It wasn't doing anything particularly interesting, <u>but the great part was that I was getting to know people who were completely different to the ones I'd known back home.</u> I really recommend taking a year out, but you need to have a firm plan or it could end up a waste of time.

Unit 16

16.1 pages 102–103

1

> **Suggested answer**
> Breakfast: cereal, yogurt, toast
> Lunch: sandwich, fruit, chocolate
> Dinner: pasta, salad, cheese, fruit

2

> **Suggested answers**
> Japan: sushi, rice, noodles
> Alaska: fish
> USA: junk food

3

> **Answers**
> **Akiko**
> | Breakfast | soup, rice, fish |
> |---|---|
> | Lunch | noodles, hamburgers |
> | Dinner | pasta, soup |
>
> **Kunu**
> | Breakfast | cheese sandwich, orange juice |
> |---|---|
> | Lunch | raw fish |
> | Supper | reindeer, fish |
>
> **Gayle**
> | Breakfast | omelette |
> |---|---|
> | Lunch | sandwich – tuna, tomato paste, non-fat bread |
> | Dinner | grilled fish, chicken |

Speaker 1: My name is Akiko and I was born in Hiroshima in Japan. I moved to England with my family when I was three but my mother always makes us traditional Japanese food. For breakfast we have <u>soup, rice and fish.</u> For lunch <u>I eat noodles, but I also love hamburgers.</u> It's very common for Japanese people to mix traditional and Western food. I'm conscious of healthy eating and I eat a lot of vegetables, but I don't worry about my weight! <u>In the evening I'll have pasta or some more soup.</u>

Speaker 2: My name is Kunu, and I grew up in Alaska, where meals are central to Inuit life. I moved to Seattle when I was seventeen, and became physically ill because my body rejected Western foods. I do eat some Western food though. <u>For breakfast I always have a cheese sandwich with orange juice. Lunch is usually raw fish, and for supper I have reindeer or fish.</u> I hardly eat any sweet foods and I exercise five times a week.

Speaker 3: Everyone calls me Gayle. I exercise for about half an hour before <u>breakfast, which is usually an omelette. For lunch I'll have a sandwich</u> – a mixture of tuna and tomato paste on non-fat bread. I eat a lot but I never eat fat. If I go out to eat I always ask the waiter to miss out the cream or cheese or oil. People are used to it in LA. I keep a journal every day to say what exercise I've done and exactly what I've eaten. <u>In the evening I'll have grilled fish or chicken.</u>

4 Look out for signposting words in the gapped sentences and the text, for example *Also* in H.

> **Answers**
> **1** H **2** B **3** G **4** A **5** F **6** E **7** C

5

> **Answers**
> **a** flavoured **b** diet **c** additives **d** portions **e** coating

6

> **Answers**
> a not available b bad c rude
> d not keen on/not having

7

> **Suggested answers**
> a I suppose if it means children will eat vegetables, it's a good thing.
> b I love rice dishes – paella, Indian and Thai curries and, above all, delicious Italian risotto with lots of freshly-grated parmesan cheese.
> c It's fairly healthy, apart from the chocolate!
> d My daughter's a vegetarian, so we eat a lot of vegetarian food. I probably could give up meat, though I'd miss fish.
> e Writing this in England, I'd have to say Roast Beef and Yorkshire Pudding, or Fish and Chips.
> f There's nothing I can't eat, but I'm not wild about heavy meat dishes.
> g Absolutely – and I had to finish everything on my plate, too!

16.2 pages 104–105

1

> **Answers**
> singular countable = waiter, lunch (a, the)
> Normally , we talk about 'a' or 'the' waiter. We can use lunch with 'a' or 'the', but when we are talking about it in general terms, we don't use an article: What time are we having lunch? (This is the same for all meals.)
> plural countable = noodles (nothing, the)
> uncountable = fish, cheese (nothing, the)

2

> **Answers**
> 1 d 2 f 3 g 4 c 5 b,h 6 a 7 e,a 8 i
> 9 j, k 10 e

Ⓑackgrounⅾ information

In Japan, and in many other countries, customers can get an idea of what to order from looking at plastic replicas of the food available. This article is about fake food in Japanese restaurants. These plastic replicas are called *sanpuru*.

3

> **Answers**
> 1 nothing/the 2 nothing/the 3 a 4 the 5 nothing
> 6 nothing 7 a 8 a/the 9 The 10 nothing 11 a
> 12 the 13 the 14 nothing 15 nothing 16 a

4

> **Answers**
> a the b – c the d – e the/– f – g – h –
> i – j a k – l – m the n the o the

5

> **Answers**
> a My husband's father (person)
> b restaurant window (kind) c OK (position)
> d a cooking magazine (kind) e OK (kind) f OK (time)
> g a cup of coffee (a container with something in it)
> h OK (position)

Corpus spot

> **Answers**
> a I prefer to travel **in** January.
> b I hope I can come again next year.
> c We are going to start next weekend.
> d We had to wait **a** long time for lunch.
> e During **the** evening she made a cake.
> f **On** Wednesday morning, I will be free.
> g In **the** afternoon we could go for a burger.
> h I played tennis **for** seven years.
> i I wonder how you get to work **on** time.
> j I enjoy spending time shopping.

Choosing the right preposition can be difficult! Remember these rules:

- *at* for times and holiday periods – at 9.30, at midnight, at Easter

- *on* for days and dates – on Tuesday, on New Year's Day, on 14 June

- *in* for months, years, centuries – in May, in 1979, in the 15th century

6 As in Unit 6, this recording is 'unscripted' and at natural speed. Don't worry if you don't understand every word. The name of the dish the man is describing is *Boeuf Bourguignon*, a French beef stew.

Answers

<u>Ingredients</u> – beef, red wine, bacon, small onions (shallots), seasoned flour, and mushrooms.
<u>Serve</u> with mashed potatoes, green vegetables or salad.
<u>Method</u>
Fry the bacon.
Add some onions and brown them.
Chop the beef into cubes.
Coat the beef in seasoned flour.
Fry the beef with the bacon and the onions.
Add the red wine.
Cook slowly in an oven for about two and a half hours.
Add mushrooms.
Cook twenty minutes more.

Woman: Tell me about your favourite dish.

Man: Right, well, it's something I tasted when I was in France, called Boeuf Bourguignon, and it's basically a stew of beef cooked in red wine. It takes quite a long time to prepare, and indeed, quite a long time to cook. You need some bacon, which you fry, then you add some very small onions, shallots, and you brown them. And then you coat the beef, which you've chopped up into small cubes, in seasoned flour, flour with salt and pepper. And then you fry that, along with the bacon and the onions and then you add red wine – that's the nice bit 'cos you can usually take a sip while …

Woman: Of course, …

Man: … while you're doing that, and the better the wine, the better the dish.

Woman: Oh really? You can't use a cheap bit that's left over from the day before?

Man: It's better if you use burgundy, which, of course, is quite an expensive wine, but it does make the best Boeuf Bourguignon …

Woman: Oh, right.

Man: … and then you put that in the oven and you need to cook it for quite a long time on a low heat …

Woman: … slowly …

Man: … so that all the juices meld, and then about, I suppose, a quarter of an hour before …

Woman: So when you say quite a long time, how many hours?

Man: Well, I think between two and two and a half on …

Woman: Yes.

Man: … on a lowish heat. Then about 20 minutes before you're going to serve it you put some small mushrooms in it and then …

Woman: Cut up?

Man: Yes, unless they're those small button mushrooms, or you can slice them up 'cos they make the liquid a little thinner, so with that you serve mashed potatoes maybe, and a green vegetable or a salad. It's absolutely delicious.

Woman: Sounds lovely.

Writing folder 8

Transactional letters and emails 2
pages 106–107

If you are asked to write a letter or email to a friend, you should use informal register throughout. Remember to develop the points given, and don't include irrelevant information – for example, asking lots of questions about your friend's family, telling your friend what you got for your birthday – as this will lower your mark.

1

Answers
1 b   **2** b   **3** a   **4** a   **5** b   **6** b   **7** a   **8** a   **9** a   **10** b

3

Sample answer

Dear Anna,

Thank you very much for inviting me to your party. I'd love to come. The restaurant sounds lovely. I love Italian food.

Thank you for the map. I shall take the train but I don't know whether to walk or take a taxi from the station. You said it was only five minutes away from the restaurant – is that on foot or by taxi? Could you also let me know the name of the road the restaurant is in as it wasn't on the map?

I will have a friend staying with me at the time you will be having the party. Would it be all right if she came too? She's called Elisabeth and she's a student from France. She is taking a course at my university and I feel it would be rude for me to disappear for a weekend while she is here. She's also 21 and very nice.

Hope to hear from you soon. What would you like for a birthday present?

Best wishes,

Corpus spot

Answers
1 accommodation   **2** advertisement   **3** which
4 believe   **5** because   **6** beginning   **7** comfortable
8 bicycle   **9** convenient   **10** embarrassing
11 especially   **12** received   **13** beautiful
14 communicate   **15** sincerely

4

Unit 17

17.1 pages 108–109

1   Read the information about Part 2 of the Speaking Test on page 7. Then, using Student A's notes, record yourself doing the task. Try to speak for a whole minute. Make sure you cover both the benefits and the problems of collecting the things shown.

   When you listen to your recording, note down any errors in grammar and vocabulary, for example subject-verb agreement, tense choice, plurals of countable nouns.

2   Remember that the other candidate has to make a brief comment, as Student A does here.

3   Here are some examples of each type of hobby.

   Collecting: stamps, postcards, shells, beer mats, cinema posters.

   Making things: model planes, science fiction warriors, jewellery, hats, furniture.

4   The picture on page 109 shows slot-car racing.

Answers
1 B   2 C   3 B   4 C   5 A   6 C   7 B   8 A

The underlined parts of the recording script confirm the answers.

1

I've been collecting fossils for about fifteen years. Lyme Regis on the Dorset coast is a good spot and you see a lot of professionals there with all the equipment, chipping away half way up some rock or other. I don't know, though. I mean I've got a special hammer, but <u>my finest pieces have been just picked up by the shore</u>, usually after a storm. 1987 was the year I found the most – the year the hurricane struck Britain. If you're not feeling at all adventurous, you can buy some excellent fossils in the shops in Lyme Regis. I was very tempted to get a magnificent dinosaur's tooth once.

2

Man: Here are those cards I bought for you in Oxford, to add to your collection. I hope you don't think they're too tatty – they must be at least fifty years old …

Woman: Thanks. The condition they're in doesn't bother me. And actually, looking at the stamps, they're older than you say, which is brilliant because I haven't got many from the 1930s.

Man: Oh, so you're looking for cards from a certain period?

Woman: Well, I collect all sorts, but I'm on the lookout for older ones <u>that have text on the picture. Like this one, which says: 'Thinking of you in St Ives'</u> …

3

I knew someone once who had an absolute passion for making things out of wood. He spent hours and hours on his hobby – whatever the object was, he always took great pride in doing it well and <u>making it unique, by choosing a special wood. He never chose the same kind twice</u>. He would make all sorts of things – a new handle for a fork, with a pattern cut into it; enough models to fill several glass cases … He even made an electric guitar, which he painted designs on – something he didn't normally do. One piece I remember well is a polar bear. The way it was carved really captured the look of the animal, walking heavily through the snow.

4

Interviewer: Jamie Eagle, who is the outright winner of today's slot-car racing, is with me now. Congratulations, Jamie, and this is now your tenth win! So where did it all begin? I know your father was also racing here today. Did he know what he was doing when he persuaded you to take up such a time-consuming hobby?

Jamie: Er, actually, it was me who persuaded him – he's only been racing this year. He's pretty hopeless at it, too! <u>No, it was my cousin who's to blame</u>. He used to take me along when he went to race meetings – I was five at the time – and I thought it was just brilliant!

Interviewer: And if your father's racing his own car, who do you have as back-up today?

Jamie: I've introduced my friend Ian to slot-car racing – at the moment he's free to help me, though next year he hopes to have a car of his own.

5

Interviewer: This is Radio QB, the phone lines are open and we want to hear about your hobbies. And here's Eleanor, from London. What are you into, Eleanor?

Eleanor: Beads. I've got several hundred, in all shapes and sizes – glass, metal, plastic ones … They're from all over the world, too: I've got a handful of beautiful wooden ones, from India, and some very unusual African ones carved out of bone. A few of them I've made up into earrings and necklaces, but what I really like doing is collecting! Especially coloured glass ones, which I've got loads of.

Interviewer: And you say you've got several hundred – how long has it taken you to get so many?

Eleanor: Not that long, really… I had lots of plastic ones when I was a kid, but I gave those away so they don't count! I suppose I got serious about beads three years ago. Since then, my family have given me tins of beads as presents, and I spend most of my pocket money on them too.

6

Now look here, you're not going to pass me on to anyone else … I have … I have been back there twice but they said I must take the matter up with you. It's clearly your responsibility – the model kit was sealed, so it can't have been the shop's fault, can it? … No, I'm quite sure. This is crazy, I mean I buy a lot of your kits, you know. Do you want me to contact Model-Makers magazine and describe the story so far? … No, I didn't think you would. Listen, you have all my details, so please get on and sort it out!

7

Interviewer: I'm with Jenny Braintree, who paints the whole world in miniature on pebbles she finds at the seaside. Jenny, you took up this hobby four years ago and …

Jenny: Er … it was four months ago, in fact. I was on a beach holiday with my parents and I collected loads of nice, smooth pebbles. When I got home, I started to paint tiny images of beautiful places like the Swiss mountains and the Brazilian rainforest. I've done 89 so far.

Interviewer : Amazing! These pictures are no more than five centimetres across and yet they contain so much detail! So what's the reason behind this, Jenny? Do you earn anything from all your hard work?

Jenny: Dad thinks I could sell them but I'm not interested in that and anyway they're too special to me. My real aim is to get better at painting because that's what I want to do when I'm older. And although I haven't been to the places I illustrate on the pebbles, it can be really good fun finding out about them on the Internet.

8

People think it's a bit odd that I spend my weekends dressed up in anything from metal armour to old uniforms, out in the open air. But it's good fun! The group that puts on these events was only formed about four months ago. I joined in April and we've already performed five battles! You learn a great deal about history, because everything is researched properly – from the costumes to the actual battle tactics. My girlfriend's not too pleased with me at the moment. I'm going to have to miss her birthday 'cos we're doing the Battle of Naseby. That's not the reason she's mad at me though. She wanted to come too but I wouldn't let her!

5

> **Suggested answer**
> Speaking personally, the hobby that would interest me least is making model planes and so on. I just wouldn't have the patience to sit down and stick all the bits together, let alone paint the model afterwards!

6

> **Suggested answers**
> 1 A dentist   B immigration/customs officer   C plumber
> 2 A sewing   B cooking   C translating
> 3 A coastguard   B detective/police   C accountant
> 4 A shiny and expensive   B dark brown   C dull and grey
> 5 A a doctor   B a gardener   C an MP/ the city council
> 6 A … my account is not in the red!
>   B … you can't stay up to watch that programme on TV.
>   C … my private life is my own concern.
> 7 A dishes, tins of food   B that your friend was lying to you
>   C distant galaxies; new stars
> 8 A someone was crossing the road
>   B a big wave was about to hit you
>   C a pot of paint was in danger of toppling over
> 9 A his older brother or sister   B a professor
>   C the head chef

17.2 pages 110–111

1

> **Answers**
> a Only some of the children were tired, so not all of them went to bed. (Defining clause)
> b All the children were tired and all went to bed. (Non-defining)
> c They decided to stay at the first hotel which had a pool, so they probably passed several which didn't have pools.
> d They stayed at the very first hotel they came to and, fortunately, it had a pool.

2

> **Answers**
> a has a non-defining clause   b has a defining clause
> c N which   d D who   e D who   f N whose
> g N (most of) which   h D that

3 The relative pronoun *which* or *that* would go after 'those cards', because it refers to them. Read the section headed **Relative pronouns** on page 204 of the Grammar folder.

> **Answers**
> Here are those cards which/that I bought for you in Oxford.
>
> a that/which I wanted to buy
> b who/that I really looked up to
> c that/which I can't stand about Harry
> d who/that you met at John's party
> e that/which we stayed at

4

> **Answers**
> a where b when c who d which/that e where

5

> **Answers**
> 1 more 2 of 3 which/that 4 where/when 5 as
> 6 from 7 every 8 ought 9 ago 10 not 11 if
> 12 would

6 The use of stress is important in English. In these examples, the speaker is able to correct an error or give a different opinion, by stressing certain words.

Interviewer: Did he know what he was doing when he persuaded you to take up such a time-consuming hobby?
Jamie: Er, actually, it was <u>me</u> who persuaded <u>him</u> – he's only been racing this year.
Interviewer: Jenny, you took up this hobby four years ago and ...
Jamie: Er ... it was four <u>months</u> ago, in fact.

7 The underlined parts of the recording script show where contrastive stress is used.

a Would you like a coffee?
No thanks – it stops me sleeping. I wouldn't mind a <u>cold</u> drink though.
b I'm going to wear my red dress to the interview.
Oh no, <u>red's</u> <u>much</u> too bright. I'd wear your <u>blue</u> one – with the grey jacket.
c Hello, Jan? Listen, I've been waiting outside the cinema but no one's turned up.
The others said they'd meet you <u>inside</u>, didn't they?
d Why is it always my turn to empty the dishwasher?
It isn't. <u>I</u> did it <u>yesterday</u> – and I cleaned the <u>cooker</u>, too.

8

> **Suggested answers**
> a Let's go and play tennis – it's not too cold, is it?
> It's **freezing!** I think we should go and see a **movie** instead.
> b Why not stay in and do your homework this evening?
> Not **again!** I'd much rather go out **clubbing**.

c Paint your room yellow – it would look really good.
Ugh! Yellow's too **loud**. I think **pale blue** would be much better.
d You know, you could have that magazine sent to you every month.
But it's so **expensive**. I think I'll just buy it **occasionally**.
e Brian's the one who's interested in model cars.
No, he isn't, that's **Jerry. Brian's** keen on **power-kiting**.
f Here's the CD I bought in town. It was only £12.99.
£12.99? I've seen it for only **£8.50**.

Exam folder 9

Paper 4 Part 4 pages 112–113

> **Answers**
> 1 B 2 C 3 B 4 C 5 A 6 B 7 A

The underlined parts of the recording script confirm the answers.

Interviewer: Welcome to *Around Britain*. On the programme today we are going to be looking at not only the pressures and problems, but also the positive aspects of life on a small island. Now, Rebecca, you were born on the island and still live there. What's life like there?
Rebecca: In many ways, it sounds idyllic – there's no crime, no roads, no unemployment. <u>The majority of the houses are grouped around the small port</u> and you can get a boat to the mainland from there fairly regularly. During the last century, however, the population fell very sharply as fishing, the main occupation, became uneconomic. Then, people from the mainland began to buy the empty houses as holiday houses. Many of these families liked the island so much they decided to stay on full-time.
Interviewer: And how do you manage to make a living?
Rebecca: Well, I had to go to the mainland for my secondary education and then I went to university to study English Literature. I did some teaching for a bit and I then got a job in London <u>with a publishing company doing editing work on a journal and worked there for a couple of years. However, because of computer technology I realised I didn't have to stay in London to do my job – I could do it anywhere.</u> All I seemed to do in London was work, work, work. I also hated the crowds of people everywhere.
Interviewer: What kind of people do you think are attracted to life on the island, Rebecca?
Rebecca: They need to be a bit eccentric, I always think. Also it needs real determination to stay on the island. For example, at some stage they will have to part with their children, which is always hard, but if they want to continue to live there, it's just a fact of life. The school only educates the children until they are nine. After that they spend the week at school on the mainland and only come home at weekends. It teaches the children independence, <u>but not everyone could cope with that.</u>

Interviewer: Indeed. And how do you see the future of the island?

Rebecca: Things are okay for this generation. However, the challenge is to provide employment for the children and their children or else they'll leave. We also need to keep development in tune with island life – we can't allow just any business to set up there.

Interviewer: I know the island is famed for its wildlife ….

Rebecca: Absolutely. That's one reason why everyone likes it. Any development would need to take that into consideration. We get a lot of tourists in summer – although they come to see us as much as the birds! – and they would disappear if any dramatic changes were made, although I believe that the islanders tend to worry too much about that and need to broaden their outlook a bit more.

Interviewer: There was talk of a large hotel complex, I believe?

Rebecca: Yes. A businessman from the mainland wanted to build a hotel which could take up to five hundred guests – there would be a spa, a swimming pool complex, an outdoor activity centre – the whole tourist thing. Most of the islanders were up in arms of course and the plans didn't come to anything in the end which was no surprise to anyone. It was a bit of a shame really.

Interviewer: Has the resulting bad feeling had a lasting cffcct on the community, do you think? IIow do you get on with your neighbours?

Rebecca: Oh people who live in a small community have to make the best of it. It's no good letting things get on top of you or starting quarrels every five minutes or you'd soon be left alone to get on with it. I guess the only downside for me is the way we live in each other's pockets all the time – there aren't many secrets there, believe me! On the whole, though, I'm glad I moved back and will probably stay on the island now for the foreseeable future.

Interviewer: My thanks to Rebecca Laing. Next week …

Unit 18

18.1 pages 114–115

1 The illustration shows a man fishing alone on the open sea; the purple fish is a marlin. From the sun and sky we know it is in a hot part of the world, maybe tropical.

Background information

Ernest Hemingway (1899–1961) received the Nobel prize for literature in 1954. Born in Chicago, USA, he spent some time in Europe as a journalist in the 1920s. He also lived in Spain for a while, and was passionate about bull-fighting. His other great love was deep-sea fishing, which is the subject of *The Old Man and the Sea*. In later life, he lived mostly in Cuba, and this is where the story is set.

2 From the reviews, we learn that *The Old Man and the Sea* is a short story which is economically written ('there is not a word too many; the writing is as tight ...'). The third review tells us that it is about an old man fishing with a line.

3 Remember that it is not necessary to understand every word in a text.

4

Answers					
1 B	2 C	3 B	4 D	5 A	6 D

Detailed explanation:

1 The answer (B) comes from 'saw a flight of wild ducks' and 'he knew that no man was ever alone on the sea'. Although A is plausible, the text doesn't say this. C and D pick up on parts of the first sentence of the second paragraph, but this is showing the old man's thoughts on other fishermen.

2 The answer (C) is confirmed in the sentence 'But we have no hurricane coming now' and in the fact that at sea, fishermen 'see the signs of it in the sky for days ahead'. A is ruled out because the text says 'now they were in hurricane months'. B, though plausible, is irrelevant, as hurricanes are first noticed out at sea. D falsely echoes the final sentence of the second paragraph.

3 This type of reference question is common in Paper 1 Part 2. The answer (B) refers to the line; 'it' is used to avoid repeating 'the line' for a third time in two sentences. A is ruled out because there is no earlier reference to the boat in the third paragraph. C is impossible, as we already know that his hand is against his thigh. The answer cannot be D, as the fish hasn't come to the surface of the water yet.

4 The answer (D) is in the second sentence of the fourth paragraph: 'I must never let him learn his strength nor what he could do if he made his run'. Although A and C are plausible, the text doesn't give any evidence. B says the opposite of the text ('they are not as intelligent as we who kill them').

5 The expression 'fast to' means joined firmly to something (for example, you can say that a label is 'stuck fast' to a bottle and won't come off). B and D reflect the content of the paragraph, but do not give the true meaning. C picks up on the other meaning of 'fast'.

6 The answer (D) is found in the final paragraph, ('But then he would see my cramped hand'), but is also echoed globally in the text. There is no evidence that the man is worried about being alone in the boat, nor that he is small. C picks up on the fish having slowed down in the water.

5

Answers
a come in for   b going without   c go through
d went after   e came up against; go through
f come out   g go in for   h gone through   i went out
j coming through

6 This task encourages you to use different adjectives and
expressions in a description of the man's hand. You will
score higher marks if you can show language range like
this in the exam.

Sample description
I imagine the hand looks like a bird's claw, or the end
of a twisted wooden branch. It is rough and scarred, and
hangs uselessly from his arm.

18.2 pages 116–117

1

Answers
a historical novel   b thriller   c play   d non-fiction
e science fiction   f short stories

2

Answers
1 a   2 d   3 b   4 f   5 e

The underlined parts of the recording script confirm the
answers.

1 All of her books are really <u>well researched</u> and they're <u>full
of amazing details about what life used to be like there</u>. I
never realised they lived in apartment buildings, for
example! The storyline is very inventive too; you're kept
guessing right up until the last few pages. This is the fifth
one I've read and I can't wait to get my hands on another!

2 I found the book really interesting, because we've got two
now. It explains their behaviour and the relationships
they have with their owners. You can find out all sorts of
things, like <u>why they purr and how they use their
whiskers</u> ... and whether they can see colour. Honestly,
I've learnt such a lot, just from one paperback!

3 Once I started it, I just couldn't put it down. The plot is
quite complicated and it moves along at a really fast pace.
What I like best is the dialogue; it's so realistic somehow.
Many people say there's <u>no better writer on crime</u> at the
moment and I certainly think so. There's lots of other
titles I haven't read yet – some of them have been made
into films, too.

4 I don't have enough time to read much at the moment,
and as I prefer to finish something at one sitting, this
book was perfect for me. There are <u>some real classics</u>, too.
I must admit that sometimes <u>I felt a little uneasy turning
the pages late at night on my own</u>, though. The worst
occasion was when I'd almost got to the end, and my cat
suddenly jumped up at me out of nowhere, which scared
the life out of me!

5 This is an excellent read! I like the way the characters are so
well developed. It's one of three, and I've got them all now.
They're so imaginative, and at the same time, they seem
strangely accurate. They really <u>make you think about our
imminent future</u>, which is not necessarily that wonderful.
One of the best people writing at present, I'd say.

3

Answers
Yes, the writer does believe the book has a future. Reasons
(in second paragraph): people have more leisure time to
read in; the book has a strong tradition; it's very practical.
1 which/that   2 as   3 would   4 besides   5 why
6 or   7 less   8 used   9 well   10 on   11 much   12 be

4

Answers
a enough reasons   b small enough
c (extra – common expressions of this type are: *funnily
enough, strangely enough*, etc. For example, *Funnily
enough, my friend had bought the same book for me*.)
d too dismissive; too much
e and by other technological attractions, too
f very badly injured; very strong pull
g so effective; so well   h last hundred years or so
i If so,   j such alternatives to books as
k such a practical tool

5 Refer to the Corpus spot on page 116.

Answers
a enough time   b large enough   c enough books
d had had enough of   e not enough people
f got enough to   g quite enough   h Funnily enough

6

Answers
1 such cold weather (that) we   2 too little time to give
3 so well you should/could   4 is very good at getting
5 takes such a lot of   6 (this is) so, a refund

Writing folder 9

The set book pages 118–119

If you plan to answer Question 5 (a or b), your answer **must** be on one of the two set books listed on the question paper. Otherwise, however good your language is, you will receive a mark of 0.

1

> **Answers**
>
> stories; containing; character; unnamed; set in; different; advertising; environment; completely; its; mixture; bizarre; surprise; particular; campaigns; Marcovaldo's; friends; neighbourhood; river; memorable

2 The essay is a reasonable attempt at the question, though the third paragraph gives too much plot description. There is no conclusion, which would have helped to link the answer back to the question asked.

3

> **Sample answer**
>
> The Old Man and the Sea, written by Ernest Hemingway, is very true to life, in my opinion. It is set in Cuba and tells the story of an old fisherman who goes deep-sea fishing for marlin.
>
> A particularly realistic part of the book is when the old man first feels the pull of the fish on his line. Hemingway's knowledge of fishing brings this scene to life – the reader is there in the boat with the old man.
>
> Far out at sea and alone, he is not in good health. He has problems with his left hand, which he cannot straighten out. Hemingway describes the old man's feelings accurately and makes the reader feel sympathetic towards him. In spite of his age, the old man is determined and strong. He takes up the challenge of the marlin, a far bigger fish than he has ever caught before.
>
> One reviewer referred to the writing as 'tight'. For me, this is why the book feels so realistic – there is nothing irrelevant, no flowery description, just the battle between the old man and the fish. The book is a twentieth-century masterpiece.

4

> **Answers**
>
> Characters: personality, qualities, defects, reputation, temper, attitude, sympathy, humiliation, determination
> Events: atmosphere, incident, adventure, episode, climate, impact, surroundings
> Both categories: mood – you can talk about someone's mood or the mood of an event; risk – you can say a person takes risks or refer to an event being a risk

5 Some sample collocations are:
shallow/weak personality
great/good atmosphere
positive/bad mood
serious/interesting incident
important/good qualities
unimportant/minor defects
difficult/dangerous adventure
good/bad reputation
concluding/final episode
strong/bad temper
enormous/small risk
narrow/negative attitude
good/bad climate
deep/strong sympathy
serious/enormous impact
final/great humiliation
strong/great determination
interesting/attractive surroundings

6 Notice the early mention of the book title and main character in the opening paragraph.

7

> **Sample opening paragraph**
> For me, the most memorable episode in 'The Old Man and the Sea' is when the fish first appears. The description of this great purple fish emerging from the sea has an enormous impact.

Units 13–18 Revision

pages 120–121

1

> **Suggested answers**
> **a** Unfortunately this is true for me and it's a pity, because I love reading and don't have any free time during the day.
> **b** Quite the opposite, I have thought about it several times.
> **c** I manage to recycle paper and glass, but I use my car too much and don't walk enough.
> **d** I think a job must interest you, whether it has a large salary or a small one, because you spend so many hours of your life doing it.
> **e** There was only one, and I have already told you about her in the notes to Unit 13.
> **f** I can't remember them saying much about me either way.
> **g** This could be true, because men have more free time than women, don't they?
> **h** True enough (see a above).
> **i** This is certainly true up to a point – but then, there are so many other things in life apart from school, aren't there!
> **j** I'm pleased to tell you that this is not true in my case – I'm quite good at cooking, actually.

2

Answers
1 A   2 D   3 A   4 C   5 B   6 C   7 A   8 C   9 A   10 B
11 C   12 D

3

Answers
a There is too much traffic in our town.
b I have such a lot of/so much work to do, I don't know where to start.
c The Netherlands and Austria are both countries in the European Union.
d Her house, whose roof is thatched, is twelfth century.
  Her house, the roof of which is thatched, is twelfth century.
e John plays the piano and football, whereas his brother prefers playing chess.
f Let me give you some/a piece of advice – don't go on a journey/trip without checking whether you need a visa or not.
g That shop has stood on that corner for ten years.
h There's a man over there who has been standing watching us for about half an hour.
i I have lived in Las Vegas for ten years and I still find it exciting.
j By this time next year I will have taught for twenty years.
k He asked me where the police station was.
l I saw a flash of lightning when I was out in the garden.
m Have you got enough information to object to the factory noise?
n He's the one to whom I gave the book.
  He's the one who I gave the book to.
o My eldest son, who lives in Paris, is a physicist.

4

Answers
1 e   2 c   3 g   4 d   5 a   6 b   7 f

5

Answers
Across
1 represent   2 sank   3 count   4 save   5 prepare
6 kept   7 raised   8 control

Down
9 organise   10 examine   11 respect   12 cut   13 start
14 accept   15 chased   16 vomit   17 produce

Unit 19

19.1 pages 122–123

2 The section in the Grammar folder on page 205 lists the structures of advice and suggestion. Note the following:

You should + infinitive without *to*

If I were you + *I would* + infinitive without *to*

You ought + *to* + infinitive

Answers
Mostly As
You are fairly healthy and have a good attitude to life. You should try to watch what you eat a little more and if I were you I'd try to do a little more exercise. Too much work and not enough play isn't good for you! I think it's about time you thought about your diet.

Mostly Bs
You are obviously in the peak of condition! I recommend you relax as you ought to get some rest even if you don't need much sleep. Overdoing things can lead to illness! Why don't you try doing more reading, or go on holiday, or have you ever thought of playing a musical instrument?

Mostly Cs
Oh dear! It's time you took a good look at your lifestyle. Missing meals and not getting enough sleep and exercise are very bad for you. My advice to you is to start right away – you'd better book a place in the gym. I also suggest cutting down on coffee and drinking more water and fruit juice. Too much caffeine will keep you awake!

Suggested answers
a I suggest holding your breath.
b You ought to see if you're allergic to anything.
c You should stop worrying.
d Why don't you take a relaxation class?
e If I were you, I would see a doctor.
f You'd better have an injection.
g What about putting your head between your knees?
h I recommend buying some spray from the chemists'.
i You should go on a diet.
j My advice to you is to run it under the cold tap.

3 Refer to the Corpus spot.

Suggested answers
a It's time you gave up smoking.
b It's time you walked a bit more.
c It's time you read a book occasionally.
d It's time you applied for another one.
e It's time you ate something healthier.
f It's time you bought your own house.
g It's time you had it mended.
h It's time you paid for something.
i It's time you bought your own.
j It's time you got up earlier.
k It's time you bought a new one.

4

Answers

1	forehead	8	stomach
2	cheek	9	wrist
3	chin	10	waist
4	neck	11	hips
5	throat	12	thigh
6	shoulder	13	knee
7	elbow	14	ankle

5   There is more than one right answer here.

Suggested answers
If I broke my leg, I'd have it put in plaster.
If I had a headache, I'd take an aspirin.
If I cut my knee badly, I'd have stitches.
If I grazed my elbow, I'd get an elastoplast/a plaster/a Band-Aid.
If I sprained my ankle, I'd put a bandage on it.
If I had flu, I'd go to bed.
If I had a cough, I'd take some cough syrup/mixture.

6   Prepositional phrases are tested in Paper 3. Look back at Unit 6 for phrases with *in* and at Unit 10 for phrases with *at*. Use your dictionary to check the meanings of *in time, on time, at times, at the same time*.

Answers
a on foot   **b** on fire   **c** on purpose   **d** on duty
e on time   **f** On the whole   **g** on sale

19.2 pages 124–125

1

Suggested answer
I think the little boy is very nervous and is expecting to feel pain as the needle pricks his skin. The patient on the right is lying face down and is probably calm and relaxed. He is having acupuncture, whereas the boy is having a Western-style vaccination against disease.

2

Background information

Acupuncture is a type of treatment that has been used in Chinese medicine for over 4500 years. It is now an important part of alternative medicine in many parts of the world. Acupuncture involves controlling the body's flow of energy, known as *chi*, in this way encouraging the body to heal itself.

3

Suggested answer
I have been seeing an osteopath because of back problems. I know many doctors are suspicious of this alternative treatment, but it has worked for me!

4   The underlined parts of the recording script confirm the answers.

Answers
1 C   **2** B   **3** A   **4** B   **5** A   **6** A   **7** B

Interviewer: Good morning. On the programme this morning we have Dr Sylvia Carpenter, who is a family doctor. Dr Carpenter, you're a great believer in Chinese medicine, aren't you?

Doctor: Yes, I am. When I was a medical student I spent a wonderful month at a hospital in Hong Kong, where they use acupuncture as well as western medicine, which is of course, what I was studying. I saw how effective acupuncture could be, especially for people with digestive disorders, asthma, back pain or stress.

Interviewer: Now, you're not qualified to practise acupuncture yourself, are you?

Doctor: Oh, I'm just an ordinary GP or General Practitioner. I work in a small community, with about 3,000 people on my list. In the past we only referred patients to specialists at the local hospital for treatment – you know, to have their chests X-rayed or have a blood test done. Now I often suggest they see an acupuncturist as well, if I feel it would be of benefit. I can't actually recommend one specifically, but I keep a list of qualified ones.

Interviewer: So, say I go to see an acupuncturist about my backache. What would happen to me?

Doctor: Well, first of all the acupuncturist will ask you for very detailed information, not just about your medical history, but about your lifestyle, what you eat, what sort of exercise you do, how much sleep you get. The treatment you need is then decided and he or she will insert needles in various parts of your body. If you have a back pain, you won't necessarily have a needle in your back, though. It might be in one of your limbs – maybe in a knee or a wrist.

Interviewer: How often would I have to go?

Doctor: It depends on your problems. For some conditions one or two treatments a week for several months may be recommended. For less acute problems, usually fewer visits are required. There aren't usually any side effects. You might feel worse for a couple of days, but that just means the treatment is working. It's quite common to feel exhausted after the first treatment, and this can be overcome with a bit of extra rest.

Interviewer: Now, the big question. Does it hurt?

Doctor: Well, it'd be wrong to say 'No'. It depends where the needles are inserted. Some areas are more sensitive than others. Once the needles are in place there's no pain at all.

Interviewer: Are any positive benefits all in the mind, do you think?

Doctor: <u>No, not at all. Acupuncture has been successfully used on cats and dogs. These animals don't understand or believe in the process that helps them to get better.</u> A positive attitude towards the treatment may reinforce its effects, just as a negative attitude may hinder the effects.

Interviewer: It's a relatively new type of treatment, isn't it?

Doctor: Only in the West. It was first discovered in China in 2696 BC! In 1671 a French Jesuit priest wrote about his experiences in China and was the first westerner to see acupuncture in use. In 1820 acupuncture was actually being used in a Paris hospital! Acupuncture received a lot of publicity in the West when James Reston, a reporter for the New York Times, was covering the visit of President Nixon to China in 1971. Reston developed appendicitis and <u>his appendix was removed using acupuncture as the anaesthetic.</u> He felt no pain during or after the operation because of acupuncture. But, in some ways, your question was right. Acupuncture is still a fairly new subject in the West, but growing all the time.

Interviewer: Thank you, Dr Carpenter. Now we're …

Grammar extra

Note that *get something done* is more informal than *have something done.*

> **Answers**
> a to do a blood test – A doctor does a blood test. You can do a blood test yourself if you know how.
> b to have a blood test done – A doctor does this to you. A more likely situation.
>
> a to have your clothes cleaned
> b to have your hair cut/washed/permed/dyed/ highlighted/trimmed
> c to have the car serviced/repaired
> d to have a dress made/altered
> e to have a suit made/altered
> f to have your nails cut/done/polished/varnished
> g to have your watch repaired/mended
> h to have your teeth seen to / checked
> i to have some furniture repaired/made

5 All four words contain 'silent' letters: *limb, though, knee, wrist.* Words like these can be a problem to pronounce, so follow the advice given in the Vocabulary spot.

> **Suggested answers**
> a knuckle, knot, knife, knight   b comb, lamb, thumb
> c wreck, wrap, wriggle   d castle, listen, whistle
> e reign, neighbour, resign   f dough, thought, thorough
> g chalk, folk, yolk   h calm, salmon

6

> **Answers**
> 1 A   2 B   3 B   4 D   5 B   6 B   7 C   8 C   9 A   10 B
> 11 A   12 B

7

> **Answers**
> a believer   b specialists, treatment   c medical
> d effective   e various   f sensitive   g successfully
> h operation

Exam folder 10

Reading skills for FCE pages 126–127

The aim of this exam folder is to make you more aware of the basic skills you will need for the Reading paper.

Background information

Candidates often don't bother to look at the title or subtitle or to read the rubric. This is a mistake as there is often very useful information contained in them. It is worth reading this background information very carefully.

> **Answers**
> The title tells you that the text is going to be about a guidebook of some kind and 'to the planet' tells you that it is a guide to one of the planets in our solar system. The subtitle then gives you more information. It informs you about the origins of some guidebooks which are called *Lonely Planet* and who started them.
> The photos give you even more information in the form of concrete evidence of what the guidebooks look like and the sort of places they talk about.

Skimming

> **Answer**
> B

Reference

> **Answers**
> a the guidebooks
> b the ferry
> c the guidebooks
> d becoming a slave to the guidebook
> e writing the guidebooks
> f Tony and Maureen
> g spending a night on a train in India / roughing it
> h spending a night on a train in India / roughing it
> i make your way from one place to the next
> j the places
> k to the places
> l the controversy

Text structure

Answers
1. a guidebook
2. once, nowadays
3. 'It helps you grow up a lot, just knowing how other people live and what happens in their countries.'
4. To show that a contrasting point is about to be made.
5. copies

Paraphrasing

Answers
a. hard to pin down
b. you become a slave to the guidebook
c. undeniably
d. to rough it
e. to grow up
f. there has been controversy surrounding the guidebooks
g. they didn't tell the truth
h. correct
i. told what to do
j. to start a journey
k. an online diary
l. to travel

Unit 20

20.1 pages 128–129

1 This is an example of the shared speaking task, Paper 5 Part 3. Follow the advice given in the Exam spot.

2

Suggested answers
a. Many crimes today are drug-related. Addicts need money to buy drugs, so steal or commit other crimes.
b. I don't think this can be proved either way, but there are certainly more violent TV programmes and films than there used to be.
c. Criminals change in prison and many come to realise that what they have been doing is wrong. Some prisoners with life sentences should be released early, as they are no longer a threat to society.
d. It depends on the crime committed. Voluntary service in the community can be a successful alternative for minor offenders.

3

Answers
a. a forensic scientist b. to prove c. guilty
d. genetic code e. evidence, the suspect
f. to cover your tracks g. taken to court

4 The article is about detecting crime. It is practice for Paper 1 Part 2.

Answers
1 H 2 F 3 C 4 A 5 E 6 B 7 G

5 This exercise practises back reference, which is often tested in Paper 1 Part 1.

Answers
a. the traces of evidence b. the old techniques c. an item
d. the dusting of surfaces

20.2 pages 130–131

1

Background information

You are going to hear a true story about three men who tried to escape from Alcatraz, a prison on an island in San Francisco Bay in the USA. The island was a prison from 1934–1963 and few people managed to escape from it.

The underlined parts of the recording cript confirm the answers.

Answers
a. Everyone had to stop talking. / The lights were switched off.
b. 10 years.
c. Some preferred to paint, others to try to learn to play a musical instrument.
d. He began to plot.
e. To cover the hole in the wall.
f. To turn into a drill.
g. By swimming.
h. They remembered to keep absolutely quiet.
i. He stopped to listen.
j. They escaped, but nobody knows if they managed to swim safely across the bay.

The long corridors of cell block B were buzzing. Behind cell doors, convicts were calling to each other, or getting undressed and ready for bed. Everyone had to stop talking at half past nine, when the lights were switched off. Frank Morris, bank robber and burglar, stared at the ceiling, alone in his cell. His world measured three paces by five. Day one of his ten-year sentence on Alcatraz Top Security Island Penitentiary was over. All around him were men regarded as the most hardened desperate criminals in the entire USA.

After lights out, the stillness was broken only by the distant boom of a foghorn and the footsteps of a patrolling guard. Morris noted the time it took the guard to walk the length of the corridor before he turned around. Already he was planning his escape.

Morris's pleasant face and friendly manner hid a ruthless determination and a brilliant brain. As the days went by he became accustomed to the routine of Alcatraz. After the evening meal the men were locked in their cells. They had four hours to themselves before the lights went out. Some liked to paint, others to try to learn to play a musical instrument.

In conversation with another prisoner, Morris learned that three years before, a large fan motor had been removed from a rooftop ventilator shaft above his cell block. It had never been replaced. He immediately saw a way of escape. Morris began to plot. It seemed impossible to reach the shaft from his locked cell but one day he saw a way.

He tried picking at the concrete around a small air vent in his cell. It was slow work and he had to hide the hole he was making with a large accordion, a musical instrument that he had bought with money he'd made in the prison workshop.

The more he plotted, the more he realised that the plan would work better if he had others to escape with. He recruited three other inmates. One of them worked as a cleaner and Morris got him to steal a vacuum cleaner, which Morris turned into a drill. This made digging much faster, but they could only use it during the music practice hour.

They knew that if they managed to get down to the shore, it would mean swimming across the bay. So one of the four managed to steal plastic raincoats to make into water wings.

Seven days before they were all due to escape, one of the four decided he could wait no longer. He forced the others to climb through the holes they had made in their cells and climb up to the roof. They remembered to keep absolutely quiet but as they were crossing the roof a slate was dislodged and fell to the ground. Below, one of the guards heard it and stopped to listen. However, he heard nothing more and continued walking.

The route from rooftop to shore passed by brightly floodlit areas, overlooked by gun towers. Carefully, they moved forward. Crouching in the damp sand, the escapees inflated their raincoat water wings, then waded through a sharp wind into the dark, freezing waters of San Francisco Bay.

Nothing was ever heard of them again. Whether they are still alive or were swept far out to sea, no one ever found out.

2

> **Answers**
> *stop* + gerund means to *cease* – They ceased talking.
> *stop* + infinitive means *in order to* – He stopped in order to listen.
> *try* + gerund – it was an experiment to see if it worked.
> *try* + infinitive – it was difficult to learn to play so it was an attempt.

3   Read the Corpus spot and the section on page 206 of the Grammar folder to check on the difference in meaning.

> **Answers**
> **a** fitting   **b** reading   **c** to inform   **d** walking   **e** to hurt
> **f** to pay   **g** telling   **h** drinking and driving / to drink and (to) drive   **i** to keep   **j** to talk   **k** to do up   **l** running

4

> **Answers**
> **1** to make off   **2** to be   **3** to fasten   **4** checking   **5** to see
> **6** to avoid   **7** carrying   **8** to take   **9** reporting   **10** lead
> **11** know   **12** to sign   **13** to turn   **14** to take

Writing folder 10

Stories 2   pages 132–133

1

> **Suggested answer**
> C ends quite well. B is rather boring. Remember you are writing a story and the reader has to be involved in what is happening. You get more marks if your story is interesting and ends well. A story that ends on a note of suspense can be successful, but you must be careful that it doesn't appear that you have simply stopped because you ran out of time, as might be the case with ending A.

A is dramatic and exciting, but the final sentence might make the story appear unfinished to the competition judges (or an examiner).

B is a bit boring and the short final sentence is not a strong ending.

2   In your story, you will generally need to use a variety of past tenses – and even present tenses if you include direct speech, as the story about Joe shows.

> **Answers**
> **1** is happening   **2** had arrived   **3** found   **4** am I going
> **5** thought   **6** had been looking   **7** had come   **8** had told
> **9** was   **10** has   **11** need   **12** had said   **13** wanted
> **14** did I decide   **15** knew   **16** had   **17** had been kidnapped
> **18** heard   **19** was   **20** was wearing   **21** have decided
> **22** said   **23** continued   **24** are   **25** hope   **26** enjoy
> **27** untied   **28** didn't have
>
> The writer changes from third person to first person in the sentences beginning *With that he untied me … swim to the shore.* It is important to write in the same person throughout the story.

3 This story is an interesting one, but the coloured parts can be improved. Note that the sentence in the question is in the third person, about someone called Joe.

Suggested answers

Place: on the cramped deck of an old fishing boat, tied up against a rusty iron railing.

Adjectives add interest. Saying that he is tied up makes it clear at an early stage that he has been kidnapped.

Person: It was an ugly, middle-aged man with a scar across his forehead, a shaved head and a ragged beard. He was wearing an odd sort of uniform – tatty brown shorts, a dirty blue shirt with gold buttons and a tie.

Use your imagination to the full!

Ending: ... With that, he untied Joe and pushed him off the boat. Luckily, Joe was a strong swimmer and he managed to reach the shore after only thirty minutes in the water. It was only later, when he told his story to the local police, that he heard about the sharks and realised how narrowly he had escaped being eaten alive. (For Joe, life at the office would never seem stressful again!)

The original story is rather confused at the end by the use of the first person. It is also better to have a strong ending – here, the sharks contrast with life at the office in the given sentence.

4

Sample answer

When Sam got up that morning he was looking forward to seeing Jack's face when he saw the huge present he had bought for him. However, before he saw Jack, Sam had to go to the bank.

He caught the bus into the centre of town and got off in the High Street. He went into the bank and joined the shortest queue. As he was waiting, he noticed that the man in front of him was doing a lot of talking to the cashier.

Suddenly the man in front turned round and nervously pointed a gun at Sam. 'Don't move or I'll shoot,' he said. Sam was so surprised he dropped the heavy parcel. It fell on the man's foot and he dropped the gun with a yelp of pain. Sam picked up the gun and took to his heels.

He ran out of the bank and into the street. He could hear the bank robber behind him and he began to panic. Sam threw the gun away and ran down a sidestreet and climbed over a wall into the park. Sam could hear no one following him, and realised that he was safe at last.

Unit 21

21.1 pages 134–135

1

Suggested answer

I really couldn't live without any books in the house – or chocolate! I'm sure I could manage without a TV, as I could always go to a friend's house to watch something. I'd find it difficult to be without a car, but I might try one day. I don't drink, so I could live without alcohol.

2

Suggested answer

The sort of things I treat myself to are special 'pick-me-ups', like a gooey cake or a new CD. I sometimes buy clothes on impulse, and usually regret it and end up taking them back to the shop to exchange for something else.

3 The underlined parts of the recording script confirm the answers.

Answers

1 B **2** F **3** E **4** A **5** C

1 Some people only buy flowers very occasionally, on impulse, but to me, a house looks bare without flowers. They brighten up your living space and they've always been important in my life. When I was small, my father travelled a lot in his job. Whenever he came home, he was always carrying an armful of flowers for my mother, even though sometimes he'd only been away for a couple of days. So I grew up with fresh flowers. After I left home, I was a penniless student. Despite being hard-up, I would still try to buy flowers, though my limit was usually a pound bunch of daffodils. Now, with a steady income, I spend at least £20 a week and I wouldn't dream of cutting back on this – I've been doing it for so long that the outlay has become part of my life, like the phone bill or food shopping.

2 For two years now, I've been going to a private gym. I used to be really unfit – I er ... liked my food rather, and I smoked quite heavily, too. My doctor told me I had to get myself in better shape and suggested dieting. Well, even though I cut down on what I ate – and cut out the cigarettes entirely – I still didn't feel particularly healthy, so I enrolled at this gym. The joining fee was quite steep, and I pay a monthly membership. While not exactly loaded, I can afford it – and I can't imagine life without my twice-weekly visit! If I do a full work-out, I use the pool afterwards. It's nice to be able to socialise a bit. When I walk out of the place I feel great, you know, totally relaxed. It's a small price to pay for feeling good about yourself.

3   There is nothing more wonderful after a difficult day than sinking into a well-made bed with freshly laundered sheets. Utter bliss! It's an indulgence I picked up when I was young. Every year we would travel to Europe as a family and always stayed in delightful hotels, with excellent bedding. After buying my own place, I was broke. My grandmother gave me all her handmade cotton sheets and pillow-cases, dating from around 1910. In spite of being given all this, I didn't use any of it for ages, because I was frightened that it might get damaged in the wash. Finally, I decided it was crazy to have it all sitting there in the cupboard, while I was in an old sleeping bag! Having it laundered gives me confidence it's in safe hands. They collect every Friday morning, and I get it back the following Friday, beautifully packed in a box. Well worth the expense, definitely.

4   My girlfriend and I work really long days, plus it takes us over two hours to get home some evenings, as the traffic's so bad. So, the last thing either of us wants to do is rush out again and do the weekly shopping. We used to, of course. It was terrible – more often than not we'd have some silly row about what to buy. We were just too tired and it got to us, whereas now it's much more civilised. Armed with a glass of wine, we sit in front of the computer in the flat, and dial up the Tesco Internet site. We can usually decide on our order quite quickly, even if we still argue over some things! It's all delivered to the door for a weekly charge of £5. I consider it's money very well spent. Anyway, with our joint spending power, money isn't exactly tight.

5   I can't remember the last time I went on public transport. I can't stand it – it's so crowded and dirty. I do own a car, although I much prefer taking a taxi. To begin with, I only used to get one after being out late with friends, because I wanted to be safe. But as my spare cash grew, so did my taxi habit. Now I have an account with Dial-a-Cab, who are very reliable. Much as I appreciate the convenience of taxis, it's the luxurious side that really appeals to me – the exclusiveness, if you like. I jump in and shut the door – and I'm in my own little stress-free world. And if I'm taking my son out for the day somewhere and can't easily park, I just add the cost of the fare to the day out without a second thought, even if it's a lot.

4

> **Suggested answer**
> Depending on a person's lifestyle, all these things might well be seen as luxuries. Imagine someone unemployed, for example – or an elderly person. It's all down to 'disposable income' and what your spending priorities are.

5   As you know, phrasal verbs often have very different meanings. Here, *cut back (on)* and *cut down (on)* both mean reduce; *cut out* and *cut off* mean stop completely; *cut across* means take a short cut; *cut in* means interrupt someone.

> **Answers**
> a cut … out   b cut across   c cut down   d cut in
> e cut off   f cut out   g cut off   h cut back

6

> **Answers**
> Good value: well worth the expense; money very well spent
> Having money: loaded, spending power, spare cash
> Cost: outlay, fee, expense, charge, fare
> Badly-off: penniless, hard-up, broke, (money) tight

7   Use adjective–noun collocations in your own writing, to show your range of language.

> **Answers**
> a account   b road   c thought   d break   e belt
> f wasp   g mood   h belief

8

> **Answers**
> 1 tight schedule   2 spare time   3 fresh air   4 safe side
> 5 steep path   6 delightful square   7 full swing
> 8 utter horror   9 tight fit   10 safe place

21.2   pages 136–137

1   Examples a and b both contain a subject and a verb – they are 'finite' clauses; c and d are 'non-finite' clauses (they don't include a verb and refer to the subject of the next clause).

Although is a common conjunction in English. It could be used in all four sentences, though c would have to be amended to *Although hard-up…* .

The Grammar folder on page 206 gives a full list of conjunctions of this kind.

2   Errors like these are typical at FCE level. (See Corpus spot.)

> **Answers**
> a despite making …   b Even though department stores …
> c whereas Iceland …   d In spite of wanting …
> e even if they …   f they usually pick up …

3

> **Answers**
> **1** been **2** although/but **3** by/to **4** like **5** this/that
> **6** it **7** Even **8** must **9** up **10** once **11** which/that
> **12** Despite
>
> Concessive clauses: *although I soon realised ... Even though they had now made ... Despite the fact that the money wasn't mine*

4

> **Suggested answers**
> If I had been Faye, I would have been very angry with the bank. If the bank let me keep £300, I'd spend it on some new clothes!

5

> **Answers**
> I knew the money wasn't mine <u>so</u> I went into the bank ... (Result)
> Two weeks later I checked my balance again <u>so as to</u> be sure ... (Purpose)
> I ... contacted head office, <u>in order to</u> sort the matter out ... (Purpose)

6

> **Answers**
> **a** Supermarkets give their customers loyalty cards so as to get more information about what they/people buy.
> **b** There weren't many stalls at the market yesterday because it was a public holiday.
> **c** Some daily newspapers cut their prices in order to get a bigger circulation.
> **d** Since I like filling the house with flowers, I buy a lot of them.
> **e** Harrods is seen as a very exclusive shop so it can charge a lot.
> **f** I went to London to buy a special present for Ellen.
> **g** It's always worth trying clothes on before you buy them in case they're too tight.
> **h** Some supermarkets create the smell of freshly-baked bread so that they (can) make a good impression on their customers.

7

> **Answers**
> **1** despite it being (so) cold
> **2** in case it doesn't
> **3** even if they charge
> **4** since it is commonly/often
> **5** whereas British people do OR whereas in Britain they do

Exam folder 11

Paper 1 Part 1 pages 138–139

> **Answers**
> **1** D **2** C **3** A **4** B **5** B **6** D **7** B **8** C

Detailed explanation:

1 The answer (D) is first suggested in the words 'they are no ordinary green' and confirmed by what the woman goes on to say in terms of colour: 'although I can make a try at it with words, trying to paint it in my sketch book is another matter altogether ... a series of zigzags in orange and red, with bluish trees'. A is ruled out because the wet season is a few weeks off; B is plausible, as the text does mention materials, but she appears to be able to use the ones she has brought; C is irrelevant, as she is painting the landscape, trees, and so on.

2 The answer (C) is found in the words 'I certainly don't want a man capable of such things looking at my own awful brush-strokes'. A is ruled out as the text refers to Royale being a sculptor; B is not suggested in the text and neither is D, though it is likely.

3 The answer (A) is confirmed by the fact that Royale doesn't want to talk about his life and considers the writer 'a fellow artist'. The third paragraph then goes on to talk about painting, ruling the other answers out.

4 The answer (B) is in the sentence 'I grew up in places like that, and I connected with it immediately'. The writer does say how much she appreciated the teacher in Wales, but doesn't go as far as saying she preferred him (A). C is wrong as the paragraph talks about her difficulty in improving in Zimbabwe, but says nothing about what happened in Wales. D is wrong because she doesn't say how many paintings she has completed.

5 The answer (B) is confirmed in three places: 'wonderfully organised … reclaim the land and rebuild the decaying farmhouse … learnt how to lay foundations'. Although the text talks about their differences, these are financial and not how they see life, so A is ruled out. We don't know how good either is at cooking (C). Scott-Thomas left London before becoming a solicitor, so D is wrong.

6 The answer (D) is implied in lines 78–81. The other options are only mentioned in passing in the same paragraph.

7 The answer is B – the holiday wasn't totally unsuccessful; although the woman meets another artist, there is nothing about learning to work with others, and the article isn't really about travel.

8 The answer is C – the article is a description of her holiday and her hobby.

Unit 22

22.1 pages 140–141

1 The two photos show a Heavy Soul open-air concert and a special event where 2,740 young musicians played in the Birmingham Symphony Hall.

> **Suggested answer**
> The basic similarity is that both pictures show music being played. The two types of music seem very different – the open-air concert is called Heavy Soul and there's a rock or soul band performing on the stage, while the other photo shows young people playing classical music and it may not be a concert at all. I've never seen so many cellos under one roof!

2 The recording is an example of the 'long turn' – Paper 5 Part 2. One candidate, Carmen, speaks for about a minute, and then the other, Jurgen, is asked to make a brief comment for about 20 seconds.

> **Answer**
> Jurgen prefers taking part whereas Carmen dislikes playing in large orchestras and enjoys listening to music at festivals.

Examiner: Carmen, here are your two photographs. They show a lot of people in one place. Please let Jurgen have a look at them.
Carmen, I'd like you to compare and contrast these photographs, and say how you would feel in each situation. Remember, you have only about a minute for this so don't worry if I interrupt you. All right?
Carmen: Yes, fine. Well, the pictures have two things in common. The first, which you mentioned, is the huge number of people. The other is that they both show music taking place. This one is at a major rock festival – it's outdoors, of course. The other one is indoors and it looks like an enormous orchestra. There must be hundreds of performers there, I mean er ... there are over a hundred cellists taking part! I don't know where it is but all the musicians are quite young, so maybe it's a concert organised by several schools?
The main difference between the two scenes is that in the first one, there is an audience – people are watching a band on stage – while in this one, everyone is a performer. I really like being part of a large audience, sitting back and relaxing to the music.
Examiner: Thank you Carmen. Now, Jurgen, which situation would you prefer to be in?
Jurgen: Oh, the orchestra, definitely. I'd rather participate than watch music. I actually belong to a large choir and we sing as a group of about a hundred and twenty. It's really good fun and because there are so many of us, it doesn't matter if you make a mistake sometimes.
Examiner: Thank you.

3

> **Answers**
> Perform: take part, participate
> Performers: musician, band, orchestra, choir
> Performance: concert, festival

4

> **Suggested answer**
> Actually, I like doing both. Listening to CDs at home can be very relaxing and going to live concerts is great. I also enjoy playing music with other people, as long as there's no stress involved – some people can be so critical, even if you play just one wrong note!
> I can appreciate all sorts of music, ancient and modern, and there's not much I dislike, apart from predictable songs with silly words.

5 This is a true story. Before Myron Kropp was arrested, he chopped at the legs of the piano with an axe.

6 Paper 1 Part 2 is covered in Exam folder 12, on pages 150–151.

7 Follow the advice given in the Exam spot.

> **Answers**
> 1 G 2 C 3 A 4 H 5 B 6 D 7 F

8

> **Answers**
> a appearing weak and unhealthy; *-looking* can be added to a number of adjectives in English in this way, for example: *tired-looking, sad-looking*
> b those parts in the piece that particularly show the pianist's feelings about what he is playing – *expressive* is an adjective; the verb is *express*; the noun is *expression*
> c having sat down on the stool as comfortably as possible
> d he didn't have much patience left – he had started to become *impatient*
> e the piano key which was sticking particularly badly
> f calmed down; stopped laughing – adjective: became *composed*
> g strongly told off
> h an idiom: meaning to reach the end of something difficult unharmed

22.2 pages 142–143

1 Try to vary the way you start your sentences, like these examples.

Answers

a 3 b 8 c 2 d 6 e 4 f 1 g 5 h 7

2

Answers

When I listen to live music (Time clause – emphasising information)

Although I like almost everything about music (Concessive clause – highlighting a choice)

Seeing blues or soul bands in concert is one of the things (*-ing* clause – emphasis through placing this information at the front of the sentence)

The adverb used three times is *really*. Other adverbs that could be used instead: *especially, particularly*

3

Answers

a As it was late, we decided not to stay for the final band.
b Beautifully hand-made, with a reddish-brown colour, the cello has an excellent sound.
c Having learnt the recorder for three years, Ellen went on to the flute.
d Despite being technically brilliant, the trumpeter's playing has no feeling.
e Due to the conductor's mistake, the soloist had to miss out a whole verse.
f This is especially noticeable in recordings of live concerts.
g Although a low-priced guitar, the Squier sounds very similar to a proper Stratocaster.

4

Background information

Frank Zappa was one of the greatest electric guitarists ever. Concerts with his band, The Mothers of Invention, were often unpredictable and the rubber chicken incident referred to is only a mild example of what could – and did – happen. Also a highly-respected modern composer, Zappa's music continues to be performed in top concert halls around the world.

Suggested answers

a Due to the delay in the band's arrival, we insisted on a refund for the tickets.
b Since the last train left at eleven thirty, we sadly had to miss some of the performance.
c Despite feeling unwell, the singer decided not to cancel the recital, although it was shortened.
d Instead of playing what was printed in the programme, the pianist improvised quite brilliantly for over 40 minutes.

e An oboe has a very suitable tone, even if it is underused as a jazz instrument.
f As the violinist suffers from stage fright, he rarely gives performances to large audiences.

5 The Grammar folder on page 206 gives further examples of complex sentences.

Answers

b is the opening sentence.

Complete paragraph:

(b) Although for the wrong reason, the Chicago Symphony Orchestra's Centennial concert was a memorable event. Three of its most famous music directors participated: Solti, Barenboim and Kubelik. Immediately before the concert, a celebration dinner was held for special donors. *(d) There were some 400 of these, each paying at least $500 for the privilege of attending.* At an event like this, it is customary to give diners a small gift, so each person was presented with an attractive alarm clock, gift-wrapped. Why some of the clocks were put in their boxes with the alarm switched on is a mystery, but this was the case. It is appropriate to remind the reader that the dinner guests went straight on to the concert, armed with these ticking timebombs! *(a) During the first half there were few problems, with only an occasional beep being heard.* However, after the interval more and more alarms were going off, so the concert had to be temporarily stopped and an announcement made. As the clocks were inside boxes and gift-wrapped, nobody in the audience had realised what the problem was. *(c) Once the laughter had died down, they were instructed to take their gifts outside to the lobby.* The rest of the evening then proceeded without incident.

6

Answers

1 B 2 C 3 D 4 D 5 A 6 D 7 B 8 B 9 C
10 D 11 C 12 A

Writing folder 11

Reports pages 144–145

1 Remember to write reports in a consistently neutral or formal register. Do not start or end them as though they were letters.

Answers

a Add something to make it clear what the report is about, for example, *on last year's festival.*
Add a concluding sentence, for example, *I hope you will find this information helpful.*

b The site
Catering facilities

c To the festival organisers
People were forced to go from one end of the site to the other when buying food and drink, which they were not pleased about.
This would give the festival useful additional funds.
It is clear that a bigger site and better-organised catering are needed, as well as some changes to the timing of the event.

d Even though there was some car parking, many people had to park ...
Although there was some choice of catering at the site, very little vegetarian food was offered.
People seemed to enjoy the performances, so perhaps each band ...
Since several members ... thought the tickets were unusually cheap, the price could be raised next year.

2 This exercise is designed to make you think about the target reader of the report, which will inform your answer.

Suggested answers
1 f, h, i   2 a, d, j   3 c, e, j   4 b, d, g

3 Make a paragraph plan before you start.

Sample answer

This report covers the main shopping facilities in Newtown.

Food
There are three supermarkets: Sainsbury's is in the centre of town near the market, and also sells DVDs; Waitrose is only five minutes from the college and has a large car park; Tesco's on the edge of town is the biggest of the three, but is difficult to get to. It is best to buy fresh fruit and vegetables in the market, which is held every day apart from Sunday.

Study materials
In Bridge Street, there are four bookshops. There is also a massive stationery shop called Staples in the main square, where you can buy everything from files and pens to CD-roms. There is a small bookshop on the college campus, which also sells basic stationery items like paper.

Souvenirs
Newtown doesn't have as many souvenir shops as London, but the castle has its own shop, and so does the museum. Additionally, the market stalls often have cheap souvenirs.

Unit 23

23.1 pages 146–147

1

Suggested answer
All four photos make me feel rather nervous. I would be especially worried in an earthquake, because they can be so severe and often happen without warning.

Answers
1 volcano – c   2 lightning – a   3 floods – b
4 earthquake – d

2 The underlined parts of the recording script confirm the answers.

Answers
1 forest fire   2 smoke cloud   3 silent   4 handle
5 the tent   6 (falling) trees   7 shirts   8 ash
9 rotten/bad eggs   10 radio

Interviewer: On the morning of May 18th, 1980, Liz Nielson was camping with a friend about 18 kilometres from Mount St Helens in Washington State in the United States. She was making coffee and her friend Dave was fishing. So, Liz, when did you realise that something was wrong?

Liz: Well, Dave lost the fish and came up to replace his line. He looked up and saw a small black cloud on the horizon and <u>said there must be a forest fire</u>. Within 30 seconds it was absolutely enormous and then it just kept getting bigger and bigger, and coming at us faster and faster, and it was very dark and black. The cloud of ash was the first sign we had that anything was happening.

Interviewer: What were your thoughts at that moment?

Liz: I'm not sure I had any – apart from maybe wishing I were somewhere else! <u>It wasn't like a smoke cloud</u>, it was as if it were alive and it was massive and dense, and very black. <u>It was the strangest thing. It was totally silent</u> until it got down into the canyon where we were and then there was a huge roaring. I remember looking at the fire and the wind just blew the flames out low along the ground, and <u>watching the handle of my coffee pot just kind of melt in the flames</u>, and then this awful cold – it just surrounded us.

Interviewer: I expect you were very frightened by then, weren't you?

Liz: Frightened! I was absolutely petrified, and so was Dave. Well, <u>we started to run back towards the tent</u>. Stupidly I thought that if only we could get in the tent we'd be safe! Then the cloud hit us. It was like an explosion of sound and I fell over backwards and was covered with dirt. I remember wishing it would stop and almost immediately it did, and then Dave reached over to me and asked me if I was OK. We got up and realised that there were trees all around us. In fact, we'd fallen down into a hole left by the roots of a tree and then <u>other falling trees had covered us</u>. Dave tried to climb out of the hole but it was too hot. Then, when we did get out we were met with such a scene of total devastation. Everything had happened so fast. When we set off it was difficult to breathe so we <u>took our shirts off and wrapped them around our heads</u>. There were flashes of lightning across the sky.

Interviewer: Was it difficult getting out of the valley?

Liz: <u>The ash was nearly a metre deep</u> and it was so hot underneath you could only stay in it for a short period of time. Then we had to get up on a tree stump and take our shoes off and unroll our trousers, but within a few minutes they would be filled up again. It gave off a <u>terrible smell – like rotten eggs</u>. Anyway, we were really lucky. A falling tree could easily have crushed us. <u>I wish now that we'd taken a radio with us</u>, then maybe we would have had some warning. Even a couple of hours' warning would have helped. We went back a few days later and found the site where our tent had been. Thank goodness we fell in that hole instead of reaching the tent!

Interviewer: A lucky escape indeed. Now in the studio we also have …

3 Following the example given, say Student B's words, with rising intonation on the first word and falling on the second.

Grammar extra

> **Answers**
> **a** very **b** very **c** absolutely **d** absolutely **e** very
> **f** absolutely **g** absolutely **h** very **i** absolutely
> **j** very **k** very **l** absolutely

4 As the Vocabulary spot says, a phrasal verb can have different meanings, which you need to learn. A good English–English dictionary will give you examples, showing typical word order. For example, with the phrasal verb *look up*, you must put a pronoun between the verb and particle: *Look **it** up in a dictionary*, but you can either say *Jane looked up **the word** in a dictionary* or *Jane looked **the word** up in a dictionary*. Unit 30 will cover the grammar of phrasal verbs.

> **Answers**
> 1 produced 2 removed 3 began the journey
>
> **a** broke off **b** called off **c** write off **d** wore off
> **e** pay off **f** put off **g** run off **h** dropping off
> **i** come off

5

> **Answers**
> 1 in 2 without 3 over 4 less 5 called/named
> 6 the 7 down 8 which/that 9 set
> 10 anything/everything 11 was 12 this

23.2 pages 148–149

1 See the section in the Grammar folder on page 206.

2

> **Suggested answers**
> I wish we had realised the mountain might erupt.
> I wish there had been a cave nearby.
> I wish we had left the area before the eruption.
> I wish we had never decided to go camping.
> I wish it hadn't happened to us.

3

> **Suggested answers**
> Wishes:
> I wish I could give up work and move to a tropical island.
> I wish I were still in bed – I'm so tired!

4

> **Suggested answers**
> I wish the teacher would stop giving us so much homework.
> I wish my parents would send me some warm clothes.

5

> **Answers**
> **a** I hope the rain stops soon.
> **b** I hope you can come to my party.
> **c** I wish I could speak Arabic.
> **d** I wish Peter would finish writing his book.
> **e** I wish I had remembered to bring the sleeping bags.

Corpus spot

> **Answers**
> **a** I hope I win the trip! / I wish I could win the trip!
> **b** I hope I can come back one day. / I wish I could come back one day.
> **c** I wish I had known it two days ago.
> **d** I wish we could find some new form of energy. / I hope we find some new form of energy.
> **e** I wish you agreed with me. / I hope you agree with me.
> **f** I wish I had more money.
> **g** If only he would stop smoking. / I hope he stops smoking.
> **h** I hope the bus will come. / I wish the bus would come.
>
> Note that the alternative sentences don't have exactly the same meaning.

6 a In the first example, you aren't an expert, whereas in the second, you are.

b

> **Suggested answer**
> **a** I'd rather go for a Chinese meal.
> **b** I'd rather do Economics.
> **c** I'd rather lie on a beach somewhere hot.
> **d** I'd rather you taught me Japanese.
> **e** I'd rather you bought me a new mobile phone.

7

> **Answers**
> 1 wish (that) I had taken
> 2 would/'d rather the children stayed
> 3 only we had seen some
> 4 wish (that) I lived/could live
> 5 wish (that) you wouldn't
> 6 would/'d rather you didn't

8

> **Suggested answers**
> **a** a knot   **b** a cardigan   **c** a knot   **d** a parcel
> **e** a secret/a clue   **f** a Roman coin, treasure
> **g** a seat belt   **h** some wool/your hair   **i** a window

9

> **Answers**
> **a** tornadoes   **b** snowdrifts   **c** gale warning
> **d** forecast   **e** overcast   **f** shower   **g** hurricanes
> **h** drought   **i** damp, humid

Exam folder 12

Paper 1 Part 2 pages 150–151

Remember that each question is worth two marks. You need to spend enough time on this difficult part of Paper 1.

> **Answers**
> 1 D   2 G   3 H   4 C   5 F   6 B   7 E

Unit 24

24.1 pages 152–153

1

> **Suggested answer**
> I prefer the painting on the left, because the colours are so bright and the perspective is unusual. Also, it has an interesting border. The one on the right is very realistic. I quite like the inclusion of the bird in the foreground.
>
> If I won the lottery, I would buy a famous painting. I really love the British artist David Hockney, who has painted in a range of different styles. In the 1960s, he painted pictures of swimming pools in Beverly Hills and there's a famous one called 'A Bigger Splash'. He uses strong colours – the water is a fantastic shade of turquoise and the sky a slightly brighter blue. There's a yellow diving board in the foreground, and beyond it, the white streaks of the splash. It's an unforgettable image.

2 The article is a true story about a boy who has made a lot of money from his paintings.

3 Detailed explanation:

1 The answer (D) can be found in 'latest child prodigy' and 'hailed as a genius'. A is wrong as Beso is from Georgia while Alexandra is Romanian. B, though likely, is not stated in the article. C is not possible, as we only know what type of paintings Beso does.

2 The answer (A) is confirmed by 'oils of human figures and faces, executed in a lively way'. B is ruled out by the words 'executed remarkably quickly'. The opposite of C is true, as he uses 'bright, sometimes almost garish, colours'. Although his pictures tell stories, the article says nothing about them being famous fairytales, so D is wrong.

3 The answer (C) comes from the quote 'I'm prepared for the verdict of time'. A is suggested by 'there are probably half a dozen or more in the world' but is ruled out because Mr Valenty doesn't know these geniuses. The article doesn't give any support for B or D.

4 The answer (B) refers back to the other kids' work in the previous sentence. The word 'none' rules out A, C and D, because they are about the children rather than the work and the article would have had to say 'no one' rather than 'none'.

5 The answer (C) lies in the sentence 'If Beso makes $19,000 in half an hour, it's because people want his work'. A is plausible, but Mr Valenty only says 'Who knows what will happen next?', which could mean an increase or a decrease in sales. B and D are likely but the article doesn't comment in this way.

6 The answer (B) is confirmed by Mr Lombardo's words 'He's structured. Sure, he'll watch television, play

baseball, do his homework ...'. from which we know he keeps up with his schoolwork. The same part of the article rules out A, because it tells us he plays baseball. C and D, though likely, are not mentioned in the article.

7 The answer (A) refers back to 'find out about these kids'. B is not suggested in the final paragraph. C is impossible as the reference to Picasso is in the following sentence. D is suggested by Beso's earlier experiences of civil war, but this is too far away in the article.

8 The answer (C) is suggested by the question mark in the title and also in the words 'Cynics like myself may question a second genius arriving so soon.' A is not supported by the article. B is impossible, as we don't know the writer's opinion of Alexandra's work. D is not stated by the writer and goes against Beso's words in the first paragraph.

5

> **Answers**
> to break a promise
> to sit still
> to get a holiday / better
> to spend a fortune / a week / a holiday
> to taste funny
> to keep a promise / still / awake / a secret
> to have a conversation / an expression / a look /
> a fortune / a secret / a holiday
> to do 20 kilometres to the litre / better
> to wear a look / an expression

6 The underlined parts of the recording script confirm the answers.

> **Answers**
> 1 A   2 B   3 C

Speaker 1: I went to see the Mona Lisa when I was in Paris. Well, it's so famous, I felt I couldn't not go, though it's better to go earlier in the day when there's more natural light. You just have to follow the crowds really – I don't think most tourists look at anything else, which is a shame as there are probably much better pictures on display there. Anyway, I went along too, <u>though it was a bit pointless really – the picture is so small, I could hardly make it out.</u>

Speaker 2: They've decided to brighten up our offices at work by letting us choose a painting to hang up. Sounds like a good idea you might think, but you'd be amazed at some of the things people have chosen. <u>I've got something fairly neutral, because of the nature of the job I do. Had I not been so high profile, I would have felt able to choose more freely,</u> like some of my colleagues have.

Speaker 3: Well, it was a great exhibition from my point of view – lots of interesting paintings, which seemed to be going down well with the public, and I saw some friends I hadn't seen for ages. The artist looked a bit down at one stage and later I found out that <u>someone had bought a</u>

<u>portrait which had sentimental value</u> – it'd been put at an astronomical price in the hope of dissuading anyone, but anyway, that's life isn't it?

24.2 pages 154–155

1 Refer to the section in the Grammar folder on page 207 if necessary.

> **Answers**
> a silly   b well   c in a friendly way   d better   e fast
> f better, well   g more carefully   h more interestingly
> i lonely   j worse   k hardly   l straight

Corpus spot

> **Answers**
> a Yesterday I visited an art gallery in London. / I visited an art gallery in London yesterday.
> b My mother often goes to the shops.
> c Never have I seen a house like that. / I have never seen ...
> d She drew the cat quickly.
> e Zoos can sometimes be nice.
> f Only I will be able to travel in July / I will be able to travel in July only. / I will only be able to travel in July.
> g Peter shook her hand politely.
> h There is always a queue for the cinema.
> i He can hardly sleep at night.
> j She works hard in an office.
> k I have never been to Paris.

3 As the Vocabulary spot says, some words can be easily confused in English. Below the answers is some information on the differences between each pair of words.

> **Answers**
> a in the end   b invaluable   c nowadays   d risen
> e Lie   f Tell   g cook   h robbed   i damaged
> j valuable   k sympathetic   l sensitive

at the end – of the story/film/book
in the end – finally

priceless – so valuable it has no price
invaluable – usually about something abstract like help; means very useful
valuable – worth a lot of money

nowadays – is happening currently
actually – in fact

to raise – transitive – takes an object
to rise – intransitive – no object

to lie – takes no object
to lay – takes an object – to lay eggs, to lay the table

to tell – someone something
to say – something to someone

a cook is a person
a cooker is a machine

to steal something from someone
to rob somewhere or someone of something

to damage something
to injure someone

sympathetic – kind if you have a problem
friendly – pleasant and sociable

sensible – full of common sense
sensitive – feels very deeply

5

Background information

Pablo Picasso 1881–1973
Born in Malaga, Spain.
Blue period 1902–1904
Pink period 1904–1906

1906–7 Cubism – helped develop this style with the painter Braque. Picasso's major work is *Guernica* 1937, a Cubist painting expressing the horror of war.

Answers
1 different 2 cheerful 3 performers 4 successful
5 inspiration 6 expressive 7 unrealistic 8 famous
9 symbolic 10 repeatedly

Writing folder 12

Articles pages 156–157

1 Note that the exam question has two bulleted parts. You must cover both of these, as the sample answer does, to score a good mark.

   Any of the three titles would be suitable. Remember to include a title if you write an article in the exam.

2 Expand the words given to produce an interesting paragraph.

Suggested answer
The walls are fairly bare and they have been painted white. There is a window high up on one wall with a basket hanging next to it. Under the window there is a table with a basket of bread, a bowl of milk and cakes set out on it. Both the jug of milk and the bowl are made of brown pottery. There are some blue and white tiles along the edge of the wall where it joins the floor. On the floor is a box containing a pot with a handle.

3 Make a plan first, like the one below.

Sample plan
Introduction – Yes, thick fog
Where – coming home from a party
What I did – got out of the car and walked slowly in front

Sample answer

Walking through a cloud

I remember very well the night I went to a party in town but had to spend six hours getting the five kilometres back home. It was my friend's birthday party and she had hired a disco. The weather was fine when we left for the party and it only took us twenty minutes to get to the disco by car. I was driving there and my brother was going to drive back.

We had a great time at the party – good music, lots of friends and a brilliant birthday cake. Every now and then someone would arrive and tell us the weather was getting worse. We just kept on partying – we weren't interested in what was happening outside. Then, around two-thirty in the morning, it was time to go home. We couldn't believe it when we got outside. Where was the car? Luckily we had parked near to the disco, so we followed the walls round to the back and went from car to car, looking for ours.

We got in and my brother drove. I had to walk in front of the car, all the way home, following the side of the road. It was a good thing that I knew the way very well.

4 It is always better to use different vocabulary, rather than repeat the same word, as this will show an examiner how wide your language range is.

Suggested answers
a large, enormous, huge, gigantic, vast, immense
b tiny, minute, little
c wealthy, well-to-do, affluent, well-off, prosperous
d badly-off, impoverished, penniless
e sweltering, boiling, burning
f chilly, icy, cool, freezing
g heavy, plump, stout, tubby
h bony, skinny, slim, slender
i attractive, charming, good-looking, lovely
j awful, terrible, unacceptable, rotten

Units 19–24 Revision

pages 158–159

2

> **Answers**
> 1 C 2 A 3 C 4 B 5 C 6 B 7 A 8 B

3

> **Answers**
> • **illness or injury**
> 1 sprain 2 cough
> • **volcanoes**
> 3 erupt 4 ash 5 lava
> • **musical instruments**
> 6 oboe 7 piano 8 guitar 9 flute
> • **serious crimes**
> 10 rape 11 fraud 12 mugging 13 arson
> 14 hijacking
> • **adjectives to describe works of art**
> 15 worthless 16 expressive 17 priceless
> 18 valuable 19 garish 20 symbolic
>
> a flute b lava c garish d sprain e arson

4

> **Answers**
> 1 not 2 of 3 few 4 enough 5 so 6 up 7 a
> 8 than 9 it 10 at 11 being 12 if

Unit 25

25.1 pages 160–161

1 The pictures show a suburb in Melbourne, Australia and a street in Greenwich Village, New York.

2

> **Answer**
> The expert is an architect – the profession is architecture.

Part 1

Presenter: Good evening. With me on tonight's edition of *Challenge the expert* are Julia Ralston and Gareth Webster. Julia is a fully-qualified architect, who works for a well known architectural practice in London. Facing her is her challenger Gareth Webster, a student at the University of London, who is surrounded by, in his own words, those eyesores that pass for modern buildings. Gareth, over to you.

3 The underlined parts of the recording script confirm the answers.

> **Possible predictions**
> 1 a person/organisation
> 2 a word that collocates with 'regulations' e.g. official, government
> 3 a type of housing, e.g. flat
> 4 something connected with new buildings, e.g. bricks
> 5 an example of an environmental requirement
> 6 something that means the same as 'urban sprawl'
> 7 a word that collocates with 'facilities'
> 8 something relating to architecture in a city centre
> 9 something that might exist downstairs in a building, e.g. shop
> 10 something in cities that may make people unhealthy, e.g. pollution
>
> **Answers**
> 1 government 2 planning 3 tower block
> 4 material(s) 5 heating 6 suburb(s) 7 out-of-town
> 8 skyscraper(s) 9 (live) music 10 (heavy) traffic

Part 2

Gareth: Right, well can I start with 1960s architecture? I walk past some awful 60s concrete blocks every day and I just can't believe how people were uprooted and forced to live in high-rise buildings against their will. Why was this ever allowed to happen, Julia?

Julia: Gareth, you're describing a time when many people wanted to be rehoused, because their living conditions were so bad. And this was a policy upheld by government, rather than decided by architects.

Gareth: But why don't planners and architects talk to the public? It's as if they feel they have the right to decide what's best for us.

Julia: The situation has changed and in my view, lack of consultation over new buildings is rarely an issue with the public. There are much tougher planning regulations nowadays.

Gareth: But the fact is that many people still have to live in high-rise accommodation. How can you expect people to enjoy life on the 23rd floor with a lift that's out of order? If we were meant to live up in the sky, we would have been born with wings!

Julia: Well, joking apart, I was in a tower block in a run-down part of Bristol for six years of my childhood, so I do know what it's like. That's largely what drove me to become an architect, actually. Yes, some 60s architecture is poor, but the point is, if it hadn't happened, we would be making similar mistakes today, whereas, as it is, we have been able to learn from the recent past.

Gareth: How, exactly?

Julia: Well, for one thing, the buildings being put up today generally have better materials than in the past, certainly in comparison to the 1960s. A lot more thought goes into this aspect, with the upside that new buildings look more attractive as a result.

Gareth: What about environmental issues, are there any special requirements for architects to meet there?

Julia: Yes, indeed. We have to design buildings that are <u>environmentally efficient, so for us in Britain that means paying particular attention to things like heating</u>. Of course, that particular requirement wouldn't be an issue for architects in southern Europe.

Gareth: No, I suppose not. … So Julia, what do you personally see as today's main problem?

Julia: Something that really troubles me is <u>'urban sprawl', the suburbs that go on forever</u>, all at a huge cost to the tax-paying public in terms of upkeep.

Gareth: What do you mean by 'upkeep'?

Julia: Basic services like drainage, road maintenance, that sort of thing. And city expansion isn't very good news for the countryside either. At the same time, there's sometimes appalling decay in the middle of our cities as a direct result of this move outwards. <u>Shops in the centre have closed because of out-of-town facilities</u>, and people are forced to drive when once they bought locally.

Gareth: And that's not sustainable, is it? So, what's the solution? I mean, any housing in central London that's nice to live in is so upmarket that it's completely unaffordable for someone like me.

Julia: Well, that depends, Gareth, on whether you would be prepared to live up in the sky. What I believe in – and what many architects are trying to work towards – is the regeneration of our city centres, but this can only happen if we think vertically – <u>design skyscrapers</u>, in other words. There's no space to do anything else! It's a really exciting development that could breathe new life into our cities.

Gareth: Back to the 1960s, then?

Julia: Definitely not! Gareth, imagine if your building was <u>a multi-use one, where you just go downstairs to see live music</u>, or across the street to pick up some late-night shopping … this is the housing of the future, where no one will need to own a car.

Gareth: Yes, but again, is that what people want? I mean having a car is every person's dream, isn't it?

Julia: Well, the success of the Mayor of London's congestion charge might prove you wrong! And it may surprise you that in a recent radio phone-in, 67% of callers thought that the car should be banned altogether from central London. I think people are ready for this Gareth, they understand that <u>traffic is slowly killing us</u>. Living in the city has to become a healthier and more acceptable option.

Gareth: Oh, I don't know, you're beginning to convince me! You do sound as though you know what you're talking about …

Background information

There is now a congestion charge for most motorists wishing to drive into the centre of London. Any chargeable vehicle entering the congestion charge zone between 7 am and 6 pm has to make a daily payment (£8 in 2007) and fines are enforced for non-payment. Several cities worldwide have referred to the London scheme when developing their own plans for city centre traffic.

5

> **Answers**
> a 3 b 5 c 1 d 2 e 4

6

> **Suggested answers**
> a There is no public concern about lack of consultation over new buildings. Again, this was an issue in the 1960s, when beautiful, historic buildings were torn down and modern concrete 'eyesores' put in their place. Nowadays, there is a proper procedure for consultation, along with stricter building regulations.
> b As cities expand, parts of the countryside are lost to make space for them. This is a great pity. It makes much more sense to regenerate city centres, make them desirable places to live once more.
> c Inner cities need to be improved and brought back to life, so that people will want to live there again. It's true that many cities no longer have living accommodation in their centres, affordable or otherwise. Paris is one exception – are there others?
> d At present, cities are noisy, polluted environments that are too often unpleasant to live in. This situation needs to change, so that people will move back.

7

> **Answers**
> i: b, c, g
> ii: a, d, f
> iii: e, h
> d is too direct for a discussion and might give offence.
> g is a rather abrupt question.

Other non-verbal strategies for directing a conversation include nodding or shaking your head; making eye contact; raising a hand; leaning forward.

25.2 pages 162–163

1 The mixed conditionals here are formed with one second conditional element and one third conditional element. See Grammar folder page 207.

2

> **Possible answers**
> a would look much worse.
> b wouldn't be starving now.
> c would be less well-informed.
> d wouldn't be stuck in this traffic jam.
> e would still be living at home.

3

> **Possible answers**
> a would have chosen to live in them.
> b would have tidied up your bedroom by now.
> c wouldn't have been so high for the last 20 years.
> d would have gone out at 3 am this morning to buy you some paracetamol.

5

> **Answers**
> 1 C 2 A 3 C 4 B 5 D 6 A 7 C 8 B 9 D
> 10 B 11 A 12 D

6

> **Answers**
> reconsider/reconsideration; reconstruct/reconstruction; regenerate/regeneration; reopen/reopening; repossess/repossession; rewrite/rewritten
>
> a regenerated   c reopening
> b reconstructed   d reconsider

Exam folder 13

Paper 1 Part 3 pages 164-165

The parts that confirm each answer are given below.

1   B   You're not just carrying bags. You're offering advice ...'

2   D   one of those awful word processors

3   C   a 50 per cent cut in guaranteed income

4   A   you're expected to jet around the world at the drop of a hat

5   C   it was a useful secondary income

6   A   gets on well with her boss

7   C   it's up to them

8   A   she can't stand flying

9   D   I'm not up with the dawn

10 B   recently recognised by European Tour Productions when they made him statistical data administrator

11 A   It seemed so shut in

12 D   it's not easy, I have to work at them

13 A   A chance meeting ... led to the offer of work ... Five years later she was in the right place at the right time

14 D   nowadays I have some secretarial help

15 A   mundane paperwork to get through

Unit 26

26.1 pages 166–167

1   The picture on the left shows an old American car. The one on the right shows a British Mini, which was a very popular car in the 1960s and 1970s.

> **Suggested answer**
> I suppose it's fairly important, although I would prefer to live without one. A car is important for getting members of your family from A to B on time, because public transport is so unreliable.

2   These are unscripted recordings, at natural speed.

> **Answers**
> Speaker 3 has to use the car every day.
> Speaker 1 would prefer not to travel by car.
> Speaker 4 claims to be a car enthusiast.

Speaker 1: I don't really use my car very much. I use it mostly at weekends when I'm getting out of the city but I don't really like driving very much so I'd much rather take the train if I could.

Speaker 2: I suppose in the week when I'm in the city I could definitely do without the car, in fact I often do and then I use public transport and it's fine. But at the weekends I go to visit my godfather who's ... who's not very well and so I have to go every weekend and really he lives in the middle of nowhere so I have to have the car then. I couldn't possibly do the journey without it.

Speaker 3: The car's used all the time now by everybody. My wife and I seem to find that we wouldn't be able to exist if we didn't have the car. We take the children to school in the morning, do the shopping because we're not near any shops any more, pick the children up from school, go to the station to pick up my parents who come down every weekend. It's like a taxi now ... it's like one of the family too.

Speaker 4: I love my car. It's a 1976 BMW 1602 in a lemon yellow colour. It's called Moosey and it's really my pride and joy. I ... I belong to the BMW members' club and I spend my weekends going to lots of rallies and I'm, you know, I'm a real car lover.

Speaker 5: Well, my car's quite important in my life although I only usually use it at weekends, taking the kids out for day trips, going to the supermarket, visiting the local DIY store. During the week, I tend to use public transport more, I mean I do use the car in the week of course, and use it for work occasionally ... but, on the whole it's weekends.

3   Refer to the advice given in Exam folder 13 on page 164. Time yourself as you do this matching task. Allow 14 minutes.

Answers
1 D   2 A   3 A   4 C   5 B   6 A   7 D   8 C   9 B
10 A   11 C   12 A   13 B   14 D   15 B

5

Answers
a get away from it all   b get the crowd behind (C)
c get the message across   d get attached to (D)   e get
your hands on (B)   f get rid of (A)   g get nowhere / not
get anywhere   h get a move on / get your skates on

Grammar extra

This exercise deals with inversion. See the Grammar folder
on negative adverbs (Unit 24), page 207.

Answers
a Not only has there been a huge increase in the
  number of private cars on the road – more goods ...
b No longer can we depend on the unlimited use of our
  cars.
c Not only does Brendan ride a bike to work, he also
  uses it to travel longer distances.
d In no way should the government weaken its
  transport policy.
e Seldom are members of the public willing to walk to
  work, especially if it's raining.
f Not only do cars pollute the air but they endanger
  people's lives too.

26.2 pages 168–169

1   Read the section on relative pronouns on page 204 of
the Grammar folder before looking at the examples.

Answers
a additional; *who* = Richard Simmons
b essential; *who* = visitors
c essential; *for whom* = the people
d additional; *whose* = the countryside
Whose does not always refer to people.

2

Answers
a Wetherby, with whom I went on several expeditions,
  was always the perfect gentleman.
b The ranchers for whom cowboys worked expected
  them to spend at least 12 hours a day on horseback.
c Apollo, in whom the ancient Greeks believed, was
  supposed to ride a chariot of flames across the sky.
d Teenagers, by whom rollerblading is seen as a quick
  way of getting around, often take unnecessary risks in
  traffic.

3

Answers
a helicopter (picture 5)   b camel (2)   c canoe (3)
d hovercraft (7)   e submarine (4)   f tandem (6)
g llama (8)

4   It is much better to join two sentences like this, showing
that you can link ideas effectively.

Answers
a The Regent's Canal in London, whose towpath is
  increasingly used by cyclists, runs between Camden
  and Islington.
b This new jetski, whose seating accommodates / can
  accommodate four people comfortably, has a top
  speed of over 100 kph.
c The hot air balloon, whose first flight was made in
  1783, was designed by the Montgolfier brothers.
d From 1983 to 1987, the number of cars and trucks in
  the United States, whose population in that period
  grew by only 9.2 million, increased by 20.1 million.
e The Brox, a new four-wheel cycle trailer whose seven
  gears allow it to go up hills and even steps easily, is
  being trialled by the Royal Mail.
f The American space shuttle, whose heat-proof tiles
  allow it to re-enter the earth's atmosphere safely, can
  be used again and again.

5

Answers

Cars and trucks	Boats and ships	Aircraft
bonnet	cabin	cabin
boot	funnel	flap
brake	hull	jet engine
cab	mast	propeller
dashboard	oar	rudder
exhaust	paddle	tyre
gearbox	porthole	undercarriage
indicator	rudder	windscreen
radiator		
steering wheel		
tyre		
windscreen		

6

Sample answers
The car, whose gearbox was jammed, crawled along at a
snail's pace.
The sailing boat, whose broken, storm-damaged mast
was useless, had to be towed home.

7

Background information

At the time of writing, Heinz Stücke is still on his epic journey. He has an entry in Wikipedia and there are various websites that feature him, including www.gluckman.com/Bikeman and www.bikechina.com/heinzstucke.

Answers
1 which/that 2 if 3 more 4 must 5 no 6 much
7 when/where 8 every/each 9 away 10 as 11 on
12 whose

Writing folder 13

Essays 2 pages 170–171

1 The answer has most relevance to Statement B, but as said, it is a poor attempt.

2

Answer
There is considerable irrelevance in the first paragraph and the statement is not adequately addressed until the start of the second paragraph.

There should have been an introductory paragraph, and the second paragraph should have been split into two (new idea, cycling as fun).

There is little use of linkers – just 'on the other hand' in paragraph 2.

The writer's view is stated, though unclearly.

There are some inappropriately informal expressions, e.g. 'oh god', 'why not', 'yes, it is'.

Corrected and improved answer

Not only does cycling provide a cheap and enjoyable alternative to the car, but it is also better for your health. This essay will consider the benefits of cycling, as opposed to the hazards of driving a car on today's congested roads.

Obviously, cycling is far less expensive, because you don't need to buy fuel or pay for repairs and insurance. Seldom does anything go wrong with a bicycle, apart from an occasional flat tyre, which can easily be repaired. In contrast, car owners often have to pay horrendous garage bills. Moreover, the price of petrol is increasing all the time.

Cycling is definitely fun, especially if you choose your routes carefully and avoid busy roads. You can see much more of the scenery from a bike and cycle paths usually go through attractive countryside. On the other hand, car drivers end up sitting in traffic jams, which is stressful and a waste of time.

In addition, cycling is very good exercise, which will help to keep you fit and healthy. It is undoubtedly the right choice!

3 All the ideas are relevant to Statement A apart from c, e and i.

4 Remember to use commas where necessary, for clarity.

Answers
a Of high priority is the introduction of tighter laws on older vehicles, whose exhaust fumes cause greater pollution.
b In the short term, it is essential to consult the public, whose concerns have never been fully aired.
c Instant action is needed to reduce the volume of cars in our cities, while in the medium term, further research should be done on alternative forms of transport.

5

Sample answer

It is obvious that there is too much traffic nowadays. Not only does this affect cities, but the countryside too. The way we depend on our cars is threatening the natural world, because of the high levels of pollution caused. Instant action is needed to reduce the volume of cars, while in the medium term, further research should be done on alternative forms of transport.

In my view, we desperately need a better public transport system, in order to cut down on the use of private cars. At present, people are not offered a true choice, as travel by bus or train is double the cost of using a car. It is also essential to advertise the services which are available.

Other measures may be needed in the short term to force people to leave their cars behind, such as higher taxes on road use. Some cities already charge for car entry and I believe this should be done more.

The government should invest heavily in research, so that new forms of transport, which are more environmentally friendly, can be developed. This applies equally to private ownership and public transport.

Unit 27

27.1 pages 172–173

1 In Unit 13, you learned various things about Madonna's life in New York before she became famous (see page 85).

Answers

Born:	1958
Place:	Rochester, (near Detroit USA)
Family:	8 children, mother died when she was young
Education:	went to University of Michigan; dropped out

The underlined parts of the recording script confirm the answers.

Part 1

Interviewer: In the studio today we have Jonas Day, who's just won an award for student journalism by writing an article about Madonna for his college newspaper. Jonas, welcome. I believe Madonna herself rang to congratulate you?

Jonas: Well, it's true that I had a letter from her PR company, but I haven't spoken to her myself.

Interviewer: So, let's start at the beginning. She was born in Detroit <u>in 1958</u>, is that right?

Jonas: Actually, <u>at a place called Rochester.</u>

Interviewer: What about her family?

Jonas: Well, let's see now, her father was an engineer. I think life was quite a battle for her. You see, she <u>was the eldest of eight children and quite young when her mother died.</u> Anyway, she did ballet, singing and piano lessons and <u>got a scholarship to the University of Michigan.</u>

Interviewer: A scholarship? She must've been quite good.

Jonas: Well, I think, on the whole, she did well. Anyway, it wasn't enough for her and <u>she dropped out after two years</u> and went to New York to find fame and fortune. I guess she didn't want to put the moment of stardom off any longer.

Interviewer: Apparently, I believe, the story is that she only had $35 in her pocket when she arrived in New York?

Jonas: I'm afraid I've never got to the bottom of that story.

Interviewer: Oh, right, OK, now tell us how her career took off.

2

Answers

taking charge of the conversation	so, right, now
correcting some information	actually
changing subject	anyway
apologising	I'm afraid
partly agreeing	it is true, but
making a generalisation	on the whole
giving some information which may not be reliable	apparently
thinking	let's see now
explaining	you see

4 The underlined parts of the recording script confirm the answers.

Answers

1 B   2 C   3 B   4 B   5 A   6 C   7 A

Part 2

Jonas: Well, of course <u>the thing most people don't associate with Madonna is the fact that she's chief executive of a large company</u> called Maverick Entertainment, which is a multi-million dollar company and earns her more than her records or her films.

Interviewer: Yes, her image is certainly different, isn't it? She's had a lot of bad publicity about her private life, hasn't she? Especially when she married Sean Penn – the newspapers really put her down.

Jonas: She said at the time that what they said in the newspapers took her by surprise. She'd believed her life to be totally under control. Everything she'd ever done had been carefully planned. You know, in order to get a record contract when she came to New York <u>she went to clubs where she knew record producers went; she even managed to get an appointment with the head of Sire records when he was in hospital!</u> He reckoned she was a very determined lady.

Interviewer: I heard a similar story about how she got her manager. Apparently <u>she asked herself who managed the biggest act in the world, and of course that was Michael Jackson's manager,</u> and she decided she wanted him to manage her too. She just walked into his office and told him.

Jonas: Well, there you have it – determination, charm, intelligence and <u>above all – talent.</u> Anyway, at the end of the eighties, she decided to move away from just being a pop star back to her first love – acting and dance. Of course, she still needed to make money.

Interviewer: I expect she did – apparently she was spending over a million dollars a month (even her dog had its own psychiatrist).

Jonas: Well that's true enough but her real motivation has been mainly to make a success of her film career. <u>Apart from Evita,</u> which won her a few good reviews and a Golden Globe award, <u>she hasn't had much success on this front.</u> She seems to have picked bad projects – things that looked like they were going to be winners and turned out to be no good. Also she put a lot of people's backs up with her desire to shock. Funnily enough it doesn't seem to have done her any real harm – I guess she realises that scandal sells! She constantly bounces back. I think she's very good at putting her ideas across. <u>Like in 1992, after a year of negotiation, she announced a new seven-year deal. Part of this deal was to operate a new multi-media entertainment company called Maverick Entertainment.</u> She was the one who signed up singers like Alanis Morissette and The Prodigy. Now the record label is one of the most successful in the business.

Interviewer : Just as well, as her own films and records haven't been wholly successful, have they?

Jonas: Quite. But she did diversify at the right time – in the nineties she started a line of clothing and bought a designer hotel, and of course, she can pick and choose in which films she would like to appear in the future.

Interviewer: Any clues about what she'll do next?

Jonas: Well, she's got married, had children, even written some children's books, and is still going on tour singing her songs. The last tour, in fact, was sold out within minutes and received rave reviews. But who knows what she'll do next? She can do almost anything because she is in charge of her own destiny and she's the type who will get on with whatever she puts her mind to.

5 Practise saying these sentences in a similar way, letting your intonation fall on the last word.

I've got CDs by Madonna, U2 and Radiohead.
I like bananas, apples, pears and oranges.
In Paper 2 there are letters, articles, reports, essays and stories.

6 If you are surprised, it is natural for your voice to rise in English. Do you do the same in your language?

7 When a question begins with a *Wh-* word or *How*, the voice falls towards the end of the sentence. If you haven't heard clearly, the question you ask will have rising intonation at the end.

8 Remember to vary your intonation, to avoid sounding unfriendly or rude.

> **Answers**
> **a** unfriendly **b** friendly **c** friendly **d** unfriendly
> **e** unfriendly **f** friendly

27.2 pages 174–175

1 As this lesson reviews tenses, it would be a good idea to look back at earlier sections in the Grammar folder:

Unit 2 (present tenses), page 198
Unit 5 (past tenses), page 200
Unit 10 (future tenses), page 202
Unit 14 (perfect tenses), page 203

> **Answers**
> 1 **a** Present perfect – She asked you at **sometime** in the recent past.
> **b** Past simple – She asked you at **a specific time** in the past which the speaker is referring to.
> 2 **a** Present simple with verbs of perception, senses, etc.
> **b** Present continuous to mean 'meeting' and for arranged future.
> 3 **a** Past simple – actions happening at the same time.
> **b** Past perfect – agreement after he had seen her.

> 4 **a** Past continuous – at some point when she was making an album she met her producer.
> **b** Past simple – She didn't make an album until she met her producer.
> 5 **a** Past simple – A general statement about the past. Possibly still true.
> **b** Past perfect – Before a given moment her life was under control. Now she no longer believes it is.
> 6 **a** Present perfect – general statement about all her record sales.
> **b** Present perfect continuous – her more recent record sales.
> 7 **a** Future simple – prediction.
> **b** *Going to* – more probable than future simple here – maybe you have evidence for this statement.

2

> **Answers**
> 1 j 2 d 3 f 4 b 5 c 6 h 7 i 8 g 9 e 10 a

3 Refer to the Corpus spot.

> **Answers**
> **a** Where were you born?
> **b** I'm flying to Hong Kong tomorrow./I'm going to fly to Hong Kong tomorrow.
> **c** I was playing football when President Kennedy was shot.
> **d** I was going to phone you, but I lost your number.
> **e** Shakespeare is/was the greatest English playwright.
> **f** It was the first time I had been to the theatre.
> **g** It is the first time I have heard that record.
> **h** After the film had finished, everyone clapped.
> **i** I wonder who makes/has made more money – Michael Jackson or Madonna?
> **j** I have been trying to explain how to do it for the past ten minutes.
> **k** This time next week I will be sitting on a ride in Disneyland.
> **l** What time do you think the plane will arrive?/What time do you think the plane is going to arrive?
> **m** He arrived at the party late because he had been working.
> **n** Madonna has produced some great records recently.
> **o** I haven't seen you for ages. What have you been doing?
> **p** This time last week I was in New York.
> **q** Where were you living/did you live/had you lived/had you been living before you moved here?

4 The alternative words and phrases are given after each phrasal verb.

5 The phrasal verbs used in this exercise have the
   following meanings:

   a postpone   b upset   c be offended   d discourage
   e save   f stop reading   g tolerate   h accommodate

Suggested answers
a Oh yes – I often put off paying bills and writing letters.
b I remember putting a friend's back up recently by
   agreeing to meet her at a certain time and then
   turning up very late.
c As an English speaker, I would be very put out.
d Nothing, apart from the fuel bills!
e I have got better at putting money by for a rainy day,
   though I don't save regularly.
f Many – the best this year has been a thriller by Arturo
   Pérez-Reverte, called *The Dumas Club* in its English
   translation. I could not put it down until I'd finished it.
g Things like leaving their beds unmade, eating up the
   last chocolate biscuit, and not helping in the kitchen …
   but I love them dearly!
h Yes, we often put friends up, even though we don't
   have a spare bedroom – they sleep on a futon in the
   living room.

6

Answers
1 grammatical   2 speech   3 extent   4 singer   5 largely
6 characteristics   7 difference   8 tendency   9 unlike
10 adjustment(s)

7

Answers
nouns
association   belief/believer   knowledge
manager/manageress/management   decision
actor/actress/action   death   announcement/announcer
operator/operation   choice
adjectives
occasional   responsible/irresponsible   famous/infamous
determined   intelligent/unintelligent   talented
successful/unsuccessful   harmful/harmless

Exam folder 14

Paper 5   pages 176–177

The section on the Speaking Test on page 7 gives
information about the timing of each part.

Think about the advice given on page 176 and then record
yourself doing each part of the test. Check the time taken as
you play back your recording.

The Part 2 photographs show:

First turn: Film star Leonardo DiCaprio out on his own and
being mobbed by fans.
Second turn: a remote village in Nepal (left) and the
Australian outback.

Unit 28

28.1   pages 178–179

1

Answers
e Sky blue is a pale blue; navy blue and deep blue are
   very dark blues; off white is creamish and pea green is
   the colour of tinned peas!
f Red is for anger – the expression *see red* means
   become angry.
   Blue is for depression – as in *singing the blues*.
   Green is for jealousy or envy – as in *green with envy*.
   Yellow is for cowardice, though this use is rather old-
   fashioned.

2

Answers
1 B   2 H   3 C   4 F   5 A   6 E   7 G

3

Answers
a a lasting/great impression
b a plan of what colours you're going to use
c blind; deaf   d basically
e a story about something that happened to you
f someone else writes your biography; you write your
   own autobiography   g a shade of red

4

Answers
a crossing things out – putting a line through parts of it
b coming out – starting to bloom
c drew out – prolonged
d held out – lasted
e make out – distinguish
f missed out on – lost
g worked out – solved
h turn out – produce

Grammar extra

This exercise covers some of the commonest prepositional errors at FCE level. Try to learn the correct prepositions that follow these verbs and adjectives.

Answers
a from, away b on c to d in e with f for
g on h with i with, for j to k about l to
m from/to

28.2 pages 180–181

1 Refer to the Corpus spot. The agreement of subject and verb in English is called 'concord'. Many errors made by candidates in Papers 2 and 3 could be avoided by checking for agreement. For example, you cannot say 'Guga play tennis really well' – you must use 'plays', the third person singular form of the verb, to agree with the subject Guga (Gustavo Kuerten, the wonderful Brazilian player).

Answers
a has b plays c watches d believe e wants
f are g has h are i are j doesn't seem
k enjoys l was formed m has found/will find/finds
n go o is p likes q is r is

2 Words with a * in the answers below can take a singular or plural verb.

Answers
A
each	*staff	*neither
every	the news	*either
no one	a series	
one of	everybody	
more than one	*none	

B
all	people	the majority of
both	*staff	*either (informally)
the police	sunglasses	*neither (informally)
a group of	jeans	*none (informally)

3 If you think of the family as individual people, then you use a plural verb, as in a. If they are used as an idea or concept, you use a singular verb, as in b.

Other words which follow the same rule include *bank, class, committee, government, orchestra, public, school, staff, team.*

4

Answers
a each b all c Both/Neither d None e either
f Neither g Every h Each i none j Each/Every
k each

5 The underlined parts of the recording script confirm where the answers occur.

Answers
1 eager to please 2 money 3 rebellion
4 30/thirty women 5 carrots 6 discrimination

Presenter: Good morning. And it's now official – blondes really do have more fun. New research has revealed that a woman's hair colour reflects her personality; redheads are wild and fiery, while brunettes have a lot of common sense <u>and are eager to please</u>.
University psychologists believe they have proved that the classic stereotypes attributed to a woman's hair colour have a scientific basis, and that changing the colour of your hair may even help change your personality. According to the research, to be published later this year, dyed blondes – typified most famously by Marilyn Monroe – start having more fun and appear to <u>worry less about money</u>.
Dr Tony Farmer, who carried out the study, said it showed for the first time that there are key personality differences between women of different natural hair colour. Whether the differences are genetic or simply a consequence of expectation is less clear. Apparently, people who dye their hair blonde <u>are making a real gesture of rebellion</u>. The researchers interviewed 93 women with natural hair colour, who answered 48 questions to establish their personality traits. <u>They then conducted the same personality analysis on 30 women before and after they changed their hair colour.</u>
Natural redheads were less likely to care about what other people thought of them and had more significant mood swings.
I decided to ask some redheads whether they agreed. First of all, Jenny Alton, the actress. What do you think, Jenny?
Jenny: Well, having red hair has caused me some problems. I remember when I was younger, <u>my classmates would call me 'carrots'</u>. Later on people would shout at me in the street – maybe that's why redheads become so bad-tempered.

Presenter: I wondered if this stereotyping was only aimed at women so I asked the redheaded writer Peter Jameson what he thought.

Peter: Well, I'm fairly famous for being irritable and intolerant, but I do think <u>stereotyping can lead to discrimination</u>. On my first day at school I was surrounded by a group of boys who attacked me so I retaliated. Of course, when a teacher appeared he immediately blamed me.

Presenter: Well, my thanks to both Jenny and Peter. Fortunately, I'm going bald so none of this applies to me. In the studio next week we ...

6

> **Answers**
> **1** as **2** on **3** is **4** such **5** the **6** been **7** if
> **8** enough **9** them **10** that **11** where **12** not

Writing folder 14

Applications 2 pages 182–183

Writing folder 7 on pages 94–95 dealt with job applications. Here, other types of application are looked at.

1

> **Suggested answer**
> Write to *Mr O'Hare*
> Don't include any postal addresses
> Include a reason for writing at the beginning
> Say why the family would be suitable
> Mention useful qualities and special experience
> Finish the letter using *Yours sincerely*

2 This letter revises many of the grammar points covered in previous units.

> **Sample answer**
>
> Dear Mr O'Hare,
>
> I **saw** your **advertisement** for a family to spend a month on a **desert** island and I would like **to** suggest my own family. **There are six people in my family** – my parents, myself (I **am** 22 **years old**), my two sisters (12 and 16), and my brother (8). We **come** from Iceland. My father is **a** doctor and my mother is **a** sports teacher. **I am doing an Economics course / I study Economics at** university, and my brother and sisters are still **studying** at school.
>
> I think we would really enjoy **spending** a month **on our own**, as we all get on very **well** with each other. We aren't the kind of **people who watch** TV all day or **need** to be **entertained** all **the** time. We are a sociable and **friendly** family who **are** capable of taking care **of ourselves**.

Last year we spent a month in the mountains camping **by** ourselves, **which** was useful experience for being on a **desert** island. As my father is **a** doctor he can take care of **any** emergencies that **might** happen. My mother is very **interested** in sport and we are all very fit and **in good** condition. I learnt **to** fish two years ago and I have a good knowledge of **which** plants are good **to eat** and **which are** poisonous.

I hope you will consider my **application** and look forward to **hearing** from you.

Yours **sincerely**,

Magnus Magnusson

4

> **Answers**
> **1** saw **2** have been collecting **3** know **4** enjoy
> **5** helps **6** write **7** would make **8** would try
> **9** criticise **10** was asked **11** held **12** will consider

Unit 29

29.1 pages 184–185

1 The headlines refer to the following stories:

  1 Soap opera star caught stealing underwear from a shop.
  2 Paparazzo takes secret photos of footballer beating his wife.
  3 Head of company resigns after being charged with bribery.
  4 Government minister's son involved in taking illegal drugs.
  5 Judge has a hideaway home with another woman.

2 The photograph shows paparazzi hounding a public figure, who is hiding her face from them so it can't be photographed.

3 The underlined parts of the recording script confirm the answers.

> **Answers**
> **1** C **2** F **3** E **4** A **5** D

Speaker 1: The first we knew about it was when the paper phoned us up and asked for an interview. Cathy had said she'd be staying with a friend in London for the weekend. She'd phoned us on her arrival – as we thought – and we were expecting her back on the Sunday evening. <u>To get the call like that out of the blue was terrible.</u> Did we know that our daughter was sailing round the Mediterranean with a bunch of drug-crazed rock musicians? How old was she? Could we let the paper have a school photo to put in Monday's edition? It was a young chap and he went on and on – I mean, he must have known that he was breaking bad news to us, but he just didn't care.

Speaker 2: I was an idiot, but at the time I suppose I was flattered, it went to my head. You know, this famous singer was interested in me, some nobody from the suburbs. I would have phoned my parents again on the Sunday evening and come clean – the yacht had all the technology obviously. I'd just turned 18 the week before anyway, so I *was* an adult – but where's the story in that? I had to become a silly little thing, a total lie of course, but then that's their trademark, isn't it? We knew something was wrong when this speedboat kept cruising round the yacht on the Saturday afternoon. Nat – the bass player – noticed one guy had a camera with a long lens. It turned out that they'd bribed one of the bodyguards the night before, who got my name and address from my passport and radioed it all through. And the rest is history – a big juicy scandal!

Speaker 3: They run stories on us the whole time – we've got this bad boy image and any dirt they can rake up on us sells newspapers – or so they believe. I feel really bad about Cathy. She's a nice kid and she didn't deserve any of this – nor did her folks. Course the paper deliberately got her age wrong, making it look as though she was this innocent young schoolgirl who was being led astray by the big bad band. You get sick to the back teeth with it, you really do. Nat's got a better attitude, he doesn't let it get to him, but I hate it – I hate *them*, hounding us the whole time. They never give up, no way. Don't suppose they ever will, while we're flavour of the month.

Speaker 4: Cathy's put a brave face on the whole thing and admits she made a mistake. When she got back last week, I visited her at home – the school's on holiday until Monday next. The family all probably thought I was going to ban her from coming back next term, but I wanted to reassure her really. I mean, the whole thing has been blown rather out of proportion, a three-day wonder. Typical media sensationalism! Cathy's a promising student who should get very good grades in her A-levels. Why let all that go to waste? Everything will have died down soon, and I've every confidence that she'll be able to concentrate on her work again.

Speaker 5: Well, I genuinely believe the public has a right to know these things, I mean it could have been anyone's daughter. It's almost a duty if you like, you know, we don't shy away from the truth, even if it is hard to find. We're ready to show these people up for what they really are. Who knows, if we hadn't got to Cathy when we did, she might not be safely back home now. Perhaps some of the people involved should think about what might have happened, then they might have a change of tune, rather than criticise us as they have done. As for the band, well they're in the public eye, so if they choose to behave as they do, they've got it coming to them. And let's face it, there's no such thing as bad publicity, is there?

4

> **Answers**
> Idioms not heard:
> break new ground (comes up in 29.2)
> keep a low profile (comes up in 29.2)
> turn something on its head (in exercise 6)

The meaning of each idiom, as heard, is given below, with the speaker in brackets:

have a change of tune (5) – think differently
flavour of the month (3) – the most popular (band) at the moment
get sick to the back teeth with (3) – get very fed up with
go to someone's head (2) – make them feel flattered or self-important
be in the public eye (5) – have a high (media) profile, usually through fame
out of the blue (1) – without any warning
put a brave face on something (4) – pretend something isn't as bad as it really is
the rest is history (2) – the rest of the story is well known
a three-day wonder (4) – only of short-term interest

6 The photo shows Camilla and Prince William.

> **Answers**
> 1 C 2 D 3 A 4 B 5 C 6 D 7 D 8 C 9 B
> 10 D 11 A 12 C

29.2 pages 186–187

1 As the advice on page 186 says, don't overuse idioms, as this can sound very unnatural. However, used sparingly in Papers 2 and 5, they will give evidence of your range of language.

> **Answers**
> 1 b 2 c 3 d 4 a 5 g 6 h 7 f 8 e 9 l 10 k
> 11 i 12 j 13 o 14 p 15 n 16 m 17 s 18 q
> 19 t 20 r

2

> **Answers**
> break new ground – do something innovative (shows approval)
> make your mark – be noticed for doing something well
> get to grips with something – finally understand or become in control of something
> come out of your shell – become less shy
> tighten your belt – economise
> keep a low profile – try not to be noticed
> get your act together – become better organised
> take somewhere by storm – be very successful
> put your oar in – give an opinion (often different to the one being expressed)

catch someone off guard – surprise someone
go out of the window – disappear completely (of a plan or idea)
put something on ice – postpone (a plan or project)

3

> **Suggested answers**
> a The paparazzi caught them off guard at their hideaway cottage.
> b The government has put many of its proposals for new road development on ice.
> c All her promises to her parents about studying hard went out of the window when she met Danny.
> d The software breaks new ground with a technique that requires much less memory.
> e Some town councils have got to grips with traffic problems.
> f Kevin has quickly made his mark in his new job.
> g The British film *Control* took Cannes by storm.
> h The argumentative politician couldn't resist putting his oar in.
> i John kept a low profile in the cinema, hoping his teacher wouldn't see him.
> j On the first day at a new school, children are very nervous, but they soon come out of their shells.
> k Caroline's always letting people down – she really needs to get her act together.

4

> **Answers**
> a on b in c in d out for e to f at g in
> h out on i with j on k at ... with l in m off

5 The four idioms illustrated are:

   1 in full swing (b)
   2 at loggerheads with someone (k)
   3 out for the count (d)
   4 in a tight corner (g)

> **Answers**
> a thin on the ground b out on a limb c pie in the sky
> d at a loose end e in a nutshell f quick off the mark
> g economical with the truth h shocked to the core

Exam folder 15

Paper 2 pages 188–189

The section on Paper 2 on page 6 gives information about the content and timing of the paper.

1 Think about the advice given on page 188 before reading the exam question.

2

> **Corrected and improved answer**
>
> This essay considers the statement about newspapers today and whether their role has changed.
> In my opinion, the answer to this depends on which newspapers you read, as some still concentrate on current affairs, while others contain only a minimal amount of news. It is clearly important for any newspaper to report what has happened, but people like to read other things too.
>
> It is also good to expose scandal occasionally, as seen recently in press coverage on the American Paul Wolfowitz. Wolfowitz abused his position as head of the World Bank in trying to get his girlfriend promoted to a better job, and this has quite rightly led to him standing down from the post. Famous people are in the public eye and they must behave appropriately.
>
> At the same time, newspapers should not focus exclusively on the reporting of scandal. Their main role is to inform and this means writing detailed reports on current news and events. I think television can often cover events effectively, with visual images and on-the-spot reports, but with a newspaper, the reader has time to read and reflect on what is printed.
>
> In conclusion, the role of newspapers today is still mainly to inform, but they should shock and entertain us as well.

Unit 30

30.1 pages 190–191

1 The first pair of photos show:
Eddie Izzard, stand-up comedian (left) and Mr Bean, played by Rowan Atkinson.
The second pair of photos are film stills of:
The Nutty Professor, starring Eddie Murphy (left) and Buster Keaton, from the silent movie era.

Record yourself doing each long turn, aiming to speak for one minute each time. Check your accuracy of grammar and vocabulary when you play the recordings back.

3 The relevant words in the texts are given beside each answer.
   1 B he found he only had about £5
   2 A he'd dropped a metal milk crate on its head
   3 D paid no attention
   4 C the petrified couple tossed all their money at him
   5 A rushed off to hospital to have their stomachs pumped
   6 D (conversation between Maxwell and the lad from Telecom)
   7 C an Italian meal on the Lower East Side
   8 B catch his train home

9   D   carried on puffing
10 B   go home or get a quarterpounder
11 D   ignoring the company's no-smoking policy
12 A   disguised the damage with … lemon and
           cucumber
13 D   You're fired!
14 C   a note saying: 'I'm real sorry …'
15 B   his card had been retained … locking away his
           delicious burger

5

> **Answers**
> **a** loomed   **b** with gusto   **c** bewildered   **d** tossed
> **e** shooed … away   **f** all the trimmings   **g** settled
> **h** fleeing

6   This is another rather unbelievable story!

Cow down below

A salesman was speeding along the motorway one
gorgeous summer's day in his new convertible, enjoying
the sunshine, the freedom and some good music on the
car stereo. Then, out of the blue, a huge black and white
Friesian cow landed in the back seat with a thud. He
managed to pull over onto the hard shoulder and tried to
remove the poor dead beast, but it was unbelievably heavy
and was stuck fast. Rather shaken, the man drove off the
motorway to the nearest village and found a garage. Once
they'd stopped laughing, the garage mechanics managed
to lift the cow out with an engine hoist, but the back of
his car was covered in unspeakable muck. They offered to
clean the car up. So, rather than standing around waiting
at the garage, he went off to the local pub for a drink. At
the pub, he got talking to the landlord and told him his
unfortunate story. As he did so, another customer came
over. 'You must have been below me,' he laughed. 'I've just
ploughed into a herd of cows with my lorry, on the bridge
over the motorway. Sorry, mate!'

Grammar extra

Rather is a very useful word in English, but you need to
learn how it is used. See the Grammar folder page 208.

> **Answers**
> **a** 1 than   **b** 3 would; not   **c** 2, 4 quite

30.2   pages 192–193

1   The grammar of phrasal verbs is summarised in the
     Grammar folder on page 208.

> **Answers**
> **b** and **e** are intransitive.
> **a** no change possible (three-part phrasal verb)
> **c** ✓ – He set down the snack …

> **d** no change possible (pronoun)
> **f** no change possible
> **g** no change possible (three-part phrasal verb)
> **h** no change possible (pronoun)
> **i** ✓ – They offered to clean up the car.
> **j** no change possible
> All four rules are true and are exemplified by the
> examples as follows:
> **1** b   **2** before the particle: c,i; after the particle: a,f,j
> **3** d,h   **4** g

2

> **Answers**
> Word order can change in *a* and *d*:
> He put up a sign …
> Jenny couldn't keep the payments up …

3

> **Suggested answers**
> **a** turn off the TV   **b** get it over with   **c** made out a car
> **d** has put me off   **e** picked up Swedish
> **f** look them up   **g** make for the beach
> **h** got behind the speaker   **i** worked out the answer
> **j** cut down on cakes

4

> **Answers**
> **1** j   **2** g   **3** o   **4** i   **5** d   **6** m   **7** b   **8** h   **9** k   **10** e
> **11** a   **12** l   **13** f   **14** n   **15** c

5

> **Answers**
> **1** bit/little   **2** during/in   **3** with   **4** at   **5** as
> **6** where   **7** up   **8** be   **9** most   **10** for   **11** since   **12** is

Writing folder 15

Transactional letters and emails 3
pages 194–195

1

> **Answers**
> • information about Larry Hatfield's performance on
>   Friday night
> • Holmes and Watson were improvising
> • Ted Grainger's humour was political but not offensive
> • not a disaster (give own view)

2 There is no mention of Holmes' and Watson's improvisation. In the exam, you must include **all** the points given in the question.

3

Answers

It has far too many idioms in it, most of which are used inaccurately. It is also badly organised.

Suggested answer

I would like to comment on the article about the Festival of Fun, which appeared in yesterday's *Daily News*. I attended this festival and was surprised by the negative tone of the article. Your reporter has been rather economical with the truth, in my opinion.

5

Sample answer

Dear Editor

I would like to comment on the article about Talentspot, in this morning's edition. I was present at the concert, which I enjoyed.

I think your paper should be more supportive of local music. Many of the bands were performing live for the first time and may have been nervous. As for the poor quality of the microphone used by Jenny Lowe, this is surely the responsibility of the organisers, as your reporter implies in the article.

Dingbats played brilliantly, especially when they added the brass section. I don't think your reporter understands the way this band performs: the arguments between the bass player and guitarist Mike Thompson are part of the act!

Talentspot is a wonderful event, which is very popular with young people. It must continue, as it gives local bands a unique opportunity to show us what they can do.

Yours sincerely

Units 25–30 Revision

pages 196–197

2

Answers

1 object to people parking
2 is (the) traffic as bad
3 first time I had bought
4 apologised for laughing at her
5 put up with people
6 haven't read either
7 all (of) the seats have
8 people live in London than

3

Answers

a Just cross out the word you spell wrongly in your composition.
b That's the man to whom I sold the house.
c I'd prefer a blue car to a red one.
d Please turn it off at once – you're making too much noise.
e The police are available twenty-four hours a day.
f Neither my father nor my mother has/have blond hair. Correct
g It's the first time I have been to the Paris Motor Show. OR It was the first time I had been …
h I believe in the trustworthiness of our police force.
i The office block had stood on this street for more than a decade when they decided to demolish it.
j What time do you think the train will arrive?
k Seldom do we see new ideas on saving energy.
l The building whose roof had been blown off by the gales is on the next street.
m If we all shared a car to work, then the motorways wouldn't be / wouldn't have been necessary.

4

Answers

a tune **b** end **c** keep **d** hands **e** ice **f** feet
g eyebrows **h** eye

5

Answers

1 calling up **2** taken on **3** taken aback **4** bring in
5 work out **6** ended up **7** put Mr Murgatroyd off
8 miss out on

Corpus Acknowledgement
Development of this publication has made use of the Cambridge International Corpus (CIC). The CIC is a computerised database of contemporary spoken and written English which currently stands at over one billion words. It includes British English, American English and other varieties of English. It also includes the Cambridge Learner Corpus, developed in collaboration with the University of Cambridge ESOL Examinations. Cambridge University Press has built up the CIC to provide evidence about language use that helps to produce better language teaching materials.